UNDERSTANDING VIDEO GAMES

From Pong to PlayStation 3 and beyond, *Understanding Video Games* is the first general introduction to the exciting new field of video game studies. This textbook traces the history of video games, introduces the major theories used to analyze games such as ludology and narratology, reviews the economics of the game industry, examines the aesthetics of game design, surveys the broad range of game genres, explores player culture, and addresses the major debates surrounding the medium, from educational benefits to the effects of violence.

Throughout the book, the authors ask readers to consider larger questions about the medium:

- What defines a video game?

- Who plays games?

- Why do we play games?

- How do games affect the player?

Extensively illustrated, *Understanding Video Games* is an indispensable and comprehensive resource for those interested in the ways video games are reshaping entertainment and society. A companion website (**www.routledge.com/textbooks/9780415977210**) features student resources including discussion questions for each chapter, a glossary of key terms, a video game timeline, and links to other video game studies resources for further study.

Simon Egenfeldt-Nielsen, Jonas Heide Smith, and **Susana Pajares Tosca** are members of the Center for Computer Games Research at IT University of Copenhagen.

UNDERSTANDING VIDEO GAMES
THE ESSENTIAL INTRODUCTION

SIMON EGENFELDT-NIELSEN / JONAS HEIDE SMITH / SUSANA PAJARES TOSCA

Routledge
Taylor & Francis Group

NEW YORK AND LONDON

Please visit the companion website at
www.routledge.com/textbooks/9780415977210

First published 2008
by Routledge
270 Madison Ave, New York, NY 10016

Simultaneously published in the UK
by Routledge
2 Park Square, Milton Park, Abingdon, Oxon OX14 4RN

Routledge is an imprint of the Taylor and Francis Group, an informa business

© 2008 Taylor & Francis

Typeset in Joanna by RefineCatch Ltd, Bungay, Suffolk
Printed and bound in the United States of America on acid-free paper by Edwards Brothers, Inc.

Library of Congress Cataloging in Publication Data
Egenfeldt-Nielsen, Simon.
  Understanding video games : the essential introduction / Simon Egenfeldt-Nielsen, Jonas Heide
Smith, and Susana Pajares Tosca.
    p. cm.
Includes bibliographical references.
  ISBN 978-0-415-97720-3 (hardback) — ISBN 978-0-415-97721-0 (pbk). —
ISBN 978-0-203-93074-8 (e-book)
  1. Video games. I. Smith, Jonas Heide. II. Tosca, Susana Pajares. III. Title.
GV1469.3.E44 2008
794.8—dc22

                                                          2007037736

ISBN10: 0-415-97720-7 (hbk)
ISBN10: 0-415-97721-5 (pbk)
ISBN10: 0-203-93074-6 (ebk)

ISBN13: 978-0-415-97720-3 (hbk)
ISBN13: 978-0-415-97721-0 (pbk)
ISBN13: 978-0-203-93074-8 (ebk)

Contents

List of figures

Acknowledgments

Knowingly or not, a number of people have helped us write this book, through discussion, comments or by contagious inspiration. For letting us pick their brains, we are indebted to our colleagues at the Center for Computer Games Research: Espen Aarseth, Troels Folmann, Gonzalo Frasca, Jesper Juul, Anker Helm Jørgensen, Lisbeth Klastrup, Sara Mosberg, Miguel Sicart, and TL Taylor. For fast and knowledgeable assistance, we owe thanks to the scholarly subscribers of the Games Network discussion list.

For encouragement, patience and love we thank Sidsel Egenfeldt-Nielsen, Marie Louise Bossow Smith, Alma Victoria Bossow Smith, Martin Selmer and Elena Tosca Selmer

INTRODUCTION: GAMES AS A FIELD

ABOUT THE READER/STRUCTURE OF THE BOOK/THE LARGER QUESTIONS

The world is changing. The world, of course, is perpetually changing, but ours is a time of impressively sudden, and varied, and deep shifts. And our age is one in which technology is often the bellwether of these cultural transitions. From minuscule microchips spring visions of the world that challenge, enthrall, and delight us, expanding our sense of our ever-expanding world.

At some time in the not so distant past, most people were content with being passively entertained. More than happy to comply, writers of the page and of stage and of screen would spin linear yarns of great, and sometimes not so great, sophistication; makeup would be applied, sets would be scouted, music would be composed, all to grip the heart and captivate our reclining bodies. Today, many are not satisfied with their couch-bound spectator status; today, many insist on a more active role.

The remarkable world of digital entertainment we know today all started, amazingly enough, with a whistling white torpedo sent floating through empty space in an MIT basement in 1961. As the torpedo crashed dramatically into the enemy spacecraft, no horns sounded and no drums shook the ground. This was the first volley of attack in what would be known as *Spacewar*. But beyond the basement, the human race at large paid no notice to the fact that video games had been born.

This conception and subsequent birth were not entirely immaculate. *Spacewar* was, in fact, a shameless derivative. Its creators, devoted fans of contemporary science-fiction books, had large-scale visions of converting their passion to the big screen, and *Spacewar* is reminiscent of many space battle movies. But more importantly, *Spacewar* merely marked the opening line of a new chapter in the larger, millennia-spanning history of games.

Creating and playing games is a basic impulse of *Homo sapiens*. The ancient Greeks, the Vikings, and most likely even our ancient cave-dwelling ancestors all had rule-based systems of **play**. These served many purposes, from entertainment to competition to education. But our new, post-*Spacewar* chapter is remarkable. In the historical blink of an eye, video games have colonized our minds and invaded our screens. From a Boston basement, video games have exploded exponentially—reproducing at an alarming rate, much like the fearful space invaders that inspired so many early games—until they are now everywhere from tiny mobile phone displays to presumptuous wall-mounted plasma TVs. And although games like the anti-terrorist, multiplayer *Counter-Strike*, or the small-time-crime simulator *Grand Theft Auto III*, are indebted to ancient predecessors, games are not what they used to be either. As the computer has offered up its sublime powers—capable of the impartial processing of even the most complex of rules and the simultaneous, dynamic presentation of sound and graphics—new game forms seem more akin to living, breathing worlds than to *Backgammon* or *Poker*.

It was inevitable that academics would eventually notice. Thus, for the last five years, scholars have unleashed traditional theories and methods of analysis—some more effortlessly, others more painfully—onto the phenomenon of video games. New theories have even evolved, coinciding with a growing number of books and websites devoted to the medium, and on the ever-growing requirements for game design professionals. Since the twin fields of game studies and (video) game design are still in early phases of construction, and since scholars approach games from widely different paradigms, much of the knowledge is not yet readily scannable—or even findable. Hence the need for this book.

In the following chapters, we aim to provide the reader with a broad understanding of video games and video game studies. We explore what we consider to be the most important developments and influential perspectives, and discuss the relations between them. We have been greatly helped by the superb enthusiasm with which experienced gamers have begun to document and chronicle the history of the game industry and of the games themselves. This deep-felt devotion to the medium has manifested itself in the publication of impressive books such as J.C. Herz's *Joystick Nation* (1997), Van Burnham's *Supercade* (2001), Liz Faber's *re:play* (1998) and Johnny L. Willson and Rusel DeMaria's *High Score* (2002). Comprehensive and extremely useful game documentation projects—like *The Killer List of Video games* (www.klov.com) and *MobyGames* (www.mobygames.com)—also serve as crucial information depots for the game scholar. Such resources nicely complement the publication of thorough and knowledgeable volumes on game design and game theory, such as Chris Crawford's now-classic *The Art of Computer Game Design* (1982), Espen Aarseth's *Cybertext* (1997), Janet Murray's *Hamlet on the Holodeck* (1997), Richard Rouse's *Game Design: Theory and Practice* (2001), Richard Bartle's *Designing Virtual Worlds* (2003), Andrew Rollings and Dave Morris's *Game Architecture and Design* (2000), Katie Salen and Eric Zimmerman's *Rules of Play* (2004), Jesper Juul's *Half-Real: Video Games Between Real Rules and Fictional Worlds* (2005) and others.

Understanding Video Games owes its existence to these predecessors. But needless to say, everything there is to know about games cannot fit snugly into one volume. Even many volumes would be incapable of documenting the astounding growth of this field. Instead, we refer liberally to original literature and to more comprehensive treatments of many of the issues that we touch upon.

ABOUT THE READER

We have written this book to serve a variety of purposes. Our primary audience is a student of games, perhaps in a program of study anchored within the humanities or the social sciences. He or she is not yet a fully trained games scholar, but has an interest in achieving a broad understanding of games. But the comprehensive overview we are striving for should find other beneficiaries as well. Those who are technically oriented or mainly interested in designing games will hopefully find much here to interest them, even if the book does not directly increase their practical skills. Similarly, one of our core assumptions is that any student of games will benefit from at least a passing knowledge of issues not specifically tied to his or her specialty. Understanding how games work and why they look the way they do requires an interdisciplinary approach. We should, in a perfect world at least, all be equally unafraid of code, aesthetical theory, and social thinking. Finally, we hope that even professional scholars will find useful our attempt to systematically map the pertinent topics in game studies.

STRUCTURE OF THE BOOK

Beyond this introduction and Chapter 1 the book is divided into the following chapters:

Chapter 2, The game industry: Explores the business side of video games, to provide a basis for understanding large-scale trends in contemporary game design.

Chapter 3, What is a game?: Introduces the reader to classic and current approaches to the study of games and play and discusses how to meaningfully group games into specific types, or genres.

Chapter 4, History: Tells the history of video games, focusing on the development of game form and groundbreaking titles. This history emphasizes the games themselves, rather than the game industry or individual designers.

Chapter 5, Video game aesthetics: Offers a formal description of games in terms of sound, graphics and use of space and time.

Chapter 6, Video game culture: Describes all the aspects of games that are external to the actual works themselves, such as the position of video games in our modern (media) culture and the discourses that both surround and embroil the gaming world.

Chapter 7, Player culture: Explores some of the cultural practices of video game players. Whereas the previous chapter explored how games fit modern cultures in a broad sense, this one examines how players organize themselves and produce culture inside and outside their games.

Chapter 8, Narrative: Recounts the relationship between video games and the art of storytelling, focusing on the role of literary theory in the study of games.

Chapter 9, Serious games—when entertainment is not enough: Introduces the reader to an increasingly important field often referred to as "serious games," and discusses topics like "games and learning," "persuasive games," and "political games."

Chapter 10, Video games and risks: Discusses the oft-mentioned and culturally divisive question of whether (or how) playing certain types of games can harm the player.

THE LARGER QUESTIONS

Many people believe that textbooks should be all-inclusive collections of knowledge on a given topic. This is not an unreasonable ambition, but can give a false impression of orderliness, and can ignore the messy, on-the-ground chaos vital to creative and intellectual advances. Such a vision implies that most issues within a field are settled and that the scholars all agree; ignored are the magnitudes of disagreement within a discipline. Game studies is a young field. It is a field that has yet to settle, systematically and convincingly, some rather important questions.

One of these is the most basic question of all: "What is a game?" Game scholars do not agree on this most fundamental issue. If this worries you, take heart—it is a condition common to many fields. Sociologists, for instance, do not all hold identical ideas about what *society* means; media scholars differ in their definition of *medium*. In one important sense, of course, the question of what comprises a game is really just a question of definition. We cannot *determine* empirically or logically what a game is. What we can do, however, is seek a definition appropriate for our questions, and be quite explicit about the meaning of "game" when we employ it in important situations.

Another question central to game studies is this: "Why are there games?" Why do we, biological entities capable of creating poetry, climbing mountains, and splitting the atom, spend so much time playing games—especially when playing these games often conflict with our basic human needs: to sleep, to feed ourselves, to communicate with our spouses? We don't know. Or rather, the question has sparked surprisingly little interest and no consensus exists. However, some answers have been proposed,[1] and, not unreasonably, they tend to be rooted in biology. They usually go something like this: the ability to play allows organisms to simulate real-life situations. Through these simulations, the organism can practice important skills in relative safety. The individual with a disposition towards play then has an adaptive advantage over those lacking this disposition; natural selection takes care of the rest. The individual who practices throwing his spear in his spare time stands a better chance of survival when a sabre-tooth tiger attacks. Such an answer, though sensible, is not comprehensive. While evolutionary biology, for instance, may explain *why* there are games, it does not explain very clearly why our games look the way they do. Nor does it explain why people like different games and display such an enormous range of attitudes about the very act of playing games.

Which leads us to the next question: "Why do some people prefer certain games?" Again, we must admit that we cannot answer this with any sort of conviction. In fact, trustworthy statistics *documenting* such preferences (or documenting *whether* there is, in fact, variation) are less than abundant.[2] We could speculate that age, gender, social status, religion or hair color correlates with game preferences, but we would then have to explain why this should be the case. We have lots of ideas, but no fully formed theory here. The expanded version of this question is also interesting: do certain types of games appeal to people in certain times or cultures, and if so, why? Again, we could speculate that there is a correlation between the rise of capitalism and the popularity of certain types of highly competitive games, but what we really need is a coherent theory of why such a relationship should be expected and rigorous testing of specific hypotheses derived from such a theory.

Lastly, there is the question uttered by everyone from pundits to parents: "How do games affect the player?" In this case there *is* research but little agreement. The question should not be confused with *do games affect the player?* They do. The former question is completely legitimate, but it is also quite difficult to answer (as we shall see in Chapter 10). Some popular variations on this question include: "Do violent games make players violent?" "Do zero-sum games make people less cooperative in real life? Can games teach children useful skills?"

These larger themes are woven throughout *Understanding Video Games*, and we attempt to answer some of the questions by synthesizing the work that has been done so far in game studies. But the reader should keep in mind the relative youth of the field. At present, video game studies may have more questions than answers, more doubts than certainties. The rules are still being formed; the orthodoxies have not yet been established. And for the curious researcher, there are many worlds in need of exploration. Of course, this is part of why the field is so thrilling. In other words, the discipline welcomes you; there is much to be done.

1 STUDYING VIDEO GAMES

WHO STUDIES VIDEO GAMES?/HOW DO YOU STUDY VIDEO GAMES?/
TYPES OF ANALYSIS/SCHOOLS OF THOUGHT?

Right at this moment, millions of people around the world are playing video games. One obvious way in which this matters is financial. The rising popularity of games translates into astounding amounts of cash. The game industry is quickly becoming a financial juggernaut. Our research may help make even better games, may help large companies increase their profits, or may offer a critical perspective on the social workings and effects of the game industry. Either way, the very size of the industry justifies our attention. But it isn't just the money that's important.

Video games warrant attention for their cultural and aesthetic elements. The aesthetic developments of the gaming industry are intense, and constant, and thrilling; this explosive evolution of creative possibility is beginning to influence significantly other types of expression. It is clear by now, after the *Matrix* trilogy, after the *Grand Theft Auto* games, that movies and games are borrowing from each other's arsenals. For the younger generations, especially, games are crucial to the way they express themselves artistically and, presumably, in the way they conceive of the world. What does it mean, for instance, when a person's self-expression moves away from linear representations, such as books and films, and they find more meaning in interactive, non-linear systems where outcomes depend on player choices? Maybe it doesn't mean anything. Maybe it means a lot of small changes are happening but no revolution should be expected. And maybe it means that in a decade or two, video games will be so essential to the creation of culture that teenagers will be unable to imagine a world before video games existed. And most likely, perhaps, is some combination of all three scenarios. Regardless, such questions need to be investigated systematically.

WHO STUDIES VIDEO GAMES?

Science is the building upon a foundation of experience, the abandonment of old theories and the revision of earlier hypotheses.

Is game research a *science* in this sense? On the one hand, people who claim to be doing game research clearly do not always live up to the highest standards of the scientific method (true for any field); further, there is even some disagreement about how to actually *do* game research. On the other hand, if we take science to mean the systematic, rigorous and self-critical production of knowledge, game research *can* and *should* be a scientific discipline.

So who are game researchers? In general, they are professionals predominantly occupied with the study of video games. Undergraduates can now major in video games. PhD programs are emerging. Dedicated journals are available and distinct conferences are held. All of this is still new, however. Espen Aarseth, editor of the *Game Studies* journal has noted that

2001 can be seen as the Year One of *Computer Game Studies* as an emerging, viable, international, academic field.[1]

A new generation of researchers consider video games their primary research interest. But the struggle for acceptance and academic credibility can still be considerable. After all, we study video games, not a phenomenon that epitomizes high-brow cultural expression. While we should acknowledge that our field of research may be frowned upon, we must also avoid any sort of paranoia. If our research is not accepted, we should not comfort ourselves with conspiracy theories nor view other fields as populated by enemies. We should instead raise our internal standards.

A series of very important developments have helped put game studies on the road to become a viable field. For instance, the last few decades have witnessed a general rehabilitation of popular culture as a worthy topic of study. Also, many scholars have grown up with video games and see no reason why they should be exempt from enquiry. But more importantly, games have grown highly complex— as has their development—inviting serious attention and creating the need for highly trained game graduates.

It has become quite obvious that many fields can contribute to the study of games and game researchers are an eclectic bunch with a multidisciplinary background. Humanist scholars with film or literature backgrounds constitute the largest single group, but game research conferences are also attended by social scientists (mostly sociologists) and, very importantly, game designers. The presence of the latter group, who are typically not academics, is noteworthy. For the time being at least, there is a relatively close relationship between game researchers and game designers. This may sound obvious, but is in fact quite a special situation. In older research fields—such as film and literary studies—the distance between scholars and practitioners can loom large, and it seems at times that the two groups barely speak the same language. This may sometimes seem to be the case in our field as well, but at least both sides are committed to making an effort.

HOW DO YOU STUDY VIDEO GAMES?

To say that there is more than one way to approach video games is to put it mildly. Most researchers, at least at present, choose to adopt methods and approaches from their primary fields. Ethnographers tend to observe players. Those trained in film studies tend to analyze the games themselves and communication scholars tend to analyze interactions between players. There is inherently nothing wrong with this tendency as long as one acknowledges the more general ideal that one should use the methodology best suited to answer the question at hand.

In order to give you a better sense of how to approach games academically, we will examine a few noteworthy studies and discuss the methodological approaches that they represent.

We will start with Dmitri Williams's study of how video games have been represented in U.S. news media over a 30 year period.[2] In order to understand the function of video games in public discourse and the relationship between the portrayal of video games and more general cultural currents, Williams searched the archives of *Time*, *Newsweek* and *U.S. News and World Report*. He analyzed 119 articles which fit his criteria, and concluded that

Consistent with prior new media technologies, video games passed through marked phases of vilification followed by partial redemption. Also consistent with prior media, games served as touchstones for larger struggles within the culture—so much so that perhaps "lightning rod" is a better term.[3]

We should note that Williams tackled not games themselves or even players, but rather secondary texts that he subjected to content analysis.

In another study, Nicolas Ducheneaut, Robert J. Moore, and Eric Nickell explored the ways in which *Star Wars Galaxies: An Empire Divided*—a massively multiplayer online game set in George Lucas's *Star Wars* universe—encourages sociability among players.[4] In particular, they were interested in how players interacted in the game's "cantinas," locations where players could meet and socialize. The observed behavior was analyzed to determine if it conformed to sociologist Ray Oldenburg's notion of "the third place," a term used for informal public places like bars and general stores. Ducheneaut, Moore and Nickell chose to combine various methodologies. They began by conducting a "virtual ethnography," that is, they spent time in the field (in the game) systematically observing social interactions in the cantinas. They also videotaped their entire game sessions (with a camera plugged into the graphics card). Finally, they recorded a log of all the interactions that occurred between players as tracked by the game, and analyzed it using specially designed software. Among other things, the authors concluded that while the cantinas did not serve as particularly sociable spaces, the entire game, due to more subtle **mechanics** than just these intentionally designed social spaces was in fact quite sociable.

Susana Tosca performed a "close reading" of *Resident Evil X—Code: Veronica*,[5] a "survival horror" game, where players have to fight zombies and monsters and solve puzzles in order to escape from an altogether unpleasant island. Tosca's study harnessed the techniques of "reader-response criticism." She employed textual analysis, closely examining the work, looking for noteworthy properties of the game's structure and teasing out the meaning of the game's story. Tosca's research is primarily concerned with using this specific theoretical toolset to explore the text of the game. Surprisingly, given the number of humanist scholars in the field, this is one of just a few detailed analyses of a concrete game title.

Finally, Jesper Juul has pursued the philosophical and ontological foundations of games.[6] One of his main goals has been to provide a definition of video games that highlights their special properties and to explore the relationship between video games and traditional games. In order to do this, Juul examined noteworthy former attempts and arrived at a "classical game model" (see Chapter 3), which enumerates the features necessary for an activity to be considered a game. The method employed by Juul is a mixture of logical deduction and induction, laying bare the assumptions which often go unnoticed when games are discussed or studied.

TYPES OF ANALYSIS

As we have seen, games can be approached from a wide range of academic perspectives and by employing a number of different methodologies. Salen and Zimmerman, in their detailed exploration of game design, suggest that games may be approached with a focus on *rules* (the design of the game), *play* (the human experience of playing the game), *culture* (the larger contexts engaged with and inhabited by the game).[7] To these three units of analysis, we add that of *ontology*, to arrive at these four main perspectives:

1   The game: here, one or more particular games are subjected to analysis. The point is to look at games in themselves and say something about their structure and how they employ certain techniques—of player reward, of player representation in the gameworld and so on—to achieve the player experience which the game designer aims for. This is often the type of analysis chosen by those with a background in comparative literature or other aesthetic disciplines.[8]

2   The players: sometimes the activity of playing games is more important than the games themselves. Studies focusing on the players usually wish to explore how players use games as a type of media or as a social space. Sociologists and ethnographers tend to favor this type of analysis.[9]

3   The culture: moving still further from the games themselves, we can choose to focus on the wider culture that games are part of. Here, we wish to understand how games and gaming interact with wider cultural patterns. For instance, we may be interested in the subcultures that evolve around gaming or in the discourses surrounding gaming, looking at public outrage to violent games as compared to earlier "media panics." Methodologically, such studies often turn to secondary sources like news media or advertising.[10]

4   Ontology: finally, some studies examine the philosophical foundations of games. These studies usually seek to present general statements that apply to all games, and may enable us to understand, for example, the relationship between rules, fiction and the player.[11] Such scholarship builds on logical analysis which is typically grounded in concrete examples but is not interested in the individual titles per se.

The following table outlines the four major types of analysis:

Type of Analysis	Common Methodologies	Theoretical Inspiration	Common Interest
Game	Textual analysis	Comparative literature, film studies	Design choices, meaning
Player	Observation, interviews, surveys	Sociology, ethnography, cultural studies	Use of games, game communities
Culture	Interviews, textual analysis	Cultural studies, sociology	Games as cultural objects, games as part of the media ecology
Ontology	Philosophical enquiry	Various (e.g. philosophy, cultural history, literary criticism)	Logical/philosophical foundations of games and gaming

Actual studies, of course, often disrespect such neat reductionism and span multiple categories. The scheme above indicates general trends, but we must remember that a certain set of methodologies and a certain set of theories need not always go together.

SCHOOLS OF THOUGHT?

To speak of schools of thought within game studies may be an overstatement, as these groupings do not usually self-identify themselves as groups nor indeed "schools." Nevertheless, certain perspectives do stand out as particularly stable.

First of all, two research communities currently perform game research on a significant scale. The first of these we can call *the simulation community*. Researchers within this group focus on all forms of simulations, including non-electronic ones like the Sumerian Game from 1961 in which the player learned about the Mesopotamia of 3500 B.C., but also consistently studies video games. This group is well established and has its own conferences and journals. The second and much newer *video game studies* community sprung into existence around the year 2000; it represents what we refer to as "game studies" in this book. The video game studies community presently revolves around the Digital Games Research Association (DIGRA) and journals like *Game Studies* and *Games and Culture*. Communication and collaboration between the simulation community and the video game studies community has so far been scarce.

Within the video game studies community, two general approaches can be identified, though most researchers do not resort solely to one of the other. A *formalist group* tends to use game analysis or ontological analysis. They represent a humanistic approach to media and focus on the works themselves or philosophical questions related to the nature or use of these works. Within the formalist group there are two primary subdivisions. One subgroup prioritizes representation while the other prioritizes rules; they are sometimes referred to as *narratologists* and *ludologists* respectively (see Chapter 8). These two have so far instigated the most intense paradigm clashes of the field.

The *situationist group* is generally interested in analysis of game players or the culture at large. They are not interested in all-encompassing statements that do not take context and variation into account. They search less for general patterns or laws and more for analysis and descriptions of specific events or social practices.

On the whole, however, game studies has so far been an inclusive field. It is unified by a certain pioneering spirit, and the understanding that the underexplored nature of games leaves room for all those interested. It is also unified in the belief that in order to understand most aspects of video games you need to play them. So we wholeheartedly encourage you, as someone who wants to understand video games, to seek out video game classics and to simply familiarize yourself with as many genres as possible. Always ask yourself the following questions. Why does this work? Why was it done in this manner? How else might it have been done? And why do players act in this way in this particular game? Love of games obviously is no requirement but it certainly doesn't hurt when entering the world of game research.

And it is to this world that we now turn.

2 THE GAME INDUSTRY

THE SIZE OF THE GAME INDUSTRY/THE STRUCTURE OF THE GAME INDUSTRY/
THE DEVELOPMENT PROCESS/ROLES IN GAME DEVELOPMENT

Most games are not casual products. Despite dreams harbored by wistful would-be-developers, video games are not typically made in someone's basement. They are made by real people—often highly trained, very smart men and women—working within big companies with real production structures. It is important to consider the mass production of games and the industrial process that makes their production possible, because both their aesthetic form and their consumption are influenced by this over-arching structure. Current **hardware**, platform ownership, the global economy, competition between publishers, and the goodwill of venture capitalists, all influence the games that are available on the market.

But the means of production are not the only element to influence the shape of the products. Game designers have to take cultural factors and trends into account if they hope to successfully sell the products. There is an interplay between production and consumption that allows for products that can be both standardized and wildly original. In this chapter, we briefly outline aspects of the industry that game students should be familiar with, to understand both why games are the way they are and how one becomes part of this industry. We also believe that academic research into games becomes more inclusive—and more valuable—when it shows an understanding of the market.

THE SIZE OF THE GAME INDUSTRY

Video games occupy a (pop) cultural niche competing most directly with the movie and music industries for the consumer's time and money. Cross-industry comparisons are often unfair since business models differ somewhat. For instance, movie business profits are comprised of box office earnings, DVD sales, rental licenses and sales to television broadcasters while the music business has secondary income such as licensing for use in commercials and movies. The video game industry essentially makes money by selling directly to consumers (whether through retail outlets or by downloads) and by subscription fees for online games. There are few sources of secondary income although movies are occasionally based on game licenses. Of course, these examples are based on "software" (i.e. games, music, movies) and if we were to include hardware sales (game **consoles**, DVD and CD and MP3 players, etc.) the picture would become even more complicated.

Sticking to software, game sales are smaller than both movie and music sales in the U.S. but show many financially promising development trends (such as increases in online subscriptions and increased proliferation of games for mobile phones). Figure 2.1 shows the development of U.S. game revenue since 1996.

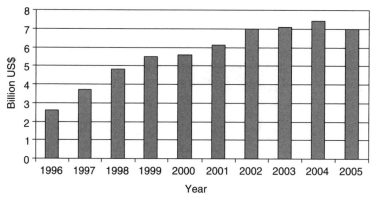

Figure 2.1 Annual U.S. game revenue (retail sales only)[1]

Looking at sales over recent years, we see that video game revenue in the U.S. has more than doubled since 1996. Interestingly, the graph also shows that constant year-to-year growth is not guaranteed, but rather depends on when new hardware is introduced, and the number of hit games published in a given year.

U.S. sales are usually estimated to make up about one-third of global sales (U.S.$21 billion in 2003[2]) as shown in the figures below. 2003 numbers are used for comparison here since, while somewhat dated, we deem them most credible.[3]

Figure 2.2 shows how that, divided by main regions, Asia and the Pacific area is the biggest market for games.

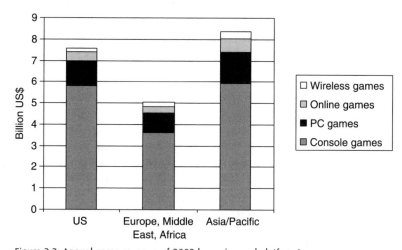

Figure 2.2 Annual game revenue of 2003 by region and platform[4]

Together, Figure 2.2 and Figure 2.3 also show how PC games are relatively marginal (in financial terms) compared to console games. But notably, the PC is an important platform for online games and almost exclusively handles important game types like first-person-shooters and **strategy games** and thus should not at all be discounted as a game platform. Also, it is worth remembering that PC games have traditionally been more prone to illegal copying than console games and for this reason the PC is in fact a more popular platform than sales data suggest.

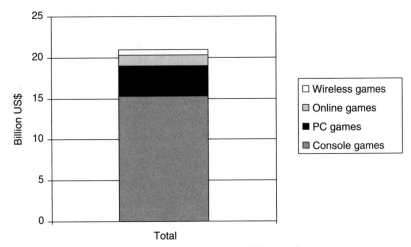

Figure 2.3 Annual game revenue of 2003 by platform (all regions)[5]

Looking at larger development trends, the U.S. game industry experienced strong growth throughout the 1990s, and has increasingly defied the so-called "console cycles." Previously, the market had operated in distinct cycles: the release of a new generation of console led to a burst of revenue from the sales of games designed for this new machine. Revenues would then slowly decrease, prompting console manufacturers to release a new machine, typically within five years. Within each cycle, the most popular machines would often be engaged in "console battles," as each company would tout the strengths of its newest model.

But interestingly, the major console manufacturers—Sony, Nintendo, Microsoft, Sega, and Atari—have never really made money on the console hardware itself.[6] The profit is in the games, as console game developers pay license fees to console manufacturers. As a result, the battle revolves around getting the largest consumer base in the three major markets: the U.S., Japan, and Europe. A large consumer base ensures large game sales, which then encourages developers to make new games for a specific platform.

At the time of writing (mid-2007), Sony has until recently led the market with their PlayStation 2 console which has shared the scene with Microsoft's Xbox and Nintendo's GameCube. Sony has seemed all but unbeatable but with the current generation of consoles—consisting of Sony's PlayStation 3, Microsoft's Xbox 360 and Nintendo's Wii—the balance has shifted somewhat. Microsoft released their Xbox 360 in late 2005, about a year before its two competitors. The PlayStation 3, admittedly an expensive machine, saw disappointing sales in its first six months (though ranking only slightly behind the Xbox 360) but the biggest surprise may well have been the undeniable success of the Wii which out-performed even the fast rise to power of the PlayStation 2.[7] Due to its year-long head start, however, the Xbox 360 has a stronger penetration than its two competitors at present (about 11.5 million sold consoles, against 3.5 million PlayStation 3s and 8.5 million Wiis worldwide).[8] The market leader in particular is able to influence publishers, distributors, and retailers, directing their focus to a particular console thus making life increasingly difficult for competitors. But the sheer size of console gaming, and of video gaming more generally, makes the market highly lucrative and tempting all but ensuring constant rivalry. For instance, *Madden NFL*—which has a new version released each year—sold more than 53 million copies from the late

1980s to 2006.[9] One of the most talked about games for the last few years has been the mostly PC-based *The Sims* series. *The Sims* sold more than 54 million copies between its release in 2000 and 2005,[10] and the PC version was the best-selling PC game in North America in 2000, 2001 and 2002. Thus, even if entering the market may seem difficult, potential sales are impressive enough to ensure competition.

THE STRUCTURE OF THE GAME INDUSTRY

Since the 1990s, the industry has consolidated, and evolved more standardized and professional structures for developing new products. Companies have been acquiring one another, and forming strategic alliances, all to handle the increasing demands of game production. More powerful hardware and a continuous arms race between game developers have resulted in larger production teams, increased development costs, and tougher competition.

All in all, video game productions have gone from being one-person projects to massive undertakings. Large-scale commercial games are often referred to as "AAA titles" and it is not unusual for such a game to involve 100 or more specialized experts, each focusing on different aspects of sound, programming, animation, graphics, marketing, game design, and production. In this light, productions of the late 1980s can seem quaint by today's standards. The MS DOS version of the 1989 hit game *SimCity*, for example, lists a fairly small number of contributors:

Original concept: 1 person

Design: 3 people

Programming: 1 person

Graphics/artwork: 3 people

Sound: 2 people

Cover art: 1 person

Documentation: 3 people

Package and documentation design: 1 person

Total number of contributors listed (including people receiving "special thanks"): 20[11]

Compare this to the extensive and much more differentiated credit list of *Halo 2*, produced in 2004:

Project lead: 1 person

Executive producer: 1 person

Engineering leads: 4 people

Design leads: 2 people

Art director: 1 person

Writer, director of cinematics: 1 person

Composer, audio director: 1 person

Producers: 3 people

3d Artists: 4 people

User interface designer: 1 person

Multiplayer and user-interface lead: 1 person

Engineering: 11

Other: more than 80

Total number of contributors listed: More than 100[12]

AAA titles, of course, are not the only games out there. The push towards ever larger budgets has initiated a strong counter-trend: the growth of independent games. Low budget games produced outside the system of big publishers have still to become a truly mainstream phenomenon (if one discounts web based games for the casual market). But they are regarded with much enthusiasm by the game developer community who sees inflated productions as a potential threat to creativity and innovation in the industry. To name one recent influential independent title, Introversion Software's game *Darwinia* from 2005 (in which the player must help eradicate a virus from a simulated world, partly by ordering around little units created by the inventor Dr. Sepulveda) gained respect from many quarters by making creative use of limited resources and by taking an irreverent approach to traditional genre divisions.

But returning to the larger scale of mainstream game publishing we see how specialization and increased complexity have resulted in differentiation.

The industry is presently comprised of the following elements:

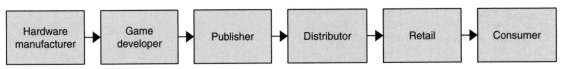

Figure 2.4 Major game industry institutions

The hardware manufacturer makes the console, or the component necessary to play the game on a PC (for example a graphic card producer like NVidia). The game developer makes the game. Small developers usually need a separate publisher and distributor (similar to the book business), while big companies perform all these functions in-house. For example *Rez*—a critically acclaimed abstract shooter game, released from 2001—was developed by UGA and distributed by Sega, while for *The Sims*, Maxis took on both roles. The games are then stored by distributors in their warehouses, before being sold to retailers (like your local Wal-Mart) and eventually to consumers.[13]

Typically, the publisher is seen as the pivotal component of the industry. Publishers buy projects from independent developers (i.e. companies who are not owned by or affiliated with a publisher), but they also usually have in-house game development sections and may at any time be searching for independent developers to acquire. To a certain extent, however, publishers are challenged by the strong hardware manufacturers, whose influence can be felt throughout the industry (for instance as demands for exclusive titles which can only be released for one console). Furthermore, various ways of making money from online gaming are emerging as serious alternatives to the standard model of game production. Thus, the dominant model of game production, described above, is under increasing pressure.

The game industry is often compared with the movie and music industries: all three share high production and marketing costs, as well as a similar reliance on blockbusters. The rule of thumb is that 90 percent of revenue in the game industry is generated by the top 10 percent of titles. These figures resemble those of the movie industry where box office revenues have been increasing in direct proportion to larger marketing budgets and production costs. It is not surprising that of the top 250 all time box office successes only two titles were released before 1997.[14]

The video game industry is dominated by AAA titles which are the ones you would see in store windows, the blockbuster titles like *The Sims, Battlefield 1942*, or *Age of Empires III*.

Console versions sell for around $49 although the price varies between countries. Typically, this sum is divided among the various players in the industry as follows: for each copy sold, the retailer gets about $17, the console manufacturer gets $8, and the distributor, the publisher, and the developer split the remaining $24. PC games are somewhat cheaper (a common retail price is $30) but the revenue is split in much the same fashion. The price difference between console and PC games reflect that console game developers must pay license fees to console manufacturers but also that PC games are the easiest to copy illegally, and thus the price must be low enough to deter some of this piracy.

By 2007 development budgets for AAA titles have soared to between $5 and $15 million or more and a typical production schedule can take anywhere from 18 to 36 months. And development is only part of the budget, as marketing can run in the range of $1 to $10 million per title. In general, these numbers are climbing, particularly as improved hardware creates consumer demand for more complex products, which in turn requires more elaborate input from more and more specialists (and the accompanying marketing savvy to make people want it).

Of course, publishers also release game titles that do not qualify for the AAA label, but which are still far more complex productions than the "independent games" discussed above. Such games may have development budgets ranging from from $0.6 million to $1 million, and similarly smaller marketing budgets in the $0.2 million range. These titles take 12–18 months to develop, but console versions usually also sell for approximately $50.

"Value titles" have even shorter development time—usually between 5–6 months—and have limited budgets of $200–300,000. The marketing is quite limited, at about $40,000, and retail prices are set somewhere between $20 and $30 depending on the platform. Interestingly, in the last ten years, value titles have been increasing in number and quality, alongside the growing availability of middleware tools—software tool sets which assist the developer in one or more areas of development—which can compete with the tools used for developing more high-profile titles.

THE DEVELOPMENT PROCESS

As mentioned above, the development time of video games varies depending on the range and ambition of the project. AAA titles will usually have the longest development cycles and involve the most detail, but almost all productions will go through a *conceptual phase*, a *design phase*, a *production phase*, and a *testing phase*. These steps are outlined in the following.[15]

The conceptual phase

First, the *game concept* is formulated, in just a few pages, in order to convey the core idea of the game and various features such as platform and sometimes concept art. Next, the designer creates a *game proposal* which functions to (hopefully) attract funding and to plan the actual production. It is much more detailed than the *game concept*, covering market analysis, technical issues, budget projections, as well as audiovisual style, and descriptions of how the game would actually feel to play.

The design phase

If all goes well, the *game concept* and *game proposal* provide the basis for further descriptions of the game's specifications. Although not always kept separate, the game designers now describe, in great detail, the *functional* and *technical specifications*. The former provide concrete details about features and how the player will interact with the game while the latter specifies how to achieve the desired design on a technical level. Together these specifications, sometimes referred to in themselves as the *design document*, may take up as much as several hundred pages depending on the scope of the project. AAA titles require very extensive documentation, while small independent productions need much less. A *design document* consists of text, illustrations, mockups, concept drawings and other details such as lists of objects in the game. It is a living document that is updated constantly as development advances. A decade ago, the *design document* might have been enough to get a publisher on board. But in a sign of how competitive/demanding/ruthless the industry has become, few investors today will give the green light to a project based on the design document only; most developers now need to produce "demo versions" of the games where the main features are already visible, and even playable to a certain extent. The few exceptions to this requirement are cases where the publishers commissioned the game, or where the parties have a lost-standing relationship.[16]

Based on the design document, the game developer makes a decision regarding the *game* **engine**. The (game) *engine* is the software which provides the basic architecture of the game but not the concrete content. For instance, a first-person-shooter engine will specify the basic of first-person-shooters (i.e. a player has one **player character**, the game world is seen from the player character's perspective, there can be other characters in the world, etc.) but not the details of how player characters must look or the structure of the actual levels in the game. Thus, a game engine is loosely comparable to a word processor which enables an author to write words of her choosing or to a theatre with props which enable a director to stage plays without building everything from scratch. More specifically, the game engine handles the **artificial intelligence** (how computer-controlled units act), the audiovisuals, and the physics (e.g. the effect of bumping into walls, and the effects of gravity). The developers may choose to build their own engine, but often a license is acquired to use a generic third-party engine. One popular commercially available game engine is the *Unreal Engine*, originally developed for the *Unreal* series but later forming the basis of games such as *Tom Clancy's Splinter Cell*, *Thief: Deadly Shadows*, and *Postal²: Apocalypse Weekend*.

Technically speaking, such an externally developed game engine belongs under the larger heading of *middleware*, discussed earlier.

Apart from the game engine, developers make use of general third-party software tools to handle elements which are imported into the engine, such as music or textures (graphical elements to be "stuck" onto elements like buildings). Many third-party tools are used in the game industry, but on the graphics side software packages such as Maya and 3D Studio Max are often used for 3D objects, while Photoshop is used for 2D.

Having made choices regarding game features, engine and other tools the next step is usually the creation of a *working prototype*, a fragment of the game that shows off its main features (and in advanced versions, may even be playable). The aim is to give developers, marketers, investors and others a feel for the game and to ensure that the core game design works and is worth pursuing further. The prototype is also used by developers to secure further funding from publishers.

Production and testing phase

Armed with design document and prototype the developers start the production proper. As one may guess, the design document only completely and effortlessly guides the production in a hypothetical perfect world. In practice, developers stumble onto unforeseen challenges and are sometimes forced (by funding issues, changes in the competitive situation, etc.) to change game elements during production.

The actual production of the game involves the writing of the game's code and the creation of different elements such as graphics and sound. This process takes several months and is done in specialized groups (in the case of large productions). When the separate elements have been individually made they are linked together to form the *alpha version* of the game. The alpha version, alpha being the first letter of the Greek alphabet, is the first version which contains all elements but which lacks fine-tuning and polishing. It is therefore only used internally to test for technical errors (bugs) and for issues concerning ease-of-use and playability.[17] Typically, this testing reveals a number of problems which are then addressed before the production of the *beta version*. This version is used for "real-world testing," typically by inviting a number of beta testers (ideally gamers as close to the target audience as possible) to play the game for an extended period and report on any problems or give suggestions. Beta testers typically are not paid for their efforts, but may receive a free copy of the game or other benefits. Apart from these core functions of beta testing, the process may also work to inspire interest and to recruit "ambassadors" who will promote the game to other gamers by word-of-mouth.

Based on input from the beta testing, final changes and corrections are made to the game and, if all goes well, the *gold master*—the first actual release of the game—follows soon after. What this means to the developer depends on the game type. Before the mid-1990s a gold master could mean the developer turning entirely to other projects. Today, however, many game productions lead directly into the production of a sequel, or the production of an add-on package. And for large-scale online games, like MMOs, the very concept of a gold master has little meaning as the sometimes gargantuan challenge of providing customer support and ensuring stability still lies ahead when the game is officially launched. Also, Internet proliferation has led many developers (particularly PC game developers) to rely on the ability to subsequently provide downloadable "patches" which must be downloaded and which fix or tweak aspects of the game. This phenomenon does inspire some disgruntlement as paying customers are arguably used as testers, but the ability to observe widespread actual use also may reveal delicate issues which are difficult, if not downright impossible, to detect under test conditions.

ROLES IN GAME DEVELOPMENT

Accomplishing the massive undertaking described above—especially in the creation of a large-scale game—requires five areas of expertise: design, art, programming, project management and testing.[18] Different companies use different titles for the same functions but the brief description below gives an overview of some of the competencies involved.

The game designer is considered the most prominent contributor, similar to a movie director. A game designer outlines the vision and describes the game in detail. Though this may seem like a very creative process, more often the designer's focus is to facilitate new ideas and continuously manage a game's identity, especially in the case of long-term franchises such as the *FIFA* series. Depending on the size of the production other participants may have the roles of *interface designer* (who handles the user interface), *level designer* (who creates detailed levels for the game, which usually involves the programming of entire areas in 3D), etc.

The graphics for the game are created by *graphical artists*. Some specialize in 3D while others focus on the 2D material. They work with sub-specialists like *animators*, *modelers*, *texture artists*, and *character animators*. Being a *graphical artist* typically requires a background in arts and deep knowledge of common game industry tools such as *Maya* and *Photoshop*. Specialist artists are often overseen by *lead artists* and even higher up by *art directors*.

Programmers are the ones who put everything together and turn the individual elements into a playable game. A typical large-scale game production can have a team of around 25 programmers focused on different aspects of the game. *Engine* and *tools programmers* create the backbone of the game. The *networking programmer* is especially important in multiplayer games, where he or she sets up the client-server architecture, writes basic protocols, and deals with online gaming issues like **latency** (the critically important period of time it takes for involved computers to communicate data) and security. The *artificial intelligence programmer* is responsible for the behavior of **game objects** (or characters) that need to respond sensibly to the player's actions (by chasing the player's character, for example, or devising counter-strategies). Other programmers will be focused on various aspects of graphics and audio. Increasingly, programmers are managed by a lead person who supervises productions and coordinates with other parts of the project.

Finally, game productions are overseen and managed by a *producer*. The producer functions as a *project manager*, keeping the project on schedule and on budget, while also ensuring that the production team has sufficient and appropriate resources.

All of this may give the impression that AAA game development is a hugely complex and time-consuming process which would be exactly right. The continuous increase in production size may well explain some of the apparent interest in creating and sharing more formalized conceptual tools for game design and development underscored by the large number of recent books on those topics. With this many people, and this much money involved, one simply cannot be bogged down by misunderstanding emanating from imprecise terminology and lack of clear responsibilities. Of course, unwieldy and financially risky productions have also—as we mentioned earlier in this chapter—paved the way for a counter-movement towards more manageable (and sometimes more creative and satisfying) productions as in the case of "indie gaming." Thus, we have recently seen, and will most likely continue to see, two parallel developments in game development: increasing AAA budgets on one side, and increasing interest in alternatives to the full-scale model on the other. The best opportunities by far for huge revenues still reside firmly on the AAA side, but with continued calls for more focus on creativity and artistic courage smaller scale development will seem increasingly attractive to many.

3 WHAT IS A GAME?

GENERAL MODELS FOR UNDERSTANDING GAMES/THE ISSUE OF GENRE

Are Poker and *Half-Life* 2 examples of the same phenomenon? The playing situation could hardly be more different. Poker is inherently multi-player and is governed by abstract rules not justified by any fictive world—a full house beats two pairs, aces are higher than jacks. Meanwhile, *Half-Life* 2 is a single-player shooter game whose rules mimic those of the physical world (see Figure 3.1). These two games are so different that it might be hard to see how they both belong to the same category.

Figure 3.1 *Half-life 2*

Nevertheless, there are similarities. For instance, in both games the player faces opposition—albeit from wildly different "foes"—and has his or her choices evaluated by the rules of the game.

In this chapter, we dig beneath the surface to examine what games are made of. We will introduce influential theoretical approaches, and their respective models. By discussing the—admittedly rare—"classics" of game studies we aim to show the different ways in which games have been theorized. We will be returning to these perspectives throughout the book. We also introduce a genre system that we shall use to distinguish between different types of games.

GENERAL MODELS FOR UNDERSTANDING GAMES

In daily life, we tend to define games informally; the general public, and even most serious gamers, don't require formal criteria in order to enjoy their games. For students of games, however, definitions are essential. Understanding the way games work and how they differ from other types of entertainment helps us choose the appropriate methods to analyze video games. If we are not specific, we run the risk of using terminology and models inappropriate to our discussion, or we risk blindness to the bias of our perspective. For instance, if we consider games to be stories we will focus on rather different things than if we consider games to be drama, or systems, or types of play. The challenge here is not so much to find the *correct* perspective but more to be aware and explicit about the assumptions we make.

Our criteria for what makes a game can have another serious consequence. Defining anything is a highly political project. Define games as narrative and the research grants are likely to end up with departments devoted to film or literature studies. Define games as a subcultural teenage phenomenon and studies of games are less likely to be funded by ministries of culture, to reach the pages of the "serious" press, or to be available in public or research libraries. In other words, definitions are tremendously important, and not just for purely academic reasons (see also the discussion of genre systems below).

Ludwig Wittgenstein and the problem of games

German philosopher Ludwig Wittgenstein (1889–1951) could not think of a common definition that would include all "games." Wittgenstein, in his *Philosophical Investigations*, famously argued that there was no common feature of the objects that we call games, and that we could hope for nothing more than "family resemblances." Wittgenstein looked at a number of activities traditionally referred to as games, including chess, tic-tac-toe (otherwise known as noughts-and-crosses), tennis, and ring-around-the-rosy. While some of these have elements of luck while others require skill, he notes that "we see a complicated network of similarities overlapping and criss-crossing: sometimes overall similarities, sometimes similarities of detail."[1] According to Wittgenstein's definition of family resemblances, while Game A shares features with Game B and Game B shares features with Game C, Game A and Game C need not share any features. This can be easily illustrated (see Figure 3.2).

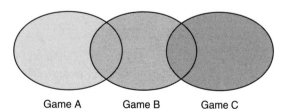

Game A   Game B   Game C

Figure 3.2 Game A shares features with Game B which shares features with Game C. Game A and Game C share no features

We must realize that Wittgenstein was not really interested in games per se, but used his analysis as an element of the larger project presented in his *Philosophical Investigations*. Nevertheless, in our context, there are two problems with Wittgenstein's analysis. First, he does not really try to find the common feature that he claims does not exist. He merely offers a few examples and notes how they do not share certain (more or less random) features. Second, Wittgenstein's analysis rests on a peculiarity of language. German, like English, does not distinguish between formal games and the informal games that children play; ring-around-the-rosy and chess are both "ein Spiel" (a game) in German. But this is not the case in Scandinavian languages, for instance. In Danish the word "spil" refers to formal games (including video games) while the noun "leg" refers to informal playful activity like playing house. Thus, Wittgenstein's argument may be quite language specific; and we should not be led by his analysis to believe that games necessarily escape sensible definition.

Johan Huizinga and the magic circle

Historically, games have been severely under-theorized. However, in the mid-twentieth century a few writers did look more closely at games than others (including Wittgenstein) had done. In 1938 Johan Huizinga, a Dutch scholar whose PhD dissertation focused on the clown figure in Sanskrit drama, published an homage to play entitled *Homo Ludens*,[2] that underscored the importance of play in culture. This study, whose title translates roughly as "Man the Player," revaluates the status of play in cultures that have historically treated it as inferior to work and other "serious" activities. Despite his approach, Huizinga has little to say on defining or understanding games. He does, however, make the important and much-cited observation that games construct a "magic circle" which separates the game from the outside world.[3] Playing a game, in this view, means setting oneself apart from the outside world, and surrendering to a system that has no effect on anything which lies beyond the circle. When you begin a game of chess, for example, you are submitting to a formally defined experience with rules that are clearly distinct from those we follow outside this special activity. The chess rules make sense in themselves and are only important within their particular context. Thus, arguably, the chess players construct (or enter into) a magic circle to engage in an activity cut off from the outside world.

Huizinga's vision of games has merit, but also clear problems. First of all, it is perhaps too closely tied to an ideological agenda. Huizinga's intention was to praise the act of play, and in his effort to protect play—from what he saw as the destructive influence of the Protestant work ethic, and a Western culture that prized seriousness over fun—he may well have overstated his case. Games are special contexts where particular rules apply, but we can apply this definition to a wide array of utterly different activities: work, family life, university classes, weddings, the nightlife of a big city. All of these situations are governed by special rules and norms that do not always—indeed, could not always—apply in other contexts. Games, then, are not *entirely different* from the remainder of our lives, and should not necessarily be treated as an aberration.

As we criticize Huizinga's philosophy, we must acknowledge that the modern game researcher's agenda, too, may in fact be ideological. For instance, economist and **virtual world** theorist Edward Castronova has echoed Huizinga's point:

As meaning seeps into these play spaces, their status as play spaces will erode. As their status as play spaces erodes, the laws and expectations and norms of contemporary Earth society will increasingly dominate the atmosphere. When Earth's cultures dominate, the game will be over; the fantasy will be punctured; the illusion will be ended for good.[4]

Castronova acknowledges that no bullet-proof philosophical argument can be made to support the idea of games as a completely separate sphere of human existence. He is arguing instead that we all, as gamers and as societies, should attempt to erect or uphold such barriers if we want game worlds to retain their unique appeal.

Apart from the ideological dimension of Huizinga's argument, we should consider whether it is really true that games do not extend into other spheres of life. Although in-game the conflicts within a game—between you and that stubborn enemy nation, for example—do not usually extend directly into other parts of your life, games do have real-world consequences. We can easily name a small number:

- *Games require time.* Games affect our lives by substituting for other possible activities, from watching television to reading a book to sleeping.

- *Games affect our moods.* Games can make us feel satisfied, or enraged, or thrilled. These and a plethora of other emotions can easily carry into other activities.

- *Games are communication media.* Games may communicate ideas and values. For instance, a strategy game may teach us how complex systems like cities or warring nation states work. Or advertising in a game may brand a certain product in our minds.

- *Games affect our behavior.* Games may make us do things that we would not otherwise have done. For instance, the American military have used the game *America's Army* as an (allegedly efficient) recruitment tool.

- *Games may directly affect the outside world.* Activities that occur in a game may have concrete effects in "real" life. For instance, objects acquired in game worlds are sold for. real money on trading websites like eBay, blurring the boundary between the two domains.

All of these aspects of gaming belie the myth that the magic circle truly separates games from the outside world. Thus, in game studies today, magic circle arguments are often treated with suspicion or seen as primarily applicable on a strictly formalist level of analysis—as when one brackets other aspects of a game to close study its design (thus speaking *as* if a game could be separated entirely from the outside world).

Nevertheless, the notion remains crucial and widely used, as we can see in the writings of Chris Crawford,[5] Katie Salen and Eric Zimmerman.[6]

Roger Caillois and the sociology of play

French philosopher Roger Caillois has articulated a more specific vision of the nature of games than Huizinga's magic circle. In his 1958 work *Man, Play, and Games,* Caillois stressed four essential qualities of play: that it must be performed *voluntarily,* is *uncertain, unproductive,* and consists of *make-believe.* He also famously divided games into four categories, according to their dominant features. The categories are: agōn (competition), alea (chance), mimicry (imitation), and Ilinx (vertigo). Additionally, he argued that all games exist on a continuum between paidia (play-fulness) and ludus (formal, rule-based game behavior).

- *Agōn (contest)*: in play of this type, competition is central and skill determines whether the player is successful or not. This includes hide-and-seek, chess, physical sports, and most video games within the action genre.

- *Alea (chance)*: here chance is the most important parameter for the play experience. Chance decides who wins a lottery or a dice game. Most video games have an element of chance and randomness, although some classic **adventure games** are entirely linear, and lack this quality.

- Mimicry (imitation): here the important play experience centers on being someone else, the ability to take on the role of a vampire, sibling, clown, or pilot. Winning is usually not an important part of this play form which is often found in traditional role-playing games and adventure video games.

- Ilinx (vertigo): this play form offers the chance to experience a pleasurable sensa-tion, often through physical activities like riding a roller coaster or carousels. In video games, it is found most vividly in racing games like *Stunt Car Racer*, and *Super Monkey Ball*.

When describing a particular game, these features can be combined to form complex play forms such as mimicry-agōn-ilinx. *Super Monkey Ball*, for example, is a video game where the player controls a monkey (mimicry), who competes against other players (agōn), and who drives fast around various tracks, and sometimes over the side and into the abyss (ilinx).

These different categories of play can be further analyzed on the spectrum between *paidia* and *ludus*. The following model illustrates the relation between paidia/ludus and the four play categories.

	AGŌN (Competition)	ALEA (Chance)	MIMICRY (Situation)	ILINX (Vertigo)
PAIDIA ↑ Tumult Agitation Immoderate laughter	Racing Wrestling } not Etc. } regulated Athletics	Counting-out rhymes Heads or tails	Children's initiations Games of illusion Tag, Arms Masks, Disguises	Children "whirling" Horseback riding Swinging Waltzing

Kite-flying
Solitaire
Patience
Crossword
  puzzles
 	
↓ **LUDUS**
	Boxing, Billiards
	Fencing, Checkers
	Football, Chess
	
	Contests, Sports
	  in general
		Betting
		Roulette
		
		Simple, complex,
		  and continuing
		  lotteries*
			
			Theater,
			Spectacles in
			  general
				Velador
				Travelling carnivals
				Skiing
				Mountain climbing
				Tightrope walking

Figure 3.3 Callois's classification of games[7]

In a *paidia* activity, one is not bound by rigid rules. *Ludus*, by contrast, refers to systems with formalized rules like chess, soccer, or backgammon. Although winning or losing is not anathema to *paidia*, these goals are not always present; who wins is much more a matter of negotiation between the players than something decided by specific rules. In *ludus* play forms. There are rules that must be adhered to and winning is a result of meeting these specific conditions. In the new field of video game studies, Callois's categories have been widely cited but his formulation has its critics. Game scholar Jesper Juul, for one, does not find Caillois's categories very useful in describing video games:

> Although it is commonly used, I find Caillois' categorization to be extraordinar-
> ily problematic. The individual categories can in many cases be useful, but their
> selection and the distinction between them are very hard to justify: while the
> distinction between paidia and ludus is more or less correct on a formal level,
> the idea that they would be opposite ends of a spectrum on an experiential level
> stems from the misunderstanding that rules are strictly limitations, and that the
> player can do nothing more complex than what the rules explicitly specify.[8]

While perhaps immediately appealing, these four game types seem somewhat arbitrary and don't always help distinguish between individual games. Take, for instance, the soccer game FIFA 2004. The game is competitive, has elements of chance (at least from the players' perspective) and simulates a sport, thus placing it in three of Callois's four categories. His claim that "sports in general" belong solely to agōn does not seem enlightening in relation to video games.[9]

You may have noticed, in addition, that the distinction between paidia and ludus is somewhat similar to the common distinction between play (as in "children in play") and game (as in "they sat down to play a game"). While a very useful distinction, it is usually best not to think of them as entirely separate. Play—even in the loose-knit form of paidia—will always have ludus elements, since even free-form play has some rules. When children play in the sandbox, they still have to—as their parents' insist—"play by the rules." These rules may be implicit, or may even be flexible, and they may not even be spoken, but they function as guidelines neverthe-less. Sandbox activity will often "be about" building the biggest, tallest, or prettiest sand creation. Most children will also be aware of the social rules that one should not take sand from the other children's sand castles, step on them or steal other children's designs and claim to be the inventor. These rules, however unspoken, shape the entire experience of being in the sandbox with others.

Forms of play with stronger ludus elements, in contrast, have precise rules and a quantifiable outcome. However, even ludus experiences contain room for inter-pretation, alteration of the rules, and some actions that are not covered by the rules. In chess, a standard rule states that once you have moved a piece the move is binding; an even stricter variant version states that you must move a piece even if you have only touched it. But in casual play, the strictness with which this rule is enforced varies greatly. This may seem like a minor detail, but chess is arguably the strictest ludus game, and an oft-cited archetype of this more severe end of the gaming spectrum.

We should note that video games differ from traditional games in the sense that their rules are enforced by the computer—rather than a gullible younger sibling or a tenderhearted older relative—and thus not open to the same type of negotiation possible in traditional board games like chess. Nevertheless, the overlap between ludus and paidia is also found in video games. One must consider video games both as rule systems and more open-ended universes. In a game like *Microsoft Flight Simulator*, for example, the player is engaged in paidia when just flying around, but when he chooses to go on a mission, the experience takes on more elements of ludus. Modern video games in particular often let the player choose between trying to achieve the goals and to simply roam the game world.

And while it is true that we cannot negotiate with our computers, we are often not competing solely against a program. Gamers don't hesitate to discuss, often fiercely, the rules of a video game, and a fundamental element of playing a video game is developing the rules about how it is played. Both before and during play, as anyone who has ever played a video game with a friend knows, it is common to try and figure out "what rules apply." It has been suggested that over time rules inevitably become less ambiguous, and that this makes games suitable for a computer platform, where the computer requires that rules be unambiguous in order to work.[10] This theory, of course, hinges on our perception of rules. In multi-player games, the negotiation of rules is often part of play, and players and develop-ers may continuously add new rules (on various levels) to the game universe.[11] For instance, players of the **real-time strategy game** *Age of Empires* II, would often spend time trying to collectively define legitimate strategies before starting a battle on Microsoft's online gaming system Zone.com.

More specifically, a certain video game type tends to encourage free-form play over strict adherence to rules and single-minded attempts to fulfill game goals. In this book, we call such games "process-oriented" (and deal with them in detail later in this chapter). An example is *SimCity*, in which the player indirectly controls the development of a city without any clear end goal.

Marshall McLuhan and games as cultural reflections

Both Huizinga and Caillois agree that games are entirely separate from the outside world. Others, however, see games as reflections of culture, and claim that a culture's most popular games can even reveal its core values. One major proponent of this position is Canadian media theorist Marshall McLuhan, referred to by some of his 1960s contemporaries as "the oracle of the electronic age." In a brief chapter of his book *Understanding Media*, McLuhan loosely defines games:

> Games are popular art, collective, social *reactions* to the main drive or action of any culture. Games, like institutions, are extensions of social man and of the body politic, as technologies are extensions of the animal organism. Both games and technologies are counter-irritants or ways of adjusting to the stress that occur in any social group . . . Games are dramatic models of our psycho-logical lives providing release of particular tensions.[12]

Here, McLuhan makes two claims: the first is that game forms are tied to the culture in which they exist, and thus reveal its nature; the second is that games release tension. An example of the first claim, from McLuhan's own discussion, is that American football is gaining in popularity at the expense of baseball because foot-ball is "nonpositional." Any player can take any position during play. Baseball, where players fulfill specific positions, represents industrial society, while football agrees "very well with the new needs of decentralized team play in the electric age."[13] He also claims that the reason why Russians surprisingly like "individualist" games like ice hockey and soccer (clearly representing a problem for his theory) is that these games have an "exotic and Utopian quality" to what is still considered "tribal" people. Although there may be some general truth to the McLuhan's claim he undermines himself somewhat by explaining away problems in such an off-hand manner.

McLuhan's second argument, that games release tension, is also not entirely obvious. Games, and in particular multiplayer games, *can* obviously provoke both anger and frustration. Beyond this, the general idea of "catharsis" (Greek for cleansing) through games is not backed up by much empirical data. The same is true of McLuhan's claim that "we enjoy those games most that mimic other situations in our work and social lives." If we look hard enough we can find similarities between most things, but we are equally likely to find examples from our list of favorite games that make this claim sound hollow. More generally, the idea of games as reflections of cultural themes remains an interesting but under-explored idea.

Gregory Bateson and play as communication

In games we are perfectly willing to accept the presence of orcs even if we would strenuously deny their real-world existence. We may even hold a series of assumptions regarding game orcs who have not even been encountered; they are likely to be evil, to not appreciate beauty and to generally be bad company.

The British anthropologist Gregory Bateson's theory on meta-communication helps us understand why we accept such fictions as meaningful (if not "real" in the strong sense). Meta-communication means communication about communication and refers to the wealth of cues we transmit and receive about how statements or actions should be interpreted. In conversation, for instance, we use body language and tone of voice to tell the other party how seriously a statement should be taken. In play, we also communicate (through numerous, often subconscious, means) that what we are doing is not to be taken at face value: We are not fighting, but *playing* at fighting. We, as animals with higher cognitive functions, are able to appreciate that an action holds different meanings within different contexts, and we come to learn this through play. As we grow older we expand the ability to meta-communicate into other areas of life and are perfectly capable of interpreting fiction (adequately meta-communicated to *be* fiction) in a different light than we would shine on reality.

Some recent games, known as alternate reality games, have challenged our ability to know and maintain the frame of play even more than traditional games. In *Majestic*, for example, part of the game consists of using real websites, fax numbers, and email addresses in order to uncover a conspiracy; the player becomes an investigator collaborating with other "real-life" players, all chasing increasingly complex clues. As play progresses, the line between what is within the video game and what is outside blurs. Huizinga would say that the magic circle is challenged, and Bateson might see increasingly subtle forms of meta-communication.

It is worth noting that alternative reality games have not achieved widespread popularity perhaps indicating that most players are not particularly interested in playing with the very boundaries of what constitutes a game.

Brian Sutton-Smith and games as play

Since the 1970s, educationist Brian Sutton-Smith has been a significant force in establishing games and play as a legitimate area of research through papers, anthologies, and conferences. Sutton-Smith never fails to stress the multifaceted nature of games, noting that "a game is what we decide it should be; that our definition will have an arbitrary character depending on our purpose."[14] According to Sutton-Smith, the variety and widespread presence of games in many cultures should not be interpreted as proof that games are inevitably a part of every culture. Rather games emerge as societies mature and develop more advanced political and social organizations. Games reflect the evolution of a society: the more complex a social system, the more advanced its games.

Sutton-Smith sees a game as finite, fixed, and goal-oriented. He defines games as "an exercise of voluntary control systems in which there is an opposition between forces, confined by a procedure and rules in order to produce a disequilibrial outcome."[15] This definition is quite broad, but it is necessary given the multifaceted nature of games. Games come in very different forms ranging from social games, to solitary games, physical games, and theoretical games. *Monopoly* is a system with rules and procedures for working out a final state—one victorious player. Each individual player tries to establish dominance by making the right moves. In soccer, players interact with each other within teams to score a greater number of goals than the opposing team.

Although Sutton-Smith has refused to give a one-line definition of play, the complexity of the challenge has not stopped others from trying, as we will see in the following sections. In fact, it seems that almost every well-known philosopher has theorized on play. For example, German philosopher Friedrich Nietzsche said that "Two different things wanteth the true man: danger and diversion. Therefore wanteth he woman, as the most dangerous plaything."[16] Psychoanalyst C.G. Jung refers to the creative aspect of play: "The creation of something new is not accomplished by the intellect but by the play instinct acting from inner necessity. The creative mind plays with the objects it loves."[17]

George Herbert Mead and role training

Social psychologist George Herbert Mead considered play to be an important ingredient in what he called the process of the genesis of the self. According to Mead, who wrote his influential work, *Mind, Self, and Society* in 1934, a self arises through a learning process in which children understand and eventually come to master normal human social activity. Social activity is all about communication, where humans use a shared system of symbols to exchange ideas with each other. Play and games, also being symbolic, are for Mead a clear precursor to adult communication.

His definition of play is mainly what others have called "make-believe," in which children pretend to be one thing or another and play a role: a mother, a policeman, or an Indian, for example. This is different from the way animals play, in that children deliberately take on another role and build a temporary self by using the symbols that indicate that role. This kind of play is usually limited to one role at a time, even though children can change from one role to another very quickly. The essential difference between this kind of play and organized games is that in games, the player has to "take the attitude of everyone else involved in that game, and that these different roles must have a definite relationship to each other."[18] This means that the player needs to be conscious about the other players' roles at all times, something that is facilitated by the rules of the game. Rules are "the set of responses which a particular attitude calls out."[19] So to go from play to game requires the individual to integrate himself into a higher level of group organization.

For Mead, an individual can only obtain his unity of self when he has internalized this "generalized other," that is, the attitude of the whole community. Games are excellent mirrors of the way that people organize themselves, where all actions are related to each other in an organic way that can be understood by learning the rules. Children experiment with many different kinds of social organizations as they grow up. The exercise of learning to belong, of learning different roles and rules, allows their personality to develop.

Henry Jenkins and the art of the game

An influential cultural view of the nature of video games has been presented by a professor of comparative media studies, Henry Jenkins.[20] Jenkins argues that video games are a new form of popular art, and game designers the artists of our century. His work is inspired by cultural critic Gilbert Seldes, who in his book *Seven Lively Arts*[21] argued that "America's primary contributions to artistic expression had come through emerging forms of popular culture such as jazz, the Broadway musical, Vaudeville, Hollywood cinema, the comic strip, and the vernacular humor column." Although some of these cultural forms have today acquired a certain cultural respectability, Seldes's focus on popular **aesthetics** instead of on the "great arts" was rather revolutionary in the mid-twentieth century.

For Seldes, the "lively arts" are mainly kinetic, that is, they seek to move people emotionally rather than to appeal to the intellect as the classical arts do. Popular artists, Jenkins explains, explore new directions and new media:

Cinema and other popular arts were to be celebrated, Seldes insisted, because they were so deeply imbedded in everyday life, because they were democratic arts embraced by average citizens. Through streamlined styling and syncopated rhythms, they captured the vitality of contemporary urban experience.[22]

For Jenkins, video games are the worthy heirs of this trend:

Games represent a new lively art, one as appropriate for the digital age as those earlier media were for the machine age. They open up new aesthetic experiences and transform the computer screen into a realm of experimentation and innovation that is broadly accessible.[23]

Jenkins reminds us that a lot of the social prejudice levelled against video games today has clear parallels to the reactions against the cinema in Seldes's time, like the vitriol levelled against the depiction of violence and sex.

He nevertheless acknowledges that many games are "banal, formulaic and predictable," following well-known recipes instead of innovating. Economical constraints are not a valid explanation for their aesthetic conservatism, as this doesn't prevent artists in other media such as film from delivering good products. (However, we must not forget that video game technology changes so dramatically every few months that designers spend a lot of time catching up instead of exploring the medium aesthetically.) Jenkins argues that games are an art form still in its infancy, but some games with advanced aesthetics already suggest that the form can provoke strong emotions. Video games have also already given us such memorable characters as Sonic the Hedgehog and *Super Mario Bros*, Mario and Luigi.

In order to understand how key developmental moments come about in video games, we need to understand them as a medium. For Jenkins, games are about player control, and the best experiences arise when players perceive that their intervention has spectacular influence on the game, such as when a *Civilization IV* player understands that her carefully planned strategy ensured her narrow but crucial victory over a warring neighbor nation.

The games he admires are those which offer players the opportunity to do things that were not possible before. For example, in *Black and White* players are gods whose every decision has moral consequences and affects the balance of good and evil in the game world.

Jenkins talks of play as a performance, where a person's interaction with a game facilitates a kind of immersion unknown in other media. In order to facilitate the player's sense of extreme control over the game he is in—vital to Jenkins' vision of a successful game—the design and aesthetics of the game is crucial. Even more than cinema, games make use of "expressive amplification," a process in which the impact of specific actions is exaggerated so that the player feels increased pleasure at executing these actions. In Jenkins' view, the artistic potential of video games will be met when designers concentrate on exploring the aesthetics of action instead of trying to imitate other media.

Formal definitions

Thinkers like Huizinga to McLuhan, as well as many others, have used games primarily in the pursuit of other questions, and are not solely concerned with creating a "formal" definition of a game. Others, however, have tried to define games in their own right. Game historian David Parlett, for instance, suggests that a game—in the sense used in this book—has two defining components: *ends* and *means*.[24] *Ends* refers to the notion that a game is a contest, with a goal that only one player or team can achieve. Thus, to Parlett, a game always has a winner. *Means* refers to the game equipment and rules. Parlett's definition is obviously both strict and broad. Many of the phenomena that we label here as games in fact do not qualify according to Parlett's concept of a game, as something that can be won, and by only one player or team.

Parlett writes mostly on non-electronic games and this focus shows. Process-oriented single-player video games, for example, cannot be won in the sense that poker can be won. The 1983 classic *Elite* is a game where the player explores deep space; part of the game's brilliance which has been copied by more recent games like is that it has no fixed endpoint, no single goal. But as a result, it would thus be excluded by Parlett's strict definition. The same goes for persistent (i.e. those which are always available and never reset to the initial state) multiplayer games like *EverQuest* (a fantasy role-playing universe where players can complete quests alone or can collaborate with characters controlled by other players); these games do not end, and in principle all players can reach the highest level. At the same time, Parlett's definition is usefully broad, since it includes activities that we would normally not consider games—auctions, for instance, and certain types of democratic elections.

A more elaborate definition is proposed by philosopher Bernard Suits in his book *Grasshopper: Games, Life, and Utopia*. He writes:

> To play a game is to engage in activity directed towards bringing about a specific state of affairs, using only means permitted by rules, and where the

rules prohibit more efficient in favour of less efficient means, and where such rules are accepted just because they make possible such activity.[25]

Importantly, Suits stresses that game rules are inhibiting, and favor "less efficient means." It is a highly compelling, though counter-intuitive, model: that to enjoy ourselves we in fact seek out rigid and restrictive structures.

Like most one-sentence truths, however, it has limitations. Think of the board game *Monopoly*. The most efficient way of moving around the board would be to just move your car as you please, without bothering about dice, cards, and other formalities. But of course *Monopoly* isn't really about driving at all. The game is about amassing wealth and ruining opponents. One very efficient way to do this would be to just to roll the dice and hand out play money according to the rolls. A simple role of the dice would decide the winner and the loser. Clearly, this would be a less than thrilling experience; we appreciate the difficulty of making money in the game, and our appreciation is evidence in favor of Suits's definition.

However, we should also stress that *Monopoly* could be far more difficult than it is. "Less efficient" certainly should not be interpreted as "least efficient," since it would appear that what makes *Monopoly* fun is not so much extreme difficulty, but rather its appealing goal—which is really quite simple—and the set of well-balanced rules we follow to try and achieve that goal. The *Monopoly* rules create excitement not just by being more difficult than our minimalist one-dice-decides-all version. The game system introduces an element of skill and encourages us to use strategy while still maintaining the importance of chance, thus keeping alive, if only barely, the hope of recovery from unfortunate situations. What is crucial—at least for our *Monopoly* example—is a particular combination of rules and chance; the rules-as-limitations concept is powerful but not without its problems.

While Suits and Parlett are not specifically interested in *video* games, others have put forth definitions that clearly take into account the rise of electronic entertainment. The first writer to seriously and systematically address such issues was game designer Chris Crawford. In 1982—several years ahead of the crowd—Crawford published *The Art of Computer Game Design*[26] an exploration of how to understand games and their relation to players. Crawford's book boldly attempts to "address the fundamental aspects of video games to achieve a conclusion that will withstand the ravages of time and change."[27] Crawford does not offer any one-line definition but rather names four features that are common to all video games: representation, interaction, conflict, and safety.

1   *Representation* refers to games being about something else; or as he writes, a game "subjectively represents a subset of reality."[28] Games model external situations—a baseball game, for example—but they are not actually part of these situations. Crawford stresses how most games, in fact, do not attempt to be truly faithful simulations; hence their representation is "subjective."

2   *Interaction*, according to Crawford, is crucial to games' appeal. The player must be able to influence the world of the game and get meaningful responses to his actions, so that he feels engaged with the game.

3   *Conflict* is the idea that a game has a goal that is blocked by obstacles, whether human or electronic. Conflict can be "direct or indirect, violent or nonviolent, but it is always present in every game."[29]

4   *Safety* refers to the fact that the conflicts in a game do not carry the same consequences as those same conflicts in the real world. For instance, losing a war
game may be humiliating, infuriating, and even costly, but it does not mean
that your actual home is destroyed. Thus, although games can have consequences, Crawford considers them safe ways of experiencing real situations.

Of these characteristics, representation and safety stand out as the most debat-
able. Crawford ties the former to the idea that games are systems, but in this regard,
representation is an odd term to use. We can have a system that is not a representation in any ordinary sense of the word. Many games do not represent real-life situations; the gold-coin filled worlds of *Super Mario Bros.*, for example, or the endless
array of puzzle games like *Tetris*. Crawford argues that while these games do not
represent any objective phenomenon they nevertheless represent something to the
player: "the player does perceive the game to represent something from his private
fantasy world."[30] Thus, the player can perceive the game action as meaningful even
though it has no reference to the outside world.

As for safety, it implies that games operate inside the "magic circle" discussed
previously in this chapter; that game events are without direct real-world consequences. Crawford's position, however, is more nuanced than that of Huizinga and
Caillois (he agrees that there are consequences; they just aren't direct) and so he
doesn't invite the criticism leveled at "strong" magic circle thinking.

More than twenty years after Crawford's pioneering book, game scholars have
recently picked up the challenge of defining games. Their commitment is notable
for its desire to seriously engage with the work that has come before. Of the resulting definitions, two are particularly useful. The first was suggested in 2003 by
game theorists Katie Salen and Eric Zimmerman, in their book *Rules of Play*:

> A *game* is a system in which players engage in an artificial conflict, defined by
> rules, that results in a quantifiable outcome.[31]

The second definition comes from theorist Jesper Juul:

> A game is a rule-based formal system with a variable and quantifiable outcome,
> where different outcomes are assigned different values, the player exerts effort
> in order to influence the outcome, the player feels attached to the outcome, and
> the consequences of the activity are optional and negotiable.[32]

These definitions look quite similar, and they are both very thoughtful. They both
stress that games are systems and have quantifiable outcomes. The most obvious
difference, perhaps, is that Salen and Zimmerman's description of "an artificial
conflict" returns us to the idea of the magic circle, whereas Juul is concerned less
with the nature of the conflict and more with describing the player herself.

Salen and Zimmerman's definition is brief and elegant, but it is not exclusive to
games. Depending on how we read "artificial conflict" it might, for instance,
include university exams. Here, the student is engaged in a conflict (to outdo her
fellow students, to prove wrong her skeptical teacher, or to overcome the "challenge" of the situation); this conflict is defined by rules (the university's laws and
regulations), and it results in a quantifiable outcome (her grade). The conflict is
artificial in the sense that the exam situation takes place within a magic circle, with
a variety of rules that do not really apply outside. (We should note that the conflict

is not, however, artificial in Crawford's sense; it is not a *representation* of a real-life situation.)

Juul's definition, on the other hand, gets around this particular objection by stipulating that the consequences be optional and negotiable. His definition is interesting for including the player in the equation; a game in Juul's terms depends on the player's attitude towards the activity. Of course, this may invite objections. Inevitably, for example, there will be players who neither exert much effort in their games nor feel particularly attached to the outcome; but we would not want to exclude such a person's game of poker—much less *the game of poker*—from the "game" category.

Juul's definition is an attempt to tease out the criteria that we intuitively use to differentiate games from non-games. To this end, he offers a model which shows our often implicit reasons for calling something a game:

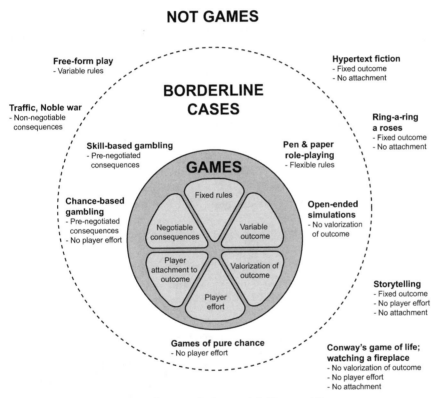

Figure 3.4 Jesper Juul's model of how standard game definitions work[33]

Juul refers to this as the "classic game model," based on his observation that certain modern video games in fact do not comply with the criteria which have traditionally been part of game definitions. The six inner slices in the model represent the classic criteria. The level labeled "Borderline cases" includes phenomena that only marginally qualify as games in terms of the classic model. For instance, pen-and-paper role-playing games do not always have fixed rules. The third level holds activities that plainly fall outside the classical model—"storytelling," for example, which has a fixed outcome, requires no effort by the player (in this case the listener) and which, according to Juul, requires no attachment. By contrast, a video game like *Lemmings*, in which the player is faced with unambivalent goals, where the rules are fixed, and the outcome is not prescribed, falls squarely within the "classic" model of games.

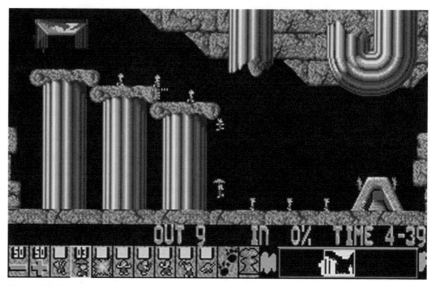

Figure 3.5 *Lemmings*

For every game like *Lemmings*, as Juul insists, we could probably find another example of a video game that proves Juul's observation about video games not fitting the "classic" criteria. In massively multiplayer **online role-playing** games like *World of Warcraft*, for example, players can set their own goals and there is no one way to win. The criteria also don't apply to wide open **gamespaces** like that of *Grand Theft Auto: Vice City*, where players can be so distracted from their missions by the vibrant city simulation that they may not ever complete the game's plot. Even certain older video games do not fit into the classic model. In *Little Computer People*, released in 1985, the player interacts with a character who performs various tasks—based on the player's treatment—as a sort of virtual pet. The program, which was of course marketed as a game, does not meet the "Valorization of outcome" criterion of Juul's model, and would therefore be classified as a borderline case.

Figure 3.6 *Little Computer People*

At a glance, perhaps, the attempts to provide formal definitions discussed above, may be appear to be relatively abstract exercises with few real-world implications. But they are important since they help us refine our thinking on what constitutes a game and thereby address subconscious biases and since they help us clarify whether the conclusions we reach are unique to games or perhaps apply to other media as well. If, for instance, we study the effects of games on learning we will do well to reflect on whether a measured effect is due to audiovisual representation (which other media have as well) or to the fact that players interact with a rule system and thus "experience" its **dynamics** (which isn't the case with books, movies or television, for instance).

Our point here is that it is more important to acknowledge and specify one's own definition than it is to try to decide on the "correct" one. However, based on this discussion we see that there is a good deal of overlap between the definitions proposed. First, they are focused on games as rule systems and are unconcerned with matters of representation. In other words, audiovisual feedback is not a requirement, and the definitions say nothing about digital computation and thus are definitions of *games* and not merely *video* games. One of the shared requirements which is most useful in distinguishing games from other activities is the notion that events or actions should be evaluated, for instance by the game assigning points to the player. Essentially, this means that a game has goals somehow specified by the game design. It is not enough that a person has a goal (say, finding a specific street address) for something to be a game; the experience must be designed. But nor it is *enough* that an experience is designed. Virtual worlds like *Second Life*, for instance, are designed but have no specific goals and thus would fall outside most of the definitions discussed. Of course, designed experiences with goals does not in itself work as a definition either (since, again, it would include university exams). It is the *additional characteristic* which an activity must display to be a game which in fact seems to cause disagreement and which is therefore all the more worthwhile to consider in one's efforts to understand games.

Having discussed formal definitions which are end-results of attempts to understand games, we turn now to definitions which—quite intentionally—are less rigorous but also serve a different purpose, as tools for actual game design.

Pragmatic definitions

The "formal" definitions discussed above aim to be as consistent and precise as possible. They are not tools for the creation of new games. Rather they can be compared to philosophies of language; they may be truly insightful without ever making anyone a better communicator. Another type of definition, labeled here as "pragmatic," has the opposite characteristics—they are meant as tools for action and not as philosophically bullet-proof concepts.

Perhaps the most famous recent game definition, famous enough to make it into most design books and onto the t-shirts of many a gamer, is that of game designer Sid Meier: "A game is a series of interesting choices."[34] In contrast to formal definitions, Meier's is less rigoros, much more casual, and perhaps intentionally simplistic. Probably, we'll actually need to amend it slightly if it is to make sense. Surely something does not cease to be a game if the choices are uninteresting? That merely makes it a bad game. So Sid Meier should be read as saying "A *good* game is a series of interesting choices." By stressing that choices must be *interesting*, Meier is pointing out (or claiming) that cases where one option is clearly better than others or where one's choice does not matter to how the game plays out are not particularly engaging to the player.

For example, in *Civilization IV* (designed by Meier himself) the player must constantly choose whether to spend resources on research, diplomatic standing, or armament. At any given time, the player has clues about which choice is likely to be most sensible, but there is no *single* correct choice. The element of chance is ever present, and the player's choices invariably depend on what she thinks the enemy is doing.

From a critical perspective, Meier's statement is very useful for thinking about strategy games, but less appropriate for action games. In *Super Mario Bros.* (see Figure 3.7) you have no choice but to jump to a certain platform, or down a particular pipe. The *choice* is not interesting in itself; the *activity*, however, may still increase your heart-rate, since the outcome depends completely on your skill. Improving your abilities and finding the correct solution to Mario's problems makes the game interesting, but there is no interesting choice as such.[35] In classic adventure games like *Blade Runner*, there may be only one correct choice and there may not even be any physical skill involved, but the investigation process can still feel exciting. Meier's definition is thus helpful, and wonderfully pithy, but not really sufficient.

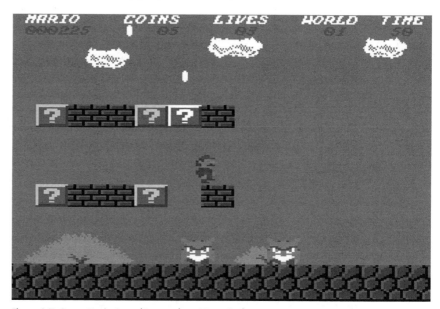

Figure 3.7 *Super Mario Bros.* (Commodore 64 version)

A simple, yet highly useful, pragmatic way of modeling games emerged out of several workshops held at the Game Developers Conference in California between 2001 and 2004. The "MDA model," developed by Robin Hunicke, Marc LeBlanc and Robert Zubeck, seeks to divide games into three separate dimensions: mechanics, dynamics, and aesthetics.[36]

Mechanics are the rules and basic code of a game. It is not what we see or hear while we play a game. Rather, "mechanics" refers to the vast amount of information that goes into constructing the world of the game—the series of algorithms, for example, that determine the reaction pattern of a computer-controlled character.

Dynamics is the way the game actually plays based on the mechanics. It is the events that actually occur, or *can* occur, during the course of the game as experienced by the player. For instance, the game mechanics may contain complicated algorithms by which the behavior patterns of an enemy soldier are determined in a probabilistic fashion, while the player is merely presented with a dangerous foe hiding behind a tree and opening fire. Dynamics are functions of the mechanics, but they may also be surprising, as complex processes interact in ways that cannot always be predicted. For instance, certain mechanics of the narrative-based shooter *Deus Ex* were flexible enough that a player could complete missions in ways not predicted by the game's designers (as we describe further later in this book under the heading of "**emergence**").

Aesthetics covers the favorable emotional responses invoked in the player as he or she interacts with the game. Hunicke, LeBlanc and Zubeck list the elements that attract us to games:

1 Sensation (game as sense-pleasure)

2 Fantasy (game as make-believe)

3 Narrative (game as drama)

4 Challenge (game as obstacle course)

5 Fellowship (game as social framework)

6 Discovery (game as uncharted territory)

7 Expression (game as self-discovery)

8 Submission (game as pastime).

A game will usually offer some of these pleasures, but not all of them. *Tetris*, for instance, emphasizes challenge, submission, and perhaps sensation, but does not offer narrative or expression. *Grand Theft Auto: Vice City*, on the other hand, affords most of the pleasures with the exception of fellowship. The categories should not be seen as "objective" as they depend on interpretation and the context in which the game is played. For instance, we can interpret both *Tetris* and *Grand Theft Auto* as providing as social framework, and we can imagine a player expressing herself through *Tetris* by modifying[37] the game and designing new background images.

The MDA model is a very useful tool for understanding—and discussing—the way games work. Although admittedly simplistic, it offers a decent distinction between the various elements of a game, and highlights the ways in which games are systems rather than linear, pre-determined structures like novels, movies or television programs. However, MDA has limitations. It is more of a designer's tool than a satisfying account of how **gameplay** actually works. Powerful parts of the gaming experience—everything from the context in which we play a game, to the culture that frames the game, to its intended or unintended links to other games, or movies, or texts—fall outside the model's jurisdiction. For instance, a teenager playing *Grand Theft Auto: Vice City* might enjoy the game's anti-establishment attitude, and might relish participating in the violent acts that have caused such a media uproar. This pleasure does not strictly emerge from the game mechanics, though there is a clear connection. Furthermore, the model is centered on the rules of a game, and except for the aesthetic category of "sensation"—which alludes to the pleasure brought about by a game's audiovisuals—MDA all but ignores the expressive side of the game.

Though not perfect, Sid Meier and the developers of the MDA model offer two of the most prominent pragmatic definitions of a video game thus providing useful "tools for thought" helpful in inspiring one's game design work.

THE ISSUE OF **GENRE**

In both popular and academic literature on games, the concept of genre tends to play a role. Observations may pertain only to certain game types and thus many game scholars and journalists find it hugely useful to establish systems for categorizing games.

Existing genre systems are based on a variety of criteria. Rigorous attempts to define mutually exclusive genres are rare, but can be found in Mark J. P. Wolf's *The Medium of the Video Game*[38] and in work by Espen Aarseth aiming to produce multidimensional genre systems.[39]

Wolf, a media theorist, discusses the relevance of various approaches to defining genre in other media. These approaches generally focus on representational, surface phenomena—what we actually see on the screen—but according to Wolf **interactivity** is more important in video games as it "is an essential part of every game's structure and a more appropriate way of examining and defining video game genres."[40] Wolf's notion of interactivity is closely linked to a game's *goals*: "In a video game, there is almost always a definite objective that the player strives to complete . . . and in doing so very specific interactions are used. Thus the intention—of the player-character at least—is often clear, and can be analyzed as a part of the game."[41] However, Wolf then goes on to outline forty-three distinct genres, many of which are only vaguely linked to his own interactivity criterion—from abstract to board games, and from educational to sports. Thus, despite Wolf's reasonable discussion we end up with a list of genres based on no discernable system of categorization.

Game theorist Espen Aarseth considers it unproductive to define a genre based on one variable (such as theme) as this is likely to have major overlaps (e.g. games that are about shooting *and* flying) or tell us nothing very interesting. Instead, he suggests that video games should be evaluated based on a series of variables. By this perspective we could decide on a game's genre by rating it in relation to each of the variables selected. This approach has the advantage of categorizing *every possible* game that could be conceived. The drawback of this system is that it is limited practical use.

Less formally, popular magazines and websites often have their own—more or less idiosyncratic—way of dealing with genres. Gamespot.com, a major games website, employs a common solution, dividing games into the following categories: action games, adventure games, driving games, puzzle games, role-playing games, simulations, sports games, and strategy games. While useful for the purposes of the website, these genres are obviously not derived from any standard principle. For instance, *driving* implies a game's theme while *action* implies a more fundamental characteristic.

Philosophically speaking, the large number of genre systems exist because there is no objective way to measure the differences between two things. An example: two books will share many characteristics (e.g. they have pages and they can be carried) but also have many differences (e.g. the covers look different, they have different titles, they don't weigh the same, and they don't have the same content). But there is no objective way of determining which similarities or differences are the most important.

The same goes for people. How different are human beings from one another? The answer is all in your perspective. Anthropologists and other students of culture may tend towards "very different," while biologists might lean towards "very similar." Neither group is right or wrong. Similarly, no one can prove that it is better to focus on differences rather than similarities, or vice versa.

Genres, then, are arbitrary. They are analytical constructs imposed on a group of objects in order to discuss the complexity of their individual differences in a meaningful way. But are genres just categories with no bearing on reality? No, the conventions of each genre create expectations. Take movies. When you watch a romantic comedy, you expect the movie to follow certain conventions and ignore others—you expect the man and woman to kiss and make up, and you are confident that a crazed murderer will not jump out from the bushes and kill them. When watching a slasher movie, you might have the opposite expectations. Perhaps more importantly, producers make movies that conform to established genres. Box office receipts may indicate that war epics do well financially, and this may influence a producer's decision to approve the next World War II movie instead of a teen comedy.

How exactly one chooses to split the cake and divide up games may be a largely arbitrary decision but some methods are more consistent than others. One way to ensure consistency is to use genre labels based on the same criterion. An example of the reverse is revealing: an *inconsistent* genre system might consist of *girl games*, *home-computer games*, *racing games*, and *sports games*. This system is not useful, as a particular title could easily fall into all four categories.

In this book, we propose a genre system based on a game's criteria for success. We ask: "What does it take to succeed in the game?" To explore this concept, let's look at two games that are quite different: the ever-popular *Tetris*, and *Myst* (a narrative adventure where the player has to explore a mysterious world and investigate the disappearance of certain characters). To succeed in *Tetris* you need fast reflexes and decent hand-eye coordination. To succeed in *Myst* you need puzzle-solving skills and deductive logic. These criteria for success are quite different. So rather than focus on criteria like theme or narrative, the system we're proposing focuses directly on a feature important to games: goals, and how to achieve them.

Another example that further illustrates this distinction is a comparison of the two soccer themed games *FIFA 2004* and *Championship Manager 4*. In *FIFA 2004* the players must wriggle their **joysticks** in order to out-score the opponent. In *Championship Manager 4* the player takes on the role of soccer coach, and concentrates on high-level strategy rather than playing in the matches. Thus, while both are "about" soccer we do not consider them to be in the same genre.

Two types of games pose a challenge to our system: single-player and multiplayer role playing games. The first problem is that these two types of role playing games are, in fact, quite different from each other. Single-player games such as *Baldur's Gate* (a fantasy-themed game where the player controls multiple characters) demand strategic skills and include puzzle solving, while online multiplayer games such as *World of Warcraft* (where thousands of players can act in the same fantasy-themed world simultaneously) do not have very explicit goals and do not generally contain puzzles, but do require social skills for dealing and collaborating with the other players. The second challenge to our system is that certain games (e.g. *World of Warcraft*) and similar games cannot be so readily categorized based on criteria for

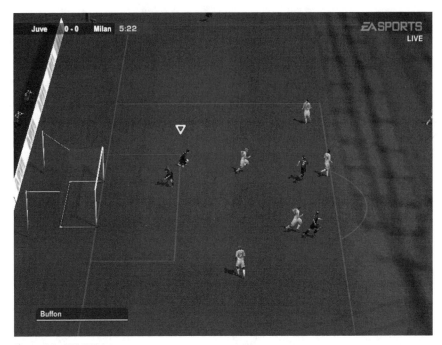

Figure 3.8 *FIFA 2004*

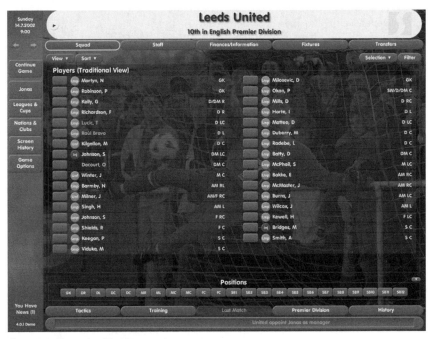

Figure 3.9 *Championship Manager 4*

success because they are not obviously goal-oriented (or at least invite players to set their own goals to a large degree). We recognize these problems as weaknesses of our genre system, and choose to group single-player role-playing games with strategy games and place games with vague goals (or no goals) in the special category of "process-oriented games." We describe the four genres in our system below.

Action games

To some, the action game is the archetypical video game. Action games are often intense and usually involve fighting or some kind of physical drama. *Pac-Man* is an action game, as is the shooter *Half-Life 2* and the racing game *MotorStorm*. What ties these games together is that their criterion for success is motor skill and hand-eye coordination. In classical **arcade** action games, the player mostly had to coordinate the movement of the on-screen character and did not have to worry about what the correct choice might be (one simply, and obviously, had to jump an approaching barrel at the right time for instance). In more complex titles like the 2003 platform game *Prince of Persia: The Sands of Time* the player must still perform challenging feats of coordination but must also put effort into figuring out how to solve the game's spatial puzzles (i.e. each challenge must be analyzed to arrive at a solution and subsequently solved in practice by a sequence of jumps, climbs, etc.).

Adventure games

Adventure games are characterized by requiring deep thinking and great patience. These skills are employed to participate in, or uncover, narratives that are often based on detective story templates. Typically, the player is represented by an individual character involved in a plot of mystery or exploration, and faces puzzles of various kinds. Quite often, adventure games are entirely devoid of fighting and of action sequences; sometimes they even lack the risk of the main character dying. To succeed the player must exhibit skills of logic and deduction. Examples of the genre, in its pure form, include *Adventure* (from 1976), *Maniac Mansion* (from 1987), and *Dreamfall: The Longest Journey* (from 2006). We also include single-player role-playing games under this heading, although we acknowledge that they have strong strategy elements. Examples of this sub-genre include *Ultima*, *Wizardry*, *Baldur's Gate*.

Strategy games

Occupying a space somewhere between action and adventure games, we find the strategy genre. The most common form is perhaps a game of war, but rather than the player being on the battlefield (a clear example of the action genre), she takes on the distant role of general. Variations on the general role can include anything from mayor to deity. The conflict is often represented on a map that resembles classic board games, and which illustrates anything from a whole continent to an urban street.

Two important sub-genres exist: real-time strategy and **turn-based strategy**. Real-time strategy games do not pause between turns but rather play out in *real-time* or, perhaps more appropriately, *continuous-time* (since a single game session may span thousands of years in the game world's internal chronology). As a result they resemble action games, in that the player's score is dependent on fast reactions and skillful manipulation of mouse and keyboard. To win, the player must carefully balance large numbers of interdependent variables, paying careful attention to signals of other players' choices and strategies. Despite their action component, these games are strategic since understanding the ways in which priorities and perceptions interplay over time is ultimately more important than one's speed with the mouse. Examples of real-time strategy games include *Dune II*, *Warcraft*, and *Dawn of War*. The other sub-genre is turn-based strategy games. Here, the action stops while players make their choices, following classic board games such as chess or risk. Examples include *Balance of Power*, *Civilization*, and *Warlords*.

Process-oriented games

Though winning seems an essential element of games, a (growing) breed of software exists on the edges of this definition of a game. Instead of giving the player one or more goals, process-oriented games provide the player with a system to play with. These products receive the game label not so much for staging conflict or competition but because they're made for entertainment purposes; they could fit the definition of a *toy* rather than actual games. Think of populating and watching an aquarium as opposed to playing chess.

There are two main approaches to the design of process-oriented games. In one type the player is a character exploring and manipulating a dynamic and ever-changing world. Another type puts the player in charge of more fundamental variables, such as taxation levels or elements influencing an ecosystem. Process-oriented games lack any standard, or consistent, criterion for success, although each game encourages certain types of play: most players will want to build a large city in *SimCity*, or try to reach higher levels in *EverQuest*. A few other examples include *Elite*, *The Sims*, and *Zoo Tycoon*.

A subgroup of process-oriented games try their best to mimic concrete, real-world experiences, such as driving a car or flying an airplane. These are often referred to as **simulation games**. While many action games do flout ever-greater levels of realism, simulation games go further than action games, and reproduce minor details even at the expense of immediate gratification. The obstacle in these games need not be any external enemy; it is often the challenge of mastering the complexities of the **interface**. The challenge of a flight simulator, for example, is learning the details of getting a passenger plane off the ground. By this definition, games such as *SimCity* or *SimEarth* are not simulation games, since they do not try to simulate a concrete experience or strive to replicate minute details. Examples of simulation games include *Flight Simulator 2002*, *Microsoft Train Simulator*, *Sub Battle Simulator*.

The four genres are summarized in table form below. We will be referring to them throughout the remainder of this book.

	Action games	Adventure games	Strategy games	Process-oriented games
Typical action	Battle	Mystery solving others	Build nation in competition with	Exploration and/or mastery
Criterion of success	Fast reflexes	Logic ability	Analyzing interdependent variables	Varies widely, often nonexistent

4 HISTORY

A BRIEF PRE-HISTORY OF VIDEO GAMES/DOES HISTORY MATTER?/A HISTORY OF
VIDEO GAMES/THE 1970s/THE 1980s/THE 1990s/THE 2000s/PERSPECTIVES

The history of video games, as we have seen, may have begun with the launching of a tiny white torpedo in an MIT basement. However, while the three creators
of the torpedo launch—more on them later—did inspire many a programmer of
the time, these three were, perhaps needless to say, standing on the shoulders of
giants.

A BRIEF PRE-HISTORY OF VIDEO GAMES

In fact, the history of video games is merely the latest chapter in the fascinating and
much lengthier history of games. If we hope to come anywhere near the roots of
this history, we must travel several thousand miles south-east from Cambridge,
Massachusetts, and some 4,600 years back in time. This will place us in ancient
Egypt during the Third Dynasty (2686–2613 B.C.); here we should be able to
observe people playing the game of Senet. As far as scholars can surmise, Senet was
a game of skill and chance not unlike present-day backgammon. Some speculate
that Senet's status changed over time, from a purely recreational pastime to an
activity with potent symbolism and religious significance. But even more remarkable is that in a culture and an era utterly foreign from our own, we find a form of
game that maintains its appeal four millennia later. Even with the omnipresence of
computers today, and their astoundingly complex technological possibilities, we
still choose to play old-fashioned board games that ancient Egyptians would have
quite an easy time learning.

Around the time of Senet, although somewhat to the East, Mesopotamians
played what is known as the royal game of Ur, an elaborate board game with an
element of chance determined by dice. Although games at various times may have
served ritual functions, it is clear that they also served the functions familiar to
us—to entertain, to delight, to create social interactions.

Nor were these two games alone. The oriental game of go was played since at
least 2000 B.C.. Dice were used as game of chance from the seventh century B.C.,
about 1,400 years prior to the first mention—in a Persian romance—of chess. This
period also marks the beginning of the Olympic Games in Greece (the first documented games were held in 776 B.C.). Like board games, sports are activities carefully framed by rules, to assign scores to the performance of participants. The
Olympic Games, then, like early known board and dice games, are testament to a
fundamental human tendency: we create games. Indeed, we even adapt most non-
recreational activities into games. Think only of how many non-game activities we
have assimilated from our own lives—or the lives of those people we dream of
being—into games: we cook and run and swim; we shoot and sail and fly.

At the time of the first documented Olympics, there existed a version of chess called chaturanga, a Sanskrit term referring to a battle formation. While not identical to present-day chess, chaturanga ranks as an undisputed ancestor; one particular piece, like the king, was all-important to victory, and different pieces were endowed with different powers. A plethora of chaturanga derivations existed, since rules diverged from region to region. The game traveled widely, and by the tenth century had arrived in Europe and Africa in the luggage of Arab travelers. Only in the late fifteenth century can we see the rules of chess undergo a process of standardization. At this time, card games—which had been known in Europe for two centuries—were given standardized card suits. Analogous to the history of Senet, playing cards took on symbolic or mystic functions in the mid-eighteenth century as they were employed in the service of fortune telling.

The idea of using board games to simulate actual real-world activities—as opposed to merely drawing upon them for symbolism—flourished in the wake of the Kriegsspiel, developed in 1824 by a Prussian lieutenant, Georg von Reisswitz.[1] This strategy game, in which players were offered a range of complex situations became popular with Prussian army personnel. Decidedly more peaceful was *The Mansion of Happiness*), released in 1843, the first commercially produced game in the United States. The board game offered a beautifully simplistic vision of the world, where good deeds were rewarded and bad deeds punished.

The Mansion of Happiness, however, will lie forever in the shadow of that singular international success story: *Monopoly*. Published in the mid-1930s by Parker Brothers, it was based on an earlier board game *The Landlord's Game* and a number of derivatives from this, but achieved a fame unknown to its predecessors. Perhaps anticipating much of the second half of the twentieth century, *Monopoly* makes no pretence of lauding in-game niceties. The game, which has sold more than 200 million copies worldwide, combines chance and strategic thinking as players vie for domination of a fictional world of real estate.[2] To the seeming delight of twelve-year-olds everywhere, the game rewards nothing as much as bold capitalist perseverance, and is a fascinating example of how games can reflect—as well as foster—cultural values. Its success also helped establish the board game as a foundational activity for family and friends, young and old alike.

In the aftermath of World War II, electronic games were struggling towards life in circuits of various types, but the launch of the tiny white torpedo was still a long way off. The 1950s, however, saw the publication of numerous strategic wargames, including the still influential Risk and Diplomacy. While the complex rules of the Kriegsspiel does live on in many of these wargames, it is worth noting that Diplomacy relies on nothing but the most minimalist of rule sets. As players battle for domination of First World War Europe, negotiation and interpersonal scheming come to the fore, thus creating a layered Machiavellian experience out of the simplest of rules.

By the mid-twentieth century, games were an established part of cultures around the globe, in myriad manifestations: we played games of chance, games of war and strategy, and games that simulated more and more aspects of the rest of our lives. One development that cannot go un-mentioned (even if it did not technically come *before* video games) is pen-and-paper role-playing games (RPGs). These did not develop in a cultural vacuum (few things do) but rather were the result of a remarkable convergence of popular trends and interests in the early 1970s. The 1960s had seen the commercial proliferation of *wargames*, tabletop games of strategy where maps, dice and figures were used to simulate battles, allowing players to recreate historical conflicts. And in 1954, worldwide publication of J.R.R. Tolkien's *The Lord of the Rings* altered the landscape of literature and introduced the world to the fantasy genre. A host of authors followed suit, recreating worlds from the medieval to the mythical, stocked with magic, dragons and heroes. These derivations, though never attaining the popularity of Tolkien's epic, catered to the many hungry readers and fostered a community of fantasy fans that continues to thrive today.

Both wargames and fantasy literature found their primary audience amongst teenage males, so it was perhaps only a question of time before the two genres merged. Soon after, fantasy-themed wargames appeared where elves and orcs replaced the armies of European empires. In fact, the mother of all role-playing games, *Dungeons and Dragons*, was directly based on a fantasy wargame called *Chainmail*. Created by Dave Arneson and Gary Gygax, *Dungeons and Dragons*, was commercially launched in 1974. Despite a slow start, it was selling 7,000 copies a month by 1979, **spawning** a multitude of sequels and inspiring untold numbers of gamers to become game designers of their own. The game's complex rules seemed to be a magnet for burgeoning designers, who adapted them in countless ways to their own worlds of fantasy.

In the medieval world of *Dungeons and Dragons*, a player chose to be either a wizard, a warrior or a cleric, and decided to be a member of one of the world's three races: hobbits, dwarves or elves. Groups of players, seated around a dining room table or huddled in a basement, conducted their adventures in hostile dungeons and castles, battling monsters, and trying to accumulate treasure and "experience points." The game revolved around a "dungeon master," who conducted the adventure and interpreted the rules for the rest of the players. Playing occurred (and still occurs) through a lot of talking: the dungeon master described the imaginary scenes the players were encountering, and controlled the endless monsters and dragons and other non-playing characters; the players, in turn, would state what actions their characters would take. The result of a player's action was then decided by a roll of the (often many-sided) dice; the result of each roll was interpreted in accordance with what was agreed in rulebooks. The dungeon master might describe a scene, for example, in which an unknown, hunch-backed troll-like creature approaches my dwarf warrior. My options are to attack or to run; I decide on the former, and roll a dice, one with twenty sides, to decide whether I hit the man based on my dwarf's abilities and skills. The dungeon master consults our rulebook, and can see that I hit the creature. I then roll again to see how much damage I do adjusted for my abilities and any spells in play. The creature then gets an attack on me where the dungeon master rolls the dice. He misses and I get another attack, where I hit the foul creature; slaying it. I then get experiences points based on the difficulty on the opponent, which in time will bring my dwarf to a higher and more powerful level.

The materials necessary to play were remarkably simple: the book of rules, sheets that describe the abilities and proficiencies of each character, and often maps and figures to create a visual representation of the adventure. Interestingly, these tools remain the basic setup for all role-playing games, although contemporary ones insist more on character interpretation, dialogue and storytelling more generally, whereas older games are more centered on the accumulation of points and treasure.

After *Dungeons and Dragons*, role-playing games seemed to grow like weeds. Some aimed to simplify its complex rules while maintaining a fantasy setting, like 1976's *Runequest*. Set in a fictional world during the bronze-age, its rules have been praised as the beginning of modern role-playing. Others introduced new settings and universes, such as the successful science-fiction game *Traveller*, from 1977. However, by the end of the 1970s there was widespread concern about the hobby of role-playing, as the news media connected cases of youth suicide or criminal behavior to role-playing games. The general public did not always appreciate a pastime that encouraged young people to sit in their living rooms and discuss the finer points of medieval weaponry and slaughtering monsters, all with a passion that struck more than a few parents as morbid and unhealthy. Especially, within religious circles role-playing games were lamented for being blasphemic. Not surprisingly, video games have become embroiled in nearly identical controversies.

Despite the flare-up of cultural controversy—and in some cases, no doubt, because of such controversy—the hobby continued to mature, with the arrival of new kinds of games, rule systems and universes. The following list gives a small sample of the diversity of role-playing games in the recent past:

- *Call of Cthulhu*, 1981. Reproducing the universe of H.P. Lovecraft's books, this was a game of investigation under the constant threat of insanity. Here, emphsis was usually put on character enactment rather than fulfillment of particular goals.

- GURPS (Generic Universal Role-Playing System) 1984. Rather than offering a specific universe, this was simply a rule system that could be adapted to any scenario. It offered great freedom to creative game masters and players, and made it easier than ever for amateur game designers to create their own worlds.

- *Toon* and *Paranoia*, from 1984. Both of these easy-to-learn games relied on humor marking another alternative to goal-fulfillment in the traditional sense (of slaying monsters, recovering treasure etc.).

- *Cyberpunk*, 1988. Though the subgenre of science fiction already had an established cult following, this *Cyberpunk* gave sci-fi its first popular RPG.

- *Vampire*, 1991. With its simple rules and its emphasis on storytelling, this game changed the hobby by introducing more serious themes and continued an emphasis on narrative over rules and goals.

If we look at sales, we can safely say that computer role-playing games have eclipsed their tabletop counterparts. It is also no coincidence that in the list above, the most recent truly noteworthy tabletop RPG is a decade and a half old. The appeal of RPGs, at least to new audiences, seems to have waned. Nevertheless, their influence is clear, as computer RPGs are often based on this early generation of role-playing games: characters grow by accumulating "experience points," which are often acquired by fighting and picking up treasure; similarly, many games revolve around simple missions (also called quests) where a player's ability to *hack and slash* is all-important, and the more subtle skills of role-playing—telling a convincing story, for example, or negotiating with other players—are optional. Incorporating more player-centered storytelling on the computer has been difficult, due to the absence of a human game master and the standardization required by video games.

Historically, as we'll see below, tabletop role-playing games have inspired two types of video games: the text adventures initiated by *Adventure* and *Zork*, and the multiplayer **MUDs** (multi-user dungeon games) and their graphical predecessors.

Text adventures have evolved into graphic adventure games (and later hybrids such as action-adventure games), and early digital multiplayer role-playing games have grown into today's huge graphic worlds of the **MMORPGs** (massively multi-player online role-playing games).

Video games, then, have a long and varied pre-history. The examples above hardly scratch the surface. But it should be clear that video games are a result of the evolution and reconstitution of various elements of games going back several thousand years. Video games let us experiment with chance and probability, partake in complex strategic interaction, and allow us to simulate things that we cannot (or do not wish to) see happen in real life. They do so by tapping into our desire for spectacle and our thought-provoking willingness to submit ourselves to strange and arbitrary rules for the sake of entertainment.

DOES HISTORY MATTER?

History, unfortunately, does not fall within convenient categories. Any historical account must leave out substantially more than it includes and these choices are always subject to debate. Since the purpose of the following chapter is to give an overview of video games themselves, we choose here to downplay important issues of hardware, business and personal achievements. Our only excuse for this choice is lack of space; those readers interested in these other elements should dig into the reference list, which contains a wealth of knowledge.

The account will be structured by decades, beginning with an introduction describing cultural and technological events significant to the development of video games. Following these brief overviews, the games themselves are described by genre.

First, however, we may want to ask: "Does history matter?" Have not video games progressed so far that comparison with twenty-year-old forbearers—who can already seem hopelessly out of date, even a little absurd—becomes highly suspect, or merely irrelevant? We do not believe that the game student needs to be a walking encyclopedia of historical game arcana. It is also clear that for many research projects game history is of little importance—if one studies how teenagers today use *World of Warcraft*, it is not essential to know how their parents played *Pac-Man*. But to understand the wider significance of contemporary games—from their aesthetics to their technology to their cultural influence—one must often look to history for explanations. Indeed, history has a habit of repeating itself.

Today's dominant game types, while technically enhanced, often take their design cues from quite early games. For instance, the 2005 game *Age of Empires* III, while employing advanced 3D graphics, is structurally tied to the pioneer real-time-strategy title *Dune* II from 1992. Indeed, it could be argued that many potential design paths are simply not options for today's designers, because real-time strategy fans have become accustomed to the conventions established by titles released a decade ago. Similarly, a MMORPG like *World of Warcraft* from 2004 builds liberally on its text-based predecessors—all the way back to MUD from 1978—copying such conventions as corpse retrieval and leveling, and largely copying the player-to-player communication interface from these much earlier games.

The cultural position video games occupy today is difficult to understand without a sense of how games were initially conceived of and marketed. Similarly, the serious gaming student will be helped by a sense of how games, through various historical phases, have moved between public and more private spheres (e.g. from arcades to home computers). For these and so many other reasons, history does matter, and can only enrich and complicate our understanding of video games and the world they've created.

A HISTORY OF VIDEO GAMES

Somewhere in the preceding pages we left a tiny white torpedo hanging in empty space. Before returning to its impact, we need to address more directly the question "What came first?" This is another of those trick questions that we have plagued the reader with a few times already. No trumpets sounded at the birth of video games, and so we must choose what constitutes the beginning. As we look for games emerging from the primordial soup, a few events breach the surface that cannot be ignored. As early as 1949, researchers at the University of Cambridge (U.K.) were operating the Electronic Delay Storage Automatic Calculator (EDSAC) one of the very first stored-program computers in the world. Back then a stored program was a revolution; today we merely know it as any program stored on a CD-Rom or hard disk. Only three years later, PhD student A.S. Douglas, as part of his research project, programmed and ran a computerized EDSAC version of Tic-Tac-Toe named Noughts and Crosses. This single-player experience, where you competed against the computer's simple program, was groundbreaking, but had limited influence on the outside world since the EDSAC was a unique machine.[3]

Another important event took place in the Brookhaven National Laboratory, Long Island. The local public, nerves frayed by the recent deployment of nuclear weapons in Japan, was anxious about the lab's cutting-edge research in nuclear physics. And as taxpayers funding this expensive computer equipment, they were unimpressed by the huge mainframes, lacking any displays, that just stood there seemingly doing nothing. In 1958, Brookhaven employee William Higinbotham thought of a way to generate more community interest in the lab: a tennis game. He developed Tennis For Two, a very basic game where visitors had to decide the angle of a ball and push a button at the right time, while certainly an electronic game it ran on analogue equipment, an oscilloscope. This precursor of the far more lauded Pong even introduced the idea of separate control equipment—what would eventually become the joysticks. Accounts of the time agree that the game was a huge success among lab visitors (for more information see Hunter, 2000).

This brings us back to Cambridge, Massachusetts. In 1961, three MIT employees divided their time between reading a series of pulp science-fiction novels by cereal chemist Edward E. Smith, watching B-movies from Asia, and working. The three men, Steven Russell, Wayne Wittanen, and J.M. Graetz, fantasized about bringing Smith's Skylark novels to the big screen. Now, much like Brookhaven, guests at MIT's annual visitors day were less than impressed with the low hum of mainframes, and the three were enlisted to create demonstration programs that would capture the minds of visitors. In a humorous and oft-quoted article[4] Graetz describes how this demand led to the development of steadily more interactive programs ranging from Bouncing Ball (which was just that), Mouse in the Maze (in which a mouse would traverse a user-designed labyrinth), HAX (a kaleidoscope based on user settings) and Tic-Tac-Toe where the player could make textual input which then generated textual output).

Though interesting, such programs did not truly captivate users, whose part in the process was obviously minor. This, and the procurement of the user-friendly DEC PDP–1 computer, led to the development of Spacewar, up and running in

February of 1962. The game was based on the three men's dreams of how their favorite sci-fi books might be adapted to movies. It featured two spaceships, named Wedge and Needle and each manned by a player, who were engaged in galactic warfare. The possibilities were quite simple. Each ship could fire torpedoes at the other, turn and increase or decrease thrust.

As previous examples make clear, *Spacewar* was far from the first video game. However, claiming that things started with *Spacewar*, as some have done, is not entirely unjustified. Here is a game that is truly novel, and relies on the actual capabilities of the computer. Also, *Spacewar*'s adherence to programming standards (as opposed to games which were directly bound to unique machines) would serve as direct inspiration for later game development.

Figure 4.1 *Spacewar*

The game was a runaway success. Its inventors did not consider it commercially interesting and simply let it spread across North America at its own pace. Over the next few years, few updated versions were created. These involved more strategy— by adding features like a star, which created a gravity pull on the ships; the possibility of hyperjumps—thus adding chance to the rule-governed universe; as well as mainly aesthetic touches such as real constellations in the background.[5] The result was a single, simple game that had an enormous influence on early programmers.

Perhaps due in part to the availability and popularity of *Spacewar* little else related to video games happened in the 1960s. One innovation, however, stands out. In 1966, television engineer Ralph H. Baer pondered a novel usage for the 80 million television sets then installed in North American homes. Why not use these sets to play games? In with this thought he lay the basic circuits for what would become the video game console. By 1967 he had a working prototype which plugged into an ordinary antenna terminal to display the pretentiously named game *Fox and Hounds* (it could have just as well been called "Spot and Spot"). The player navigated his "fox" to try and capture the "hounds." Baer and his employer were pleased and the project was continued. New technologies would soon enable users to play a light sensitive shooting game, as well as *Firefighter*, in which the player tried to prevent the TV screen from turning red by rapidly pumping a single fire (or in this case, "water") button.[6]

With the bold addition of a third "character" (or object such as a ball) Baer's team was even capable of sports games, most obviously *Ping-Pong*. In 1968, they had a saleable console but encountered serious resistance from TV manufacturers. Through a combination of stubbornness and luck, they finally landed a deal with Magnavox. Nothing, however, would come of this until well into the next decade.

Almost all the games mentioned here belong to the action genre. Early video game designers may have preferred this genre because of its immediate appeal to players without detailed instructions and without the need for advanced audiovisuals.

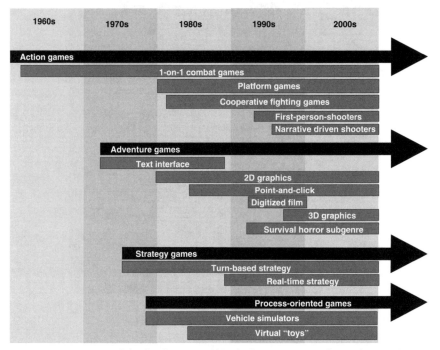

Figure 4.2 An overview of the development within the four genres. Gray bars indicate major trends in content or technology

THE 1970s

Although the previous decades had several possible beginnings of video games, the 1970s saw them grow explosively. This decade marked the birth of video games as an industry, and paved the way for gaming consoles much like the ones we use today. Most importantly, perhaps, the 1970s established video games as a cultural phenomenon to be reckoned with (**arcade games** featured in movies as early as 1973, for example in the American movie *The Last Detail*). And during these years the subculture of gamers was born. Those gamers, mostly young men, would gather in newly created arcades, large rooms both wondrous and dank that housed this new cutting edge digital entertainment.

The most important producer of video games was Atari. Electrical engineer Nolan Bushnell had quickly perceived the financial possibilities inherent in *Spacewar*. It was obvious to him (although not to many others) that people would pay money to play such games in the right setting. Around 1970 the technology to realize this ambition was becoming available. The result was *Computer Space*, the world's first proper arcade game, and very much inspired by the original *Spacewar*. While not successful, it paved the way for *Pong*, which would soon rocket Bushnell's new company, Atari, to the head of the video game stratosphere. While the company earned about $3 million in 1973, only two years later that figure had risen to $40 million. In 1976, the company was bought up by Warner Communications; severe changes in the previously informal work environment upset a number of employees, not the least Bushnell, who left in 1978. This would be the first of many conflicts between the often laid-back culture of game creators and the far different atmosphere of corporate America.) With successful consoles and games however, Atari continued to thrive, and in 1979 gross income rose to $200 million.

Video games in the 1970s also entered the home. Ralph Baer's arrangement with TV manufacturer Magnavox spawned the Odyssey console in 1972. The system was heavily hyped, with Magnovox marketing the promise of nuclear family fun for only $100. Some potential buyers, however, were confused since Magnavox hinted that the system required one of the company's own TV sets to work. A total of about 200,000 Odysseys were sold.

In that vein, Atari went domestic in 1975 with *Home-Pong*, a highly successful one-game-only console. More technologically interesting was the Channel F console, which hit the market in 1976 and was the first console to use plug-in cartridges containing individual games. Previously consoles were shipped with one or more built-in titles, which the player chose by flipping switches or inserting cards that held the appropriate settings. During its four-year lifespan, twenty-one games were published for the Channel F. Atari soon followed suit with the Atari Video Computer System (the Atari 2600) which would remain successful well into the next decade.

Two other events that would have substantial bearing on gaming occurred in those same years. On a technological level, few inventions rival the microprocessor in importance. Invented in 1972, and commercially interesting a few years later, the new technology of the microprocessor would influence heavily not only arcade games and consoles, but also the personal computers about to make their entrance. Perhaps equally important for gaming culture was the publication of the pen-and-paper role-playing game *Dungeons and Dragons* in 1973. As we have discussed, D&D introduced players to procedural (as opposed to goal-oriented) fantasy world role-playing, and would share a (sub)cultural niche with video games for a long time, appealing to the very same subset of young, predominantly male, players.[7]

Action games

The world's first arcade game was a failure. Inspired (heavily) by *Spacewar*, Nolan Bushnell drew many wrong conclusions from the game's design, and certainly failed to appreciate the desires of his audience. He was not producing a game for dedicated computer scientists, but rather for crowded smoke-filled bars and the technologically innocent. Not surprisingly, *Computer Space* did poorly. The game's graphics resembled *Spacewar*, but the game was single-player and featured a spaceship battling against two UFOs. In addition, the game controls were hard to master, creating a learning curve too steep for new players who were unfamiliar with the very concept of video games.

Bushnell, however, learned his lesson and learned it well. His follow-up product, *Pong*, singlehandedly launched the video game as an industry. Released in 1972, its success was massive. Whereas the first version of *Computer Space* had been single-player, *Pong* was multiplayer at its heart. Furthermore, the complex controls of the space battle were sacrificed for simple paddles, and the rules were summarized in a single line, "Avoid missing ball for high score," offering a Zen-like exercise in simplicity. As in previous games, the player's perspective was detached and omniscient. All objects of the game—two white paddles, one ever-bouncing ball—were contained within a single screen.

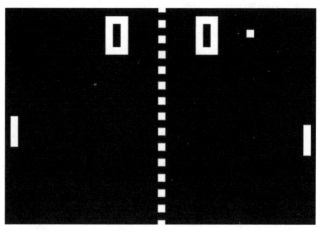

Figure 4.3 *Pong*

Arguably, *Pong* was itself highly derivative and the slew of *Pong* clones that followed, in arcades as well as in homes, relativize any claim that copying proven games is in any way a modern phenomenon. In 1973, Atari followed up on the success with a two-player race through space, appropriately entitled *Space Race*. The players each navigated a spaceship through a meteor field in order to reach the top of the screen. Again we see a very simple, competitive two-player game formula which served as a template for so many early game successes.

Marking a return to the shootout theme of *Spacewar*, players in 1974's *Tank* would attempt to shoot each other in a mine-strewn black and white maze. Much the same concept, although with restricted horizontal movement and different obstacles, made *Gun Fight* a success in 1975. The perspective remained centered while two players took on the roles of Wild West gunslingers.

The year after would see more dramatic developments. On the level of design, Atari's *Night Driver* from 1976 was one of the first games to challenge the dominating third-person, one-screen perspective. This driving game was among the first to employ a first-person perspective, placing the player directly behind the wheel, so to speak. In addition, the game world only gradually revealed itself to the player as the road curved ahead into the horizon. While not a standard case of scrolling, the effect was very similar.

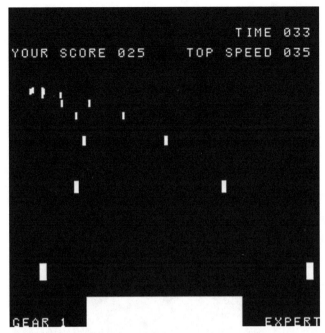

Figure 4.4 *Night Driver*

This design development cannot be taken lightly. It was suddenly clear that the third-person omnipresent viewpoint was not the only possibility. Drawing comparisons to another modern form of expression, this is not dissimilar to when movie makers "discovered" the moving camera and the point-of-view shot.

Later that same year, however, another game would more loudly draw attention to itself. *Death Race* marks the end of innocence for arcade games and the beginning of a long-standing tradition of public outrage and worry over the morality of games and their players. *Death Race* centered on two cars running over stick-figure people who, when hit, turned into crosses. However, the crude graphics allowed for the possibility that the stick-people were "gremlins" (as the developers insisted) and thus not technically alive. Much controversy ensued. Thus was born the concept of the video game as public spectacle, and as a symbol of cultural ailment, to developments that continue to our day.

Though not revolutionary in any obvious way, two action games published towards the end of the decade would become benchmarks for much later design and earn their seats in any unofficial game history hall of fame. The first of these was *Space Invaders* from 1978. This single-player game upholds the most basic video game conventions—on the surface it is even comparable to *Computer Space*. However, the controls were much simpler than its forebearer, and the gameplay compelling. The player controlled a tank moving horizontally at the bottom of the screen. The objective was to shoot down a formation of aliens slowly approaching, while utilizing four shields to create tactical advantage. If the aliens shot the player or reached the bottom of the screen a life would be lost. Repelling one wave of attackers brought forth a new armada, this one moving slightly faster. The explosive success of *Space Invaders* did much to draw games from dimly lit arcades and into the florescent light of cafés, shopping malls, and convenience stores around the United States.

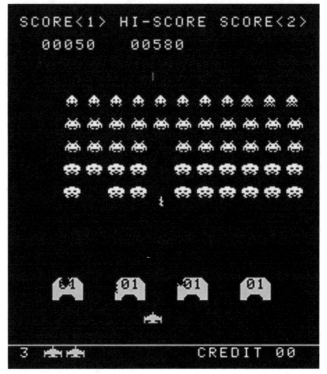

Figure 4.5 *Space Invaders*

Though it had a smaller cultural impact, Atari's 1979 hit *Asteroids* made even more money than *Space Invaders*. *Asteroids*, too, focused on gameplay over fancy graphics—although the stylized and incredibly simple visual components are note worthy for their trancelike qualities. This effect was to some degree a consequence of early **vector graphics**, first seen in 1977 in *Space Wars*, and already used by Atari with some success earlier in 1979 in *Lunar Lander*.

In *Asteroids*, a single-player game, a lonely spaceship had to fight its way through an asteroid belt visited by the occasional enemy flying saucer. Shooting an asteroid would split it into many pieces that then each had to be destroyed. The legacy of *Spacewar* is obvious in the wraparound, seemingly never-ending space, and the feel of gravity's tug on the ship.

The *Spacewar* template was highly visible here, and even in the more varied surfaces of many successes to follow, not least of which was the first true color arcade game, *Galaxian*, from 1979. Considering these triumphs, we can conclude that although various design experiments were conducted through the decade, action games didn't evolve much beyond the beautifully simple standards set by *Spacewar* eighteen years before.

Adventure games

Although it might have seemed so at the time, not all games in the 1970s were action games. There were plenty of reasons to try different approaches to game design. Action games held limited possibilities for storytelling, and basically appealed to people who enjoyed games that challenged motor skills. The more contemplatively

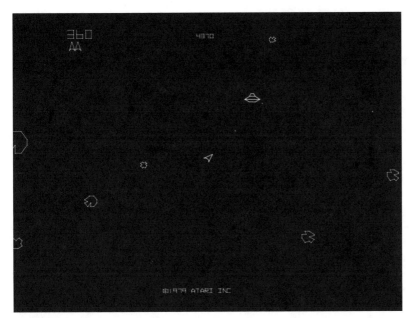

Figure 4.6 *Asteroids*

minded might not be thrilled by fire-button thumping and a reliance on good reflexes. And some designers likely lacked the skill or resources to actually produce a state-of-the-art action game. For these and no doubt for other reasons, text adventure games started showing on mainframes in the early 1970s, and a few years later would be easily and enthusiastically ported to personal computers.

The founding father, arguably, was *Hunt the Wumpus*, written by Gregory Yob in 1972. This simple construction placed the player in an underground cave system plagued by the presence of a clearly evil wumpus—a subterranean monster—with little interest in peaceful dialogue. The player, using only written commands, typed in his intention of either moving or shooting. Through the purely textual interface, the game would give hints as to the location of pits, bats, and the monster itself. No graphics meant modest demands on the player's hardware; the program was light, easy to understand, and addictive to more than a few people in whose imaginations the evil wumpus sprung to life.

More influential on game design was *Adventure*,[8] originally constructed by programmer William Crowther around 1972, and then expanded and improved by Don Woods at Stanford to be widely distributed in 1976. *Adventure* combined Crowther's interests in cave exploration, fantasy role-playing and programming. The purely textual game led the player through a world full with events and imbued with objects and creatures, each with their own properties. The player would write his commands in "natural language," typically as a combination of verb and noun (such as "examine building"), and the program would offer a result. Thus, the beginning of the game could read:

At End of Road

You are standing at the end of a road before a small brick building. Around you is a forest. A small stream flows out of the building and down a gully.

[Player input] *Examine building*

It's a small brick building. It seems to be a well house.

Traveling through the textual world, the player would encounter small puzzles and creatures, armed only with a series of simple commands to interact with them.

Adventure was distributed for free over the ARPAnet, a rudimentary precursor to today's Internet. Simultaneous to free distribution, video games were beginning to make money, and *Adventure*'s successor—Zork—was considered a commercial opportunity almost from its inception. Designed by a group of MIT students, the game was more ambitious and in some ways technically superior to its recent ancestor. Spurred on by the game's popularity among their fellow MIT students, the designers founded Infocom to handle the production and distribution (for the history of Infocom see Briceno *et al.*, 2000) Nevertheless, the first *Zork* game did travel widely across the ARPAnet, although the game's code was partially restricted to prevent other designers from copying features directly.

Both *Adventure* and *Zork*, of course, were heavily influenced by the era's fascination with Tolkien and the growing popularity of fantasy role-playing. *Dungeons and Dragons*, more perhaps than later role-playing games, held obvious appeal to the technically interested; hand-drawn paper maps of dense dungeons and foreboding forests were pored over by D&D and *Zork* players alike. In early adventure games, as in early tabletop RPGs, the game experience was centered more around puzzles or logic than around narrative. Playing *Zork* involved not only solving puzzles within the game but also guessing what written commands the game's input interpreter could comprehend.

Although the focus on logic and puzzles fascinated many, these themes would be downplayed throughout the next decade. Beginning the trend towards narrative was Ken and Roberta Williams' *Mystery House*, published in 1979 for the Apple II. While the game structure didn't rival *Zork*'s, *Mystery House* sported crude graphics to enhance the player's textual experience. Based on the success of *Mystery House*, the two authors went on to found On-Line Systems, which would soon become Sierra Online, a company that would strongly define the genre in the decade to come.

Strategy games

Several games of the 1970s circulated as ideas or snippets of code; multiple designers might expand on these bits, so a game could exist in multiple incarnations at any given time. One such game was *Hamurabi* (occasionally spelled *Hammurabi*, and sometimes known as *Kingdom*). In this text-based game, the player was a ruler managing a nation's resources. With each command, the player would have to balance his country's various resources and also attend to popular opinion.

More complex and more influential was Walter Bright's *Empire* from 1978, in which the player attempted to conquer an unexplored world, using a series of military units. Another game of the same name, written by Peter S. Langston, was a yet more complex multi-player game with a notable economic system. Compared to action and adventure games, strategy games did not go undergo dramatic development in this decade, perhaps because they already had a considerable history (in terms of board games) which was mostly built upon and adapted to video game format.

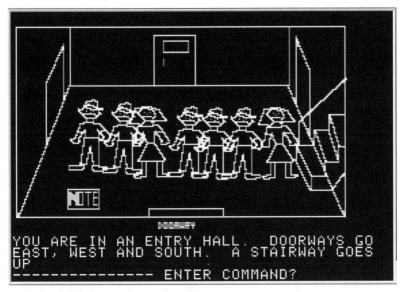

Figure 4.7 *Mystery House*

Process-oriented games

Looking to digitize the role-playing experience, others went in somewhat different, and less commercial, directions than the makers of *Zork*. At Essex University, Roy Trubshaw and Richard Bartle, in the last years of the decade, were working on a system called MUD. The multi-user dungeon was essentially a multiplayer version of the *Adventure*/*Zork* template. Users would connect to the game, which ran on a server (i.e. a central machine which players could connect to via their own machines), and could then interact with the objects in the system as well as with other players. The world of the game, which would cyclically continue for a considerable period and then reset to the initial state, incorporated the actions of every player, and quickly became far more dynamic and unpredictable than the static worlds of single-player adventure games. MUD, which would turn into the label for the whole subgenre, was a success, albeit a local one, since only a few people had network access at the time. Its influence, however, would be wide-ranging and is clearly detectable in the massively multiplayer online role-playing games (such as *EverQuest* and *Star Wars: Galaxies*) of today. Before these, however, a wide range of MUD manifestations would serve as the playing ground of many hobbyists and academics, primarily through the 1980s and early 1990s.

THE 1980s

The 1980s was marked by rapid technological progress, a number of novel approaches to game design, and the proliferation of personal computers. The decade was also marked by what is sometimes called the Great Videogame Crash of 1984. Though dramatic and sudden, the "crash" was actually the result of a combination of factors. In the first third of the decade, the industry exploded and everything seemed promising. By 1984 one in four American homes housed a game console. Game sales had more than tripled (to $3.2 billion) from the previous year and there were few, if any, alarm bells ringing. One potential—though ignored—warning was the 1981

Atari 2600 adaptation of the arcade smash hit *Pac-Man*. The adaptation was legendarily poor, with very few of the aspects that made the original so popular. Following up on this artistic (if not commercial) disaster, Atari released *E.T.: The Extra-Terrestrial* that same year, a game so poorly designed and so rushed through production that it became one of the largest flops of the industry. The failure was underlined by Atari dumping and destroying huge numbers of E.T. cartridges in the New Mexico desert.[9]

Figure 4.8 *E.T.: The Extra-Terrestrial*

Atari, though controlling two thirds of the industry, then attempted to stifle third-party competitors by taking them to court arguing that independent development for Atari machines should be illegal. Bushnell's old company lost which led to an explosion of third-party publishers, and the market was soon flooded with huge numbers of games of uneven quality.

The final, and perhaps largest, nail in the coffin was home computers. In the early years of the decade, a variety of personal computers became available at prices that could compete with the game-dedicated consoles. As consumers realized the potential of home computers, and the growing number of games sold on 3.5 inch floppy disks, there was little reason for acquiring consoles that were less versatile. The Apple II—produced in 1977 by former Atari employee Steve Jobs—supported a large catalog of games. For price conscious gamers, Commodore's Vic 20, was a big success at under $300, as was its more powerful younger brother, the Commodore 64.

In very little time the console industry virtually ceased to exist (Atari itself avoided bankruptcy but never regained its strength). Investors grew wary of anything videogame-related, and it would be another two years before the Japanese company Nintendo kick-started the console business once again. In 1986 they released their Nintendo Entertainment System (NES) in the U.S., a version of the Famicom (short for "family computer") which had already done very well in Japan.

By the end of the decade Nintendo had assumed the crown as the most successful console manufacturer emphasizing their victory with the success of their handheld GameBoy (launched in 1989) which outperformed Atari's handheld Lynx released that same year.

Action games

Before 1984's "crash," Atari released action games at a brisk pace. Following up on their earlier successes with vector graphics, *Battlezone* (1980) put the player inside a tank fighting other tanks in what today looks like an abstract landscape of geometrical shapes. The game was so successful—and was considered so realistic—that the U.S. Army commissioned a special version for training purposes. This Atari–Army collaboration continues to shape present-day debate about the military's use of games.

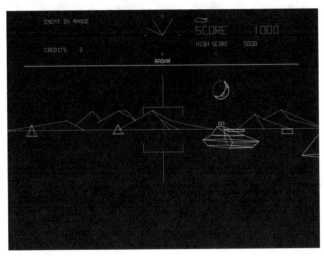

Figure 4.9 *Battlezone*

The same year saw the release of yet another space shooter, although this one less faithful to the original mechanics of *Spacewar*. In *Defender*, the player protected small, inanimate humanoids from aliens who swooped down to the planet's surface, picked up a humanoid and carried him to the top of the screen, where he would transform into a mutant alien. The player had use of a laser, a number of "smartbombs," which would destroy all aliens onscreen, and could also hyper-jump to a different part of the screen (a feature well known since a late iteration of *Spacewar*). Whereas *Spacewar* employed a wraparound space made famous by *Pac-Man*, *Defender* used a different version of the same concept. The scrolling game world was circular; going far enough in one direction would place you back in your original position without any apparent relocation of your spaceship. Helpful in the battle was a radar illustrating your position in the game world. While a few years before, an arcade game had been considered successful if 15,000 cabinets were sold, *Defender* approached sales of 60,000.[10]

The thirst for space shooters must have seemed insatiable. Building upon the *Space Invaders* theme, *Gorf* from 1981 was the first arcade game to offer (somewhat) different levels; it also introduced the concept of battling a big bad something at the end of each level—in this case the Gorfian mother ship. Other small innovations included a flickering force shield that would slowly be destroyed by enemy fire, the limited vertical movement of the player's ship, and the ability to shoot only one torpedo at a time (shooting another before the first exploded would cause the previous torpedo to disappear).

After 1980, however, the abundance of *Space Invaders* clones were literally eaten away. *Pac-Man*, deliberately cartoonish and quite simple to play, was a remarkable success in Japan and was then exported to the U.S. Originally called *Puckman*—considered too tempting for English-speaking vandals—*Pac-Man* was the name of

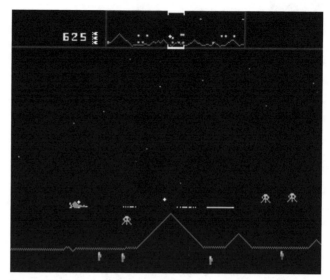

Figure 4.10 *Defender*

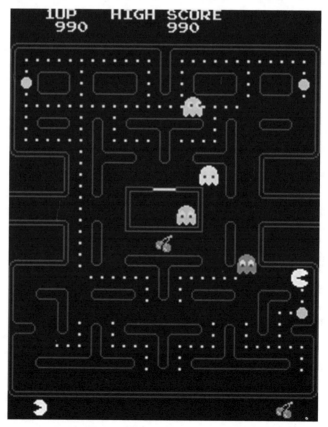

Figure 4.11 *Pac-Man*

a small pizza-like wedge which had to gobble up a maze of small dots and floating fruit, while alternately avoiding and (with the help of "power-ups") attacking the four ghosts that stalked the game space.

As with the earliest games, the player was omniscient and the game was confined to one screen. Thus, although technological advancements were numerous, many successes of the early 1980s were quite conservative. *Pac-Man* was revolutionary, though, in one essential aspect. Unlike all previous game hits, this one had an identifiable main character. Pac-Man was quickly licensed to appear on merchandise—from towels to t-shirts—at no extra cost to Namco, the game's developer, or Bally/Midway, the U.S. distributor. Like cartoon characters, Pac-Man did not develop a Hollywood ego, nor did he demand a cut of the licensing income. The game and the Pac-Man character were so popular as to warrant an ABC TV show (*The Pac-Man Show*) and a slew of clones, copies, and sequels. Of these, *Ms. Pac-Man* was the most important, and became a large success in its own right. Another sequel, *Pac-Land*, transported the adventurous wedge into a sidescrolling world where he had to navigate a series of platforms and obstacles. This piece of the Pac-Man universe exemplifies several important trends in arcade games, particularly the triumph of so-called "platform games," as we'll see below.) With over 300,000 units sold,[11] *Pac-Man* is considered the best-selling arcade game of all time and with the astounding success of character-based cuteness it seriously challenged the powerful sci-fi templates which had long dominated the industry.

Alongside the dominant single-screen game, these years witnessed the beginning of the "platform game," as mentioned above. The game that launched this sub-genre was *Space Panic* from 1980, in which the player controlled an astronaut who climbed ladders and dug holes to combat enemy aliens.

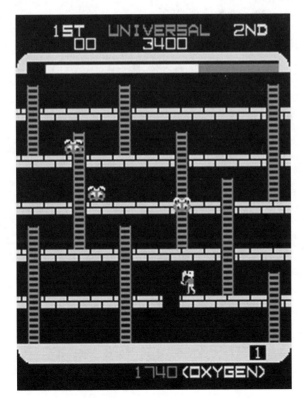

Figure 4.12 *Space Panic*

On a superficial level at least, Nintendo's highly successful arcade game *Donkey Kong* from 1981 (before Nintendo's console successes) drew obvious inspiration from *Space Panic*. Mario, a heavyset and conspicuously mustached plumber, had to move from the bottom of the screen to the top by navigating a series of ladders and obstacles, all to rescue his fiancée from the clutches of a large gorilla. The game launched designer Shigeru Miyamoto's career, and would be the cornerstone of Nintendo's coming success in America. Mario returned, along with his brother Luigi, in 1983's *Mario Bros.*, where they did some actual plumbing. In this non-scrolling platform game, the brothers were out to combat the turtles and other beasts thriving in poorly maintained pipes. Each player bumped his head into the floor below a turtle, flipping it onto its back, and the plumbers could then kill the turtle by running into it. The game's revolutionary possibility—for players to cooperate against a common foe—had been introduced the year before in *Joust*, and would be used to great effect in 1985 in *Gauntlet*.

In *Gauntlet*, up to four players could cooperate in ridding a dungeon of monsters. The four characters—a warrior, an elf, a wizard, and a valkyrie—each had different abilities, betraying the concept's roots in pen and paper role-playing. The game in fact earned Atari a patent, confirming the company's invention of "multi-player, multi-character cooperative play video game with independent player entry and departure."[12]

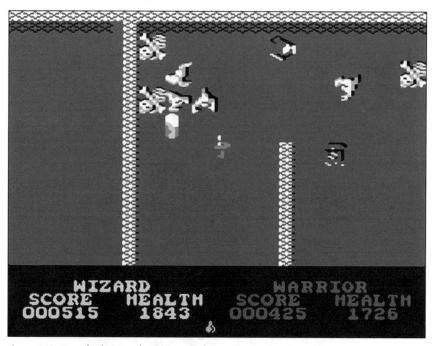

Figure 4.13 *Gauntlet* (Commodore 64 version)

Mario Bros. was followed by *Super Mario Bros.* in 1985—which, like *Pac-Land*, scrolled horizontally—as Mario and Luigi fought to rescue the Mushroom Princess from the evil turtles. This time around, enemies could also be killed by landing on top of them. This version kept a crucial feature of the original—that the player had to decelerate before turning around—even though the ground did not appear to be slippery. This exact mechanism was in turn a legacy of the original space shooters, from *Spacewar* to *Asteroids*.

As the decade continued, platform games became a staple of the action genre with notable examples being *Elevator Action, Impossible Mission, Wonderboy, Rainbow Islands, The New Zealand Story, Ghosts'n Goblins, Prince of Persia,* and *Sonic the Hedgehog.* These introduced a variety of gaming elements—like the need to time your jumps between platforms, to name one of many—which would be standard practice for years to come.

The merging of sideways scrolling and jumping could also be combined with classical space battle themes, as seen in *Moon Patrol* from 1982. Here the player drove a purple vehicle across a futuristic lunar landscape, while fighting alien spaceships above and avoiding holes and rocks (some of which could be blasted away). The game featured "parallax scrolling," in which background layers passed across the screen at different speeds to create the illusion of depth.

Figure 4.14 *Moon Patrol*

In the early 1980s, driving—particularly race cars—had been a popular electronic pastime for several years. Building upon successful games such as *Sprint 2* (from 1978) and the first-person driving games that followed the success of *Night Driver, Pole Position* swept through arcades in 1982. The player raced a car around a circuit, competing against other cars and the clock. Rather than a bird's-eye view, the perspective of the game was from behind the car, which of course constitutes the first of many variations on the first-person driving game.

The intensity and intuitive controls of racing games helped ensure the popularity of this subgenre, along with a string of commercial successes: *Pole Position* was followed in 1983 by games such as *Pit Stop;* the split-screen, two-player sequel *Pit Stop 2* one year later; the stylish *Out Run* in 1986; the motorbike racer *Hang-On,* fast-paced *Lotus Esprit Turbo Challenge,* and the *Test Drive* series that stretched from 1987 to1999. (Later games, such as the *Need for Speed* Series starting in 1995, and the *Gran Turismo* series, first published in 1997, ensured that driving would remain among the most popular electronic simulations of "real-life" activities.) Other racing games focused less on realism, and more on abstract or cartoonish aesthetics, such as *Bump 'n' Jump* from 1982, *Spy Hunter* from 1983, *Super Cars II* from 1991 and *Mario Kart* from 1992.

Another subgenre that burst onto the scene in the early 1980s was sports games. While individual sports had been simulated many times, a new breed inspired by the 1984 Olympic Games offered the player a variety of disciplines. Following the arcade game *Track and Field* from 1983, Activision published *Decathlon* for the Commodore 64 that same year. The Commodore 64 soon boasted Epyx' "Games" series, inaugurated by *Summer Games* in 1984 and followed by *Summer Games II*, *Winter Games*, *World Games*, the highly popular *California Games*, and others.

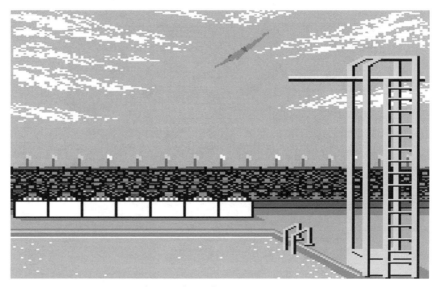

Figure 4.15 *Summer Games II* (Commodore 64)

Shooting games continued to evolve. A noteworthy experiment with form was *Zaxxon* from 1982 which introduced the "isometric perspective." In *Zaxxon*, the scrolling game world is watched from above but at an angle; as the player flies through a heavily guarded enemy fortress, the spaceship's altitude and horizontal position is crucial for survival, making the isometric perspective integral to the game. This perspective was rarely used in action games, with a few notable exceptions like *Blue Max* for the Commodore 64 (from 1983) and 1988's *Paperboy*. More consistently popular in shooters was the standard third-person perspective in a scrolling screen, with games more or less equally divided between a vertical scroll—*Xevious* and *1942* are prominent examples—and a horizontal scroll—*Scramble* and *Blood Money*.

Although cooperative games were quite successful, and sports and other simulation games began to reshape the industry, the classic one-on-one fighting game—with obvious echoes of *Spacewar* and *Gun Fight*—was still very much alive in the 1980s. *Karate Champ* from 1984, for example, was the first two-player karate game. Each level was set in a new arena, a visual convention which would be followed for decades. Similar fighting games following in the mid-1980s include the single-player game *Yie Ar Kung-Fu*, *International Karate+*, and *Street Fighter*, as well as later games from *Mortal Kombat* to *Tekken* to *Soul Calibur*.

Figure 4.16 *Zaxxon*

The cooperative versions of these "beat'em up" games typically featured a horizontal scroll. One illustrative example is *Double Dragon* from 1987, in which Billy and Jimmy Lee battled a host of street-fighting thugs to save Billy's girlfriend. In an obvious parallel to early moviemaking, the archetypal rescue-the-damsel-in-distress storyline was widely used in 1980s games, including *Donkey Kong* and *Super Mario Bros*. *Double Dragon*, however, was not a feel-good buddy game: players were able to hurt each other (accidentally or not), and at the end had to fight over who got the girl (a feature evident in later strategy games, where victory is handed to the "last man standing").

Strategy games

Games requiring careful analysis and strategic thinking are obviously ill suited for noisy arcades, where games rarely lasted more than a few minutes. However, with the triumphant entry of home computers, games of strategy found an obvious home, and an eager audience.

Strategy games in the 1980s were, to a large degree, direct adaptations of board games or highly inspired by their cardboard brethren. As is still the case today, the genre was built mainly of wargames, although there were important exceptions. The distributor SSI dominated the market in board-game inspired wargames. *Kampfgruppe*, *Gettysburg: The Turning Point*, *Storm Across Europe* and the fantasy-oriented *Sword of Aragon* all expanded (or just copied) the boardgame formula without adding revolutionary new elements.

In 1987, Walter Bright and Mark Baldwin published an updated version of *Empire* (originally from 1978). As in the original, the player began with few resources and

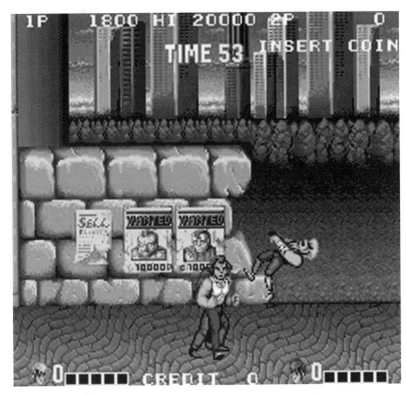

Figure 4.17 *Double Dragon*

explored the game world to find, and hopefully defeat, enemy nations. Although now considered a wargame classic, Bright had serious problems finding a willing publisher. One publisher, Microprose, rejected the game because they were currently looking for action-oriented "real time" strategy simulations. Bröderbund did not find the story original enough nor the graphics advanced enough, and Epyx did not consider it appropriate for their favored platform, the Commodore 64. When released by Interstel, however, the game did prove highly successful.[13]

Several wargames experimented with diplomacy and political maneuvering. In 1985, *Balance of Power* addressed the acute Cold War tension of the era. The player assumed the role of a super power leader trying to win the world over to his side without fatally provoking his opponent (either the computer or a second player) into a nuclear attack. The entire nail-biting experience was made possible by nothing more than graphics of a world map; this economical design approach has enhanced the game as a classic. Although, strategy games interfaces were adapting to the point-and-click era and graphics were becoming more detailed, the genre has traditionally relied very little on impressive visuals compared to other genres.

A small breed of strategy games took the pillars of the genre—the poring over battle maps, the consideration of endless interdependent variables—less seriously. The French game *North and South*, for example, published in 1989, was blatantly cartoonish and focused less on maps and more on utilizing the full visual and audio potential of the Commodore Amiga. The game, based on the comic book series *Les Tuniques Bleues*, was set during the American civil war and would alternate between a strategic level and action sequences. The latter would unfold once the player made the strategic decision to attack a fort or board a moving train.

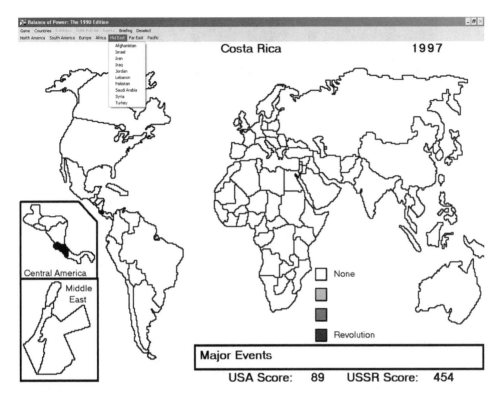

Figure 4.18 *Balance of Power* (1990 version)

Equally colorful but more satirical was *Nuclear War* from 1989, which carica-tured real-world political leaders and their simple-minded responses to nuclear threat. Most hardcore strategy gamers were unimpressed; the jokes overrode atten-tion to gameplay, as the computer opponent was capable of only very simple strate-gies, and the consequences of the game's choices often seemed random.

North and South was not the only game to mix strategy with action sequences. The developer Cinemaware was especially prolific with this hybrid strategy, seen in late-1980s games such as *Defender of the Crown, King of Chicago*, and *Lords of the Rising Sun*. The first, remade in 2003, featured groundbreaking graphics and situated the player as a post-Robin Hood British lord vying for control of the country. With limited strategy components, and a reliance on action sequences which seemed to imply that strategy along couldn't keep players entertained, these hybrid games never found universal acceptance by hardcore strategy gamers.

One game that did effectively combine strategy and action was *Herzog Zwei*, released in 1989 for the Sega Genesis (known in Europe as the Sega Megadrive) a strong competitor to Nintendo in the console business at this time where the Genesis was marketed as a cooler and more adult-oriented machine than the Nintendo Entertainment System. In *Herzog Zwei* the player defends and expands his territory while managing resources and creating various military units. In an important departure from all other strategy games (and their boardgame origins), players competed without taking turns. In other words, players made choices simultaneously and without interruption (as they would in any action game like *Pong*). *Herzog Zwei* thus qualifies as the first real-time strategy game, a subgenre that would prove both hardy and prolific in the decade to come.

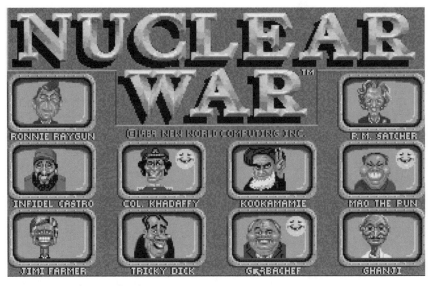

Figure 4.19 *Nuclear War* (DOS)

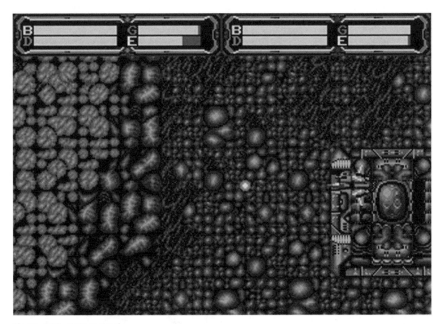

Figure 4.20 *Herzog Zwei*

Two other highly important strategy games helped end the decade with a flurry of creative activity. One of these was Bullfrog's *Populous* from 1989, which combined the real-time concept with an isometric perspective (this would later become a standard combination for the subgenre). The game positioned the player as a deity thriving on worship and capable of godly deeds of wonder and destruction. The second noteworthy entry from the end of the 1980s was the legendary

SimCity, from 1989. Although it featured many strategy elements, it was the culmination of the decade-long merging between the strategy and process-oriented genres, and will be discussed with the latter.

As the 1980s came to a close, the strategy genre looked radically different than it had a mere ten years ago. These games experienced an adolescent-like explosion, moving in a short period from an almost total reliance on text and crude graphics to a wide range of gaming experiences that pushed against the very boundaries of the genre. Strategy game designers had dutifully explored the possibilities offered by board games, and seemed ready to burst into new arenas. Spurred on by the enormous promise of the home computer, the possibilities were endless, though two phenomena stood out, and would continue to alter the genre: real-time strategy and the influence of process-oriented games.

Adventure games

Over the 1980s, multi-user dungeon games (or MUDs) would remain constrained by the lack of networked computers; meanwhile, however, Zork and its many offspring would find happy new lives in the rapid proliferation of home computers. The adventure world offered something fundamentally new, and both the technical and the popular press displayed great interest. In 1980, Infocom designer P. David Lebling described Zork in Byte magazine as not a video game but a "CFS (computerized fantasy simulation) game," defining it as "a new art form: the computerized storybook." He was simultaneously skeptical that Zork could be enhanced by the use of graphics: "the player's imagination probably has a more detailed picture of the Great Underground Empire than could ever be drawn."[14]

The connection to literature, and the player's storytelling imagination praised by Lebling, was essential to ensuring the cultural acceptance of the genre. In what is likely one of the first reviews of video games in its august pages, the New York Times Book Review in 1983 described Infocom's Deadline as "more like a genre of fiction than a game . . . Infocom has been a major pioneer in such games, which have been called 'participatory novels,' '**interactive fiction**' and 'participastories'."[15] The hesitant use of the label of "game" is both intriguing and revealing, as it demonstrates how different the text-reliant adventure games seemed from their contemporary arcade shooters.

Infocom continued to cultivate their literary image, and many adventure games designers thought of themselves as different—and perhaps more sophisticated—than other game designers A distinct image, of course, had marketing advantages: "old media," like the New York Times, might be more interested in a new "art form" than just another video game; and computer owners who didn't consider themselves gamers might be more willing to try a game sold as "interactive fiction." Similarly, early film makers sought to enhance the legitimacy of their medium by associating it with already admired forms of expression, particularly classical theatre. But marketing concerns aside, adventure games were highly innovative (though stubbornly bound to a pure textual interface) and Infocom led the genre for most of the decade.

The aforementioned Deadline was the genre's most significant follow-up to the foundational success of Zork. Moving the adventure genre out of Tolkieniesque dungeons, Deadline drew upon the whodunits standards of mystery novels and movies, as the player maneuvered a New England colonial estate to solve the murder (or was it suicide?) of Marshall Robner. The Witness, also from 1983, drew upon many of the same principles, as the player had only twelve hours to solve the crime story. The same concept was recycled in 1984's *Suspect*, in which the player must defend herself against false murder charges.

Dungeons and detectives were complemented by science fiction plots in *Planetfall* and *Stationfall*. Of these, *Planetfall* is best remembered, as it featured the robot Floyd, one of the industry's first examples of a convincing and dramatically important character who was not a player. (At one point in the game, Floyd would even sacrifice its life for that of the player.)

Other adventure designers, in contrast to Lebling, didn't believe that the player's imagination—weaving visions entirely from text—was crucial to the genre. In 1980, Sierra Online had already introduced the possibility of a graphics-based adventure game with *Mystery House*. This was followed in 1981 with *Ulysses and the Golden Fleece*, set in ancient Greece and featuring color graphics illustrating the player's situation.

So far, however, the nascent use of graphics had merely described events and locations within the games. These static images could not be manipulated but this would change dramatically in 1984 with *King's Quest*. The player assumed the role of Sir Gawai, traveling the magical land of Daventry in search of three treasures. Gawain was represented by an on-screen **avatar** who could interact with nearby objects—which had of course been common in other game genres since the birth of gaming. The player, however, could still only interact with the game via text, and still had to guess the correct combination(s) of words in order to create the necessary commands. Graphic innovation, however small, was rewarded, and the *King's Quest* series became a steady success, with new installments as recently as 1998.

Fueled by this development, Sierra released *Space Quest: The Sarien Encounter* in 1986. Its unlikely hero, Roger Wilco, had survived an alien attack by napping in his janitor's closet, and now had to set things right. The humorous tone struck a chord with many soft-core gamers and the *Space Quest* series lived on until 1995 (with constant rumors of more games being developed since then).

With gamers not traditionally drawn to the genre, Sierra's best-known games may be the *Leisure Suit Larry* series (based on *SoftPorn* from 1981). Larry is an ambitiously dressed and balding wannabe, a lady's man anti-hero who seeks love in a world of pretence, smooth surfaces and low comedy. *Leisure Suit Larry in the Land of the Lounge Lizards*, the first of the series, seemed a commercial failure when released in 1987, but word of mouth made it a slowly building bestseller as well as an informal classic. The third installment, *Leisure Suit Larry 3: Passionate Patti in Pursuit of the Pulsating Pectorals* from 1989, added a novel twist: the player alternated between controlling Larry and his (ex)girlfriend Patty.

Through the first half of the decade, the literary Infocom and the less purist Sierra dominated the genre. However, a development was on the horizon that would do more than add pictures to the stories. In 1987, a gamer's endless search for the right combination of words, long the frustration of text adventures, found an alternative as LucasFilm Games (later known as LucasArts) released the humoros horror story *Maniac Mansion*.

In addition to requiring the player to switch between teenage protagonists, the game introduced the point-and-click interface to the genre. Instead of typing commands, the player would be offered a series of verbs that could be combined with graphical elements in the game by use of mouse or joystick. The player was more constrained than in text adventure games with large vocabularies, but no longer had the aggravation of guessing the right word combinations. The creators

Figure 4.21 *King's Quest I: Quest for the Crown* (2004 remake by Anonymous Game Developers Interactive)

Figure 4.22 *Maniac Mansion* (2004 remake by LucasFan Games)

of 1990's *Loom*, which followed *Maniac Mansions* newfound interface, explained: "[We] think you like to spend your time involved in the *story*, not typing in synonyms until you stumble upon the computer's word for a certain object."[16]

Building on the template, LucasFilm Games soon released the equally witty *Zak McKracken and the Alien Mindbenders*, and followed with *Indiana Jones and The Last Crusade* in 1989. The latter saw the guest appearance of Chuck The Plant, an unusable object from Maniac Mansion, and introduced the phrase "I'm selling these fine leather jackets," which would resonate through later LucasArts games. These intertextual mini-jokes served to reward fans for their loyalty. But more important than this cleverness, the point-and-click interface proved massively appealing, and soon textual interaction was on the decline. A new breed of adventure games was born, and would prosper until midway through the next decade.

Meanwhile, the role-playing branch of adventure games was also blossoming. Through the 1980s, these games remained loyal to Tolkienesque fantasy, and were the genre's most obvious heirs to the *Dungeons and Dragons* legacy focusing on large explorable worlds and relying on the concepts of hit points, skill levels, trade, and random encounters far more than the games produced by Infocom, Sierra, and LucasArts.[17] Especially towards the end of the decade, RPGs also replicated the concept of the adventuring party, in contrast to the genre's reliance on the single protagonist.

Designer Richard Garriot began the decade with *Akalabeth*, which he followed later in 1980 with *Ultima*. Launching a series that would continue until 1999, *Ultima* offered a bird's eye view perspective on the simple graphics that made up the world of Sosaria. Other series soon followed. *Wizardry: Proving Grounds of the Mad Overlord* featured first-person dungeon exploration in 3D vector graphics and inspired a large number of sequels. *Tales of the Unknown, Volume I: The Bard's Tale*, from 1985, colorfully mixed 2D and 3D graphics (two sequels followed). We should also note that RPGs were not confined to home computers. In 1987 Nintendo fans could enjoy (the misleadingly named) *Final Fantasy*, which kicked off a series that would proliferate across platforms for at least the next two decades.

Although not dissimilar in structure to standard adventure games, the openness of computer RPGs would ensure them a very different fate in the decade to come.

Process-oriented games

Much like adventure and turn-based strategy games, process-oriented games were unthinkable in a fast-paced arcade but seemed born for home computers. Indeed quick and intense arcade-like experiences are usually anathema to process-oriented games as many strive for realism while some focus more on recreating the physical experience of dealing with a real-world system—and pay less attention to the game's accessibility or how fun it is, or even if it has a clear victory condition.

Of course, it wasn't only process-oriented games which strove for some sort of realism. One arcade game also lauded for its faithful representation of reality was *Battlezone*. While the 1980 game does simulate a battle tank, it focuses on shooting and the complex controls of the vehicles are downplayed. This was not so in many process-oriented home computer games. In the case of the Microsoft Flight Simulator series, which had a remarkable twenty-one-year run, from 1982 to 2003 the manual for the first game was adamant that "Microsoft Flight Simulator is a

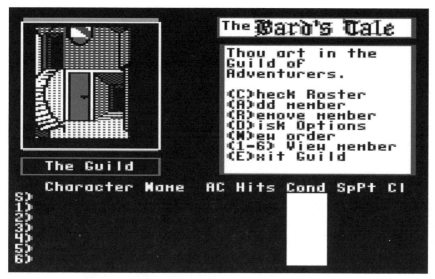

Figure 4.23 *Bard's Tale 1* (Commodore 64 version)

highly accurate simulation of flight in a single-engine aircraft. Its working instruments, panoramic out-the-window graphics view and real-time flight conditions will give you the excitement of flying in a real plane." It also stressed that "Flight Simulator gives you full use of the flight instruments and controls. This instrumentation is so accurate that it meets the FAA regulations (part 91.33) for day and night, visual and instrument flight conditions."[18]

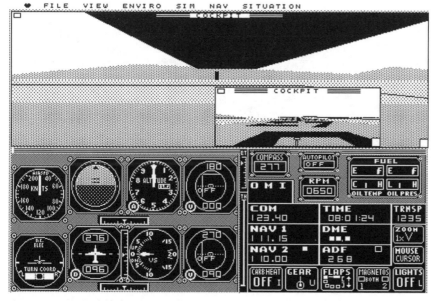

Figure 4.24 *Microsoft Flight Simulator* (1986 MAC version)

The game had a steep learning curve, as players had to slowly familiarize themselves with the complex controls, and succeed in a long flight across fairly monotonous land in order to land at the next airport.

Other process games added action elements to broaden their appeal. Sierra's *3-D Helicopter Simulator* saw itself as "computerized flight training with realistic action!" as it put the player in control of the McDonnell/Douglas "Apache" military helicopter. The 1987 game was also significant as the first to introduce head-to-head multiplayer combat, via the then-impressive technology of a telephone modem.

With the exception of flight simulators many "vehicle" games had optional action modes. You didn't have to engage with the action elements, but could choose to perform them to your liking. Submarine simulations such as *688 Attack Sub* from 1989 and *Sub Battle Simulator* from 1987 took clever advantage of limited processing power. The murky, vague graphics enhanced the paranoia of being in a confined space underwater; just as in the depths of the ocean, there was often very little to see while playing this game, and the player's limited perception of the surrounding world added to the anxiety of playing the game.

One landmark game combined strategy and action more seamlessly than many contemporary genre hybrids—the 1983 space merchant classic *Elite*. One of the first home video games with **polygon** 3D graphics, *Elite* also sported a pompous (if technically simplistic) 2001-style classical soundtrack. The player was plopped into a huge universe (seemingly constructed at random) with a modest spaceship and limited cash. From these humble beginnings the player had to engage the worlds around her with some combination of trade, smuggling, bounty hunting, and quest-solving. Approaching a floating, three-dimensional, semi-abstract space station at low speed was an experience unparalleled in game history. With no storyline or set goal, the game created a unique sense of vastness and unlimited opportunity, and was among the most revolutionary home video games of the time.

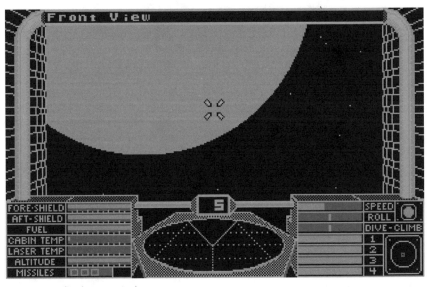

Figure 4.25 *Elite* (DOS version)

Figure 4.26 *Sid Meier's Pirates!* (2004 PC remake)

The idea of open-ended games lacking clear conditions for victory slowly caught on. One innovative game, which offered dynamic world (although it did have a goal and could, in fact, end), was *Sid Meier's Pirates!* from 1987. As an aspiring pirate, the player traveled the Caribbean in search of treasure and fame. You could follow various plot strands, with their resulting ebb and flow of alliances, which created the impression of being just one person in an evolving world.

Despite their landmark innovations, the fame of *Elite* and *Sid Meier's Pirates!* pales next to *SimCity*. In this 1989 game, the player assumed the role of mayor, and managed a city that would grow or diminish almost organically in response to the player's choices on everything from zoning and construction to taxation. Angry citizens might protest and leave the city, while a content populace would settle down, have more children and generate more income. Since all parts of the game's world interacted, a fairly small number of game settings and variables would elicit complex behavior from the system. Apart from this complexity, of course, the design draws upon the *Hamurabi* legacy (see p. 58) of managing a world, though the popularity of *SimCity* would influence not just design of future games, but the role of the entire industry within American—and world—culture.

Meanwhile, various MUDs had descended from the original, and some manifestations of the genre belonged more to the process-oriented category than to its

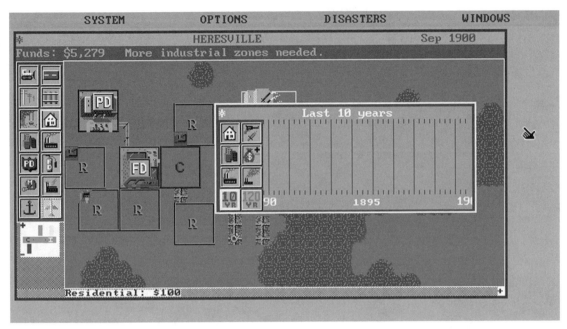

Figure 4.27 *SimCity* (DOS)

adventure brethren. Of these, *Habitat* stood out, applying the LucasFilm ethos of moving away from text and towards cartoonish graphics. Launched in 1985 for the Commodore 64, its players logged in via modem and encountered a graphical world full of social interaction and quests. The concept was very ambitious, and encountered equally difficult technical and social challenges.[19] Though plagued by these problems, many of the lessons learned (as well as the actual features used) inspired "social worlds" for years to come, including *There.com* and *Second Life*, both launched in 2003.

At the end of the 1980s a great deal had happened. Many genres and subgenres had solidified into formats still going strong today (perhaps most evident in the case of single-player RPGs). Also, the console-based business had fallen from legendary pre-1983/1984 heights against most predictions, only to resurface within a few years to co-exist with home computer gaming. Video gaming itself had become a staple of pop culture which most children—and sometimes indirectly their parents—had experienced and worried voices had been raised about the influence of gaming on young minds.

At the end of the decade game production was also quite a different undertaking than in earlier days as increasingly powerful hardware formed the backdrop of an audiovisual arms race and necessarily more complex game production processes. This latter trend would continue with great strength into the 1990s and beyond.

THE 1990s

Though most video games relied upon already established genres and conventions during the last decade of the twentieth century, a few developments were truly signif-icant. In the technology arena, the personal computer (by now universally referred to as the "PC") awoke fully as a hardcore gaming platform due to major advances in sound and graphics hardware. A well-equipped PC rivaled the audiovisuals of all but the very newest consoles at any given moment. In addition, the spread of network technology and the rise of the Internet created both explosive growth and broad diffusion, which would change both the experience of playing a video game and the game design templates themselves. Meanwhile, the commercial introduction of the CD-ROM as a software storage medium simultaneously destroyed the floppy disk and swiftly increased the size of a typical game. And in the realm of graphics, by the decade's end 3D polygon graphics would replace two-dimensional graphics as the industry standard. By 1990 text-input interfaces were only seen in marginal examples of the adventure genre and in MUDs (although home computer games usually rely on a combination of keyboard and mouse).

In terms of genres, the classical adventure game would start a long decline in the late 1990s, and action games would be forever marked by the arrival of the first-person shooter template around 1993. More generally, the four genres, as we have described them here, begin challenging their own boundaries. Towards the last third of the decade, hybrid games became the norm instead of the exception. Action games would employ strategy elements, strategy games would lean towards action (most notably in the prolific subgenre of real-time strategy), and adventure games would continue to spice up their puzzle-solving with action sequences.

As to consoles, the Nintendo Entertainment System (NES) still dominated at the end of the 1980s, but began to encounter unprecedented competition from Sega's Genesis. Nintendo, which used gray plastic cartridges for storage, had succeeded partly by a tight control over game production, to avoid flooding the market with low quality games. Sticking to cartridges, however, meant costly products and harsh publishing rules regarding content and quality made life difficult for many developers. Furthermore, as Nintendo strove to maintain their machine's family-friendly image, Sega contrasted their own console as cool and radical (embodied in the early 1990s slogan, "Sega does what Nintendon't"). The same strategy would also be used by upstart video game producer Sony, as their 1994 PlayStation outclassed the Sega Saturn and two years later continued to sell well against the Nintendo 64 (which was further troubled by Nintendo's loyalty to cartridges). Sega, in 1999, did well with their Dreamcast console (the first to be designed for online play) although within just a few years the competition became too harsh, and they changed strategy towards developing game titles only.

The growth of local area network technology (computers close to each other sharing a network) across the globe, and the emergence of the World Wide Web, created the perfect conditions for multiplayer gaming. The wiring of the world also to some extent meant the return of the arcade—now in the form of gaming cafés (more pervasive in some countries than others. Whereas home computers had isolated players in some ways, network technology brought them back together.

Action games

The action genre displayed limited creativity or originality at the decade's outset. In 1992, however, change appeared in the shape of *Wolfenstein 3D*. The game, based on an earlier 2D game, was the original first-person shooter (although it was preceded two months earlier by *Ultima Underworld: The Stygian Abyss*, the first modern-looking 3D action game with a first-person perspective). In *Wolfenstein 3D*, the player was a lonely soldier invading a Nazi castle; the gameworld was seen solely through the

Figure 4.28 *Wolfenstein 3D*

eyes of the protagonist. Although the player could move freely in the game world, the graphics were not technically 3D, since they consisted of 2D objects and not of three-dimensional polygon shapes.

Though popular, the game could not prepare the world for1983's *Doom*. The player assumed the role of a lone no-nonsense solder defending the universe from the unfortunate, and seemingly unceasing, onslaught of the hordes of Hell. Since such creatures are not known to engage in constructive dialogue, the player was required to use varied weaponry to send them all back to where they came.

As with *Wolfenstein 3D*, the developers at id Software released the first version of *Doom* as shareware, meaning it was available for free on the Internet. The game's server was quickly and then persistently overloaded.[20] And as with the previous game, *Doom* was easily modified, causing an intense interest among serious and casual game designers alike; altered versions of the game thrived on online bulletin boards and as separately marketed productions (which required the original to play).

Its striking difference from mainstream action titles, as well as its creative and efficient use of sound and graphics, was enough to ensure *Doom*'s fame. However, it also became one of the earliest mainstream games to make good use of local area network technology, as players could fight head to head in the slime-ridden hallways.

Doom made a huge imprint on action games from the mid-1990s onwards. *Doom II* updated the original's success. *Hexen* used the *Doom* setup for fantasy purposes. *Quake* embellished the concept with true 3D graphics. *Unreal* introduced more story elements, while *Half-Life* played successfully with alien/conspiracy pop culture themes. A subset of the now ubiquitous first-person shooter—the tactical shooter—arrived in 1998 with *Delta Force*, which relied more fundamentally on multiplayer gaming and required cooperation and coordination skills.

A subgenre born into great popularity in the previous decade—the platform game—converged in 1996 with adventure structures and 3D graphics in *Tomb Raider*; this action-paced archeological expedition also represented a very different merger, between the video game industry and pop culture, as it introduced one of gaming's most famous virtual personalities, adventuress Lara Croft.

Figure 4.29 *Doom*

Figure 4.30 *Tomb Raider II: The Dagger of Xian*

In "The first real 3D interactive exploratory adventure," as the game claimed, the player guided Lara, scantily dressed and wearing her two trademark guns, as she hunted through temples and jungle levels to find a lost artifact. While competently designed, the Lara Croft personality (and indeed appearance) was far more important for the popularity of these games. Lara became a symbol of cool,

Figure 4.31 *Mortal Kombat* (DOS version)

appearing in life-style magazines and throughout the media landscape; she was both a favorite icon of the era's girl power movements as well as an academic object of desire for cultural studies of various persuasions. By all accounts, Lara paved the way for other female game protagonists, such as Jill of the *Resident Evil* series and the female prisoner of *Unreal*. The limited creativity of the game and its sequels eventually diminished its cultural relevance, but not before it provided the basis for one of the most commercially successful game adaptations for cinema, first in 2001's *Lara Croft: Tomb Raider* and then in the follow-up *Lara Croft Tomb Raider: The Cradle of Life* two years later.

Sometimes, of course, one does not need to be creative to make an impact. Violence, quite often, will do the trick. This was one of the principles behind the one-on-one fighting game *Mortal Kombat* from 1992 (which we will return to). The game looked like many other action titles, but was distinguished by noticeable features, which horrified many and delighted more than a few: each character had a number of "fatality moves," and with a few dexterous combinations of the **controller**, your defeated opponent could be killed in various gruesome ways. The parental and media outrage to follow would become a cornerstone in the U.S. Videogame Rating Act of 1994, which forced the industry into establishing a system for rating games.

Another game that fueled the same fears was *Carmageddon*, which built heavily on standard racing templates, and used mechanics reminiscent of *Death Race*, but offered far more lifelike casualties. Apart from this, subgenres such as racing games, thrived during this decade but did not make any noteworthy conceptual changes. And while action games did make use of the increased storage capacity represented by CD-ROMs, this change was quite gradual, and its fruits would not truly be seen until the following decade.

Adventure games

Continuing their innovative approach to interface design, LucasArts in 1990 published the intriguing *Loom*, in which puzzles were solved by the use of magic operated by use of music (notes were selected with the mouse to construct brief musical snippets with various effects). That same year they released an adventure game classic, *The Secret of Monkey Island*. The game, a pirate parody stuffed with pop culture references, obviously needed sword fighting. So what could one do if one doesn't want actual action sequences? LucasArts introduced us to "insult sword fights," where the player dueled using a series of proposed insults that had to outclass her opponent's taunts.

A large splash was made by the 1993 arrival of *The 7th Guest*, a haunted house story that was one of the first games to utilize the storage capacity of the CD-ROM medium. The game in no way challenged the boundaries of the adventure genre, but it was technically ambitious as its graphics were digitized film clips populated by real actors. This was impressive to many, but bought at the price of limited flexibility in terms of player actions. The game also began a tendency towards marketing games by their size, notably followed by Sierra's *Phantasmagoria*, which also starred real-life actors and spanned seven CDs.

The genre's technical evolution is also embedded in Sierra's *Gabriel Knight* series, featuring the decade-long investigations into the occult matters of "shadow hunter" Gabriel Knight. In the first game, *Gabriel Knight: Sins of the Fathers* from 1993, all graphics were 2D and hand drawn in the style of *King's Quest* from a decade earlier. The sequel, 1995's *The Beast Within: A Gabriel Knight Mystery*, leaped to the use of digitized film on background photos, and the latest game—*Gabriel Knight 3: Blood of the Sacred, Blood of the Damned*, from 1999—mixed several types of graphics but relied mostly on the 3D polygon mode. These changes are indicative of adventure game design in the 1990s. As designers began to utilize the increased capacities of CD-ROMS, and as possibilities for three-dimensional graphics grew, the look of adventures games became far more complex and mesmerizing. The genre's most famous development was the

Figure 4.32 *The Secret of Monkey Island* (DOS)

digitized "interactive movie" experiences of the middle of the decade; games like *Ripper, Phantasmagoria*, and the second *Gabriel Knight* installment, flirted heavily with Hollywood, often using popular screen actors as the basis of the game's characters, and designing the game using classical cinema conventions.

Before all of this, however, *Myst* happened. Released in 1994, *Myst*'s strong narrative and atmospheric world made it one of the most famous and bestselling home computer games ever. Its appeal to the literary-minded is obvious: in addition to the thematic focus on books and reading, the ability to wander through this world offered an altogether meditative experience. The game was taken seriously by the media, and widely reviewed in the literature sections of newspapers and elsewhere.

Myst, like the decade's other adventure games, did have one large problem. It was decidedly single-player, and since it was based on tightly woven narratives that didn't allow for much (if any) unexpected interference, it couldn't take advantage of the explosion of network technology in the second half of the decade. Though plenty of successful adventure titles were released during the 1990s—*Alone in the Dark, Day of the Tentacle*, and *Under a Killing Moon* are just a few of the other most popular ones—the genre in its classical form was struggling for air.

Role-playing games, on the other hand, let nothing stand in their way. SSI kicked off the decade with a series of games based directly on *Advanced Dungeons and Dragons*[21] rules and game worlds. While some, such as *Champions of Krynn*, from 1990, were classic *Ultima* style games (using the isometric perspective) others such as *Eye of the Beholder* employed the first-person perspective as the player traversed dungeons fighting monsters in real-time. Other older series were continued side by side with stand-alone games; most of these, like 1992's *Darklands*, were based on standard RPG conventions.

Figure 4.33 *Myst* (2000 remake)

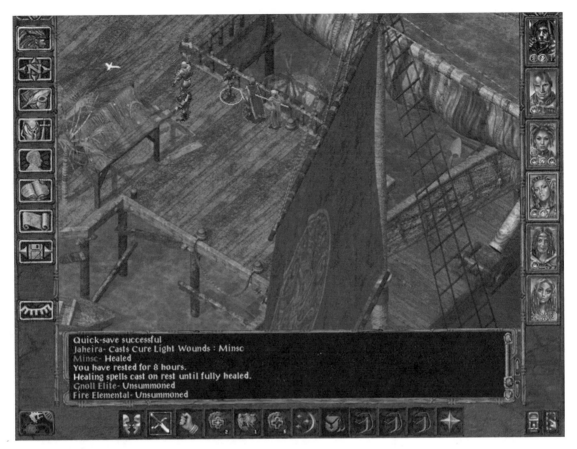

Figure 4.34 *Baldur's Gate II*

A few other adventure games deserve individual note. Complexity and creativity were beautifully merged in the post-apocalyptic *Fallout* from 1997, and 1999's philosophical amnesia thriller *Planescape: Torment*. As was the norm throughout the decade, these games used the isometric perspective, probably because it affords a clear sense of space in combat situations while keeping the player close to the protagonist(s). While not structurally innovative, *Baldur's Gate* from 1998 set many new adventure standards, because of its impressive size and extraordinary freedom of choice within the game, as the player decided whether and how to complete quests and engage with the world's many subplots.

Many continued to appreciate the virtues of this game type, even if it did not truly adapt well to multiplayer play.

Strategy games

At the start of the 1990s real-time strategy games had just blinked into existence. With *Dune II: The Building of a Dynasty* this subgenre would find a form so powerful that today's games are merely more complex variations. Later games include *WarCraft: Orcs and Humans*, *Command and Conquer*, *Age of Empires* and *StarCraft*. These games differ in their speed and complexity, but typically focus on eradicating the enemy while building up an economy based on one or more resources (spice in *Dune II*, for example, and food, wood, stone, and gold in *Age of Empires*).

Figure 4.35 *Dune II*

And unlike their adventure cousins, Real-time strategy games adapted smoothly to the new possibilities of network technology, becoming hugely popular for online or LAN play. As the complexity of these networked worlds has grown, various features have been introduced to help players keep track of their nations. But in an interesting lack of innovation, real-time strategy (unlike almost all other games) remained a 2D pastime; only in the following decade would they experiment with polygons. The basic gameplay of most of this subgenre, however, remains much like that of *Dune II*.

Turn-based strategy games, however, did anything but roll over and die. *Warlords*, for example, was a popular 1990 game that allowed up to eight people to compete on the same computer. It was quickly overshadowed the following year by Sid Meier's *Civilization*, which was an international smash hit. The player chose from among a series of historical civilizations to lead towards glory. The game's fame arose not because of its features, but in the way it combines familiar gaming elements in highly entertaining ways, creating a wide range of playing styles and strategies.

Adding various elements and a new theme to the sub-genre, 1994's *Master of Orion* dropped the player into a galactic battlefield, where he had to command a race for domination of the universe. From the same publisher, Microprose, came *X-COM: UFO Defence*, in which the player desperately defended Earth from alien invasion. The game offered two distinct modes: on the "Geoscape" level, the player managed and deployed assets, while on "Battlescape" the player fights the aliens in turn-based combat with an isometric perspective.

Process-oriented games

Though the standard adventure games like *Myst* didn't take advantage of the newly wired gaming world, other entries—that existed between the adventure and process-oriented genres—did adapt to the demand for multiplayer experiences. Certainly, *Ultima Online* from 1997—the first mainstream large-scale persistent[22] online game world—did look much like its single-player brethren. The game built

Figure 4.36 *Civilization*

on the foundation of 1985's *Habitat*, but also on the semi-successful *Meridian 59* from 1996, which (not unjustly) had introduced itself as "The First-Ever Internet-Based 3D MUD."

Ultima Online, like the MUDs, invited players to create characters and explore a universe of adventure housed in servers around the globe. As opposed to most MUD creators, however, Origin—the developer of *Ultima Online*—had a serious business plan. Players would buy the game box, including the client software, and also pay a $10 monthly subscription fee to play. The game, not quite as pretty as its offline contemporaries, used the isometric perspective and a highly complex character and skill system. *Ultima Online*, much to the surprise of most observers, had 100,000 paying subscribers within the first year. Ten dollars multiplied 100,000 times is, of course, a substantial sum and other developers followed suit. Problems quickly arose, however. Origin quickly learned the difference between friendly, bug-tolerant MUD users and paying customers, as a group of disgruntled players filed a lawsuit against the distributor for negligence, breach of contract, and intentional misrepresentation. The case was settled out of court, but offered the first look at the brave new world—and the many accompanying problems—faced by the makers of such technologically innovative games.

THE 2000s

At the time of writing, a series of trends is giving shape to the current decade of the video game industry. First of all, hardware capability is increasing rapidly, creating the possibility of evermore technically ambitious games. In the last few years, the game production process is taking on the proportions of film production. The production and marketing costs for a full-scale game currently reached a staggering $25 million for the most expensive game projects and with such large sums of money floating around, these games can only be created by experienced professional teams with a broad range of skills. Some have argued that since failures are so costly, a conservatism is overtaking the industry.[23] There are indeed an astounding number of sequels released today. However, sequels are nothing new; we need only recall the number of *Pong* clones that flooded the market at the birth of arcade gaming to realize that the industry, in all of its stages, has always tried to ride the wave of success.

Although production of full-price games becomes more and more expensive, we have seen an opposing trend which should give pause to those lamenting the conservatism of game designers. The World Wide Web has become a raging river of experimental and independent game production as various software products enables anyone with a PC and a modicum of skill to create and publish her own games. Furthermore, through the publication of astounding numbers of game design books, designers have begun—at an unprecedented scale—to share their hard-earned experience and converge their vocabularies. A few of the most significant of these titles have been discussed in the current chapter.

The growing breadth and depth of gaming knowledge coincides with the steady growth of university programs on game design. The start of the twenty-first century also marked the explosive birth of video games as an academic object of study. For some time considered unworthy of critical analysis video games are now working their way into academia with the growth of our field witnessed in journals like *Game Studies* and *Games and Culture* and in the diverse scholarship presented at conferences like the bi-annual conference of the Digital Games Research Association.

Returning to the rudiments of the games themselves, the industry's hardware is the site of more and more intense battles for control of the market as mentioned in Chapter 2. Three video game consoles presently compete for market shares: Microsoft's Xbox 360 (2005), Sony's PlayStation 3 (2006) and Nintendo's Wii (2006). To most people's surprise Nintendo is beating both of the top dogs in terms of units sold with their fresh and innovative Wii that bets on a truly new interface that inspires new forms of playing.

The PC, it seems, is becoming less economically important for game publishers. Only 16.6 percent of games were sold for the PC in the U.S. in 2005.[24] This marks a decrease from 27 percent in 2001 although the PC remains an important platform for online games. Piracy may explain the decreasing commercial importance of the PC, as it is much easier to copy and distribute PC games than console games; access to pirated games may mean, in fact, that the PC as a platform is still more popular than game sales would imply. Another crucial development—at least in the minds of financial forecasters and investors—is the rise of mobile gaming, which has come on the heels of the cell phone boom, and aided by the increased processing power of PDAs and the growing number and capacity of handheld video game consoles especially the PlayStation Portable (2004) and the Nintendo DS (2004). Mobile gaming has yet to feature truly novel designs, although it has re-established an interest in how to design games under severe size constraints; looking towards the future mobile game concepts which make use of the player's location and context show considerable promise.

On a broad level, the business of video games is booming. U.S. sales have more than doubled in less than a decade, rising from $3.2 billion in 1995 to $7.0 billion in 2005.[25] The rest of the world is also experiencing growth with Europe especially slowly catching up with the U.S. market in sales. The industry's economic vitality is all the more remarkable considering that no design revolutions are yet apparent in the current decade. Instead, genres keep merging, and tried and true designs continue to be incrementally improved.

Action games

The offspring of *Doom* live on. First-person shooters are everywhere. In the last few years the trend has moved towards team-based (rather than single-player) tactical shooters. World War II is a hugely popular setting, as seen with *Return to Castle Wolfenstein Battlefield 1942*, and *Medal of Honour: Allied Assault*, to name but a few. Exceptions, however, abound, the most significant being *Halo*, which successfully accompanied the launch of Microsoft's Xbox in 2001, and was then followed by *Halo 2* in 2004. *Halo* is a story-driven first-person shooter in a science fiction setting, in which two players can cooperate in slaying the alien hordes. The game was almost universally praised, and took home a whole series of the Interactive Achievement Awards bestowed by the Academy of Interactive Arts and Sciences in 2002.

Halo's success has also resonated beyond the game's own profits. Since one obvious disadvantage of the Xbox was its release without an existing game library (in contrast to the PlayStation 2 which could run existing PlayStation games) the success of *Halo* in all probability did much to ensure its acceptance.

Figure 4.37 *Halo* (PC version)

With 2003's *Max Payne II: The Fall of Max Payne*, shooters began exploring their interactive environments in earnest. With increasingly advanced engines, objects in most game worlds—from barrels to tables—are now programmed to interact with other objects (or characters) in realistic, often unpredictable, ways. Whereas *Max Payne II* may have been a pioneer in creating the feel of a "living" world, this vibrancy felt more integrated with the gameplay in releases like *FarCry* (from 2004) and *Half-Life 2* (from 2005).

The continued success of consoles has had the consequence of encouraging non-tactical shooter games. Until recently, consoles were mostly confined to offline play, and the result has been a design focus on viable, single-player formulae. One sign of these constraints is the growth of "survival horror" games in this decade as in the previous one. The most famous of these are the *Silent Hill* series, released between 1999 and 2003, and the *Resident Evil* series released between 1996 and 2006. These games which pitch a single player against a creepy, often zombie-ridden, environment need only relatively simple controls.

The action genre—and the industry as a whole—has also been shaped by the growth of exclusive distribution rights, where a developer will make a game for only one console. Existing consoles have had notable exclusive hits—*Halo* and *Project Gotham Racing* for the Xbox, *Metroid Prime* and *The Legend of Zelda* for the Gamecube.[26] But with the exception of *Halo*, these do not compare with Sony coup in acquiring *Grand Theft Auto III*, its offspring *Grand Theft Auto III: Vice City*, and later *Grand Theft Auto: San Andreas* from 2004. *Vice City* in particular, which started humbly as an expansion pack,[27] has reached legendary status on two very different fronts. The game's questionable moral code have made it a favorite target of those who protest against violence, and the original version has been banned in several countries. The protagonist is a gangster who undertakes various shady assignments and acquires funds in rather unethical ways (the most infamous is having sex with a prostitute and robbing her afterwards). Had this been the game's only claim to fame, however, it would have been little different from controversial titles like *Death Race* and *Mortal Kombat*. To many, *Vice City* is also an astounding piece of game design. It reaches new levels of openness, allowing the player unprecedented use of the objects in the game world, and also displays a coolness of style alien to many games as it parodied (or paid homage to, depending on your interpretation) bad police fiction of the 1980s. Thus, the game to cause the loudest outrage in recent time also became America's best selling console game of 2002 (followed the next year, in fact, by *Grand Theft Auto III*).[28]

Nintendo offered a bold alternative to the decade's barrage violence—shooter and otherwise—with the 2001 release of *Super Monkey Ball* for the GameCube console. The game soon joined their large number of successful franchises, though the gameplay itself was novel, as four players each guided a monkey inside a ball through various obstacles. The game highlighted the difference between Nintendo's and Microsoft's approaches, as the former stressed casual light-hearted play and the latter tended towards hardcore game formats. *Super Monkey Ball* also embodied the growing popularity of non-realistic, (mostly) non-violent games, suitable for group play at a party as much as for the solitary gamer. Another explosive example of these alternative action titles are rhythm games, such as *Dance Dance Revolution* from 2001. Originally popular in Japan, they have received increasing international attention in recent years, even being praised by school systems in the U.S. as a means to combat childhood obesity.[29]

Adventure games

In sharp contrast to the obvious importance of the action genre, classical adventure games today struggle for life. The struggles, however, are sometimes quite heroic. Third-person sci-fi story *The Longest Journey*, which featured the female protagonist April Ryan was lauded as an honorable specimen when released in 2000. The same critical praise befell *Syberia* two years later, a game that also used colorful pre-rendered backgrounds and relied largely on 2D graphics. This somewhat nostalgic

Figure 4.38 *Grand Theft Auto III: Vice City* (PC)

Figure 4.39 *Syberia*

form is not dominant, however, as witnessed by 2003's *Broken Sword: The Sleeping Dragon*, which featured a 3D world of free-perspective.

Offline role-playing games continue to thrive, mostly in the form established in previous decades. A notable exception was 2002's *Neverwinter Nights*, widely praised for offering a player the chance to act as gamemaster, similar to the days of D&D play around dining room tables (in truth, *Vampire: The Masquerade—Redemption* introduced the feature first, two years previously). In both games, one player could thus control various aspects of the game's scenario as it unfolded. *Neverwinter Nights* was sold with an invitation from the game's ambitious developer for the players to create their own adventures and share them with the user community. *Star Wars: Knights of the Old Republic* did nothing this innovative when released in 2003, but did introduce true 3D graphics to the RPG subgenre and was almost universally heralded as one of the best of the (many) games based on the *Star Wars* license.

Strategy games

Real-time strategy games have recently embraced 3D graphics, as illustrated by the 2002 releases *WarCraft III: Reign of Chaos* and *Age of Mythology*. But little else has changed in the genre, although *Warcraft III* did offer some alternative pleasures, by including role-playing elements and focusing on small battalions as opposed to massive armies.

Meanwhile, some turn-based series have experimented with multiplayer modes, like *Sid Meier's Civilization III: Play the World* from 2002. Another breed of turn-based strategy caters to those war gamers eager for complex and credible simulations of epochs or specific conflicts. Among the industry's best examples of this intricacy are the *Europa Universalis* games (2000–2007) and *Hearts of Iron* from 2002.

One strategy game that does stand out is Lionhead Studios' *Black and White*, from notable game designer Peter Molyneux. The game caused a stir in 2001 due to its novel design, and initially received rave reviews, although it later made number one of GameSpy.com's list of twenty-five most overrated games of all time.[30] No-one, however, denies that the game was innovative. In a parallel to *Populous*, the player assumes the role of a deity and is given a nation and a magical creature, which develops its own personality and knowledge based on how it is treated by the player. At the same time, the player's choices affect how his subjects perceive him, leading to various possibilities and constraints.

Process-oriented games

In recent years, developer interest in massively multiplayer online games has skyrocketed. Presently around 170 MMORPGs exist or are in development complemented by a significant number of large-scale online multiplayer games in other genres.

The most ambitious Western titles in the decade's early years were Funcom's science fiction themed *Anarchy Online*, Vivendi's *Dark Age of Camelot* and Sony's *Star Wars Galaxies: An Empire Divided*. Of these, *Anarchy Online* faced tremendous technical trouble at launch, while *Dark Age of Camelot* is often described as something of a miracle in terms of flawless launches of ambitious online games.[31] None of these rebelled against the standards established by *EverQuest* and others, although variety in the specific mechanics did lead to somewhat different game experiences. Many believed that the large number of fantasy themed games available had satiated that particular niche, but they were proven wrong by Blizzard's extraordinarily successful *World of Warcraft* in 2004. With little that was radically new, *World of Warcraft* geared its dynamics towards more casual play and quickly attracted more than

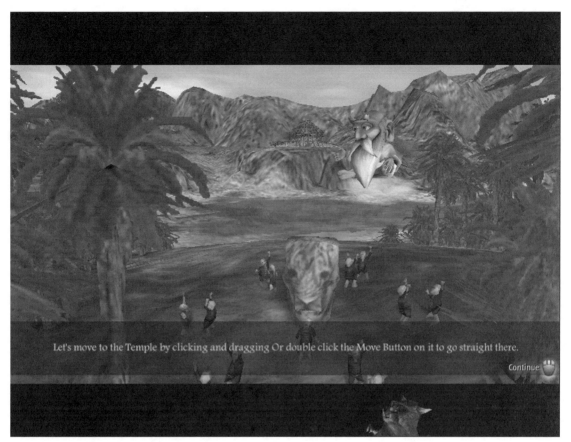

Figure 4.40 *Black and White*

twice as many users as *EverQuest*—until then the most popular Western MMORPG—had ever had.[32]

It is curious that MMOGs[33] have been mostly confined to their region of origin. As a general rule, Western games have enjoyed very limited success in Asia and vice-versa. In Asia, the game *Lineage: The Bloodpledge*, released in 2001, drew players in numbers which surpassed even the most successful Western MMORPG of the time though later surpassed by *World of Warcraft* (although differences in how subscriptions work make comparisons difficult). Graphics were two-dimensional, not unlike those of *Ultima Online*, and the game focused on battle. Other Asian MMORPG successes include Gravity Corporation's *Ragnarok Online*, a stylized animated-inspired 2002 release, *Final Fantasy XI* from 2003, and Lineage's successor *Lineage II: The Chaotic Cronicle* from 2004.

These titles, however, may just be the beginning given the large number of MMOGs (massively online games) Ccurrently in production. However, it seems that certain strong design conventions have already been established such as the use of fantasy settings and the focus on player characters working toward higher levels.

In mid-2007, the website MMOGData which collects statistics on MMOG subscriptions estimates the total number of MMOG subscriptions to be 20 million (up from a select few in the mid-1990s). Figure 4.42 shows number of subscribers for the most popular games.

Figure 4.41 *World of Warcraft*

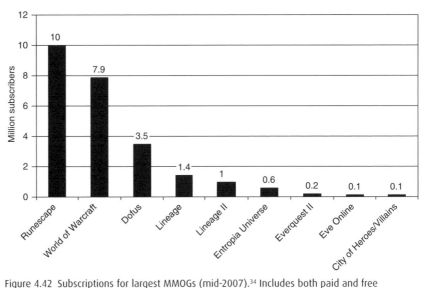

Figure 4.42 Subscriptions for largest MMOGs (mid-2007).[34] Includes both paid and free subscriptions

We see how presently *Runescape* (which offers free subscriptions) has more players than any other game and that *World of Warcraft* is the most successful paid-subscription-only game in the world by far.

Apart from MMOGs, non-competitive vehicle simulators remain an important niche in the process-oriented genre. Microsoft continues to publish reality-faithful simulators, like the 2001 *Microsoft Train Simulator*. Here, the player controls various train types and is able to operate everything from a variety of brakes and horns to windshield wipers. To ensure realistic representation Microsoft has teamed up with actual railroad operators, with the sole aim of mimicking the experience of actually running a train.

PERSPECTIVES

Where are video games going? Although certain trends seem evident, the industry's only true constant has been rapid change; as a result, large-scale predictions about the future of games are likely to be the butt of ridicule in a matter of years.

In the absence of fortune-telling, then, let's outline some intriguing trends. First of all, it seems that a belief common in some quarters at the turn of the century—that video games would rid themselves of narrative trappings to embrace their core "gameness"—has been thoroughly debunked. The success of games like *Grand Theft Auto III* (2001), *Hitman: Codename 47* (2000), *Max Payne II* (2003) and *Half-Life 2* (2004) has shown that storytelling is as essential as ever. This group exists in some opposition to another growing subgenre—the world-oriented, massively multiplayer role-playing games. These manifest many contrary characteristics, and are for example much less rigid about their definition of success, and much more open as to playing styles. The latter group, which has arrived with high expectations and much discussion, has not become the instant goldmine that some dreamed of. While *World of Warcraft* has become immensely popular, others have not captured the masses like they were supposed to—the disappointing sales of 2002's *The Sims Online* exemplifies that the potentially lucrative game format is not a sure recipe for success.

Another split runs between active hardcore PC gamers—who are willing to spend time and money altering and expanding their favorite games—and console gamers, typically content to be entertained by less demanding game types. If the financial importance of the PC as a gaming platform declines further this may lead to the PC not being automatically supported by certain genres of game developers.

Sticking to the dichotomies, both console and PC games have generally increased in size, complexity and development budgets. Meanwhile, the World Wide Web has become a training ground for would-be game designers of all levels. Adding to this renewed focus on simple, sometimes minimalist, game design is the rise of mobile platforms (particularly cell phones), which have fueled a special creativity brought on by severe limitations. Thus, while AAA titles grow in size and marketing force, each new day sees cascades of simple, experimental independent games being released on the web. To say that design development in the *broad* sense is being stifled by growing budgets is blatantly incorrect. This pessimism is as inaccurate, in fact, as the fallacy that old games were better than new games, or that game designers today—more than their predecessors—rely on true and tried formulae. Great specimens have always been copied, but development is not about being uniquely creative each time. It is very much about the slow accumulation of knowledge—technical and otherwise—about building on past effort, copying the masters, and learning from the success and failure of one's peers. The successful development of new work, as we have seen time and time again in this chapter, is ultimately about understanding the history of video games.

5 VIDEO GAME AESTHETICS

RULES/GEOGRAPHY AND REPRESENTATION/NUMBER OF PLAYERS

We have already tried to reach an understanding of what games are—to give a sense of the formal qualities that we can use to decide what constitutes a game. In this chapter, we will look more closely at how to understand major game features like interactivity, rules, and gamespace.

By aesthetics we are referring to all aspects of video games which are experienced by the player, whether directly—such as audio and graphics—or indirectly—such as rules. Thus, importantly aesthetics as used here is not limited to how a game looks or sounds but more broadly to how it *plays* as a function of the various design choices of the developers. Or put differently, Chapter 3 was about describing games as a phenomenon in contrast to other phenomena whereas this chapter is about describing the elements that actually make up games.

- *Rules*: these defined limitations determine what you (and other characters in the game) can and cannot do, and which actions or events increase or decrease the player's score. In chess, for example, there is a rule that one cannot place one's own king in a position of check; in the snowboarding game *SSX 3* there is a rule that a certain aerial maneuver gives the player a particular number of points.

- *Geography and representation*: like the cardboard playing surface of a traditional boardgame, a video game's geography "physically" blocks certain actions (you generally cannot pass through walls), while allowing others (you may be able to jump from one platform to another). The world of a video game is typically represented to the player by means of graphics and sound. Within the realm of representation is an enormous variety of design possibilities: For instance graphics may be two- or three-dimensional, sound may be realistic or cartoonish, and the perspective may be isometric or first-person.

- *Number of players*: in terms of design and development single-player games differ greatly from multi-player games. In the former type, computer-controlled opponents—or the environment itself—must respond entertainingly to the player's actions, while in the latter type designers must ensure level playing fields, efficient communication features, etc.

On a very abstract level, these three elements could be independent of one another. One set of rules, for example, could be attached to a variety of game representations (we could have a game of *Star Wars* chess, which in fact we do). But as we shall see, the choices regarding one of these elements tend in practice to shape choices on other levels.

The issue of narrative and setting is not mentioned here since it will be dealt with separately in Chapter 8.

RULES

Recall, if you can, the 1983 blockbuster film *WarGames*. The characters of Matthew Broderick and Ally Sheedy have come amazingly close to destroying the world—all by playing a video game. As an out-of-control military supercomputer ticks down to an imminent nuclear war, they race to reach the one man who may be able to help them, Dr. Steven Falken. Reluctant to help, Falken instead lectures them on game design. "Did you ever play Tic-Tac-Toe?" he asks Sheedy. She answers yes, but adds that she doesn't play it any more because it is a boring game and always ends in a tie. Falken agrees: "There's no way you can win." As most of us eventually realize, Falken is right. Unless one player makes a mistake—or is too young to grasp the structure of the game—Tic-Tac-Toe will always end in a draw.

The savvy Broderick realizes the beauty of Falken's simple lesson, and proceeds to save the world by forcing the nuke-enabled runaway computer to play repeated games of Tic-Tac-Toe. The goal is to teach the computer that a nuclear war between the superpowers cannot be won. In the nick of time the computer catches on and proclaims: "Strange game, the only winning move is not to play."[1]

Although deliciously dramatic, the movie's logic is hardly flawless. Strictly speaking, one does not, of course, win Tic-Tac-Toe by not playing it. The perfect analogy would require either a cost or a disadvantage to playing the game in the first place (in the movie's plot, for example, the disadvantage would be analogous to the cost of engaging in a nuclear war).

Nor is it obvious why the computer should generalize its new-found understanding of Tic-Tac-Toe to the Cold War as a whole, when it has played hosts of other games where one side actually *can* win. Nevertheless, the film demonstrates how Tic-Tac-Toe, despite its design "flaw," is a compelling example of the functions of a game's rules.

Let's look at the incredibly simple/mundane rules of this paradigmatic non-electronic game. In Katie Salen and Eric Zimmerman's formulation,[2] they are:

1   Play occurs on a 3 by 3 grid of 9 empty squares.

2   Two players alternate marking empty squares, the first player marking Xs and the second player marking Os.

3   If one player places three of the same marks in a row, that player wins.

4   If the spaces are all filled and there is no winner, the game ends in a draw.

Most of us would agree that these are indeed the rules of Tic-Tac-Toe. However, these rules alone do not guide the way we play of the game. Stephen Sniderman reminds us, for example, that in standard Tic-Tac-Toe rules as stated above, "nothing has been said about time. Is there a time limit between moves? Normally, we both 'understand' that there is, and we both 'know' that our moves should be made within a 'reasonable' time, say 20 seconds."[3] If you realize that you have made a mistake and will lose on the other player's next turn, nothing in the four basic rules would seem to prevent you from actually never making your move, thus halting the game forever. But as Sniderman puts it:

> Anybody who seriously resorted to such a tactic would be considered childish or unsportsmanlike or socially undesirable and would probably not be asked to play in the future. This behavior seems to violate some fundamental but rarely stated principle of the game without any of us ever having to discuss it.[4]

The implication, as Salen and Zimmerman underline, is that it is not possible to state all the rules that apply to most non-electronic games. Video games, however, are somewhat different in this regard. A game of *Microsoft Solitaire* on a Windows computer has fewer unstated rules than our paper and pencil game of Tic-Tac-Toe since everything taking place within that game must have been made possible (and legal) by the game code. Nevertheless, you could of course choose to avoid the embarrassment of quitting a hopeless game by cutting the power to the computer.

What, then, is the relationship between a game and its rules?

In a very important sense, a game is its rules.[5]

Rules, arguably, are the most defining characteristic of games; they are the element shared by everything we usually understand as a game, and are the element that sets games apart from linear media such as novels or movies. (A novel, for example, has its own geography, its own representation—text—and its own narrative and setting.) An important feature of rules is that they are not tied to one particular type of material; in other words they are *transmedial*.[6] Thus, the game of chess does not rely on black and white pieces moving about on a physical game board. It is possible, as many die-hard Lucas fans know, to play chess using pieces representing *Star Wars* characters; it is just as possible to have real geographical features function as a board, and have people function as the pieces, or to have the whole thing taken care of by a computer. Thus, no matter how and where you choose to represent the chess conflict, as long as you follow the rules you are still playing chess.

If we accept the limited definition that a game is its rules, then all games are transmedial. But this does not mean that the rules of a game can be transferred into anything that someone has classified as a medium. You cannot play chess on/through a movie (although a movie can tell the story of chess, or can depict a specific chess match). The transmedial nature of games simply tells us that although a game cannot be played through any medium, a game is not tied to a *specific* medium.

Do you agree with the above concept? If not, perhaps you are envisioning a game of chess played using various types of Barbie dolls in a forest divided into grids— such a game would *feel* extremely different, no doubt, from a classical chess match with its elegant, almost minimalist, setup. In other words, you might feel that the context of the game is crucial to determining the experience of a game. You would be absolutely right, of course. But here we need to distinguish between the formal and the phenomenological levels of a game. As Salen and Zimmerman put it: ". . . the formal system of a game, the game considered as a set of rules, is not the experience of the game."[7] Context is clearly important to any player, but when analyzing games we must sometimes bracket this acknowledgment when discussing how games are alike or different in terms of their more basic aesthetics.

A definition of rules

Science fiction author and game critic Orson Scott Card has said:

> Remember, gamewrights, the power and beauty of the art of gamemaking is
> that you and the player collaborate to create the final story. Every freedom that
> you can give to the player is an artistic victory. And every needless boundary in
> your game should feel to you like failure.[8]

Card's declaration will make immediate sense to many gamers and certainly has
merit as a piece of game design advice. But if we believe that interactivity is central
to the enjoyment of a game, does it follow that enjoyment is closely linked to
player freedom? Not necessarily. Stephen Sniderman notes that "To play a game is
to pursue that game's object while adhering (more or less) to its constraints."[9]
Similarly, Salen and Zimmerman are adamant that one of the essential qualities of
rules is that they limit player action.[10]

Many may instinctively think of rules as bad, or constraining, or a burden. We
seek to fight against rules, to find ways around them. But we would do better to
acknowledge that rules are an essential component of a game. These limits on our
freedom as players are actually what give a shape and a drive to the playing of the
game; they are what challenge us in the game world, they are what enable us to feel
satisfaction when we win. Perhaps what we should hope for is not no rules at all,
but rules that limit player freedom in entertaining ways. More formally, a rule is an
imperative governing the interaction of game objects and the possible outcome of
this interaction.

Types of rules

Despite the brevity of the definition above it can be difficult, in practice, to determine
which aspects of games belong under the heading of rules. Helpfully, a number of
authors have specified different *types* of rules. Gonzalo Frasca, for example, has
proposed a dualism of rules: "ludus" rules relate to the conditions by which a player
wins, and "paidia" rules refer to game procedures (such as "pawns move one square
at a time" in chess).[11] As you've probably guessed, both terms are borrowed from
Roger Caillois, who used them in a slightly different sense (see Chapter 3).

For a more formal approach, we can turn to Jesper Juul's three levels of rules:[12]

1   *Game state rules*: these rules cover the basic aspects of the game state (i.e. the exact
    condition at a point in time of all game elements).

2   *Outcome valorization rules*: these rules define which outcomes are considered posi-
    tive and which outcomes are considered negative.

3   *Information rules*: these rules determine what information the player receives
    during play about the game state.

As with Frasca, we find a distinction between rules that determine processes, and
rules that relate to the outcome of the game. Juul's third category allows us to
consider another important aspect of game systems: the amount of information
that the player is given about the state of the entire game. To Juul, the player of *Pac-*

Man has perfect (or *complete*)[13] information—he can see the entire screen, and cannot be surprised by any new information; an *Age of Kings* player, immersed in a world bursting with unexpected occurrences is in a quite different position.

However, we must add that the amount of information given may be clear, the significance of this information may not be. One piece of information may support multiple interpretations of the game state. Imagine, for instance, that our *Age of Kings* player comes upon a nearly depleted and abandoned gold mine. What does this tell him about the game state? Technically, it tells him only that there is a nearly depleted mine at certain coordinates. But it may also lend credence to one or several additional hypotheses, such as "Player B has mined gold here but was disturbed, and is apparently too busy or too rich to mine the remaining gold." Thus, the information which a player actually *understands* can be quite different from the information that the player *receives*.

A rather different typology is suggested by Katie Salen and Eric Zimmerman. They too, have three rule types:

1   *Operational rules*: these are what one would typically describe as the rules of a game. In a combination of Juul's "game state" and "outcome valorization" rules, they govern both a game's processes and its conditions for victory.

2   *Constitutive rules*: these are the underlying formal structures of a game which define its basic dynamics. For instance, some games (were one to disregard their presentational aspects) may be reduced to core logical/mathematical problems.

3   *Implicit rules*: these are all the unwritten rules that we take for granted when playing a game.

These three levels describe well the rules of non-digital games. For video games beyond a certain level of complexity (say, anything more advanced than *Tetris*), this typology is still useful but works less well in practice. The concept of constituative rules, for example, is not often applicable; it is not easy nor necessarily meaningful to describe *Halo: Combat Evolved*—a game of vast complexity—in terms of underlying formal structures.

We are free to employ whichever typology is the most useful. But in writing this book, we have found it most useful to merely distinguish between two types of rules, along the lines of Frasca's proposal. The first type, what we call the *interplay rules*, determine the relationships and the properties of elements in a game. These correspond to the physical laws of the gamespace. They determine what can be done and, combined with player input, determine what happens. The second type, the *evaluation rules*, decide which occurrences are rewarded and which are punished. For instance, in *Super Mario Bros.* one interplay rule states that Mario will jump to a certain height when a player presses "A" button on their controller; one evaluation rule is that killing enemies by landing on them gives you points.

Gameplay

The term "gameplay" is often used but rarely defined. As commonly employed it refers to the game dynamics, or more simply, "how it feels to play a game." Although this feeling is influenced by a game's audio and visual aspects, gameplay is usually considered a consequence of the game's *rules* rather than its *representation* (which we'll discuss in the following section). Using this basic definition, we can say that the gameplay of chess is deliberative and while the gameplay of *Burnout 3* is frantic and easily accessible.

In line with common use of the term, we will define gameplay as: *the game dynamics emerging from the interplay between rules and game geography.*[14] These dynamics may be entertaining, or not, and they may be more or less predictable. Let us look at some examples. In *Super Monkey Ball* (see Figure 5.20) the rules and geography combine to ensure that the game will be hectic and competitive and fast-paced. *Age of Empires II: Age of Kings* (see Figure 5.1), on the other hand, contains many potentially successful strategies, and depending on the aggregate choices of the players involved, a game can be quite hectic or far more deliberative and defense-oriented.

Figure 5.1 *Age of Empires II: Age of Kings*

In part, this variety in gameplay stems from the different conflicts staged by the two games. In the racing sub-game of *Super Monkey Ball*, each player largely plays against the game system (even though it may not feel that way); the actions of the other players are mostly irrelevant, because your main concern is to get that monkey through the level as fast as possible. *Age of Empires II*, on the other hand, provides a more chess-like geography for what is essentially a conflict between *players*.

Game balance[15]

With very few exceptions, game designers attempt to achieve "balance" in every game. Essentially, this means that winning a game should be a function of player skill plus any element of randomness or luck that the game employs, but should be unrelated to the game's initial conditions. In chess, for example, if black began the game with three more knights than white, the game would not be balanced. We should note that balance can exist both within the game itself (called "in-game balance") and also between players ("player-player balance"). But sometimes the term also refers to a designer's attempt to balance various strategies and game units (such as soldier types) against each other in interesting ways. In a real-time strategy game, even if this applied to all sides (so that the game was technically fair), it shouldn't always be best to simply concentrate on one particular unit type or strategy.

Staying with real-time strategy games, we can see how difficult it can be to achieve balance. Since each player typically can choose amongst various races or civilizations—each with different strengths and weaknesses—the developers must plan carefully and test meticulously to ensure that all potential interactions are balanced; furthermore, these interactions must remain fair even across the different types of maps available, and regardless of whatever ingenious strategies players bring to the game. Examples of failure in balance are not difficult to find. In 1994's *Warcraft: Orcs and Humans*, for instance, the Orc player producing warlock units will almost always win.[16] Similarly, in *Age of Kings* some civilizations (mainly the Teutons) were often considered too strong compared to others, and players often agreed to not choose these over-powerful civilizations.

One classic way of achieving in-game balance is the use of intransitive relationships. The principle is well-known by anyone familiar with the hand game *rock-paper-scissors*:

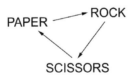

Figure 5.2 *Rock-paper-scissors*. Arrows stand for "defeats", e.g. rock defeats scissors

Rock-paper-scissors has only three strategies available to the player. But the success or failure of choosing rock, paper, or scissors depends entirely on what the other player chooses; and just as importantly, no strategy is inherently better than any of the others. For *Age of Empires II*, we can plot a simplified relationship between the game units (i.e. the types of soldiers, etc., that a player can create and use) as shown below.

As we follow the arrows, we can see that the cavalry is very effective against archers and siege weapons but are vulnerable to pikemen. Adding to the complexity, each of these characters (or units) has a production cost (it requires a certain amount of wood to build heavy infantry, for example, and a different amount of gold): and a production time (e.g. siege weapons take longer to build than footmen). These factors are further influenced by the specific map being used (on maps with few forests, units requiring wood are effectively more expensive to build), as well as the civilization chosen by the player (each civilization has particular advantages such as special units). In other words, achieving in-game balance is quite complex.

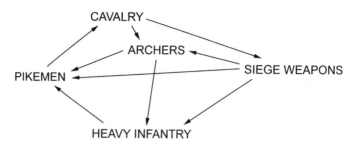

Figure 5.3 Relationship of *Age of Empires II: Age of Kings* units

When considering game balance, the field of economical game theory is helpful. Game theory is a discipline (or perhaps more accurately, a set of techniques) that originates in economics, and uses the terminology of games in order to model situations of strategic interaction.[17] Of particular interest here is the concept of the *Nash equilibrium* (and the related concept of *dominant strategies*). Simply put, a game has an equilibrium state if playing a particular set of strategies produces a situation where no player can benefit from changing his strategy (assuming that the strategies used by the other player(s) remain constant). Players tend to gravitate towards this equilibrium and once there, no one will budge (because there is no incentive to do so). In certain real-life situations this is very useful (everybody gravitates towards driving *either* on the left *or* on the right side of the road), but it is a problem for game design, because such a game will tend to be played in the same way every time. The related term *dominant strategy* refers to a strategy that simply is the best one to choose, regardless of what the other player(s) are expected to do. The existence of such a strategy usually saps the game of the potential for choice, thus making it boring.

Economic game theory, while not originally intended as a tool for video game development, is highly useful for grasping the dynamic of how different rules create different player relationships. Concerned as it is with *choice*, it helps us (whether we are designers or analysts) understand balance and the related concept of strategy. Thus, the reader interested in these issues is encouraged to seek out (economic) game theory literature, even if it is not directly tailored towards video game analysis.

GEOGRAPHY AND REPRESENTATION

The splendid sunsets of today's massively multiplayer online role-playing games seem only distantly related to the primitive (if groundbreaking) two-color visuals of *Spacewar*. This section provides a systematic account of the various strategies of geography and representation employed by game designers.

Obviously, the way the game world is laid out is related to the way it looks. If you're roaming a three-dimensional city and the way ahead is blocked you will typically notice something large in front of you (as opposed to just suddenly being stopped by an invisible barrier). But there is also a difference between geography and representation. In the 1982 arcade game *Moon Patrol*, the player patrols a lunar surface for aliens while, in the background, futuristic buildings scroll by. These buildings have no direct in-game effect; for instance they don't block the player's movement or provide cover. They are simply there for the visual effect. Similarly, the "splendid sunsets" referred to above have no direct bearing on the player's possibilities. They mostly add to the atmosphere, provide a sense of realism and generally make the game world seem alive.

Game students and scholars who focus closely on rules run the risk of delegating audiovisuals to the category of surface phenomena. Graphics, in particular, is sometimes treated as mere window-dressing, eye-candy providing an enticing way of interacting with the actual game beneath. As we shall see throughout the following that view is much too simple as graphic types have different properties and afford different gameplay styles. Also, a graphical style may *ideally* be chosen for its ability to support the game mechanics but in the real world graphical style the causal arrow is sometimes reversed as graphics determine the mechanics. For instance if a game designer starts out with a preference for a certain graphical style, this preference is likely to influence the kind of game she will make.

Imagine, for instance, a game designer who has access to graphical tools developed for a first-person shooter. All other things being equal, she is unlikely to produce a real-time strategy game. Similarly, if she sets out to make a real-time-strategy game, she may debate whether to incorporate 2D or 3D graphics, but she is likely to choose a third-person perspective.

Geography, representation, and gameplay are interrelated and to see this more clearly let us look at the way in which games have developed over the years. Concerns over the relative merits of 2D and 3D game engines were not pressing on the minds of the *Spacewar* developers in the early 1960s. Working under severe hardware constraints they were forced to limit the number of on-screen objects and to limit the details of these objects. Nothing, however, forced them to create the game's puzzling wraparound space, which ensured that a spaceship leaving the right edge of the screen would materialize on the left. It would be odd, yes, to have the ships crash against the screen edges (space is supposed to be infinite, after all) but there certainly is no logic demanding that the ships make this odd and unexplained transition to another position in space. Although hardware was important, this was one of many design *choices*, with great implications for the gameplay of this and many other games to follow.

We see the action of *Spacewar* from an abstract position—rather than from the perspective of one of game's protagonists—so we can say that the game employs a *third-person perspective*. The alternative to this would be a *first-person perspective*, where the player sees the game from her character's perspective, as is the case in first-person shooters.

The galactic shoot-out takes place on a single plane, in which the spaceships can move in any of the cardinal directions, but not down or up away from the plane. This is equivalent to a space battle carried out on a game board—lacking any depth—and is of course not realistic in any way. Thus, we say that the graphics are two-dimensional. The action takes place on a simple coordinate system and the position of an object can be described using only two coordinates (see Figure 5.4). This is opposed to three-dimensional graphics, which also have depth, much like the physical world.

Spacewar was a competitive two-player game where the players (typically) were watching the same screen and thus it would be difficult to have the

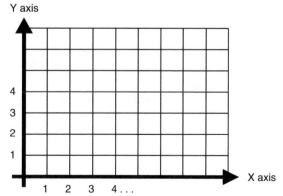

Figure 5.4 Two-dimensional graphics entail that the game action is limited to a simple coordinate system. The position of any object is determined by the values of X and Y

Figure 5.5 *Bomb Jack*

Figure 5.6 *Time Pilot*

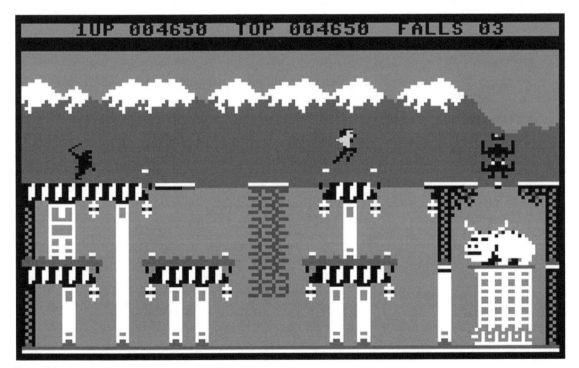

Figure 5.7 *Bruce Lee*

perspective move to follow one of the players. Thus, the *Spacewar* world did not "scroll." Scroll refers to the movement (typically horizontal) of the perspective to follow the action, somewhat like the the gradual unrolling of the contents of a paper scroll, or a camera on a track which rolls alongside a scene.

Multi-player one-display games which *have* scrolled have typically been cooperative action games like *Golden Axe*, *Gauntlet*, and *Double Dragon*, where it is to the players' advantage to move in synchrony. Thus, *Spacewar*'s non-scrolling perspective may have been a function of gameplay details, but another choice made by the designers, not required by the logic of the game or its technological constraints, is the game's off-screen space. Because the playing field wraps around to meet itself, *Spacewar* technically has no off-screen space. Thus, the players can see all the objects in the game at all times, and do not have to worry about anything lying beyond the screen. Again, hardware limitations might have played a role, but this design choice also suggests the pervasive influence of classical board games. In chess, *Stratego* and *Risk*, for example, nothing exists beyond the board. Through *Spacewar* is simple, the types of choices faced by its designers are similar to those faced in later and more complex game productions.

Below is a table of basic geographical and representational characteristics that we shall use to distinguish between aesthetic strategies in games followed by a detailed description of each.

Perspective	First person			Third person	
Dimensions	2			3	
Space type	Torus		Abstract	Free	
Off-screen	Dynamic		Static	None	
Scroll	Vertical	Horizontal	Free	None	
Exploration	Forced		Free	None	

Figure 5.8 Basic graphical/spatial game characteristics. The table does not indicate relationships across the rows

Perspective

Excluding text-based games and abstract puzzle games (in which perspective is irrelevant), all video games employ either a first- or a third-person perspective (or the ability to toggle back and forth between the two). In addition, games can also employ either an isometric perspective (similar to an architect's sketch of a building) or a top-down perspective (also known as a bird's eye perspective).

In the first-person perspective, we see the game action from the point of view of the protagonist—it is as if the player himself is experiencing the action. In the third-person perspective the player watches whatever it is that he controls, which can be an on-screen object (a character, a vehicle), a number of objects (an army of soldiers, a group of villagers) or various settings (such as tax rates or city zoning). In the case of games like SimCity, the player is not even directly represented in the game world, suggesting that we can enjoy interacting with a system without the need (so obviously present in narrative film, for instance) to identify with actual characters. If we consider video games as an extension (or variation) of classical board games, we won't be surprised here. Card games, dice games or board games such as kalaha or backgammon are engrossing without any human-like representation of the player.

What is more surprising is that video games seem to work equally well in both the first- and third-person perspective. Nor is there any indisputable difference

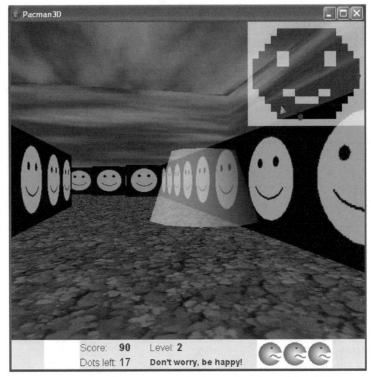

Figure 5.9 *Pac-Man 3D*: first-person perspective version of a traditional third-person game[18]

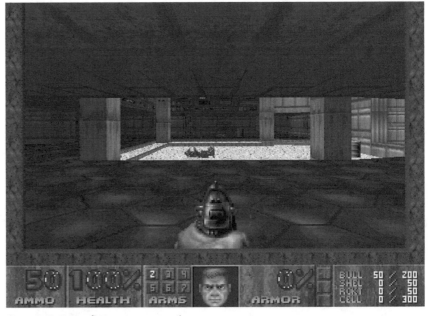

Figure 5.10 *Doom*: first-person perspective

between the experience of playing the two. It is easy to assume that the first-person perspective offers a unique, visceral and hectic experience, but this is belied by the blood-pumping enthusiasm that many players have brought and still bring to even the simplest of third-person action games (like *Spacewar*).

One general statement we can make, however, is that genres and subgenres (as discussed in Chapter 3) consistently adhere to one or very few perspective(s). For instance, real-time strategy games always employ the third-person perspective. The same holds for turn-based strategy games and for most action games, which require the careful coordination of physical activities by different players. We can imagine the difficulty, for example of maneuvering the vine swinging and pyramid climbing of archaeological adventuress Lara Croft while seeing the gameworld through her eyes.[19] In comparison, almost all modern action games that revolve around shooting are tellingly referred to as *first-person shooters*; it would be hard to imagine these in the third person. Multi-player third-person shooters, however, are far less unlikely than a first-person strategy game. The reason for this is that strategy games do not have single protagonists, making such a design experiment rather meaningless.[20]

One subgenre not clearly linked to either perspective is role-playing games (whether single or multiplayer). Throughout the subgenre's history, both perspectives have been used. In *The Elder Scrolls III: Morrowind*, where the player assumes the

Figure 5.11 *The Elder Scrolls III: Morrowind*

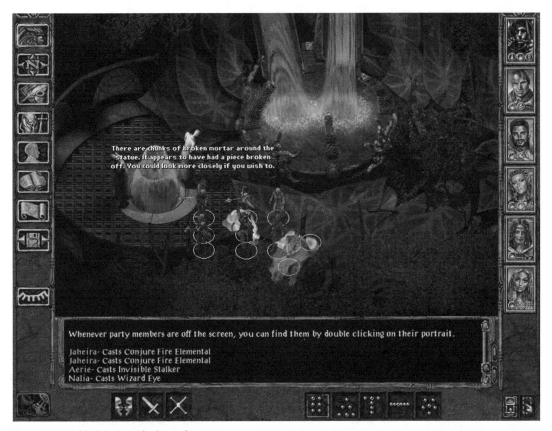

Figure 5.12 *Baldur's Gate II: Shadows of Amn*

role of a single character, she is mainly offered a first-person perspective of events (but can shift to third person). In *Baldur's Gate II: Shadows of Amn*, where the player is responsible for the wellbeing of an entire party of adventurers, the player must content herself with a third-person perspective. Similarly, MMORPGs usually "prefer" the first-person perspective but always offer a multitude of different perspectives.

Some other games seek the best of both perspectival worlds: they avoid the strict first-person perspective (seeing through the character's eyes) in favor of a point of view placed *very close* to the object controlled by the player.

As we follow the historical evolution of video game design, we should increasingly not cling to a strict division between first- and third-person perspective; rather, we should discuss a game's *point of perception*,[21] the point from which the player perceives the gamespace. Importantly, a game may offer varied, often overlapping, points of perception. Real-time strategy games, for instance, offer maps of the entire gamespace, which coexist with the standard view chosen by the player.

What makes the difference is often the *distance* of the point of view from the game action. In *Half-Life 2* the point of perception is that of the player character, which offers only a very limited portion of the game world as a whole. This ensures very limited knowledge and a frantic, non-strategic approach to problem solving. *Baldur's Gate II: Shadows of Amn* (see Figure 5.12), on the other hand, uses the so-called isometric perspective.

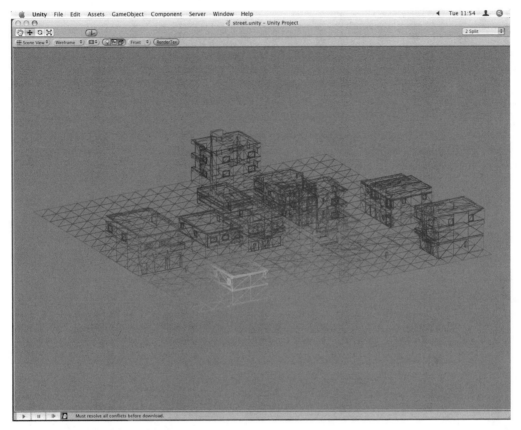

Figure 5.13 Example of the isometric perspective

The isometric perspective is a technique normally used for architectural draw-ings, as a method for presenting three-dimensional objects in a two-dimensional form. Technically speaking, the angles between the projection of the three axes (X, Y and Z) are all 120° and there is no vanishing point (see Figure 5.13).

The isometric perspective is not necessarily more effective or engaging than a top-down perspective, but it does allow for a less abstract perception of the game space. We can see this by comparing the isometric perspective of *SimCity 2000* (Figure 5.14), to the top-down perspective of *SimCity* (Figure 4.28).

Two early uses of the isometric perspective were the 1982 arcade space action game Zaxxon and the 1984 ZX Spectrum game *Knight Lore*, in which a werewolf roamed a magical castle in the hopes of lifting the curse upon him. Notable later games to employ the isometric perspective include *Paperboy* (1984), *Diablo* (1986) and *The Sims* (2000). Today, the perspective is a staple of the real-time strategy subgenre, although early examples—such as *Dune II* and *Warcraft*—in fact used a top-down perspective. Role-playing games with a third-person perspective (such as *Baldur's Gate* or *Lineage the Bloodpledge*) always also use the isometric perspective. Probably because is facilitates identification with on-screen characters and simulta-neously allows for a strategic understanding of the gamespace.

Perspective is of great importance in game design since it directly shapes how we perceive the game world and how close we can get to its characters and objects (and if we can even relate to individual characters at all).

Figure 5.14 *SimCity 2000*

Dimensions

Although we shall soon discover the grey areas, in essence all computer graphics are either two-dimensional or three-dimensional. We have already seen examples of both but now is the time to be more specific.

Two-dimensional graphics are somewhat comparable to paintings. They are created in computer applications, like *Adobe Photoshop*, originally designed to facilitate drawing, sketching and image processing. They can be printed on paper without losing essential qualities (unlike 3D graphics which, if printed, would obviously no longer be rotatable, etc.).

Elements of a 2D image may consist of either *vector graphics* or *raster graphics* (to name the most important possibilities). Vector graphics are geometric models described as mathematical statements. Thus, they can be turned, twisted, rotated and resized without any loss of quality. Raster graphics (or bitmap graphics), on the other hand, are rectangular maps of pixels (points of color); each pixel endowed with a color value. When thousands or millions of these individual pixels are grouped together, they create a comprehensible image. Raster graphics are used to transfer photographs from a digital camera onto your computer screen and cannot be resized—at least not made bigger—without obvious quality problems.

3D graphics are fundamentally different: as we saw above, they add the Z-axis and 3D graphics objects thus become spatial (see Figure 5.15).

Also, the computer will typically store 3D objects as *models* (see Figure 5.16) which can then be rendered wherever appropriate in a game, for instance as running right next to the player character with sunlight illuminating one side of a face.

Such on-the-fly computation is so demanding that modern games typically require 3D-dedicated hardware to render the graphics but often the level of detail is adjustable making the game playable on systems without the latest graphics cards. Figure 5.17 and Figure 5.18 show examples of games with 3D graphics.

There are creative ways of achieving 3D-like effects using 2D graphics, to create a feeling of depth without the complexity and cost of real 3D or simply because it fits one's aesthetic purpose. For this purpose designers most often use the isometric perspective, as we discussed above. *SimCity 2000* (Figure 5.14) uses 2D graphics but attains depth by using the isometric perspective.[22] In an interesting innovation, *Wolfenstein 3D* uses a first-person perspective but

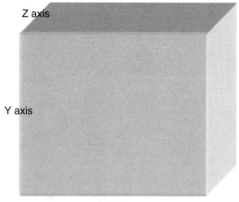

Figure 5.15 In games with three-dimensional graphics, the gamespace can be thought of as the inside of a box. The position of any object is determined by its value X, Y and Z. Most gamespaces, however, can be said to consist of only the bottom of the box, as vertical (Y-axis) player movement is often limited

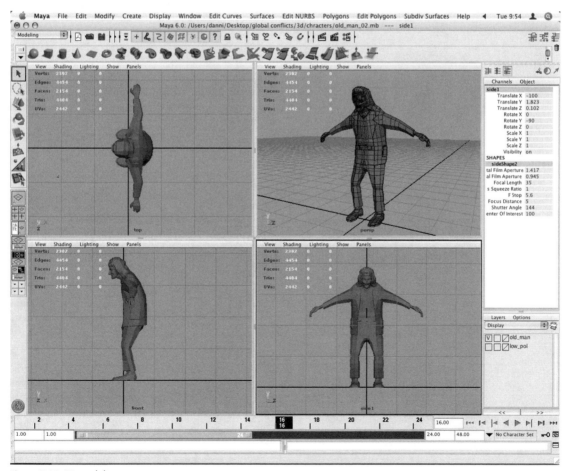

Figure 5.16 3D model

Figure 5.17 *Tomb Raider*

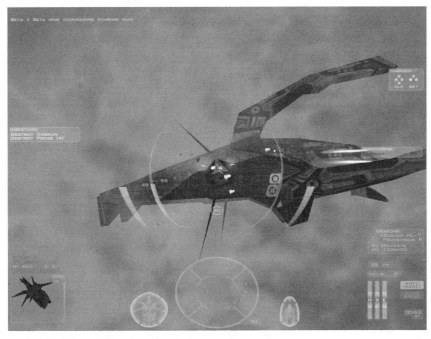

Figure 5.18 *Freespace II*

"fakes" a three-dimensional effect by use of 2D models (see Figure 4.29). Simply put, the enemy soldiers are merely bitmap figures scaled to match their distance from the player's point of view (a visual conceit quote obvious if you look for it). These enemy soldiers have no backsides—so it's fortunate that they always face the player. A related technique—known as parallax scrolling—provides depth to an image by moving layers at different speeds. Thus, objects "close" to the player move faster than more distant objects. This technique is used, for instance, in *Moon Patrol* and *Shadow of the Beast*. Since two-dimensional processes can be used to fake three-dimensionality, distinguishing between whether graphics are *technically* 2 or 3 D is not vital for our discussion of game form. Thus, in this book we categorize any game as 3D any game that allows for movement in three dimensions—that is, up and down and into the gamespace.

What, we might ask, is the relationship between a game's perspective and the number of dimensions it uses? Since 3D can be faked using 2D, there seem to be none. While there are no rules about this relationship, nearly all games follow similar standards. A game with third-person perspective can exist in two dimensions or three. But it is hard to imagine a first-person game that did not use (or at least fake) three dimensions. Again we see how aesthetic aspects that are technically only loosely related in game design practice tend to be tied together. It is by appreciating the existence of such conventions and by considering how one may innovatively challenge them that creative game design tends to happen.

Space type

Most non-abstract games of recent vintage occur in a "life-like" space comparable to that illustrated in Figure 5.15. But early games like *Spacewar*, as we have seen, used 2D graphics and had a somewhat idiosyncratic gamespace. When the player-controlled spaceships left the gamespace at one side, they immediately appeared on the opposite side. This gamespace by its nature is abstract. Another interpretation, however, is that the gamespace was in fact circular, or torus-shaped (see Figure 5.19). Thus, going far enough in one direction lands the players back at their starting point.

The *Spacewar* approach to gamespace was copied by many later games such as *Pac-Man*, and the arcade hit *Defender* (see Figure 4.11). In *Defender*, without any real explanation, the player navigates a torus (possibly the alien-ridden planet is extremely small and the player merely circles it). This approach has fallen out of fashion in recent decades as the technological capabilities of game platforms have increased exponentially—and perhaps, in turn, a player's desire for a more "realistic" gamespace to navigate.

And yet, modern games which typically let the player roam more freely do not allow immediate access to the entire gamespace. We have already discussed how most games limit vertical movement and most also divide the gamespace "box" into various levels of action which the level may move between at certain points in the game.

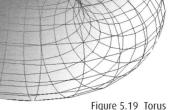

Figure 5.19 Torus

Figure 5.20 *Super Monkey Ball*: player-controlled monkeys inside balls traverse obstacle-filled levels and may sometimes move between different levels of elevation (relative to the ocean surface below)

An important element of space is the sheer size of the gamespace. Early games, like *Spacewar* and *Pong*, were limited simply by what one screen could hold. But soon, games started transcending the one-screen gamespace (e.g. *Night Driver* and *Bump'n'Jump*). At least three alternative approaches emerged early on (along with a number of combinations): unconnected levels, zone-based multi-screen spaces, and seamless multi-screen spaces.

In games with *unconnected levels*, when a level is cleared the player-character is merely transported to a different place; there is not necessarily an implication that the two places are physically connected. Examples of this approach include *Pac-Man* and and *Bomb Jack*.

In the case of zone-based multi-screen spaces, the player-character exits through one side of the screen and the perspective then jumps to show the player-character on the other side of the next screen. For instance: reaching the right side of the screen the perspective skips to show the player standing on the left side of the next screen facing right (the implication is that the perspective has moved, not the player character).

This type of space was popular with many early graphical adventure games, such as Warren Robbinett's *Adventure* from 1978.

Finally, seamless multi-screen spaces use a scrolling perspective, so the player gradually reveals the gamespace as he moves. This is the case in games like *Ghosts'n'Goblins*, *Time Pilot*, and *Commando*. The space type has clear consequences for gameplay. With a one-screen gamespace, all of the objects in a game are usually visible at all times. When all elements are visible, a player may concentrate all resources on that which is known. The player doesn't need to save energy for unexpected situations or use precious mental capacity to plan for various contingencies. The same holds true for games with unconnected levels, although when these levels are linked in terms of the game's goals (even if not geographically), the player may still have to worry about getting hold of objects needed at a future level, for example, or conserving energy for the final show-down.

In seamless multi-screen spaces, quite the opposite is true. Here, projections of what might come must inform the player's choices. In the racing game *Bump'n'Jump*, for instance, the player has to consider what the odds are that various obstacles (such as pools of water) may be looming ahead, and then must play accordingly.

Off-screen space

The concept of off-screen space originates in cinema. If a movie scene shows two people meeting in an office and the soundtrack contains the sound of traffic in the street below, then that street is part of the scene's off-screen space. In video games, there are two distinct types of off-screen space. We can refer to them as *passive* and *active*. In passive off-screen space nothing really happens. This is the case in a game like *Spy Hunter*; see Figure 5.21.

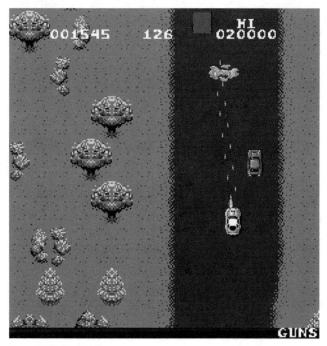

Figure 5.21 *Spy Hunter*

The player controls a weapons-laden car as it barrels down an unfolding road, shooting enemy vehicles. We know that the gamespace is larger than what fits in any one screenshot, and as the road scrolls past we encounter enemies appearing from both below and above. But when they are not visible on the screen, the other vehicles are irrelevant; their behavior and accompanying fate is processed by the game only when they are on-screen. The off-screen space, then, is passive: logically it exists but nothing happens out there.

Unit under attack.

$ 10000

Figure 5.22 *Command and Conquer: Generals*. Bottom left a map of the gamespace is shown

This is not the case for games in certain other genres. Since real-time strategy games rely heavily on active off-screen space, let's take a look at one representative example—*Command and Conquer: Generals* (see Figure 5.22).

As the player's budding warlord lays the foundations of his glorious fortifications on one side of the gamespace, other characters (controlled by additional players or the computer) are doing the same in unseen areas of the game's world. What happens beyond the frame inevitably affects the course of the game. Thus, the off-screen space here is radically different from that of *Spy Hunter*. It is dynamic, living, or *active*.

The extreme approach to active off-screen space is of course that of MMORPGs in which the player at any one time experiences only a miniscule portion of the vast gamespace. Also, in MMORPGs the game is processed even when the player is not even present in the game world.

Modern games tend towards more active off-screen space, while almost all arcade games had passive off-screen space; but the distinctions are not always clear-cut. Take, for instance, *Grand Theft Auto III: Vice City* (see Figure 4.39). While often applauded for its breathing game world and the openness of its gameplay, *Vice City* is not, in fact, a living simulation of an entire city. At any given moment, objects that are not directly related to the player character (those that are very close or on the screen, or are being tracked by the player's radar) are not being processed by the game. An example: the player hi-jacks the car of a poor city dweller. The victim does not then, for example, lose his job, become a criminal and pose a danger to the player in dark alleys. Instead, he or she just disappears when the player-character has reached a certain distance from the crime scene. Similarly, a dramatic car crash does not slow down traffic in other places in the city, or leave nearby streets unguarded by police. A similarly partial approach to off-screen space is found in virtually all recent action games such as *Thief: Deadly Shadows* and *Half-Life 2*. The rarity of an active off-screen world in action games—in sharp contrast to the abundance of living that takes place off-screen in MMORPGs and real-time strategy games—reflects the different priorities of these genres. The former prize the intensity of conflict above all else—the bigger world is quite literally, peripheral—whereas the satisfaction of MMORPGs and real-time strategy is in figuring out the ramifications of the endless possibilities of human (and non-human) interaction.

Scroll

As we have seen in earlier, scroll refers to the gradual unveiling of game space. A game can scroll horizontally or vertically, or freely, which means both vertically and horizontally; or not at all. In scrolling games, the perspective is typically centered on the player character. The concept is not usually applied to first-person games, which do not have an "implied camera" tracking the game action.

Horizontal scroll was common to many arcade games of the 1970s and 1980s. Often, the player character would fight his way from left to right, by either battling or avoiding opponents. Examples of early horizontal scroll abound: *Defender* (1980), *Scramble* (1981), *Kung-Fu Master* (1984), *Ghost'n'Goblins* (1985), and *Wonderboy* (1986).

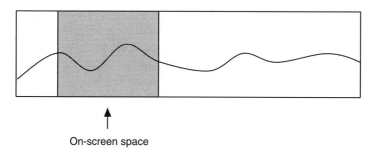

On-screen space

Figure 5.23 Horizontal scroll

Vertical scroll was slightly less common in early games, but could be found in both personal combat-style games and aircraft shooters. Examples include: *Spy Hunter* (1983), *1942* (1984), *Commando* (1985), and *Rainbow Islands* (1988; see Figure 5.24). Some arcade games scrolled both ways. Certain ones, such as *Time Pilot*, scrolled freely (within the gamespace), while in others, such as *Gauntlet*, movement was restrained by walls or other features of the gamespace.

Mainly, it seems that platform games (where the player must jump between platforms) work best with horizontal scroll, one of the only actual exceptions being *Rainbow Islands* which did not set an influential precedent.

Scroll is typically only used in the context of 2D graphics, since 3D gamespaces usually are not gradually revealed in the same paper scroll-like manner.

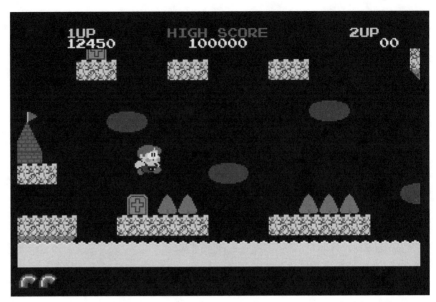

Figure 5.24 *Rainbow Islands* (Amiga version): using rainbows as weapons, the player character must try to get to the top of the gamespace

Exploration

In a given game, is the player free to explore the gamespace at her own pace? Or are there constraints on her—a ticking clock, to name one prominent example. Most arcade games employ the latter principle. Arcade games make more money the more often they're played, so a moving perspective that literally pushes the player forward quickly became the standard. This variation of scroll we call "forced exploration." In the vertically scrolling *Rainbow Islands* mentioned above, for example, the bottom of the screen slowly filled with water, forcing the player upwards. Forced exploration, was even more common in vehicle-based shooters, like *1942* or *Scramble*, where the forward propulsion of the airplane (or spaceship) forced the player to keep moving. In sharp contrast to arcade, gameplay time is not an issue on consoles or home computers. Here, with the exception of certain flight games, exploration tends to be un-forced, and the player is free to navigate as quickly or as slowly as he desires. Having examined how space is created and used in video games, we turn now to an equally important feature: time.

Time

Time in a video game is also an aesthetic aspect, that is something experienced by the player. It is also largely under the control of the designer, who controls many aspects of time such as whether or not it can be sped up during trivial tasks (such as traveling).

Compared to the interest bestowed upon game space, research on the issue of time in games is limited.[23] While time has been a very important topic in literary and film studies, especially from a structural perspective, it draws little attention in game studies. But as Jesper Juul suggests,[24] looking at game temporality can help us understand how different game genres are influenced by different aesthetic conventions, and can even shed some light into the historical development of the industry. If we look at the beginnings of game history, coin operated arcade machines offered a distinct sense of time compared with today's games: as we mentioned above, the arcade games were fast-paced and designed for short playing sessions, in order to maximize the dropping of coins into that bottomless slot. With the arrival of PC games, designers found a very different set of parameters, which allowed for longer playing sessions and encouraged "slow" genres such as adventure games (although such games had been pioneered on earlier machines).

Inspired by concepts of discourse and story time, and how they create a sense of narrative, Juul proposes that we distinguish between *play time* (the "real" time a player spends playing a game) and *event time* (the time that passes in the game world during this game). These two concepts only apply to games that project a fictional world; in abstract games, the concept of event time does not make much sense. The relationship (or "mapping") between these two "times" is, Juul suggests, highly variable. For example, in action games such as *Quake* or *Unreal Tournament*, play time and event time are equal, which means that every action the player takes (moving with the mouse, or shooting a bad guy) immediately affects the world inside the game. In this case, we say that the game happens in *real time*. By contrast, strategy and process-oriented games often compress event time so that player action can span across years and even centuries, and a few hours of play can make or destroy civilizations. For example, in SimCity, we might play for two minutes of real time (play time), and two years could pass in the game world clock (event time). In some of these games the player can adjust the event time according to their desired speed (typically quicker if they are experienced players, and slower if they are still learning how the game works).

Games that contain **cut-scenes** represent an interesting anomaly our sense of time: the relation between play time and event time is interrupted, while at the same time cut-scenes contribute to the construction of event time (for example, by showing what happened in an ellipsis of five years). Another interruption of play time in many contemporary games is simply a consequence of technology: the player has to pause—for a few seconds or a few minutes—while the console loads the game's many levels. The inevitable wait is considered a negative player experience by some game designers. Juul calls these interruptions of play time "violations." Another prime violation, in Juul's opinion, is the much discussed possibility of saving games. Does the ability to return to a game later on ruin the aesthetic experience of playing? Is it a necessary evil in order to complete difficult games, or is it simply a design feature which can be both used and abused? This is an aesthetic debate among designers, and not one with an obvious answer.

The dichotomy between play time and event time points to how players understand the mapping between their actions and the game's fictional world, but it does not tell us a lot about the gameplay itself, since in principle, every game is played in *real time*. Even slow adventure games offer an immediate connection between player action (clicking a mouse, for example) and events in the game world (character movement, dialogue, decision making). The significant difference, then, between play and event time is actually in *pace*. Think of the reaction speed that different games require of players, and the fact that every genre has conventions of pace and speed that the player must learn to be successful. For example, many of the early (and also abstract) arcade games are about learning to react *on time* to the same challenges again and again, so that players become *quick enough* to complete each level.

Time becomes even more significant when we realize that we already categorize several types of games based on how they use time aesthetically. Turn-based games, sport games, and multiplayer action games are all founded upon the particular way that time passes. An even more extreme example is MMORPGs, where a huge time investment is required by the player in order to build a character skilled enough to truly explore the game. Many intriguing questions about time in video games have not yet been explored in detail. Time, however, is such a basic human tool for understanding our place in the world that it continues to be a significant (if unconscious) tool for game designers. Further study of time's many ramifications should only further our understanding of the building blocks of a video game's design.

Graphical style

In the pages above we have glimpsed the variety of elements that a designer must decide between—from perspective to space type to the passage of time—each of which has obvious implications for gameplay. But designers must also decide on graphical style—literally, how the game should express itself visually. For instance, *Warcraft III* and *Rise of Nations* are both real-time strategy games, and share a number of design elements; but to the player they feel rather different, in large part because of their divergent graphical expressions. *Warcraft III* copies a cartoonish graphical style, and makes no pretence of realism, while *Rise of Nations* portrays characters and buildings in a mostly realistic manner.[25] Game scholar Aki Järvinen[26] has identified three graphical styles that have dominated video game design since its inception: *Photorealism*, *Caricaturism*, and *Abstractionism*. We will discuss the three styles briefly below.

Photorealism

All media and art forms have at one time or another been employed in the service of realistic representation. In painting, for instance, it was common at least until the mid-nineteenth century for artists to attempt as faithful as possible a rendering of reality on the canvas (the subjects, of course, could be imaginary or fictitious, but the style was realistic). Starting in the 1860s the French Impressionists Manet, Renoir, Monet and others dramatically challenged the dominant style by attending to subjective, fleeting moments (an idea that seems quite conservative, of course, compared to what came after). In the 1960s, following multiple schools of abstraction, came photorealism: a style of painting that tried to completely mimic photographs. Computer graphics have similarly been unable to resist the lure of the "real." We could argue that video games have attempted to depict reality from their beginnings, but were long hampered by insufficient technology. A dominant branch of video game graphics development has craved improved hardware able to process more and more details. Nowhere in video games has such an attempt been more obvious than in the "interactive movies" of the early to mid-1990s (see Chapter 4). Believed by many at the time to be the culmination of games' search for realistic graphical expression, these adventure games typically saw Hollywood actors performing pre-filmed action sequences in filmed environments. Illustrative examples include *The 7th Guest*, *Ripper*, *The Beast Within: A Gabriel Knight Mystery*, and *Under a Killing Moon*.

Photorealism has given birth to two subcategories: *Televisualism* and *Illusionism*. The former is a graphical style that attempts to faithfully mimic the aesthetics of television, usually in the case of sports. Such games mimic multi-camera productions and use sports TV features such as instant replay. These games copy an evolved form of representation clearly suited to the sport at hand (though not necessarily optimal for a game in terms of control or identification).

Games aiming for *Illusionism* use photorealistic graphics in the service of non-realistic content. For instance, a science fiction game may attempt to present aliens and unearthly machinery in a fashion that seems "life-like," even though the objects presented have no real-life counterparts. For instance, the looming metallic tripods of *Half-Life 2* seem to move with menacing realism although the player has no real-life experience of such monstrosities.

Caricaturism

Long a favorite of political cartoonists, caricatures attempt to present the essence of a person or object by exaggerating its most prominent features. In recent years, a few games have taken this approach often achieving the feeling of a cartoon.

Despite their departure from reality, and their similarity to cartoons, these games are not always intended for younger audiences. Many games based in caricaturism are gripping, which belies the notion that immersion is intimately linked to realism in any direct sense. The *Crash Bandicoot* (see Figure 5.25) games take a caricaturist approach, as do the *Zelda* games and the *Jet Set Radio* games.

We can make a few generalizations about the relationship between graphical style and genre. With exceptions like the realistic play of *Jet Set Radio*, caricaturist games are mostly unrealistic (or semi-abstract) in their gameplay. Thus, most platform games fall within this category. Other subgenres—such as 3D shooters and racing games—cling tightly to photorealism. But many genres resist graphical categories, and contain games in a range of graphical styles. In the case of real-time strategy games, for

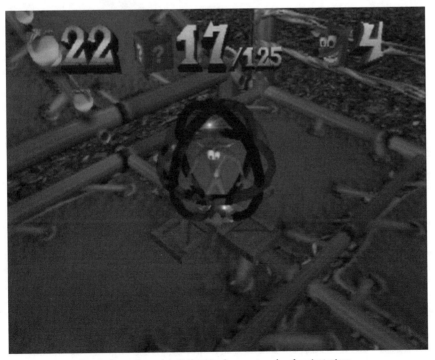

Figure 5.25 *Crash Bandicoot 2: Cortex Strikes Back*: an example of caricaturism

instance, games such as *Rise of Nations* or *Command and Conquer: Generals* are photorealistic, while *Warcraft III: Reign of Chaos* is caricaturist.

Abstractionism

Our third category is a visual style that does not try to represent people or real-life objects. Though rarely seen in commercial titles, it is far from unimportant in the industry's continuous experiments with game form. At heart, abstractionism can be said to be "about" form.[27] A prime example here is the legendary Soviet smash hit *Tetris* (Figure 5.26), which began its world-wide reign in the mid-1980s.

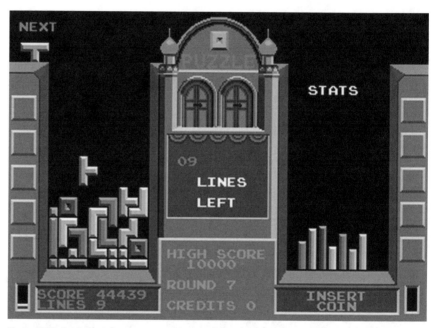

Figure 5.26 *Tetris*: the player must manipulate falling bricks to form complete horizontal lines. The existing implementations of the game are legion

Long before *Tetris*, however, there was 1981's *Qix*, in which the player draws rectangular shapes while avoiding Qix and Sparx, the game's abstract, line-drawn enemies.[28] And a year earlier, and more famously, there was *Tempest*, in which a yellow, three-dimensional crab-creature valiantly defended a barely delineated world from strange abstract beasts that continually emerged from a tunnel. More recently, abstractionism saw a brief resurgence of interest with the courageous *Rez*, a rhythm-based shooter game in which the player traverses a psychedelic game-space populated by colorful shapes and figures. While scoring big with critics and the experimentally minded, Rez was less than a commercial success.[29] The game's lack of influence led Järvinen to worry that "abstractionism might end up as a marginal [footnote] in the history, and future, of an audiovisual cultural form also known as computer and video games."[30]

The overarching problem with abstract games, not surprisingly, is that they are hard to market. It is difficult to create hype purely around a game's mechanics (as opposed to its amazing story, or its sexy lead character); and next to impossible to make money on merchandise (not to mention movie rights); and a trailer of an abstract game is unlikely to wow the marketers and buyers at game fairs. Equally important is the fact that contemporary games seem to attach increasing importance to narrative; just as film and literature have proven over time, despite ongoing murmurs of experimentation, humans seem ineluctably drawn to the simplest form of all—the story. For all these reasons, abstractionist games will probably for a long time be confined to low-powered devices like cell phones, or to experimental circles.

Game audio

Think about your favorite game. Now try to describe what it sounds like. Unless you are unusually analytical about your video games, you will likely be (a) unable to remember the sound and music clearly or (b) unable to analyze the sound design in any detail. When we want to approach game sound systematically, we face two problems. One is a broad, and embarrassing, tradition of ignoring the audio side of audiovisual media. In film studies, for instance, sound has received extremely limited attention relative to its importance for the experience of a movie.[31] The second problem is that we are generally not taught how to describe the qualities of sound. In fact, our common vocabulary does not even include many terms that can be used to differentiate sound types. This causes a problem for interaction designers—professionals who design interfaces in the widest sense—who want users to state their sound preferences or comment on sound design. To comment systematically on this important element of games, one must become familiar with a complex language in order to speak of sounds (*transparent*, *narrow*, and *full*, for example, are just a few of the adjectives used to describe sounds verbally).

The sound landscape in video games may be understood by applying the following categories:

- *Vocalization*: these are the voices of the characters in a game (including voice-over speech and other off-screen elements).

- *Sound effects*: these are sounds made by in-game objects (for instance, the sound of a gun being fired).

- *Ambient effects*: these are non-specific sounds contributing to the game atmosphere (a bird calling, the distant sound of machinery).

- *Music*: this is the soundtrack of the game. Music is usually used to add to the atmosphere of the game (or set the mood), but can also be directly tied to the game world[32] (in *Grand Theft Auto: Vice City*, for example, the soundtrack is provided by car radios).

Whether we notice or not, music and sound play a truly important role in game design. Modern game credits often list several people responsible for various aspects of sound, and game audio today requires the collaboration of a number of specialized professionals. But it wasn't always so. In the very beginning, games did not have sound at all. In the 1970s it became possible and practical to store and play sound files. Some systems could play actual sound recordings while others used MIDI-like formats (in the MIDI format a sound file is simply a series of references to sounds that are then played back by the sound card, analogous to a sheet of musical notation, which requires instruments, players, and interpretation to actually make sound.

By 1980, game designers still faced severe limitations as to sound design. Whether stored directly or in a MIDI file, game sound typically consisted of a few basic sounds or rhythms complemented by various *event sounds*, which would be played when a certain condition was fulfilled. For instance, in *Pac-Man* a brief introductory jingle gives way to a ambulance-like sound that plays throughout the game. On top of this layer of sound, the characteristic munching sound is triggered each time Pac-Man eats a dot. Distinct event sounds are triggered. You eat a ghost, or when a dead ghost (if you will) returns to the ghost headquarters. When *Pac-Man* is killed, another jingle is heard. Whereas the introductory jingle ascends in pitch, the death jingle mimics an object spiraling downwards, or the sound a ball makes when bouncing toward a standstill. The audio of *Pac-Man* is obviously context-dependent. However, it is also very simple. The sounds themselves are rudimentary, and they do not influence each other nor vary according to secondary conditions.

Another good example of the creative use of primitive audio was *Asteroids*. A heart-like beat would slowly increase in intensity over time. Exploding missiles made pleasant thumping sounds, and the abstract majesty of the gameplay was suddenly interrupted by the shrill alarm sound of alien spaceships. The only other sounds were the thrust of the protagonist spaceship and the explosions of asteroids breaking onto smaller parts.

In the 1990s, most storage constraints fell away (at least for PC games). Thus, the size of the sound files became less important. The epic multi-voice choir scores of *Phantasmagoria* from 1995 and its contemporaries testify to this development. However, for all platforms (each of which dedicated different amounts of resources to sound processing) processor speed was a serious constraint on developing fully dynamic game soundtracks. Thus, while epic compositions could be played back, very little on-the-fly processing could be done to the sound. For instance, the designer of a survival horror game might want the tempo of a tune to increase as the monsters get closer. In this case, the processor would have to calculate the physical relationships between the characters and shift the audio playback accordingly. In another case, our designer might want sound effects to reflect present game conditions, like the altered pitch of a car as it speeds through a tunnel. As the speed of console and PC processors have caught with to the explosion in storage capacity, more and more dynamic sound processing has become feasible.

As illustrated by the examples above, today's games use sound to do far more than simply reflect the action on screen. Ongoing developments mean that sound effects in contemporary games can also be affected by:

- *The environment*. For instance the size of the location, the material of the walls, the characteristics of the carrying medium (i.e. air, water etc.), the weather conditions.

- *Spatiality*. Sounds are situated in space. Thus, the sound of a monster 30 yards to the left and concealed by trees is different from the sound of the same monster one yard behind you.

- *Physics*. The sound may be affected by relative movement etc. (e.g. Doppler shift).

Although technically challenging, the above advancements merely mean that game designers strive for a realism similar to that of a movie soundtrack. While describing the rules of sound generation is quite different from adding sound effects to a movie in post-production, the principle is not hard to grasp and we will discuss this development in the following.

The quest for dynamic music generation

Much as a video game narrative is not predetermined but generated dynamically based on the actions of the players, so auto-generated music is music created (from fragments of various size) to match present game conditions. While presenting a considerable challenge we should remember that some forms of pre-electronic music—like jazz—are at their heart improvisational; likewise, live music is often adapted to local conditions. Also, as with system-generated narrative, system-generated music is a rather old idea. A famous example, celebrated during the Romantic era of literature (in the decades around 1800) is the Aeolian harp. The Aeolian harp basically consists of a sounding board with strings attached lengthwise across two bridges. Depending on how the strings are tuned, music (of a sort) is created when the wind blows across the strings.

Video game designers typically want the music to adapt to the present circumstances of the game. There are two important aspects to this. First, a single piece of music can be modified to fit changing conditions. Say a certain tune is attached to a non-player character. The tune might then be altered to reflect the protagonist's relation to the character, or the character's state of health, or both. If the NPC has turned from enemy to friend but is badly wounded, the tune might be played in a desperate (or perhaps mournful) tempo.

But this designer might not be content to merely playback a piece of music when some single condition is fulfilled. In more open-ended games, sound designers attempt a much more dynamic soundtrack by describing more basic relationships and principles. Certain music files, for instance, may be split into various sections and looped for various periods of time. Specific conditions—anything from the protagonist's state of health to the type of on-screen action—may combine to inform the game what music is most appropriate; similarly, built-in rules may tell the game how and when to shift from one composition to another.

This is not dynamic music generation, strictly speaking (it is merely rule-based playback of pre-composed music). Asking the computer to generate music itself, we encounter what has been called "the computer music problem."[33] Whereas computers are extremely potent at processing rules and analyzing large amounts of data, we are not very good at formalizing creative and high-quality music performance and composition (if indeed this can be formalized at all). Thus, we are incapable of telling a computer how to go about composing good music.

The function of sound and music in games

Sound and music is essential to enhancing the gaming experience. They do so mainly by informing the player about the state of the game world and by cuing emotions that enhance the immersiveness of the game. Music, in particular, can have a visceral link to our emotions, and when used effectively can instill feelings from excitement, to melancholy, to desperation. Certain kinds of music seem to have nearly universal emotional associations; high tempo cuing activity and outward-directed feelings. Most traditional/conventional music, in fact, uses tempi that lie within the normal heart-beat patterns of adults. The cues offered by other pieces of music, however, can vary widely depending on context. The grand strains of a classical orchestra, for example, have long been used by filmmakers to connate an epic narrative; the sound of a lone saxophone, meanwhile, might connote the mournful loneliness of a big city.

In a designer's many uses of sound, we must note that the aim is not realism in the strict sense. What sound design should achieve, apart from increasing a player's sense of immersion, is the *feeling* of realism.[34] In the case of video games, this feeling of realism actually requires randomization. As sound designer Marty O'Donell says: ". . . the biggest tip off to the listener that something is artificial is when the crow always caws just after the leaf rustles and before the frog croaks every thirty seconds or so."[35] Thus, generating the sensation of realism is not just a question of faithfully reproducing the sounds of actual object (such as gunshots). It is a more complicated question of creating an aural world that mirrors the complexity of the visual one.

We shouldn't be surprised to discover where game audio takes many of its conventions from. In the conventions of cinema—and the many video games that follow suit—sound and music is used as the glue that ties together different shots. Thus, the image may change dramatically but because of the continuous sound (and use of editing conventions), the sense of continuity is not broken. Apart from the continuous music, "sound bridges" also prepare the viewer for a change in perspective by actually starting up the sound of a new shot before the image of the old is replaced. In games that use cinematic aesthetics, the role of sound is just as essential as it is in a movie. For instance, the survival-horror game *Resident Evil 4* has a very memorable sound design in which the destruction of monstrous enemies is accompanied by detailed (and gruesome) sounds. Anyone playing a game such as *Resident Evil 4* can observe just how much atmosphere audio can mean to the game experience.

Emergence

Emergence is a phenomenon where the interaction of simple principles on one level creates complex results on another, higher, level.[36] Certain species of ants, for instance, doing no more than acting on their simple genetic dispositions, will create towering mounds of sand that look like the results of a very careful design. Similarly, flocks of birds moving in complex and seemingly coordinated patterns are no more than the emergent result of each bird following basic "rules" of behavior. One compelling example of emergence in simulations is John Conway's famous *Game of Life* from 1970, a simple simulation of population dynamics in which very basic relationships create interesting patterns.[37]

In game design (as in so many other fields) the concept has been en vogue for some years. Here, emergence refers to the fact that game dynamics (in the sense of the Mechanics-Dynamics-Aesthetics design model) may arise without being planned for. The archetypical example is taken from 2000's *Deus Ex*. The game's lead designer, Harvey Smith describes how

> . . . some clever players figured out that they could attach a proximity mine to the wall and hop up onto it (because it was physically solid and therefore became a small ledge, essentially). So then these players would attach a second mine a bit higher, hop up onto the proximity mine, reach back and remove the first proximity mine, replace it higher on the wall, hop up one step higher, and

then repeat, thus climbing any wall in the game, escaping our carefully pre-defined boundaries.[38]

Here, the rules (in the broad sense) of the game interact to create possibilities that the designers themselves had not predicted. Such emergent possibilities have grown recently, due to the increasingly advanced physics engines in modern games, and a strong focus on making game worlds feel more alive.

It is not that the concept, while fascinating, is new in itself. Again, consider chess. The simple rules of chess combine to create a (practically) infinite set of possibilities, so that not even a grand master can know for certain how a game will progress (although it gets increasingly easier as the game goes on).

Another way to look at emergence (and the opposite) is to consider games in terms of their degree of openness. This can be thought of in a number of ways. For instance, certain games are world-centered as opposed to protagonist-centered. In the case of the former, the game is a world with its own active laws of physics, and here things occur without the protagonist necessarily being involved (generally in the *active* off-screen space).

In protagonist-centered games, however, the entire game system revolves around the protagonist; nothing noteworthy takes place beyond the radius of the protagonist's action. In her humorous account of U.S. video game culture *Joystick Nation*, game journalist J.C. Herz referred to the former approach as the "Old Testament approach to game design" stressing that the designer here creates the basic material and the basic rules (analogous to the laws of nature). This, she contrasted with the " 'Pirates of the Caribbean' syndrome, where you feel like you're on some kind of monorail through the game."[39]

Another, and more precise, distinction was made by Jesper Juul who described games as being on a continuum between two basic structures: "emergence" (as described above) and "progression."[40] Emergence, to Juul, is "the primordial game structure, where a game is specified as a small number of rules that combine and yield large numbers of game variations. . . ."[41] In progression games, on the other hand, "the player has to perform a predefined set of actions to complete the game."[42]

Clear-cut specimens of the latter include adventure games such as *Myst* (1994) and *Gabriel Knight* 3 (1999). Juul stresses how the progression form of gaming is practically unique to video games, since most board games, card games, and other forms of entertainment remain interesting precisely because their few rules offer many potential outcomes.

NUMBER OF PLAYERS

In terms of player experience, and in terms of game design, an important difference is that between single-player and multi-player games. The discussion here is kept brief as many issues concerning social interaction between players are addressed in Chapter 8.

The differences between single-player and multi-player games affect a number of game elements, from artificial intelligence to the importance of communication features and the issue of cheating in games. But before we tackle those issues, let's start with a simpler task. Can you name one non-electronic game that only requires one player?

Chances are you eventually thought of solitaire. But other answers are few and far between. There are, in other words, strikingly few non-electronic games which do not require the presence of several players. Video games thus represent an anomaly in gaming—which historically and culturally has been a fundamentally *social* pastime. As witnessed in Chapter 4, the history of video games is full of titles that pit man (in the singular) against machine.

Many video games today are designed with options for soloplay *and* multiplay. *Doom III*, for instance, features an elaborate single-player campaign but it also contains two multiplayer modes, which emphasize either collaboration or take-no-prisoners mutual destruction. Thus, the single- and multiplayer game forms are not fundamentally at odds, but they do contain some important differences.

This design choice can affect the form of the game. Single-player games often function as obstacle courses (*Half-Life*, *Donkey Kong*, *Pikmin*) or procedural systems (*SimCity*, *Pirates*, *Railroad Tycoon*). Multi-player games, by contrast, can be thought of as playing fields as known from team sports; i.e. spaces endowed with rules and structural features to create an interesting competitive experience (*FIFA 2004*, *Tekken*, *Warcraft II*). Most progression games, in Juul's sense, are single-player games, since progression games are typically player-centered.[43]

Single-player games usually require what game designers refer to as artificial intelligence (AI). Such systems do not constitute attempts to create anything as complex as human intelligence but rather consist of virtual entities endowed with response patterns enabling them to respond flexibly and with *apparent* intelligence to game conditions (particularly, the actions of the player). The behavior of one's soccer opponents in the *FIFA* series is an example of game entities which may seem to know exactly what they're doing while being guided by relatively simple rules of behavior. Particularly in action games, the "intelligence" of enemy non-player-characters has improved remarkably in the since the mid-1990s (see Figure 5.27).

Figure 5.27 *Far Cry* (2004): enemy soldiers adapt (somewhat) to player choices, showing far more intelligence than the monsters of *Doom* for instance

For certain genres, the computer's "intelligence" is crucial. Success in real-time-strategy games, for instance, is far easier if the player can trick a gullible computer-controlled enemy. Generally, computer-controlled players in such games employ a very limited number of strategies and are unable to learn from their own mistakes. Thus, experienced human players will often have very little trouble beating even the highest level of computer-controlled resistance (unless the AI "cheats" by gathering resources unnaturally fast, for instance).

Designers of multi-player games, on the other hand, do not have to worry about AI as their players face other gamers who are (often) smarter than even the most advanced of AIs. On the other hand, multi-player games face crucial balance issues that single-player games don't. To be enjoyable, the playing field must be truly level (without being boring) as in successful levels for *Counter Strike* which do not merely look the same from the starting point of both teams. And if the game features a variety of characters, each needs to have its own unique features but none can be innately superior to all others since that would spoil the fun.

The biggest challenge for developers of multi-player games, however, may be to facilitate constructive social interaction between (sometimes) large numbers of players. In *Spacewar*, the social dynamics of the game world were limited—you met physically, played one or more rounds and that was that. Today, large multi-player spaces (with the players typically not in the same physical location) are social systems which invite both cooperation and conflict.

6 VIDEO GAME CULTURE

HIGH CULTURE AND POP CULTURE/PUBLIC PERCEPTIONS OF GAMING/
IDEALIZATION OF PLAY/GAMES AND OTHER CULTURAL FORMS/
VIDEO GAMES AS CULTURAL OBJECTS

This chapter will map the cultural position of video games. We will describe the cultural relationship between video games and other (older) media, and we will discuss both how public perceptions of games have evolved, and how video games are used by different groups for different ends. Though our focus is primarily is on the United States, we will also compare the situation here with examples from around the globe.

More than four decades ago, media theorist Marshall McLuhan wrote that:

> The student of media soon comes to expect the new media of any period whatever to be classed as pseudo by those who acquired the patterns of earlier media, whatever they may happen to be.[1]

It is certainly true that the history of media development shows an almost instinctive skepticism leveled at the new media of the era. It has been true of radio, true of movies and it certainly has been true of television, which has long fought against the perception that its only role was to entertain, rather than to enlighten. (If you immediately responded to the previous statement—whether in agreement or in defense of television's capacity for art and intellect—you have just demonstrated the depth of television's cultural clash.) Many issues factor into the battle for cultural acceptance that most new media must fight. A strong visual (as opposed to written) basis usually does not help, for instance, as this hints that the medium may be one suited for the illiterate. In addition, relying on serial formats—as opposed to self-contained finished "works"—also clashes generally with classical Western perceptions of culturally worthwhile pursuits (or "art"). Consider the way in which serial books—whether written by Stephen King or Mark Twain—are almost never deemed as worthy of the high cultural praise which, in the field of literature, is typically reserved for single, "unique" works. Another important factor is the perceived intentions of the producers. Media that are seen as primarily market-driven fare poorly in the quest for acceptance as good taste. Meanwhile, we believe that "art" is not (or not only) driven by such worldly motives. German author Franz Kafka, for example, can be praised as a natural artist, as he did not publish most of his work before he died and even asked a friend to have that work destroyed after his death. Thus, he could not in any way be suspected of material motives.

While these issues of cultural perception matter, we must also consider how expressions of taste or distaste about a new medium may be strategic or power-related. French sociologist Pierre Bourdieu in his book *Distinction* argued that taste is an altogether social phenomenon.[2] His empirical argument opposed the commonly held idea that taste is an individual matter. Taste, Bourdieu demonstrated, is a means to establish group boundaries, by signaling one's membership to a certain social group. Those in power will praise their own tastes in music and books and media in general, and will tend to label other media as un-civilized or otherwise problematic. And in contrast, marginalized groups have historically rallied around certain activities (or cultural expressions) in order to establish a counter-culture that prizes their own values and tastes.

The above ingredients by no means tell the entire story of how different media interact. But as the reader has likely already guessed, video games are one of the world's most explosive examples of new media; not surprisingly, they too have been immersed in these cultural battles. In the pages below, the historical difficulties faced by new media will offer a useful key to understanding the intense and often mysterious cultural dynamics surrounding video games.

HIGH CULTURE AND POP CULTURE

Cultures around the world tend to distinguish between forms of expression that are intrinsically worthwhile and those that are not. In Western societies, for example, painting, literature and sculpture are traditionally considered more dignified, more worthy of careful attention, than television and games (whether analogue or digital). During the middle part of the twentieth century, however, the traditional hierarchy was challenged by artists who drew upon objects and images from pop culture (this trend was exemplified by the pop art movement). A foundational example of this is Andy Warhol's series of portraits of Marilyn Monroe. The boundaries between high and low culture were decisively blurred, and to the delight of some and the horror of others, Western culture has been unable to fully separate the two ever since.

Meanwhile, theoretical and scientific developments in the second half of the twentieth century pushed in the same direction. For instance, cultural relativism (the idea that cultures should be understood on their own terms) led a trend across the social sciences to acknowledge the biases and "imperialistic" overtones that had long colored academic approaches to foreign cultures. The rising discipline of media studies challenged the idea that certain media or genres were inherently better than others, particularly within work inspired by semiotics and ethnography. One such movement was the widely influential cultural studies school, which studied contemporary cultural phenomena—often using a neo-Marxist perspective—to understand their meaning and relationship to power structures and the wider culture. Such approaches were typically girded by the belief that all cultural phenomena could be "read", that is *interpreted*, and that no particular type should be privileged. The movement also coincided with a growing number of empirical studies which showed how media users appropriated all types of media products for their own purposes and often used (or interpreted) them in ways not necessarily connected with the type or class of products. An example of this could be the popularity of *slash fiction*, as studied by Henry Jenkins in *Textual Poachers: Television Fans and Participatory Culture*. This is a particular kind of fan fiction where people write stories about homosexual love between characters of television series or films, where no such thing occurs in the original series, like the relationship between Captain Kirk and Spock from *Star Trek*. This kind of media use further undermines the idea that media or genre can be categorized using fixed criteria that do not take users into account.

All these developments have served to blur, but not erase, the distinction between high culture and pop culture. Games are still categorized within the latter—and still lower—sphere. Many of us—scholars and gamers alike—have argued that games are underrated as an art form, and that games only lose out in comparison to other arts because the criteria are not suited for their particular qualities. Such arguments (following McLuhan's observation above) tend to under-line the arbitrariness of distinctions between art and non-art, and expose the unfairness of denying the status of art to a form of expression just because it provides entertainment and aspires to a mass market.[3] This position has merit; it would be difficult for even the most conservative cultural critic to deny that games are at times judged more on their alleged differences from "worthy" art than on their actual qualities. But we must also clarify the limits of the video-game-as-high-art argument. Whether something is actually art can never definitively be settled through analysis and debate. The question is really more significant in the battle for legitimacy, be this academic (whether computer games be studied in universities), cultural (whether the average newspaper allocates resources to computer game reviews like it does with books or movies) or political (whether game developers apply for public funding in the same measure as other artists). Just like our other efforts to define and discuss games, the question "Are video games art?" has endless answers. The question is at once meaningless—since it merely depends on our definition of art—and of exceeding practical importance, as the answer has consequences for everything from the establishment (and relative importance) of academic departments, to the government's regulation of the video game industry (by for example censuring content through ratings), to the cultural obligations of that industry, that will conceivably develop in different ways if it is a part of the establishment or if it is denied legitimacy. And if nothing else, the question is at least an intriguing one, since today's games are mired in a heated argument over what they mean and how we should feel about them.

PUBLIC PERCEPTIONS OF GAMING

In present-day Western societies, video games occupy a contested cultural niche. On the one hand, they continue to slide into the mainstream. The number of people who have never played a video game, from first graders to retirees, seem to be inex-orably dwindling.[4] On the other hand, video games still are consistently considered to be: unsophisticated in their form; problematic in their content; the cause of health problems—from obesity to addiction; and inculcated in amorphous cultural fears—like the seemingly ever-present scourge of anti-social, aggressive teenagers. The first video games raised few cultural eyebrows—perhaps because so few people ever played them, or perhaps because their few pixels were so abstract that they left little emotional impact. But it wasn't long before this new form of entertainment raised suspicion. Video games entered into into America's culture wars in 1976; as we'll see below, *Death Race*—and its goal of running over tiny human-like figures—sounded the first alarm. For the following three decades, the concerns surrounding games have remarkably consistent, with a few slight developments.

Consider the following quotation from a 1981 *Newsweek* article:

> For all their winning ways, video games have been bombarded by controversy. Critics contend that they squander allowances and study time, glorify violence and encourage everything from compulsive gambling to tendonitis (*Space

Invaders wrist). Taking a cue from the pool-troubled elders of the mythical River City, communities from Snellville, Ga., to Boston have recently banned arcades or restricted adolescent access; one legal challenge to the ordinances will be heard by the Supreme Court this week. Boosters counter that video gaming is helpful as well as fun: it speeds eye–hand coordination, sharpens driving and math skills and shields against technological future shock. "Kids are becoming masters of the computer," says Bob Doyle, a Cambridge, Mass., astrophysicist who designs electronic games. "When most grownups talk about computers, they fear the machines will dominate and displace. But these kids are learning to live and play with intelligent machines."[5]

It is striking how many of the issues mentioned here still resonate twenty-five years later. Critics of video games still wish to censor (or restrict access to) violent games, and game proponents still refer to the alleged positive effects of game-playing as part of their defense. (The one irrelevant issue is that games train children to be competent computer users. This defense has been used only rarely since the mid-to-late 1990s. most likely because computers have become both easier to use and more widespread.)

Reports from U.S. popular media in the early 1980s were often fascinated with the growing subculture of gaming. But from early on reporters and commentators alike expressed ongoing concern about the detrimental effects of gaming, whether physical or moral. The question of moral harm was raised as early as 1976, when the violence of *Death Race*—and the seeming glee with which the player could barrel into other creatures—sparked a media outcry and the game was banned.[6]

Concern over the violence in games, and the endless argument about whether computerized violence can spill over into violence in the real world, has repeatedly spurred academic and cultural research (see Chapter 10). The results have further fed public discussion, from government think tanks and outraged parents to the kids themselves. An example of this is *Video Games and Aggressive Thoughts, Feelings, and Behavior in the Laboratory and in Life*, Craig A. Anderson and Karen E. Dill's 2000 study of the effects of violent games. The study begins with the following: "On April 20, 1999, Eric Harris and Dylan Klebold launched an assault on Columbine High School in Littleton, Colorado, murdering 13 and wounding 23 before turning the guns on themselves."[7] The authors thus framed their work as part of the investigation into what caused the tragic school shooting.

In their short forty-year history, games have been connected to a wide variety of (often contradictory) effects. Since the experts themselves so often disagree, it is even more difficult for the rest of us to know what to think. As one editorial in the *British Medical Journal* mentioned, game-play has been connected with aggression and addiction and "case studies have reported adverse effects of playing video games, including auditory hallucinations, enuresis, encopresis, wrist pain, neck pain, elbow pain, tenosynovitis, hand-arm vibration syndrome, repetitive strain injuries, peripheral neuropathy, and obesity."[8] Meanwhile, news media regularly report that games have been linked with positive effects like improved hand-eye coordination (see Chapter 9).

Given that even early arcade games—with their primitive graphics and barely human protagonists—sparked full-fledged controversy, there is no direct link between a game's realism or content and cultural concern. Nevertheless, most of these flare-ups have occurred in the last decade, and are often tied to particularly violent titles. Controversy became especially intense in the U.S. in the early 1990s. This was just when the console producer Sega sought to distinguish themselves from Nintendo by publishing much more provocative games. While Nintendo's games were family friendly, Sega tried to appeal to older audiences by betting on adult themes and graphic violence. A number of publishers were more than happy to comply, and launched games which seemed bound to cause alarm.

Mortal Kombat (see Chapter 4) in particular, was released for the Sega console in 1993[9] and quickly symbolized the trend towards ruthless on-screen violence. Acclaim, who released the game for both the Sega Genesis/Megadrive and the Super Nintendo, were told by both Sega and Nintendo to tone down the violence; but Sega allowed players, through the use of codes to unlock the game's full-scale violence.

> Newspaper articles described Mortal Kombat as "offering children exciting new ways to maim, dismember, and murder unsavory opponents in a sadistic martial-arts tournament" where "it is considered a mark of success . . . to rip the head and spine out of an opponent and wave it in the air while the blood flows to the ground" (*Montreal Gazette*, August 7, 1994). With such stirring imagery, it was only natural for parents to be concerned about video games as more than a thief of a child's attention.[10]

America was thus already primed to get upset over *Night Trap* (1992), a horror game inspired by the already disreputable slasher film genre, which had been released a few months earlier and that raised such controversy that it was withdrawn from some U.S. shops in 1993. Moving beyond a reliance on graphics, this game actually used full-motion video to bring to life the player's efforts to save a group of female college students trapped in a lakeside house full of vampires. The game contained both scantily clad screaming young women and lots of blood, so it was a sure recipe for scandal.

The wake of these and other troubling games washed all the way to Washington, D.C., and in July 1994 the U.S. Congress debated on how to respond to such violence. The result was the creation of the Entertainment Software Rating Board[11] (ESRB), which at the prompting of Congress was established by (what is presently called) the Entertainment Software Association. (The ESA is a trade group for American game publishers founded in 1994.) Since 1994, the ESRB has rated every video game published in the U.S. The anonymous raters[12] assign a game one of a number of six age ratings—from Early Childhood (3+) to Adults Only (18+)—and a series of content descriptors (there are more than thirty) such as "Drug reference," "Nudity" or "Strong Language." A similar system, the Pan European Games Information (PEGI),[13] exists in Europe with aims and procedures comparable to those of the ESRB. The U.S. rating system, in particular, has been surrounded by some controversy as its methods and rulings have become issues in the continuing debate about how we define violence and immorality. A regular complain is that any inkling of sex will cause games to be rated as "Adults Only," while games with high doses of violence will receive lower ratings.[14]

More recently, cultural outrage has centered around the *Grand Theft Auto* series. The series's last six games from *Grand Theft Auto III* (and specially sequels *Vice City* and *San Andreas*) have all courted controversy because of the player character's criminal and violent behavior against police and other citizens. After its 2001 release, *Grand Theft Auto III* was criticized for its focus on crime (carjacking in particular); in 2002 *Vice City* became infamous for a game mechanic allowing the player to have (off-screen) sex with prostitutes. Afterwards, the player could assault the prostitute and steal her money. Though the mechanic was purely optional, such actions were made possible by the game, and arguably encouraged, since the player received a health bonus by having sex. What critics couldn't see is that these games were also popular because of their biting irony and satire; their game-worlds have been inspired by gangster movies and, particularly in the case of Vice City, made abundant use of pop culture. To the initiated, the game played like a living pastiche of TV cop shows from the 1980s. Though these sources of inspiration had long made their way into the cultural mainstream, these video games (and perhaps the industry as a whole) were still too new, and too discomforting, to be accepted.

Two years later, *Grand Theft Auto: San Andreas*—inspired by California gang life in the early 1990s—came under attack in a case curiously similar to the *Mortal Kombat* scandal almost fifteen years earlier. The game contained a sex minigame that even though it was unaccesible in the published version, it could be unlocked by installing the PC hot coffee mod.[15] While the developer, Rockstar North contended that installing the mod brought the content into the game and was a violation of the user's end agreement (and they therefore couldn't be held responsible), the truth is that the content is also present in the console versions of the game. This prompted the ESRB in 2005 to re-rate the game to "adults only" and some shops to withdraw it from their shelves. Rockstar hurried to produce a version without the *Hot Coffee* content and got the game back to the mature rating, but had lost a lot of money in the process.[16] Later that year, high-profile politicians like Senators Hillary Clinton and Joe Lieberman used this example in their call for further regulation of computer game content.

Though public reactions to video games arise, as we have seen, from a host of factors, the role of media panic is essential. With *media panic* we are referring to the public's reaction (through traditional media such as newspapers or television or through associations) to the form or content of new media; typically, the novelty is seen as inherently dangerous for people (readers/viewers/players, depending on the medium), who are thought incapable of distinguishing fantasy from reality.

In 2004 the British tabloid press caused an uproar about a seventeen-year-old boy who was allegedly obsessed with the game *Manhunt*, and who killed a friend in a manner similar to that of the sadistic murders of the game. Reporters seemed to cement the link between the game and the murder, dabbling in psychiatry and speculating about the troubled boy's motivations, and casting a clear cause and effect relationship between the two. (It later turned out that it was the victim, not the murderer, who was a player of the game.)[17] There are countless examples of alleged links between video games and extreme violence in the media: the Columbine High School massacre mentioned above is regularly invoked. Michael Moore plays with the absurdity of media panic reactions in his film *Bowling for Columbine* (2002), where he explains that the two teenagers also bowled regularly, wondering if that should be linked to their crimes as well.

The scientific evidence linking videogame (or other media) consumption to real world violence is highly contested (we'll discuss this connection further in Chapter 10). As Henry Jenkins puts it:

If video game violence was an immediate catalyst, we would have difficulty explaining why none of the shootings involving teens have occurred in movie theaters or video arcades where the direct stimulus of game playing would be most acute. Instead, these murders have tended to occur in schools and we need to look at real-world factors to discover what triggers such violence . . . Media activists strip aside those careful qualifications, claiming that the computer games are "murder simulators" teaching our children to kill.[18]

Dmitri C. Williams has analyzed the representation of video games in major American news magazines.[19] His results show that media discourse on video games is plagued with misconceptions and frequently vilifies the games themselves. These attacks have little to do with video games per se, Williams argues, but reflect basic conservative fears about new media, and even show the same historical progression of anxiety than other media before them have suffered: "first were fears about negative displacement, then health, and then antisocial behaviors like aggression and violence."[20] He notes that "at the same time as games were drawing the ire of conservative society, they were also used as a means of reinforcing social norms and power relations. This was particularly evident for gender and age,"[21] where women players and older players are ignored by the media, so that the picture they present is still tied to the negative image of the male antisocial teenager.

On the one hand, these examples testify to the general struggles any new medium has to go through before it gains wide social acceptance. The violence in the media debate is much older and bigger than video games, and it taps into some of the most deeply rooted fears in our society: of the young running amok, of law and order breaking down and giving way to chaos. On the other hand, the examples also show the gap between the public's perception of video games, and that of game designers and players. Video games has for many years been a specialized hobby, and for those in the know, a mature medium that can play with conventions and use irony and distortion to depict adult themes such as violence and sexuality. There is of course an unnecessary and purposeful intention to shock in some games, but while players can distance themselves from, or even enjoy, the controversy and appreciate the games for their playing value, the general public cannot get past the initial panic towards the unknown, because they don't understand the language of the medium. We can illustrate this by again using film as a comparison. If the 1939 film audiences that loved *Gone with the Wind* had been exposed to Quentin Tarantino's *Pulp Fiction*, of 1994, they would have been horrified. Not only would they have been unable to understand the nonlinear plot, but the exaggerated and grotesque violence would have shocked them to the bone, and they would never have interpreted it ironically or metatextually. In game terms, it is as if the general public were no more medium-savvy than the film audience from 1939, and as if game designers and players were already in 1994. But this gap will eventually close as more and more people become players, and as computers and game consoles become even more widespread in the average home.

Branding and marketing

Marketing can be seen as the intentional shaping of public perception, the industry's effort to infuse their products with symbolic meaning in order to make them more attractive. This is especially true of entertainment products. Video games are self-contained objects that have no inherent value—they cannot feed us, for example, or give us shelter. In this respect they are akin to the arts and "high culture"; but unlike the opera or a poem, interpretation is not enough for their consumption. Games require the user to engage in play—a very particular type of activity that is not only interactive but also distinct from "real life." Thus consumers need a very particular set of reasons to indulge in such an activity. Not surprisingly, the promise of sex and violence and glory on the electronic battlefield are all tried and true marketing methods.

But game manufacturers also have to deal with the social stigma attached to games, and market their products in a way that doesn't inflame public opinion and the media. The depiction of gaming in print advertisements and television commercials has changed over the years, as the industry has continually tried to adapt to society's changing views. The most common strategy has been direct appeals to gamers—as people who are "in on the secret"—since the industry's negative associations have as of yet prevented complete mass appeal (and thus mass marketing).

Video games started to creep into the consciousness of the public in the early 1980s, with the birth of Pac-Man, Space Invaders and other classics. Atari launched a campaign that framed their console and games as family friendly; their slogan, "Have you played Atari today?" was sung by happy voices, and the commercials depicted family members of all ages enthralled in gameplay. As the personal computer conquered the world, it similarly was advertised as a useful tool to do one's homework, help with finances or learn languages; but invariably, playing games was presented as the most attractive feature, in a series of advertisements from Atari proclaiming things like "We brought the computer age home."[22]

Starting in 1989 in America and the next year in Europe, Sega launched its new console (Genesis in the U.S., Megadrive in Europe) with a lot of slick advertisements and the successful "Sega!" scream idea.[23] The market war between the console manufacturers went public:[24] in America, the console was advertised under the slogan "Sega Genesis does what Nintendon't".[25] At the same time, Sega created Sonic the Hedgehog, a character intended to rival Nintendo's ambassador, Mario.

The movement from subculture to mass-market continued in 2001, as the major players introduced their third generation consoles—Sony's PlayStation 2, Microsoft's Xbox and Nintendo's GameCube—appeared within a short period. The three companies launched broad marketing campaigns that for the first time directly targeted the up to then reluctant "general public." Games were not the dominion of geeks or children any more—according to the promotional websites, television spots, and reams of print ads—but a creative pastime suitable for all fashion-conscious young people. Consoles certainly earned their place in the public conscience, especially around Christmas. The three competing companies— Sony, Microsoft and Nintendo—launched original commercials on television that caught a lot of public attention and in some cases even generated scandal. For instance, the "Champagne" Xbox advert, which featured the violent birth-propulsion of a baby into space where he would age in flight and finally crash into a tombstone as an old man under the slogan "Life is short. Play more," was considered distasteful and banned in the U.K.[26] The most curious thing is that none of the campaigns (with their slogans "Life is a game," "The third space," and Play more) concentrated on the playing activity itself. The adverts were dreamlike and surreal, depicting aestheticized universes that emphasized the high quality of escapism offered by their machines: the possibilities for leaving this reality behind and entering another one that was ultimately more satisfactory.

The fourth generation consoles (2005–2006) advertising has continued this trend towards "normality," away from the darkened male teenager room. The Sony PlayStation 3 uses the slogan "This is living," and the Nintendo Wii shows healthy families playing together. The Microsoft Xbox 360 was launched with adverts such as the "Jump in" series, showing young people playing with water balloons or a jumping rope that link the new console to new healthy, non-white audiences (and that don't show the console at all).[27]

These campaigns are the first sign of a possible change of public opinion and a more appreciative view of video games. As the first gaming generation is now in their thirties and forties, games and consoles can be advertised as legitimate entertainment with a cool edge, as desired objects of modernity.

Cultural reactions to games

The way people react to video games varies greatly by culture. While similarities exist, different media climates and traditions greatly influence how gaming is perceived and what sort of cultural niche games fall into. Some countries—Germany, Norway, and Australia are good examples—have strong histories of regulating media; enforcing limits on video games, then, is just part of a much broader—and quite routine—effort at monitoring many forms of cultural expression Other countries—like the United States—herald their own history of freedom of expression (though there are inevitably caveats to what can be expressed and how).

Although widescale public worries about video games have occurred around the globe, the official reactions of different countries have varied widely.[28] In 2002, the twenty-one-year-old American Shawn Wooley committed suicide, a death widely linked to excessive EverQuest play.[29] People around the country were shocked and concerned, but the alleged game addiction of Wooley and others has not led to any legislation in the U.S. Similarly worrisome cases have been reported in other countries. In South Korea, online gamer Kim Kyung-jae died in 2002 of exhaustion after playing online for eighty-six hours.[30] Based on this and previous cases, the game-friendly South Korean government chose to provide funding for computer addiction centers.[31] Similar problems have become prevalent in Thailand, and in 2003 the government imposed a gaming curfew, by blocking access to certain game servers between 10 p.m. and 4 a.m.[32]

In China, the government in 2005 banned anyone under the age of 18 from online games where players could kill other players' characters. A government official explained that "Online games that have PK (**player-killing**) content usually also contain acts of violence and lead to players spending too much time trying to increase the power of their characters. They are harmful to young people."[33]

Even more restrictive was the law passed by the Greek parliament in 2002, which banned electronic games entirely in an attempt to combat illegal electronic gambling. The law was later revised to target more specifically gambling activities.[34] Another example is the Chinese government banning the game Hearts of Iron I and II for "distorting history and damaging China's sovereignty and territorial integrity,"[35] due to the game's depiction of Tibet as an independent state.

It is clear that video games have the capacity to provoke strong reactions in many countries. The field of game studies has noted basic similarities and differences in these national outcries, and has documented some anecdotal and statistical evidence. The scholarship, however, has not yet made any persuasive links between reactions to video games and cultural differences. It seems to us that the video game industry is stumbling through the same gauntlet of cultural acceptance that all new media has to face, just as governments of all political and ethnic and ideological stripes are trying to react to a mysterious and growing behemoth in their midst. As video games secure their position as a global phenomenon, the ways that different cultures both accommodate and protest against these games (and the children who love them), promises to be a fascinating field of inquiry.

IDEALIZATION OF PLAY

Western culture has a tendency to idealize play.[36] We see it as frivolous fantasy, a symbol of youth and innocence, as creative expression detached from the troubles of the world. Hopefully, if we try hard enough, we can remember the feeling of being so deeply involved in a game that the sense of time and space is lost. It is almost a religious experience. Such reverie can shape our perceptions of what children *should* be doing or what play *should* look like. Despite widespread public concern, video games are not entirely exempt from this trend. But when studying video games, it is important not to fall into the trap of idealization, even though the fact that video games are played indoors already takes away some of the romanticism connected with free outdoor play.

The idealization of play is perhaps innate, as we look at the play of children and feel nostalgia for the days of youth. But it is also a consequence of early academic theories of play, which were promulgated in the mid-nineteenth century, and based almost exclusively on middle- and upper-class life. Here, only certain forms of play were considered appropriate—tennis, for example. One of the many purposes of these games was to provide a proper upbringing for children, which meant distinguishing them from the more base pastimes of the lower classes. Play theory for many years helped enforce this separation. In this elitist vision, play was seen as positive, innocent, and free from outside interference.[37] But it also ignored the reality that when not observed, the play of upper-class children was probably not that dissimilar to their working-class brethren. Within video games, such a vision of play would be analogous to only focusing on very free-form games—like *The Sims*—which in no way represent the breadth of gaming.

Thanks in part to cultural relativism and the other intellectual developments discussed above, we are developing a far more nuanced understanding of our recreation. We now acknowledge that play is an astoundingly mixed palette of activities. Play can no longer be seen simply as positive and innocent; it can also include degrading activities, and can sometimes have sexual undertones. There is also a great deal of power involved in play: in a group of children—not unlike adults—play is often staged by the strongest, and does not always include everybody. The majority of play activities in kindergartens, according to one study, involve themes of escape, power, attack, and defense.[38] We can take this observation one step further and stress that play—in children and adults alike—is often dangerous and reckless. Examples include climbing trees, make-believe fights, and racing bicycles down a steep hill. And this list doesn't even include the far end of the play spectrum: shooting BB guns; torturing small animals; or jumping in front of trains, with regular newspaper deadlines about accidental teenage deaths. Compared to these types of play, shooting aliens on screen may seem harmless; but video games provoke strong responses nevertheless.

When we idealize play, we tend to ignore these darker—but equally important— aspects. Such idealization limits us from, if you will, a three-dimensional understanding of this vital human occupation. More recent play theory, for example, emphasizes the importance of social dynamics in play—we now see that these interactions can run the gamut from kind to mean, but even more important, the ways children relate to each other are crucial for the richness of play, as well as for child development.[39]

Cultural theorists have gone further and introduced the concept of *evil play*.[40] Evil play is characterized by a loss of control, where children end up in situations that require outside interference—typically the intervention of an adult. A classic example is a child's fascination with the line between life and death. Many children have torn the wings off of flies, or have pulled the cat's tail. This child is not necessarily acting out of cruelty; rather she is exploring (and sometimes crossing) the limit of what is permissible, and acknowledging the intensity of their own—sometimes violent and negative—emotions. Evil play acknowledges that children sometimes need guidance from adults—with video games and any other form of play.

Play does not have to be hazardous, but often the potential danger is an important part of the attraction. The thrill of the illicit is, not surprisingly, essential to the magnetic attraction many of us feel for video games, and also to the equally strong repulsion that they elicit in many parents and authority figures. Video games challenge our visions of play—since many of us adults still idealize play. Video games typically require us to sit indoors and stare at a screen. They cut us off from the outside world. They excite us more than the food our mother has just prepared. They sink us into worlds of violence and fantasy, worlds where we are free to do things impossible in our own lives—anything from slaughtering an enemy army to perfecting a 720-degree spin on a tricked-out skateboard.

Not surprisingly, video games revolve around exactly the themes that parents and teachers and politicians lose sleep over. The culture of childhood can be a scary place, and adult culture doesn't like to acknowledge these dark corners. Most adults hesitate to think of violence, aggression, sexuality, and autonomy as intrinsic qualities of childhood. When kids use media to explore these concepts—especially when it is new media, utterly different from the novels and television shows that adults remember from their own youth—it is hard for adults not to get anxious.[41] Perhaps the most unnerving truth about video games is that they reveal the enormous divide between the perceptions of adults and the desires/realities of children.

GAMES AND OTHER CULTURAL FORMS

As we've discussed, video games have applied the conventions and language of earlier media—particularly cinema—in order to emulate the kind of visual representation our culture appreciates. The visual language of video games themselves has evolved so much in just the last four decades that we are already able to distinguish between quite a number of audiovisual styles and sub-genres, each of which are in turn influenced not only by cinema but other media from comics to literature to television. Perhaps more surprisingly, the aesthetics of video games have proven so powerful and so innovative that they are already beginning to influence other media, from cinema to music videos to performance art.

In the fever that surrounds video games, however, we must judiciously examine the scope of their cultural influence. Despite lots of breathless commentary to the contrary, video game aesthetics have not yet made a substantial innovation in the language of cinema language, on par with, for example, the birth of sound or the technological innovation of **CGI** (computer generated imagery) for cinema. One standard argument is that video games are the cause of the growing sophistication of computerized special effects and animation techniques in film. For example, a 2003 white paper from the Entertainment and Leisure Software Publishers Association (ELSPA) states:

. . . it is possible to argue that films such as *The Matrix, Terminator II* and *T3* are structured like video games, each with plots that feature levels of increasing difficulty. The hero battles past one set of enemies to win entry to a new world and another set of foes. Waiting at the end is an über-villain who's extremely hard to dispatch.[42]

Such an argument may seem convincing, but we must keep in mind that video game promoters like ELSPA have a vested interest in exaggerating the social sig–nificance of their product. The fact is that this kind of "Hero's Journey" narrative structure can be found in many Hollywood films (like the *Star Wars* movies), and even in classic literature like *The Odyssey*; these conventions are far from the exclusive realm of video games. It is easy to link the spectacular action sequences of contemporary cinema with video games, as Geoff King has noted, but this kind of spectacle serves different purposes when you are watching a movie or playing a game, so that such connections are too simplistic.[43] We should also keep in mind the fact that because video games are already vilified in our culture, they become an easy comparative tool for those who want to criticize the poor quality of Hollywood films.

That being said, those who dream up movies—like all forms of artistic expres-sion—draw on a wide variety of influences. Video games are certainly on this list. We can see in certain martial arts films, for example, the marginal influence of video games. Leon Hunt has noted that in the film *Romeo Must Die* (2000), Jet Li's fight sequences incorporate the "ultra pain mode," a series of "computer animated X-ray shots used to represent internal injuries inflicted by Li's character." We get to see, for example, an opponent's spine being shattered, a convention very similar to the detailed violence of *Mortal Kombat*.[44] The film was very badly received by fans of the genre, who thought this exaggeration worked against Jet Li's talent as a martial artist. Hunt traces this trend to *The Matrix* (1999); in one scene the protagonist Neo (played by Keanu Reeves) downloads a kung-fu program directly into his brain, and after a few seconds is suddenly a kung-fu master.[45]

There are even a few films that use video games as a direct inspiration in their construction. The best known example is the German production *Run Lola Run* (1998), which contains different alternatives to the story of a girl who has to find a sum of money in twenty minutes in order to save her boyfriend from being killed by the mafia. The movie presents three versions of the story, depending on different decisions of the main character; the viewer sees them one after another, and is left to decide what really happened in the movie. The fast pace of the film and its sudden and abrupt rhythm is punctuated by pulsing techno music; the film plays on its arti-ficiality also by showing some scenes in cartoon form. For Margit Grieb, the film is a landmark in the way that it "fashions itself according to computer game aesthet-ics," while retaining an overall filmic structure: "Run Lola Run attempts to engage the viewer in the production of meaning rather than simply playing to the 'passive' audience generally associated with this popular entertainment form."[46] The idea of the multiple endings is a seductive one, but it is not unique to video games, as we explain below.

Other films associated with game aesthetics are *The Double Life of Veronique* (1991), in which two women (played by the same actress) have mysteriously linked lives; *Sliding Doors* (1998), where a young woman's two possible lives are explored, based on whether she gets on or misses a train one morning; and *Time Code*, where "a story unfolds through the dialogue of four characters on a split screen. The viewer has to concentrate hard—they often speak at the same time—but eventually a coherent narrative emerges."[47] All of these films are explorations of the idea of multiplicity, that a story can contain several versions and points of view. These concepts have also fascinated hypertext literature authors and critics since the beginnings of electronic literature in the 1990s, not to mention the prevalence of "Choose Your Own Adventure" books in the 1970s and 1980s. Again, though the very public presence of video games today encourage these comparisons, we must not forget the wide variety of sources that can influence new expression.

Looking at other media, we find that video games have slowly gained significance as generators of art, even if it is still at a small scale. Some of the most prestigious orchestras in the world have recorded music for video games, and some record companies have begun to use video games to promote forthcoming artists and bands.[48] In addition, a number of art exhibitions have featured video games, such as the 2002 exhibition held at the Barbican Museum, London that later toured Europe.

Finally, video games have been the inspiration of performance art, with projects such as *Tekken Torture,*[49] *Pac Manhattan,*[50] in which games were used as conceptual frames in projects that reflect on our contemporary society.

Another example, more directed at the **game community**, are projects of artistic modding such as *Velvet Strike.*[51] According to their website,

> *Velvet-Strike* is a collection of spray paints to use as graffiti on the walls, ceiling, and floor of the popular network shooter terrorism game "Counter-Strike." Velvet-Strike was conceptualized during the beginning of Bush's "War on Terrorism." We invite others to submit their own "spray-paints" relating to this theme.[52]

This intriguing adaptation actually contradicts the violent impulses of video games (or at least of *Counter-Strike*), and encourages the players to use the game to articulate their own feelings about war. *Velvet-Strike's* creators clearly believe that gaming is a mature enough cultural form that it is ready to be subverted—and perhaps even that gamers are now ready to consider the real-world implications of the violence they participate in. Video games are now reaching a fascinating precipice, where they can be utilized not only by other very divergent media, but also in the service of more conceptual goals, like political expression.

Finally, a new form of games has emerged in the past few years that is not only inspired by other cultural forms, but that also operates within their codes and parameters to create a meta-form of gaming. This new kind of experience has been called "pervasive gaming," "alternate reality gaming" or even "cross-media gaming." The concept is derived from the idea of ubiquitous computing, which emphasizes that computers are omnipresent in our society, and control even the smallest aspects of our everyday lives. *Majestic* is perhaps the best-known example of these pervasive games, which may begin in your computer but then use other media to exist beyond the screen. For example, a player of a pervasive game is walking through their town and gets a message on her mobile phone; she is warned (thanks to location technology) that a player from the game's enemy faction is in the same square. The two players can then choose to "battle," using their mobile phones to send their attacks; afterwards they can each go home to check the number of points their team has earned during the day, communicate with other players and then decide their next strategies. In this case, the game uses video games and mobile phones as tools, while the physical location of players also plays an important role.

However, the aspect of pervasive gaming that has so far been most intriguing for researchers relates to the game's ability to "mix" with the real life of players; these games not only happen at any time during the day (including the working hours of players), but also use the same devices that constitute daily communication. In a mixed-reality game, players can get phone calls, emails or faxes from characters in the game, see messages related to the game in the screen titles of films or television programs, and search for information on game-based websites that look just like real websites. For example, in the game launched in connection with the release of *The Matrix Reloaded* (2003), players could start by visiting what looked like the authentic corporate website of Metacortex,[53] where the main character, Neo, worked. From there, they could investigate further and uncover dark secrets.

The most successful of pervasive games has been *The Beast*, released alongside Steven Spielberg's film *AI* (2001), where thousands of players followed clues buried in the film trailers, Internet sites, and even newspapers, trying to uncover a murder conspiracy. This player community thrived online, where information was exchanged in many fora across countries and languages. Speculation was made into an art. Jane McGonigal, a game researcher who has worked extensively on this kind of game, has reported how a group of *The Beast* players, the Cloudmakers, treated the very real events of 9/11 as if they were part of the conspiracy in the game, and talked about "solving" 9/11. Though these players might seem delusional, McGonigal explores their sense of agency, and how new social networks emerge where people can engage in different kinds of social action.[54] Although still marginal in most cases, all these examples testify to the raising influence of video games, as if they were passing the test that each new medium must face on its way to cultural acceptance.

VIDEO GAMES AS CULTURAL OBJECTS

Not many authors have dealt theoretically with games as a cultural form, with the notable exceptions of Johan Huizinga, Roger Caillois and Brian Sutton-Smith.[55] These three authors have framed the serious study of games as an interesting cultural object[56] in itself; beginning from considerations about games as a separate sphere from the *real* world, but actually of major importance in the shaping of the culture of any given society.

As we saw in Chapter 3, Dutch historian Johan Huizinga considers play (competitive play in particular) a fundamental basis of civilization and culture. He argues for its role in the cultic, religious, and ceremonial activities that are the backbone of civilizations. He is best known for his work about the Middle Ages, but it is his 1938 book, *Homo Ludens*, that has made him current again as video game theorists look to the past for inspiration on the serious study of games.

> The spirit of playful competition is, as a social impulse, older than culture itself and pervades all life like a veritable ferment. Ritual grew up in sacred play; poetry was born in play and nourished on play; music and dancing were pure play . . . We have to conclude, therefore, that civilization is, in its earliest phases, played. It does not come from play . . . it arises in and as play, and never leaves it.[57]

Animals also play, but humans have developed play into extremely complex forms of social interaction (from the piety of religious rituals to the romance of poetry). For Huizinga, play is more important than seriousness, and it offers a way to go beyond hard rationality and logic, an excess of which he treats as a sign of deca-dence in a culture. In his opinion, the culture in Europe in the 1930s was decadent because it was so far from play, particularly in what regards war.

What would contemporary culture look like if video games didn't exist? The impact and significance of play on culture is nearly impossible to measure with any assurance, but Huizinga offers a good guideline: he stresses that play both reflects and changes our culture.[58] *Grand Theft Auto III*, for example, may be said to reflect America's romantic view of gangster life, or be an enjoyably satirical depiction of our popular (and misguided) ideas about who gangsters are. Similarly, it has been suggested that *Civilization III* has risen above mere entertainment, and significantly altered its players' perception of history.[59] We would like to adhere to Huizinga's perspective and suggest that video games should be seen as informing and reflect-ing culture, even if that influence is only at its beginning, and not just as empty entertainment.

In his 1958 book, *Man, Play and Games*, Roger Caillois criticizes Huizinga because his work is not a study of games as such, but "an inquiry into the creative quality of the play principle in the domain of culture."[60] We discussed his defini-tion of play and games in Chapter 3. For present purposes we should remember his division of play and games into four categories (*agōn* or competition, *alea* or chance, *mimicry* or simulation, and *ilinx* or dizziness). He connects each of these categories to a particular kind of society. He sees the preference for a certain kind of game over others as a major indicator of the nature and quality of social life; so that some societies would be, in his words, corrupted and therefore prefer games with real-life stakes, such as gambling, while the better games are those with no real conse-quences, such as sport. Of course, strictly following the rules of a game is the preferred form of play, so that Caillois advocates an organized kind of leisure gaming not unlike present-day video gaming as we know it. Video games are both strictly organized in form of rules, and also have no real-life consequences, so that they are pure leisure.

A general trend with those who have studied play has been to consider it in an utilitarian manner, that is, as training for children for their future life as adults. Brian Sutton-Smith wants to go beyond this in *The Ambiguity of Play*, where this utilitarian view would only be one of the seven typical rhetorics when approaching play (rhetorics of play as progress, as fate, as power, as identity, as the imaginary, of the self and as frivolous; see the *Play Theory* chapter for an extended explanation). Examining these rhetorics, he insists on the ideological values they represent and the intricate different ways in which they are present in our culture:

> Much of the time such values do not even reach a level of conscious awareness. People simply take it for granted, for example, that children develop as a result of their playing; or that sports are a part of the way in which different states and nations compete with each other; or that festivals are a way in which groups are bonded together; or that play is a desirable modern form of creativity or personal choice; or that, contrary to all of these, play is a waste of time.[61]

Sutton-Smith has another interesting point about the historical nature of these categories, showing how some have been predominant in certain times. For example the rhetoric of fate was common in the ancient world, whereas the rheto-ric of progress can be seen in the work of contemporary psychologists. We can easily discover these rhetorics at play in the various ways that society—everyone from the media, to parents, to educators, to the players themselves—conceive of video games as an activity (we'll discuss this further below).

We began this chapter by exploring how video games are considered a part of "popular culture"[62] which links them (for better and for worse), to Sutton-Smith's rhetoric of play as frivolous. Their pop culture status is manifested in several ways: as a mass-produced object that is liked and bought by many people; as something opposed to high culture; and for some people, a bad product that is unworthy of attention. While play and games have been of interest to anthropologists and ethnologists because of their "spontaneous" nature, the industrial nature of video games has made them be considered in the light of other industrial cultural products designed to entertain late capitalist society.

Video games are linked to pop culture for another crucial reason: they are inextricably seen (again, for better and for worse) as entertainment. Entertainment plays a crucial—and much-debated—role in contemporary life. It is often considered a synonym of escapism, which has very strong negative connotations as it is associated with an unhealthy flight from reality through means such as drugs.

But we can also adopt a wider notion of escapism, one that includes any human activity not immediately geared toward survival. In this definition, video games are certainly escapist, but so to is literature and indeed all of the fine arts. The time that is "left over" in our struggle for survival can—and perhaps should—be filled with another reality, one that is more pleasurable and offers relief from the difficulties of living.[63] As critic Andrew Evans writes,

> When we look at the range of recreational activities that are popularly considered escapist, we can further note that most of them are "leisure industries" promoted by heavy advertising. Such advertising emphasizes the whole idea of "getting away from it all", "leaving your troubles behind", having a "weekend break".[64]

Evans differentiates between escapist activities, as some are passive (like watching bad television), while others are active (like gardening). Games would belong to the active category (to return to Sutton-Smith: the rhetoric of *play as the imaginary*). Evans does not consider games a negative activity, since the healthy or unhealthy quality of escapism does not depend on the activity itself, but on its context and the way it is performed. (In principle, any kind of escapism can become an addiction.) He considers games a necessity, both for mankind as a species and for children in their psychological development, and looks at the future of advanced console gaming with positive curiosity about new possibilities for simulation and what they could offer us.[65]

Western society has—at least since Plato—been suspicious of play and entertainment. The dominant influence of the Protestant work ethic, among many other things, has made it very difficult for adults to justify play and games. Video games have inherited this prejudice, along with all of the other suspicion that is heaped upon new media. But nevertheless, video games continue to be popular. Children and adults alike are drawn to them. And in the midst of these conflicting assumptions—about what we should do with our time and what we want to do, between whether games have a purpose or whether they just expose us to danger—the video game has become a cultural object fraught with importance. Not unlike the many-sided die of the old *Dungeons and Dragons* games, video games yield many answers, depending on how you look at them, and reveal many different things about us as a people.

7 PLAYER CULTURE

REASONS FOR PLAYING/THE SOCIAL SIDE OF VIDEO GAMES/COOPERATION AND
CONFLICT IN GAME COMMUNITIES/METACULTURE/CONCLUSION: THE CULTURAL
TURN IN GAME STUDIES, BREAKING THE MAGIC CIRCLE

We have just seen some of the myriad ways in which games are a cultural force.
They are everything from an instrument that influences culture to a body of knowledge that is influenced by the culture(s) surrounding it; they interact with media
and other cultural trends in complex ways. But we must also acknowledge the
culture of the people who make the gaming industry possible—the gamers themselves. Men and women, young and old, rich and poor—players don't just play
these games; from the merging of a game (or a genre) and its players spring many
different cultures and subcultures, each with particular interests, values, norms,
and sometimes even languages.

In other words, players organize themselves in groups and behave in ways that
are based on particular games, or a particular genre, or the broader phenomenon
of gaming. But what is essential to realize is that the new cultures born of this
enthusiasm are not in any way reducible to the individual games themselves. If you
take a look at a discussion on a game forum, for example, the core of the conversation will likely be the game itself, but chances are that eventually talk will stray into
widely different topics. A mere analysis of the game itself would not be able to
predict the variety of topics that emerge.

We should note that not all players of video games are a part of these cultures.
We are talking about players who spend considerable amounts of time outside the
actual game, discussing, interacting and sometimes modifying their favorite games.
Though they might be frightening to the uninitiated, these activities are usually seen
in a positive light by the field of game studies; these gamer cultures exemplify
creativity and self-organization, and demonstrate how people can use the capitalist
ambitions of multinational companies (in this case, the gaming industry) and make
something of their own. Gamer culture testifies to the desires of these players to
be active creators rather than passive consumers. Only a modest percentage of all
players are truly active in this sense, whereas many are content to "merely" enjoy the
games as provided by publishers. However, even the players who are not so active
are a part of game culture in that they need to know the conventions of a particular
game community in order to be able to enjoy the games. As a player of *World of
Warcraft*, you might have never participated in an online forum about the game and
you might not want to be part of a guild, but still you need to know how to talk to
other fellow players if you are to form groups that help you reach the highest levels
when playing the game.

It is also worth noting that gaming communities (like all other communities)
are often exclusive. A player has to prove her worth, by living up to community
norms and developing a certain amount of social capital. Gaming communities are
also prone to some conflict, as we will see below; socializing has a negative side as

well when people are mobbed or cannot agree about what constitutes appropriate behavior.

Then there is the extreme end of player culture. Here we find a growing number of players who do not merely play to enjoy themselves or share tips and resources with others online, but who consider themselves professional gamers, as we will see below.

Video games have now become a way for people to identify themselves, to find like-minded individuals, and participate in a world that merges with their "real life" in new and exciting ways. With so many motivations, and so many desires, player culture is a fascinating world, and a crucial element of understanding video games today.

REASONS FOR PLAYING

Most of the people reading this book, like us, are at least intrigued by the world of video games, if not players themselves. But we should not forget the befuddled spouses of the world, not to mention the aggravated fathers and the protective mothers. These people ask a very important question: "What are you doing spending all that time staring at a screen?" And they have a point. Although some people play video games very casually, other gamers seem to live for little else. They play with an all-consuming passion. They spend hours tucked away in their rooms or clustered in Internet cafés, punching buttons and staring at a screen, fascinated by the unending possibilities of video games.

So what is it that makes this activity so fascinating? A number of psychologists have tried to give an answer. Juan Alberto Estallo has compiled a number of explanations based on reinforcement theory, or the boost of self-esteem felt by those who become good at playing. Moreover, players assign symbolic value to the games they play, so that they find their own subjective rewards in the act of playing. Estallo is aware that any self-esteem boosting activity is prone to provoke addiction in certain kinds of people, but he rejects that video games per se are a cause of sociopathologies. He actually stresses the positive qualities of video game players, such as a high level of creativity and extroversion, and a heightened capacity for learning.[1]

Estallo's theories are borne out by the empirical experience of several authors—namely Sue Morris and Talmadge J. Wright—who have written about first-person shooters. In Morris's *Online Gaming Culture*, she argues that some video games provide a degree of "authorship," understood as creativity and autonomy lacking in many other available forms of recreation (as we will see below about the modding community).[2] Wright, Boria and Breidenbach have studied player communication and conclude that it "can both reproduce and challenge everyday rules of social interaction while also generating interesting and creative innovations in verbal dialogue and non-verbal expressions."[3] Video games would thus allow players to escape alienation in different ways, and to engage in a kind of activity that goes beyond consumerism.

Mihaly Csikszentmihalyi's book **Flow**: *The Psychology of Optimal Experience*, has often been referred to to explain the joy people find in video games. His concept of "flow" describes a state of concentration and satisfaction that a person experiences when performing an activity—anything from playing a musical instrument to climbing a mountain—she enjoys very much, and that becomes an "optimal experience." Flow usually refers to activities that fall outside daily routines, and include a certain sense of playfulness. People will achieve it through completely different activities, depending on their preferences. The optimal experience is "an end in itself. Even if initially undertaken for other reasons, the activity that consumes us becomes intrinsically rewarding." The experience of flow is characterized by the following elements of enjoyment:

- a challenging activity that requires skills (not something spontaneous, but but goal-oriented and with rules);

- the merging of action and awareness (attention totally absorbed by the activity);

- clear goals and feedback;

- concentration on the task at hand (forget about everything else);

- the paradox of control (the sense of exercising control in difficult situations where your abilities are pressed to the limit, not losing it of course);

- the loss of self-consciousness;

- the transformation of time (either time passes very quickly or a second at a key moment of the activity is experienced as lasting for a long time).[5]

Csikszentmihalyi suggests that in order to turn an activity into a flow experience, the first step is to make it a game. He suggests that a person establish her own rules, objectives and rewards, and lets herself be absorbed by a powerful goal. But this goal will only work if it is balanced with the person's abilities: the task should not be too difficult or we will experience anxiety, nor too easy because we will then get bored. The reward of flow is the ability to lose oneself and experience ecstasy, understood as a total detachment from the world outside the activity, so that the actor becomes the event.

The theory of flow can help explain why people enjoy playing video games; these games often adapt to the expertise of the player,[6] so there is a innate match between ability and goal, and anyone who has tried to get the attention of someone immersed in a game knows how the player can lose awareness of every-thing outside the game. But flow is simultaneously such a general concept that it could explain any other activity equally well. The theory ultimately does not offer a a specific explanation of why video games are fun to engage with—why don't players seek flow through other available activities?[7]

Another direction of inquiry is Sherry Turkle's work, Life on the Screen, one of the only examinations to date of simulated identity and interactions in "inhabited" game worlds.[8] Turkle's book contains an enormous amount of empirical informa-tion in the form of stories told by participants in multi user dungeons (MUDs) and role-playing games of various kinds. She looks at textual MUDs as spaces where people have a chance to experiment with different identities, and ultimately, the medium allows us to realize—and directly experience—the notion that there is no unified self. Reality is just another window, just like the window of the computer screen; what one experiences online has real-life implications and consequences. This is seen as something positive, as Turkle insists on the illuminating and even curative properties of this kind of play, even though she acknowledges that some players experience a dangerous fragmentation of their identity from too much play.

Her work on MUDs is certainly relevant to all social gameworlds where players adopt a fictive identity, and is a powerful testimony to the profound ways that video games can influence one's sense of self.

People also play games because of the emotions they elicit. Multiplayer games in particular can create a whole palette of "social feelings" in the gamer; a player might run the emotional gauntlet during a game, feeling anything from rage to joy to betrayal, all because of the trials and tribulations of his on-screen persona. These emotions—even the negative ones—can offer a powerful incentive to keep playing. Jonathan Baron has explored the emotions attached to this kind of game and how simple responses are a powerful element either to motivate or discourage players according to their degree of success in the game.[9]

There are even players who find joy in destroying the game experience for others, These *grief players* are a part of every gaming community, from the early textual worlds to the gameworlds of today with hundreds of thousands of participants; and more to the point, such "players" are a part of every human community. In the world of multiplayer games, these players may wreak havoc, for example, by playing only for the purpose of killing other players or stealing their property. Developers have become more and more aware of the fact that social games not only will encourage people to play nicely together, but will also open the door for a lot of "undesirable behavior." In recent years designers have altered the configuration of games precisely to curb this brand of spiteful activity.[10] Jonas Heide Smith, in his analysis of group behavior in social games points to the trade-off designers face between allowing a large degree of freedom and restricting action to avoid grief play. His article "Avatars you can trust—a survey on the issue of trust and communication in MMORPGs" presents indicative data of players' perception of different kinds of sabotage in online games, showing how players think sabotage is a big problem, as it can totally spoil their experience of the game.[11] The presence of the grief player reveals the potentially negative reasons why some people, luckily very few, are drawn to video games and can be linked to the negative effects videogame playing can have in some predisposed individuals, as explored in Chapter 10. We will deal with this topic in the "game communities" section of this chapter.

If we move further outward in the range of parameters affecting players, there is another dimension influencing the ludic experience, which we call *metaculture* following Aycock. It includes all the factors that go beyond the psychological experience of playing and are defined by a playing community. Aycock uses chess as an example to ask why winning is sometimes (when playing an ex-world champion, for example) more satisfactory than others. The answer lies in the metaculture of chess, which can include everything from the international rules, tournaments, and ratings, to journals about the game and the equipment used in the game. All of these elements are significant because they help determine, for example, how important a single game can be, or how players can achieve fame that lasts beyond the actual game. For instance, the World Cybergames (WCG) website hosts a "Hall of fame," where pictures and small biographies of the WCG heroes are kept. This title "is given by WCG committee to the players who have won the Grand Final two or more times. WCG and all the world's gamers will remember them forever."[12] Winning, in this case, means much more than just playing a good game.

The metaculture around a game is an array of meanings produced and endorsed by the playing community, something that also occurs for video games, as we will see in the next section. Considering the metaculture around a game completes our understanding of the act of playing, because without it, theories of framing such as Csikszentmihalyi's flow as explained above, remain insufficient to specifically grasp the experience of playing as a whole.

THE SOCIAL SIDE OF VIDEO GAMES

Many have observed that analyzing a game's structure (the text of the game) is quite different from analyzing the actual act of gaming.[13] The computer code of the game in effect gives birth to a much bigger world, the world that we have termed "player culture." In order to better understand its parameters, we consider player culture in two forms:

- *Game communities (within the game)*: this refers to the relations between players as afforded by the game, as members of a team, for instance, who communicate to arrive at the best strategy and align their movement. Such relationships are not always sufficient in current video games, so players extend these communications with informal rules, extra tools, and places to relate beyond the game, such as websites.

- *Metaculture (around and beyond the game)*: this refers to fan sites, discussion forums, game magazines, and other places where players discuss a variety of content related to the game. It also covers modding, poaching and the more formalized side of gaming, from competitions to professional players.

This distinction is a bit artificial, since many activitites clearly overlap both categories, but it is a way to stress how player culture is born within the games and then expands further and further. It is players who form game communities, and it is game communities that through their actions define the metaculture around a game.

Game communities

In our ever-more-networked world, there is a substantial amount of research into virtual communities—which as opposed to real-life communities, don't meet physically but over the Internet. The research on virtual communities typically focuses on MUDs, and social networks of various kinds, from website forums that talk about their favourite soaps to dating sites.[14] To understand what constitutes a "game community," let's explore the characteristics of a virtual community as described by researcher Tom Erickson,[15] since game communities would mostly be virtual.[16] Erickson has condensed a lot of research on virtual communities and come to the conclusion that most definitions contain the following elements: membership, relationships, commitment, collective values, shared goods and duration. If we apply them to a persistent online game, *EverQuest*, we will obtain some parameters to understand the kinds of communities that originate around video games, as well as help us distinguish between them. *EverQuest* is one of the best-selling fantasy games of all time, *EverQuest* was first published in 1999 and still has an online community of hundreds of thousands of players; because of its size and durability, it offers a good case study in the dynamics of a game community.

- *Membership*: all players must sign up for their own account in order to participate in *EverQuest*. In contrast to the vague standards of some other communities—like an online forum, for example, where people can post anonymously and come and go as they please—membership in a game like EverQuest is a pre-requisite to enter the online world. It has to be noted that membership is tied to the player and not the characters, and one membership account allows a player to maintain several characters at the same time.

- *Relationships*: the fictional world of EverQuest, called Norrath, is governed by a set of rules—explained in the game's instructions and on numerous websites. These rules also determine the social relationships between players. A player begins the game by choosing a race and a class (profession) for his characters; this decision determines everything from how other races and classes will view them to what territories they can and cannot venture into (at the risk of being killed in hostile territory). Relationships among races are determined partly by the fictional history of Norrath provided by the game creators, and partly by fantasy literature unspoken conventions (e.g. dwarves do not like elves). The abilities of the player characters also play a role, in that a higher level means a higher social status. Relationships become formalized when players organize themselves in guilds and acquire rights and obligations towards the other members of the guild. For example a guild might want to make a raid one night and need all its members to participate in order to have a chance of success; this can put pressure on the players to log on, even though they might have other real life commitments, like a sick child, that make it difficult. These social bonds can thus affect the real-world relationships of players.

- *Commitment and generalized reciprocity*: commitment to EverQuest is simple: the game demands hours of your time. Dedicated players spend a great amount of time in the fictional world, and usually expect a similar level of dedication from fellow players, especially if they adventure together in *ad hoc* groups or organized guilds. Generalized reciprocity means respecting the rules of the game. These rules can be "hard"—the type that game administrators will enforce—like that you are not supposed to kill another player unless you're in a PvP (**player versus player**) server; but they can also be "soft" rules—either informal or unwritten—you shouldn't talk "OOC" (out of character) in a guild meeting as it can annoy fellow players. Different groups of players will share different "soft" conventions.

- *Shared values and practices*: EverQuest players are mostly interested in advancing their characters (character advancement is the main goal of the informal genre of "role-playing games," and thus the most common practice). Secondary goals can be anything from exploring the virtual environment to engaging in conversation.[17] Players advance their characters with very similar strategies: usually solitary quests and easy killings (rats, snakes) in the first levels, and then more complicated group quests as the levels increase. The shared values of a game community are manifested through game behavior (it is for example usual for experienced players to help new ones with their initial quests, and even give them pieces of equipment as a gift) and in the websites and fora where players discuss the game and how people should or should not behave.

- *Collective goods*: the main shared collective good is the world of Norrath, duplicated in several servers around the world. Characters also have similar ways of collecting goods; for example by looting enemy corpses. Sometimes players trade with items from their own inventories. This collective exchange of materials was not intended by the designers of the original game,[18] since every object is supposed to be acquired by a person's "labor" in the game (by killing a monster, for example, or completing a quest). Sharing and other creative exchanges raise the interesting question of who owns the virtual goods in a game world.[19]

- Duration: this is one of the main concerns when considering typical digital communities. Can they be called communities if they do not exist all the time, but only in limited timeframes (i.e. through emails or sporadic chat meetings)? For some, only the persistent ones are communities, while the majority of researchers are willing to call more sporadic interactions a community. The EverQuest world is available twenty-four hours a day, seven days a week, so a player can join whenever she likes. Even if no other players are online with you, the illusion of a living community still holds as you can nevertheless explore the world, go on individual quests, and interact with numerous characters controlled by the computer (called **bots**). The community's frontier is also extended by the player's participation in the game's metaculture, as we'll see below—out-of-the-game fora, where players use email or instant messaging or Internet chat rooms to discuss various aspects of the game.

Game communities are thus virtual communities where a computer game is the object of interest. As we can see from the above, we can use Erickson's parameters to distinguish between different kinds of game communities. For example, if we look at the parameter of "duration," some game communities have a persistent universe like EverQuest, while others exist only on websites and discussion fora, such as the one for Age of Empires.

We can easily see how the dedicated fans of MMORPGs have created thriving game communities. But these gamers are not alone. Other genres, particularly shooting and strategy games, have given birth to communities around games like Counter-Strike, Quake, StarCraft, and Age of Empires II. The loyal fans of these games belong to clans, maintain dedicated homepages, and participate in intense discussions. Clans and guilds[20] are interesting mini-societies where power is organized, fought for and exerted, actions are discussed and plans, and dedication levels are high.

The strength of the in-game communities is often tied to the persistence level of a game, or the amount of time average players dedicate to it. A commited EverQuest player can immerse himself for hundreds of hours in the many quests of the game. However, even if the game world itself is not persistent—as is the case, for example, for most shooters—the community of fans can utilize the game space to create a sense of continuity. Thus, in a shooter like Battlefield 1942, players will create individual derivations of the game with specific rules. A group of people who all play on a particular server might settle on certain rules of behavior, and ways to enforce these. For example, a group of Battlefield 1942 players might agree that camping[21] is not allowed, even though the game rules cannot prevent it. As more and more groups follow suit, what emerges is a series of subcultures built around the game but each with their own peculiarities, which in turn increases the devotion of its players.

What does all this accomplish? According to a study by Florence Chee and Richard Smith, game communities provide players with positive values absent from their real lives. They argue that the game helps fulfilling a need, but it doesn't create it and certainly presents no danger for players.[22]

COOPERATION AND CONFLICT IN GAME COMMUNITIES

Multiplayer games are a balance of cooperation and conflict between players, and that is a crucial point in the formation of player culture. Common definitions of computer games usually stress that games imply conflict.[23] In their account of game design fundamentals, Salen and Zimmerman write, as mentioned earlier, that "A game is a system in which players engage in an artificial conflict, defined by rules, that result in a quantifiable outcome."[24] And as you may also remember Brian Sutton-Smith and Elliot Avedon define games as "an exercise of voluntary control systems, in which there is a contest between powers, confined by rules in order to produce a disequilibrial outcome."[25]

Though these definitions leave out games like *World of Warcraft* or *The Sims*, they do capture the fundamental competition that girds most games. This competition, we should note, takes a number of forms. It can be strictly zero-sum as in the case of most strategy games where you either win or die trying or more ambiguous as when players of a console RPG must cooperate to achieve overall goals but also compete to some extent for resources. These examples all qualify as *intra-mechanic*, that is, they concern player relationships that are shaped by the actual game code.

There is also a type of conflict that is *extra-mechanic*, that does not stem from the rules of the game itself (though can be influenced by the game). It is usually this type which causes serious strife and not, for instance, that Player A shot down Player B in a competitive game. In other words, conflict *itself* is not a problem. A few examples serve to illustrate the issue.

In September 2003, game developers Blizzard chose to cancel 400,000 accounts at their Battle.net gaming portal. These accounts had been associated with "a hack or a cheat program" and the players involved were seen as harmful to the status of Battle.net as a "fun and safe place."[26] These suspended players were accused of gaining unfair advantages by use of third-party helper applications or by taking advantage of flaws or vulnerabilities in the games.

Players themselves largely agree that there is a problem. In one informal survey, 41 percent of the respondents felt that multiplayer gaming is "troubled by sabo-teurs (player killers, cheaters etc.)" either "often" or "all the time."[27]

Developers have learned this lesson the hard way. Soon after the 1997 release of the early MMORPG *Ultima Online*, massive tension developed between players who did not agree on the norms of behavior.[28] As one critic commented, the world soon resembled "Afghanistan after the Soviets left: unremitting random violence, feuds, continual victimization of the weak by the strong. . . ."[29] Since then, most online game designers have usually gone to great lengths to limit possibilities for destructive play. Often this has taken the form of severely limiting player options.

Clearly, there are infinite ways in which players may upset other players; and anecdotes abound from practically every online game. Here we shall focus on three main categories of the most common offenses—cheating, grief play, and the violation of local norms.

Although noticeably significant to the understanding of gaming, the world of cheating has received limited academic attention.[30] We can define this transgression as any behavior that gives the cheater an unfair advantage over opponents, and/or anything that runs contrary to the spirit of the game. The terms "unfair" and "spirit of the game" are clearly subjective, and make cheating itself an alto-gether social construction.

However, some consensus exists and the term is not used in an entirely arbi-trary way. First of all, the advantage must be somehow "unfair." If your brother was an expert *Tekken* player and you had never tried the game before, using those skills to crush you in battle would not be unfair (although it might not live up to higher ideals). Re-ordering chess pieces while you were distracted, however, would constitute cheating: since it is unfair (you have not had a similar chance, since the other player has not been distracted), and goes against the spirit of the game (in which strategic skill should decide the winner).

Some techniques may run against the spirit of a game without being techni-cally unfair These are in fact the most common. The phenomenon known as *camping* is one example. Camping refers to the less-than-brave tactic of placing one's first-person shooter character in a highly secure spot, and then waiting patiently for the enemy to come close enough to be surgically dispatched with. Camping is not technically unfair since the option is equally available to the enemy (in which case the game would grind to a halt). In fact, since camping is such a probable success-ful strategy, many a player will argue that it actually does not go against the spirit of the game (that is, the intentions of the designers). If so, then camping becomes a question of local norms.

Having the core rules refereed by an impartial machine, video games clearly offer far less cause for confusion about winning conditions than do traditional games. But despite the seeming clarity offered by a computer's algorithms, multiplayer games are still often dependent on players reaching a mutual understanding on how the game should be played. Such implicit rules are the subject of intense debate among players. Often such discussions go directly to the question of the "spirit of the game," while at other times discussion hinges on the interpretation of specific local rules or player actions as regards these rules. For instance, a player of a real-time strategy game may not like his choices of civilizations. If this game's player community finds that one or more particular civilizations are comparably too powerful, a player might not be accepted for entry into the game if she has chosen one of them. Should the player insist strongly, she may end up being evicted from the game in question.

Interestingly, when an implicit rule reaches a certain broad degree of consensus it is often built into the actual rules of game sequels or later games in the same genre. For instance, *Age of Kings* players would often attempt to draw up an agree-ment that attacks should not be launched before a certain period of time had passed in the game. Such agreements were obviously often shaky, and could be easily broken. However, the designers recognized this flaw, and in the later game *Rise of Nations* from 2003, the ability to make early attacks impossible was built into the game.

The broad category of *grief play* includes any player behavior that intentionally causes stress in another player, and which is typically unrelated to the winning conditions of the game. A common example is unprovoked harassment through an in-game chat channel.

If stress-inducing behavior is a consequence of a player pursuing a personal goal, Chek Yang Foo and Elina M.I. Koivisto have suggested that the term *greed play* is more appropriate.[31] They give an example:

A player persistently camps a high level mob for an item he wants. But because his character isn't advanced enough, this mob kills the player, and proceeds to kill other neighbouring players. The others are unhappy and feel their gaming is being affected, but this player refuses to leave the area and continues to fight the high level mob, as he wants that item.[32]

In this case, the player may be unscrupulous but his actions are not motivated by a wish to harm innocent bystanders.

Grief play, in other words, can be understood as the intentional cause of distress in another player. There are gray zones, however, since all players are represented in a game space by some type of avatar. Thus, if one player has created an explicitly anti-social character, it can obviously be difficult to distinguish between behavior which is aimed at displeasing another player and behavior which merely (though it may hurt other game characters) is actually consistent with the character's identity.[33] In general, we should note that grief play is not surprising. It is simply a manifestation of deviance, a gaming parallel to real-world situations that happen every day.

METACULTURE

Serious players do not content themselves with just the game. The game, and the typically rudimentary communication it offers between players (such as limited-length text chat in many shooters), is simply not satisfying enough. And so, meta-culture is born. In order to bring a game beyond the screen, so to speak, players construct elaborate out-of-game meeting places; these devotees can do anything from discussing a given game to creating ranking systems for evaluating their performances. Modding and official competitions also spring out of these group efforts, which range from fully official (for example, a "community" that is based on the game developer's own web page), to semi-official (e.g. websites with formal links to developers such as http://heavengames.com), to other websites that are fully independent of the game's creators (this is the case for most "clans"). The existence of such Internet support can prove essential to the longevity of a game. So even games that have no online component (or only a weak one) may be deeply affected by the existence of the World Wide Web.

Often dedicated players will keep a game alive long after its release (and after the developer has turned its efforts to marketing other games). An example of this is the website *Age of Kings Heaven*.[34] Whereas the original game was released in 1999, players remain active (in mid-2007) posting news stories, strategy guides and other materials, and participating in forum discussions. The main forum contains over 200,000 posts testifying to a level of player interest that goes way beyond a mere desire to play the game itself.

Such fan dedication means more than sharing information and discussing strategies. As players congregate, they form sub-cultures centered around a specific game but which also place the players in the wider culture of a specific genre and in the culture of gaming itself. For instance, avid *Halo* players can feel a sense of belonging when interacting with fellow *Halo* fans. They will develop particular sub-cultural slang. Such slang will only be fully intelligible to other devoted *Halo* players, will be partly understandable by fans of other shooters, only vaguely understandable by fans of other genres (like the strategy genre) and close to unin-telligible to non-gamers.

Undoubtedly, game-specific lingo is a form of metaculture that emerges because it is an efficient way of communicating for the initiated. But it also highlights one's seniority within the social strata that builds around a game. Your language is a way of distinguishing between the experienced and the newcomers and thus a way to assert one's position. In other words, even if it was not invented for that purpose, subcultural language becomes a social stratification tool. Nowhere is this more clear than in the case of "leetspeak."[35] Leetspeak or just "leet" is a code (or more precisely, a cipher) which specifies alternative ways of writing English words.[36] A phenomenon such as leetspeak may well be understood as a reaction to the mainstreaming of gaming—a way to recreate some of the subcultural exclusivity enjoyed by (some) gamers in the past. Certainly one's command of leet, like any other "in-the-know" form of speech, is a signal of one's seniority within gaming.

Another example of metaculture is *poaching*. The term *poaching* refers to any activity where fans creatively re-use content from other media. A classic example is a fan writing fiction using the characters from their favourite television series, as Henry Jenkins reports in *Textual Poachers: Television Fans and Participatory Culture* (1992). Andrew Burn has studied different kinds of fans "poaching" with video game texts: "writing walkthroughs," creative writing that expands game universes, and the drawing of manga comic strips inspired by characters or events in games.[37] Walkthrough writers create a scene-by-scene re-enactment of the experience of navigating your way through a game, telling players what to do at each turn.[38] They present themselves as "experts" in the community, the best known ones will be downloaded by many, and they will become authorities on a particular game. Creating walkthroughs is an extremely time-consuming activity with uncertain rewards, since nothing guarantees that other players will endorse one's version of the game. On the other end of the scale, creative fiction writers and manga artists who are inspired by games are not interested in gameplay at all, but only in the narrative, or rather, the possible narrative inspired by a particular game. They will elaborate on a character's history, re-tell events that happened in the game adding explanations and feelings, and even write poetry based on their favorite characters. Stories, poems and drawings expand the emotional universe in ways that the game cannot do. Here is a Halo fan poem called "Hymn to the Fallen."

> Like the sunflower leaning towards the sun,
> So trivial is life.
> Let us retrace our steps,
> From which all this chaos derives.
> We have fallen,
> We have prospered.
> Among the distant suns we long to live,
> But do not realize the mistakes we have made.
> Mistakes that have cost millions of lives.
> We honor our fallen heroes,
> For they have protected us,
> Against an enemy so deadly, so ruthless,
> That our own imaginations couldn't comprehend.
> Protect the mother planet,
> So we say.
> But what is there left to protect,
> After the devastation these barbarians have caused?
> Nothing.

All we have left is our own lives,
Which we must struggle to cherish.
We will never forget the ones,
The brave ones, the strong ones,
Who have saved us from further destruction.
Hope is what remains of an empire,
Put down upon its knees,
Torn apart by parasites and floods.
Our faith in God must be strong,
Otherwise, the spirits of the dead ones,
Will haunt us through the long, cold and cruel nights,
That have set their domination among us.
Faith is what makes us stand united,
Is what makes us survive.
The nightmare is far from over.[39]

A very special genre of fan-fiction that we could call "flash movies" has also spread quickly across the Internet, and gotten a lot of attention from the gaming community. These rely on the software program "Flash," which enables people to make their own animated films. Fans make movies that re-use characters, settings and storylines from games, usually with some humoros or ironic purpose, such as the famous "All Your Base Are Belong To Us."[40] This movie is based on the 2001 Internet craze of gamers quoting the often nonsensical sentences from the Japanese videogame, *Zero Wing*. The game's terrible translation into English turned it into a cult object, and fans started altering photographs from all sorts of situations to include the sentence "All your base are belong to us." The pictures were exchanged and commented upon in many fora. Eventually, a series of these pictures was compiled in a flash movie that was downloaded thousands of times by delighted fans.

Other flash movies take their inspirational material to new heights. Alexander Leon's very popular "Mario Brothers" movies[41] feature Nintendo famous brothers Mario and Luigi, in original sprites (two-dimensional figures) from the game, as they engage in an epic journey to save Princess Peach. The five movies create a surprisingly palpable sense of drama, as the cartoonish, almost detail-less images of the two brothers are given gravitas with original dialogue and emotional music. The author, who posted the first movie as a joke in 2003 was very surprised by their success. All these semiotic expansions are the varied efforts of a very active fan community; the result is that favorite games are kept alive as cultural texts far longer than the usual "shelf-life" calculations of industry would predict.

Mods are modifications to or extensions of commercial games; they are created by players and then exchanged with other fans in active online fora. Though players have typically focused most of their modding efforts on shooting games, more recently all types of video games have been modded, from *Civilization* to *Grand Theft Auto*, from *SimCity* to *Europa Universalis*. As with poaching, an important effect of this kind of practice is that it extends the life cycle of successful games. *Half-Life*, a single-player shooter, for example, gave birth in 1999 to the most successful mod of all: a multiplayer version of the same game called *Counter-Strike*. In modifications like this one, fans can correct bugs in the game, construct new levels and maps, create new *skins* (or character avatars), and even modify certain rules so that the result is a different game *entirely*.

Modding can probably be traced to the beginning of video game history, and enthusiasts were already tinkering with Commodore 64 titles in the 1980s. But it was not until the early 1990s that the phenomenon started to spread, when the first modified versions of *Wolfenstein 3D* began flooding the net. Game developers rapidly realized that this activity could be beneficial, and started facilitating modders' work in various ways. The most significant example was in the mid-1990s when developers began to separate the main program of a game from the media files (such as skins), so that modders would not destroy the original program. (The first game to allow for this was *Doom* in 1993.[42]) Some modders have been hired by game companies, and this is increasingly recognized as an acceptable way to get a foot inside in the industry.

With the launch of *Neverwinter Nights* in 2002 and its accompanying *Aurora Toolkit*, game developers tried to accommodate player creativity directly in the game world. A player could construct a game scenario with stronger tools than were normally available in commercial games, where an occasional map editor had been the norm. Here, the developer BioWare tried to merge the mainstream fan's interest in making scenarios for his favorite game and the modding community's more elaborate changes of the game's code in search of a completely new game. In *Neverwinter Nights*, a player can construct her own scenario, invite players, and be the game master to take them through the adventure. The player/gamemaster is free to script potential dialogue and customize everything from scenes to avatars, and can then share the scenario with other players. This is the culmination of many previous efforts, including 2000 *Vampire: The Masquerade—Redemption*, which was the first computer role-playing game to include a gamemaster function and to allow gamemasters a great degree of control over the creation of adventures and plots.

A further example of metaculture—which also furthers the connection between devoted fans and the game industry—is beta-tester events. Today, most video game producers use large numbers of so-called beta testers while developing a game. The beta-testers are usually dedicated players that try new online games, and both help tweak the formal rules and seed the ground for the more informal culture in the game. From a game developer perspective, this hotline to the game community is crucial to ensure the success of the game, and also to reduce the cost of testing the game,[43] as opposed to hiring lots of people and paying them a salary to test the games. As we can see, gamers integrate themselves deeply into the culture surrounding games and gaming. And as the discussion of modding above makes abundantly clear, the resources of fan culture are becoming increasingly important in the games business and culture.

The last example of metaculture is the profesionalization of play. Just like those who play "physical" sports (for lack of a better way to differentiate), video game "athletes" train by playing a game (or games), find corporate sponsorship, enter gaming tournaments and hopefully win prizes and recognitions. As early as 1999, the Descent 3 Championship Tournament had a $50,000 grand prize,[44] and since 2000, the World Cybergames (WCG) have been held. There are many other championships, but this is the only one where people from six continents play against each other. In 2007 they can boast of "a rapidly growing international olympics in which nearly one million players complete against one another for the title of world champion in separate events."[45] "With over $2,5 million in cash and prizes," winning the WCG Grand Final is the "highest mark of distinction in the world by gamers."[46]

These numbers give an idea of how tournament play—also referred to as "E-sports"—has come a long way since starting about a decade ago. Many countries now have their own associations and leagues, such as the E-Sports Entertainment Association,[47] which organize tournaments and serve as information clusters for teams and sponsors. The ESEA (E-Sports Entertainment Association) describes themselves as follows:

> E-Sports EA was created to help promote professional gaming and mitigate the risk and uncertainty that surrounds much of the gaming community. We are creating the infrastructure needed for professional gaming teams, players, news sources, and other mediums that are needed to develop gaming into an attractive marketing tool. Through strategic partnerships and affiliate programs, companies will be able to use different gaming outlets to promote products and services and in turn, allow teams to compete in events around the world.[48]

Apart from helping their members with "lessons" on how to play each game or giving them the chance of posting videos of their best game sessions online, the organization has a clear market goal, aimed at making e-sports as big as traditional sports:

> Spectators fly into different locations just to be amongst the best players, and watch them compete. Media coverage is beginning to catch on, from traditional news venues like CNN, ABC, and the New York Times to more focused coverage like PC Gamer and Tech TV. With an ever-growing industry in our hands, we must keep feeding the fuel to fire. There is no limit to where competitive gaming will lead to.[49]

From these quotes it is clear that money is still a paramount concern, even when the targeted audience is dedicated gamers—perhaps especially when they are the target! And the cash prizes that await the end of a tournament are no doubt a primary motivation for some of these players. But we should not let simple capitalism obscure what is at work here, since gaining fame and glory through playing is an incentive as important as money, if not more. Competitions give players the chance to excel at something which might be frowned upon by their families or the general public, but that this way becomes legitimized as a desirable skill and a worthy enterprise.

Gender and video games

The video game industry is overwhelmingly dominated by men. If we are to fully understand the culture created by those who play video games, we must examine the role of gender in the industry. Though there are a few well-known female designers—such as Brenda Laurel or Roberta Williams—men control both in the production and consumption ends of the industry, with the products themselves mainly targeted at a male audience. However, there is a female game audience: in USA and Western Europe, female gamers constitute respectively 39 percent and 25 percent of the total active gamers; and in Japan, 36 percent of players are women, and nearly 70 percent of all women have a game machine at home.[50] There have been some attempts by the industry to attract young female players, usually by giving games a more girl-friendly appearance. For example, there is the well known case of *Ms. Pac-Man*, a game that was similar to the very popular *Pac-Man*, except that the main character had a pink bow on top of her head. Nintendo has also marketed a pink version of their Gameboy, so that girls would also buy it, even though the content of the games themselves was the same as those for boys. For many years, video games based on the Barbie doll, such as *Barbie Fashion Designer*, have been typical girl best-sellers, even though neutral games such as *Tetris*, *Myst* or *Frogger* have allegedly enjoyed enduring female attention. Other games that have contributed to open up game culture to girls are the new music-based games such as *Parappa the Rapper* or *Fluid*, dancing games such as *Spice World* or *Beatmania*,[51] and games that involve the entire body, such as games built around Sony's Eye-Toy technology. Some of the massively multiplayer online role-playing games like *EverQuest* have an important fanbase among women; according to Nicholas Yee, *EverQuest* players are 16 percent female.[52]

From this varied list of games, it is difficult to extract a set of characteristics of the kinds of games girls prefer. There seem to be some games which attract both boys and girls, although the two genders display different playing strategies, as reported by Kafai about the game *Where in the World is Carmen Sandiego?* She has studied the differences in children's attitudes to video games by asking boys and girls to design games that would teach mathematics and science to younger children; concluding that gender differences might be more context dependent than innate.[53] It is impossible to say if these results can be extrapolated to games in general, but they indicate the importance for empirical research to take into account the context in which players are observed, for example changing a parameter like the genre of the game can produce totally different results.

Nevertheless, Schott and Horrell have conducted a series of interviews with girl gamers and have been able to isolate several characteristics:

> Specifically, girl gamers identified a preference for third-person role-play games that contain animal/creature based characters rather than highly gendered human figures. In addition to these factors, games also needed to allow girl gamers the freedom to explore the virtual setting of the game. This was supported by the finding that girl gamers rejected games such as sports games and violent, combat focused games that are not open to creative interpretation.[54]

Girls in this study were also aware of the sexism in games and wished gender representation was more balanced and realistic.

The concerns of these girls reflect the two main types of academic research into the area of gender and video games: that which deals with representation of women in video games, and often work from a cultural studies or literary perspective; and that which deals with women as players of games, usually from a sociological or ethnographic perspective.

From the former, we have a number of studies that analyze the content of video games to discover how women are represented. These studies are usually very critical of the medium, finding in video games the worst kind of social prejudice and objectification of women. Their arguments are very similar to those of feminist critics dealing with cinema or television, as they concentrate on the symbolic weight of representation. Common themes are the stereotypical representation of male and female bodies and behaviors[55] or the male gaze.[56]

For example, the study conducted by Tracy Dietz in 1995 analyzed representations of women in the most popular thirty-three games of the time. These portrayals ran the gamut: from sex symbols or a prize, to victims of male power, to heroes and action characters. The study also considered the use of violent themes in the selected games. However, the analysis concludes that the most common depiction of women in games was that of "damsel in distress":

> In one example, The Adventures of Bayou Billy (1989), the beginning of the video game shows a woman in a low-cut, red dress. This woman has large, well-rounded breasts. A man is holding her and has a knife placed at her throat. Apparently, this man has kidnapped Annabelle and Billy's mission is to save her. In another similar example, Double Dragon (1985), a woman, also depicted with large breasts and wearing a mini-skirt, is walking down the street when a man hits her, knocking her down on the sidewalk. He subsequently throws her over his shoulder and carries her away. Once again, the goal of the game is to fight your way through the stages of the game to rescue her.[57]

In the games analyzed, all women characters had insignificant roles (or very stereotypical ones, in the case of villains), apart from the victim or sex object role described above. The author considers that engaging with this kind of representation is harmful to children of both sexes, "since they will internalize these expectations and accept the idea that women are to be viewed as weak, as victims, and as sex objects."

The study, however, does not present or refer to any empirical material that supports this claim. This is a typical problem of content analysis studies, which usually fail to provide empirical evidence of how content actually affects players. Other studies are even more problematic in that they fail to consider video games in their specificity as a media form; for example Urbina Ramirez et al. (2002)[58] base their conclusions about the subordinate and stereotypical position of women in video games in an analysis of their covers, without actually having played the games themselves.[59] Video games are not analyzed as such but rather seen as representational media only, and this can be very problematic in a cultural form that is so much more than representation.

We could, for example, make a content analysis of the character of April Ryan in The Longest Journey. We would immediately comment on her tight clothes, her full breasts and her big innocent eyes and sensuous mouth and it would be easy to conclude that she was a sex object and a passive figure.

However, this would be far from the truth. April Ryan is an independent and resourceful character, who is not only the protagonist of the game, but also makes decisions that can alter the fate of the world and engages in dangerous action without depending on men. She is part of a trend of strong, beautiful women in a variety of media (the prototypical modern example is the Sarah Michelle Gellar's depiction of the title character in the television series "Buffy the Vampire Slayer"). The point is that exclusively using content analysis to evaluate the cultural role of video games will never give us a full and fair picture.

The case of Lara Croft, the gun-toting, pin-up character of the Tomb Raider series, is paradigmatic of these concerns. The character has drawn the attention of theorists for years, but their analyses have not always paid attention to the game as such.[60] Helen Kennedy's Lara Croft: Feminist Icon or Cyberbimbo? On the Limits of Textual Analysis summarizes these arguments, and Lara Croft's ambivalent role as both an action heroine (finally a female character with an active role in a videogame!), and an eroticized object of the male gaze with a great deal of voyeuristic appeal.

Figure 7.1 April Ryan of *The Longest Journey*

Kennedy argues that watching Lara is not the same as playing as Lara, that is, video games foster a "complex relationship between subject and object."[61] On this same topic, Mary Flanagan has argued that playing (that is, manipulating) Lara's body takes us a step further than watching it: "More than the indulgence of looking at these stars within filmic worlds, we now embrace the very real pleasures of controlling these desired bodies: Lara is at the apex of a system in which looking manifests into doing, into action."[62]

But things are slowly changing: after Lara Croft and other pin-up heroines, some games have portrayed female protagonists who not only are resourceful and valiant, but also more realistic in their physical representation. Aida from *Unreal II* and Jade from *Beyond Good and Evil* are two good examples. According to more recent research, and in contrast to older studies such as Dietz's, Jeroen Jansz and Raynel Martis have conducted a survey of games and found that though a majority of them are dominated by male protagonists, there has been a growth of female protagonists or co-protagonists with active roles. Also, they stress that both males and females are portrayed as stereotypically beautiful.[63] Other related topics such as race, age or class representation in video games have deserved much less attention.[64]

On the other side of the screen, there is also significant and fruitful research into women and girls as players of video games. A seminal early work in this area is the book co-edited by Justine Cassell and Henry Jenkins *From Barbie to Mortal Kombat*.

Gender and Computer Games, which appeared in 1998 and compiled a series of contributions from researchers and interviews with women in the game industry and players. The book paints a wide picture of the world of girls and games, going beyond stereotypes and examining what kinds of games girls play and why. It both looks into games specifically produced for girls, and to how girls play games that are traditionally boy-dominated. Since the authors are worried about girls being "left out" of the computer revolution, an aim of this book is to offer some answers as to how girls could be integrated into the world of video games without necessarily having to adopt boys' culture, but rather modify the culture itself so that there is space for everybody. The editors believed that female-run and female oriented game companies could transform the market in what they called "the girl's game movement," something that has not happened yet, even though, as Jenkins argues, the success of games such as *The Sims* might indicate an industry shift.[65] For Jenkins, *The Sims* incarnates the ideal version of a game for girls as described by Brenda Laurel:

- Leading characters are everyday people that girls can easily relate to, and are as real to girls as their best friends

- Goal is to explore and have new experiences, with degrees of success and varying outcomes

- Play focuses on multi-sensory immersion, discovery, and strong story lines

- Feature everyday "real life" settings as well as new places to explore

- Success comes through development of friendships.[66]

If these features become more interesting to both girls and boys, the industry might progress towards genre-neutral gaming, according to Jenkins. However, there are still significant differences in the way males and females approach play. Both girls and adult female players dedicate less time to this activity than their male counterparts. In the case of girl gamers, the explanation might lie with the scarcity of attractive game content and the girls' perception that it is a male-dominated culture. In the case of adult players, it is very clear that other commitments (such as housework) are prioritized, and women seem to have more mental barriers to finding time to play than men.[67] This is confirmed by statistics about female players' hours of gaming, where younger players spend more time on games than older ones.[68]

Beyond game content and the demographics of players, there is another important aspect to consider in relationship to girls and video games: the gendering of game spaces and gaming practices. According to Rutter and Bryce, public gaming spaces—namely the arcade—are typically male-dominated,[69] and research has found that women prefer playing in domestic spaces. As a result, women are less likely to play certain games such as first-person shooters. Alongside the spaces where games are played, we should also consider the formation of groups of female gamers and the development of their own communities. Jo Bryce and Jason Rutter present a useful introduction to the multifaceted nature of the intersection between gender and computer gaming in *Killing Like a Girl: Gendered Gaming and Girl Gamers' Visibility*.[70]

In her report "Women Just Want to Have Fun—A Study of Adult Female Players of Digital Games," Aphra Kerr, after empirical studies with women gamers and game producers, and an analysis of gaming industry advertising strategies, concludes that women gamers are "largely invisible to the wider gaming community and producers."[71]

But why do women play? What pleasures do they derive from engaging with, mostly male oriented, games? In her *Multiple Pleasures: Women and Online Gaming*, T.L. Taylor offers an explanation based on empirical data gathered through extensive ethnographic and interview research centered on MMORPGs, arguably the favorite genre of online female gamers (with the exception of traditional games—from cards to puzzles to trivia-based games—that many people play at their work-places[72]). Looking at *EverQuest*, Taylor found that women enjoy a very varied range of activities in the game. Some of these won't surprise us such as socializing or exploring the game world, but other activities are typically associated with male players, including an interest in game standing and progress, identity performance, advancement in the game by way of improved skill, team sport and combat. Of this list, it might be striking to some that girls also seem to enjoy competition, and that they do not abhor violence, even as stylized as it is in this game. Also revealing is the fact that female *EverQuest* players "often struggle with the conflicting meanings around their avatars," due to their stereotypical appearances; so that, while they enjoy being able to choose an original appearance (instead of a pre-made avatar) they often ignore it during play. What the success of MMORPGs demonstrates is that "games that simply focus on friendship and sociality may overlook the fact that girls are looking for games which also push them to take risks and where there is a chance to be absolutely and unequivocally dominant."[73]

The gender discussion in computer games studies is by no means over. We have here questioned the validity of some of the content analysis studies or empirical work that extrapolate about the influence of video games on a girl's sense of identity. This is not to say that the topics are uninteresting, what is needed is empirical work that understands the medium of the video game and does not make assumptions about its representative value without taking into account that playing a game is not watching a movie or reading a book, as some of the more recent work points to. As to the actual women players, Taylor's work suggest that women players might be a more complicated subject than hitherto explored. Women are an increasingly important part of gaming culture, and we will see their influence grow in the coming years, both in game content and cultural formations around games.

CONCLUSION: THE CULTURAL TURN IN GAME STUDIES, BREAKING THE MAGIC CIRCLE

This chapter draws on a growing body of scholarship that puts players at the forefront of research. Game studies was born as a structural discipline, where scholars were mostly worried about defining the essential properties of the medium, as we have seen in Chapter 3. The later years have witnessed a turn where questions of identity, gender, player activity in MMORPGs and cultural contexts have become more interesting than those about game genres or rule definitions. This turn can be seen in the calls for papers and final programs of the major conferences in the field, as well as in the number of new works that have appeared. As Jason Rutter and Jo Bryce put it, this approach moves "away from any basic assumption that digital games have a meaning or form which can be discovered through applying the right analytical cipher to the appropriate game code in a manner removed from social, economic and political contexts." Games are "cultural artefacts which are given value, meaning and position through their production and use."[74]

There is no game without its players. Recent scholarship challenges the idea of the magic circle where games would be separated from real life, as presented earlier in this book. They have mainly observed MMORPGs, where there are numerous examples of what Geoff King and Tanya Krzywinska define like this:

> Gameplay does not exist in a vacuum, any more than games do as a whole. It is situated instead, within a matrix of potential meaning-creating frameworks. These can operate both at a local level, in the specific associations generated by a particular episode of gameplay and in the context of broader social, cultural and ideological resonances.[75]

Some of these meaning-creating frameworks become apparent in the struggles around player avatar creation and ownership, as well as in the fact that MMORPGs economy extends into the real world. There are also moral and ethical questions attached to player's behaviour.

What, for example, is an avatar? Is it comparable to a chess piece, or is it in fact an extension of the player, somewhat comparable to a virtual limb? It took the present generation of MMORPGs to accentuate the problem as it became increasingly clear that their game-status (in the magic circle sense) was anything but clear-cut. The status of player activity in these worlds is contested. Does it constitute work (and is therefore taxable and protected by standard laws) or is it innocent play? The game end-user-license agreements a user must sign before playing usually take the latter position—not surprisingly, since game manufacturers want to make it as easy as possible for players to do nothing more than play. But obviously when they do so, players can spend significant amounts of time and resources living in the gameworld—building characters, acquiring objects, and anything else the brain can think of. Many players attach a certain value—even if just a gamer's pride—to their activity.

And others agree. Trading websites like eBay serve as markets for game objects and characters (often traded at high real-dollar prices). The monetary value of in-game activities can then actually be measured precisely. In *EverQuest* during 2001, the characters in the game combined to produce to gross national product an annual per capita GNP of $2,266 per capita, or roughly that of Russia.[76] While this inspired dramatic headlines we should be clear however, that this does not mean that *EverQuest* is a rich nation (the number of inhabitants is too small). Giving a rough estimate, Edward Castronova has suggested that the combined economies of all virtual worlds may have an impact on the global economy comparable to that of Namibia or Macedonia.[77]

There are, however, other signs that many virtual worlds cannot be kept separate from real-world influence and legislation. In South Korea more than half of all reported cybercrimes reported in the first half of 2003 were related to online gaming.[78] In late 2003, a Chinese court ruled that the developers of the online game *Hongyue* were liable for the losses of virtual property suffered by a player. The bereaved (one Li Hongchen) argued that the developers had neglected server security leaving his account vulnerable to hacking.[79]

Meanwhile, in *The Sims Online*, professor of philosophy Peter Ludlow discovered an in-game brothel with a number of employees controlled by under-age girls. The story made headlines in the *New York Times* (Harmon 2004), but following Ludlow's claims his account was cancelled, on the charges of having advertised his blog within the game (the game developers do not allow the in-game advertisement of real-life goods or services).[80]

Such events all highlight the difficulty of separating two spheres of reality and make it still harder to maintain magic circle notions of the status of games. Players live between the two worlds. In an influential paper on the topic of how legal thought applies to games, Greg Lastowka and Dan Hunter note: how "Though virtual worlds may be games now, they are rapidly becoming as significant as real-world places where people interact, shop, sell, and work."[81]

We would like to end this chapter on how players create culture by adhering to T.L. Taylor's words: "My call then is for nondichotomous models. One of the biggest lessons in Internet studies is that the boundary between online and offline life is messy, contested, and constantly under negotiation."[82] Games are of course designed and produced industrially, and have meaning as aesthetic artifacts, but they are transformed by players, who are producers of culture,[83] and how this happens is likely to occupy game scholars for many years.

8 NARRATIVE

STORYTELLING/RECEPTION: THE PLAYER'S EXPERIENCE OF STORY/A BRIEF
HISTORY OF LITERARY THEORY AND VIDEO GAMES/THE POETICS OF GAME
DESIGN/MAJOR THEORETICAL ISSUES

Let us now move away from the cultures created by games and their players, and
back into the substance of the games themselves. This chapter explores the importance of narrative in video games. Critics, scholars, and parents alike have found
many reasons to dislike/criticize video games. One argument is that the medium
cannot tell a story; much current theory centers on what many perceive as an
incompatibility between gaming and storytelling. This stands in sharp contrast,
however, to the avid nine-year-old fan of *Zelda*, who can offer a point-by-point
recitation of the adventures of Link as he travels through the land of Hyrule. So we
are left with a basic question: are video games stories?

> The rain has been falling like a dense spittle for weeks now, and as you cruise
> above the metropolis in your spinner, the neon lights blur below like artist's
> pastels on a sidewalk. Back on the ground to pursue your mission, the babel of
> cityspeak washes around you. The last warm smile you can remember came from
> a geisha grinning off the side of a stark high rise, and that was about as genuine
> as one of those android snakes they're hawking down in Chinatown . . .[1]

You are a blade runner. As you search for clues in your first mission, life is not kind
in the city. The sound of rain accompanies your character's footsteps; you can nearly
smell the food as you step into Howie Lee's bar to ask the owner a few questions.
Using your mouse, you click on the screen image of Howie and a menu pops up:

• LUCY PHOTO

• RUNCITER CLUES

• EMPLOYEE

• SMALL TALK

• DONE

These are your options. What will your next step be? You've just returned from the
Runciter shop at the other side of L.A, where an animal murder has taken place,
and there you have found a pair of chopsticks with the name of the bar you stand
in now. Is this just coincidence or an important lead? As you contemplate this, you
notice that the bulky employee behind the bar looks a bit like one of the suspects
from the shop's security system. You use your mouse to click on "SMALL TALK,"

and ask Howie Lee about his employee. He cannot tell you anything, so you click "EMPLOYEE," and the program guides you around to the back to talk to the guy yourself. He claims to have maybe seen the girl whose picture you are showing him, but then he suddenly throws a boiling pot of water towards you and runs away through the back door. Can you dodge the water? Will you follow him or go back to Howie?

If this were a movie, the main character would probably run after the suspect in the alley; you as the spectator would not give this interchange a second thought. He might even say something witty as he jumped beyond the arc of the boiling water. You would not need to click over and over again on a simplified list of commands. You would sit back and watch the action unfolding in front of you, pondering connections between the story's elements and wondering what might happen next.

However, this is a video game, so nothing will happen unless you act. You need to decide whether to move or wait, choose conversation topics, shoot a suspect or not, arrest suspicious persons or not, and you need to always look for the clues that might be hiding on the edges of the screen. You are a blade runner. The year is 2019, and in the grim Los Angeles, your job is to chase runaway replicants, human-like androids that are a threat for the human population. Or are they? Just like in a movie, the decisions of the main character—in this case, you—occur within the context of a bigger story. There are characters with individual motivations and personal agendas, a mystery to be solved, a whole city to be explored, and histories to uncover that have shaped your character. And finally, if you are successful, there is a solution—you discover that the girl was a replicant and kill her together with all her friends, or you are killed by your policemen colleagues that think you are a replicant yourself. No matter what happens, it is an outcome that you have helped create. You cannot play *Blade Runner* without paying attention to the story, as you wouldn't know what to do next at almost every turn. *Blade Runner* is *more* than a story—it is a game—but we can't deny that it is *also* a story. Video game genres (and individual video games) are so different from each other that it would be folly to suggest that a story-centered analysis is always a good idea, but there are many cases in which it is, as we will demonstrate in this chapter.

Blade Runner belongs to the genre of adventure games, a direct descendant of text adventures (see Chapter 4), and arguably the genre where story is most important. There are other sub-genres where stories are very significant, such as role-playing games or the so-called action-adventure games. In the beginning of video game history, only text adventures could be said to integrate stories and games (even though many games used the frame of a plot as advertising); but nowadays there is no popular genre that doesn't use some sort of explicit fictional framework (these terms will be defined below). Early video games were simply too abstract for plot to be a central concern—we can only imagine the triangle ship of *Asteroids* as involved in so many plot-heavy adventures.

But as computing processing power has grown, the industry has tended towards the production of more representationally sophisticated games. Good graphics have translated into painstainkingly detailed and sometimes beautiful worlds, while better AIs allow for more advanced response to player's action, including more interesting non-player characters and better simulations—all of these advances make the gameworld seem more alive, and each, in turn, changes the possibilities for storytelling.

Narrative is so pervasive that there are video games based on nothing more than a tangential connection to stories in other media; the most popular of these are games directly created from other cultural products such as films. These games can sometimes have a narrative element, but often the film ends up being a thematic excuse for a platform or action game. Consider, for example, *Star Wars Episode I: Racer*, developed in connection to the movie *The Phantom Menace*. The game draws on the fictional universe of the *Star Wars* series, but is based on only one scene from *The Phantom Menace*. As a typical racer game, it contains almost no story, but it nevertheless prompts the player to "take the controls as Jedi-to-be Anakin Skywalker."[2] There is only a suggestion that makes the player frame her actions within the game as part of this specific fictional universe; the act of playing itself will not reproduce the sequence of events as in the movie, but allows for many other combinations.

Figure 8.1 *Star Wars Racer*

Even the genres where stories are not part of the gameplay at all, such as strategy or simulationoneones, fictional worlds prompt players to imagine that their actions take place within a meaningful frame. For example, Microsoft's successful *Age of Empires*, a strategy game based on the management of resources in the classic setting of "civilization-builder," where your tribe has to develop from nothing to an empire, all while competing with others for world dominance. The theme of advancing your empire gives a reason for abstract resource management and provides the frame for the game's graphics, settings and action. Without these descriptions, it would be very difficult for the player to understand what she has to do. Themes and plots—however vague—enable players to figure out game interfaces and the rules of the game: what actions are available to me as a player?—and that is why most games use them. *Age of Empires* has a final goal: *advance your culture and dominate all others*, but even video games without any goals, such as the toy-like *The Sims*, coat the simulation with a fictional varnish. In the promotional materials for the game, you are invited to play God in an adult version of a doll house:[3]

> Create simulated people and build their homes, then help your Sims pursue careers, earn money, make friends, and find romance . . . or totally mess up their lives. Test your "people skills" as you deal with family, friends, careers, and chaos! There is no right or wrong way to play this game.

Clearly, stories are everywhere. And we will use the general term "narrative video games" to refer to any games in which stories play a significant role. But to avoid the confusion which has haunted many discussions about the role of narrative in games, let us define our concepts carefully.[4] So far, we have been using the words *story, narrative, fictional world* and *fiction* in what seems like an interchangeable manner, something that would no doubt horrify many literary scholars.

Narrative can be defined as a succession of events. Its basic components are: the chronological order of the events themselves (story), their verbal or visual representation (text), and the act of telling or writing (narration).[5] For example, the novel *Dracula* tells us a *story* of how an ancient vampire comes to England, wreaks havoc in a small community and is finally destroyed. This story—which is not always clear or chronological—is found in the *text*, written by Bram Stroker. In this text, Bram Stoker (whom we cannot see in the text) creates the *narration*, both through his own descriptions and through the voices of the characters, who "speak" through their letters and other writings.

Though "story" and "plot" are technically "ingredients" of narrative, they both concentrate on describing a succession of events, and we will therefore use these terms interchangeably. When we talk of stories, plots or narratives in video games, we are referring to a scripted succession of events that the player has to perform in a specific order. (In *Blade Runner* you have to find the chopsticks before you can go to Howie Lee's bar.) The events that make up the whole story/narrative/plot of this kind of games usually allow for minimal flexibility in the order of completion.

The other components of narrative—text and narration—are not as essential to our discussion of video games, mainly because these games lack a static text. No matter how many times a book is read, for example, by no matter how many different people, the text is always the same; but in a video game, no two game sessions will be exactly the same. As for narration, the non-fixed text of video games makes it difficult for them to have a a single telling; the exception proves the rule here, as there is a very short list of games, such as *Prince of Persia: Sands of Time* or *Max Payne*, that feature a voice-over narration as you might see in a movie, which frames the player's actions within a narrative framework that has already been fixed in advance. But this is a trick, of course, because the voice-over only concerns itself with the main lines of the story, and it would still be possible to have different playing sessions in which minor things were done slightly differently.

As we can see, the above terms are concerned with the structural description of a narrative. We should also mention the broader category of fiction and fictional worlds. Fiction is not an uncontested term, but we can make a pragmatic distinction between *fiction* as events that have not occurred in "real life" (the basis for novels, films), and *non-fiction* as documentation of events that have occurred (as seen in news items, autobiographies, and film documentaries). Nearly all video game stories are fictional, although there are also games, such as *Battlefield 1942*, based on real World War II battles, that simulate historical events.

A fictional world is an imaginary construct created by the descriptions of a text. Readers—and viewers, and players—infer that there is a make-believe universe in which the events they are reading about (or viewing or performing) make sense. For example, from reading the tale of *Little Red Riding Hood* we can imagine a premodern world, where people lived close to forests, had tight family relations, and where animals could talk. From our own experience, we know that grandmothers and granddaughters are usually fond of each other, and that little girls shouldn't talk to strangers. This is much less detailed than, say, the fictional world that J.R.R. Tolkien creates in *The Lord of the Rings*, where he invents languages, and carefully describes continents, races, animals, plants, and an entire mythology. But these two narratives can similarly affect us as readers; the point is that we do not need much descriptive prompting in order to ascertain what kinds of events make sense in a concrete fictional world. As we read, or view, or play, we unconsciously and immediately apply what we know from our own world if it is a realistic setting, and from other fictional worlds if it is not. For example, the player of *Half-Life* assumes the role of a scientist trapped in a secret research facility, where an experiment has gone horribly wrong and brought evil aliens into our world. The player quickly recognizes the science fiction–conspiracy theme (from novels or Hollywood movies) and can almost immediately guess the plot to come: the government will try to eliminate him and all other surviving witnesses, and his only hope of survival is to kill everything in his way. *Half-Life* is full of cues of all kinds: visual, in the dialogues, and in the kinds of actions that we can (and can't) perform with our character. The fictional world is immediately recognizable, and thus believable, because it is similar to many stories we have seen and read before.

Most games have a fictional world, however minimal, and the success of this imaginary creation nearly always influences the player's enjoyment of the game. *Star Wars Episode I: Racer*, as we saw above, wouldn't be as engaging if instead of pods and the characters from the *Phantom Menace* movie it featured cars and an unknown set of colored animals as characters; with the visual clues from the movie, the player can imagine her actions as loosely connected to a broader *Star Wars* story that is outside the game. It still would be a racing game without the pods, but the link to the movie is what made thousands of fans buy it; the fictional world taps into their knowledge and enjoyment of the *Star Wars* universe, even if the gameplay is no different from that of any other racing game. Fictional worlds matter even when they are barely there, or highly abstract, or don't refer to any recognizable story. *Super Monkey Ball* is a good example. The game takes place on a stylized world of platforms that loom above colourful scenarios of forests, water or undetermined places. Nevertheless, people react to the cute characters of the game by identifying with them and enjoying their sketched personalities.[6] These fictional clues (a minimal setting, some emblematic characters . . .) certainly stimulate the player's imagination to turn the playing experience into a kind of narrative-related experience, even if this is not explicit.

We can see that most video games evoke a fictional world that is independent of the rules of the game, but nevertheless extremely important for the player experience.

We can also state that narratives always occur within these fictional worlds. However, there can be fictional worlds that don't contain a specific narrative, understood as an organized sequence of events. Narratives are made of events, and usually contain settings and characters, but both these ingredients can appear on their own, without being tied to a specific narrative, so that players can imagine how setting or characters fit in the fictional world, refer them to an external story (like *Star Wars*) or simply use them in order to narratively thematize their enjoyment of the game (*Super Monkey Ball*).

We should point out that it is easy to confuse fictional worlds with narratives. This is because one of the ways we understand a narrative is by filling in the gaps: we postulate connections between events, we interpret the motives of characters, and so forth. In other words, we project an imaginary world. In the same confusing way, when video game designers talk about narrative, they usually refer to the introduction of elements that prompt the players into imagining fictional worlds—which could be anything from excellent characters to detailed environments. As we will see below, many designers abhor the scripting of programmed sequences of events in games, which would actually form a narrative in the literary sense.

A lot of the scholarly discussion around narrative and video games deals with the perceived difficulties of combining a playing experience that feels free with the necessary constraints of the narrative structure: in other words, the problem of letting players act freely while ensuring that their actions produce an interesting story. This chapter will first introduce some of the concepts that are important when looking at video games from a narrative perspective, both about narrative as sequence of events and the creation of fictional worlds, in the section called *Storytelling*. There we will also offer our own view on how story and gameplay are integrated in the playing experience through the analysis of a particular game. Then we will present "A brief history of literary theory and video games," a summary of the authors who have dealt with these issues, including game designers. The final part of the chapter is an overview of major theoretical issues around narrative, where the main topics of discussion in the video games-narrative community will be addressed. This chapter should give you an idea of everything that has been done in the area, as well as hopefully demonstrate that a consideration of narrative is a useful tool for understanding video games.

STORYTELLING

We will here introduce interesting elements of narrative that are relevant to video games. Here we have divided the concept of storytelling into three broad categories, which can be thought of as the *who* and the *what*, the *how*, and the *why* of a narrative. The categories are: "the fictional world," which includes the story's settings and actors; the "mechanics" of the narrative, or how the action of the story is organized; and the "reception," or how players experience the story.

The fictional world: settings and actors

As we explained above, most video games are placed in a setting that not only helps the player frame her actions, but is also engaging enough so that it has some value in itself. Players of *Myst* marveled at the beautiful landscapes and eerie atmosphere of the deserted islands. Fans of *The Last Express* no doubt still remember the animated life of the train where the game takes place, full of characters that go about their business with no regard for the protagonist. And those players steeped in *Counter-Strike*, where enemies can appear in any doorway, and where danger lurks around every corner, may even find themselves fantasizing about combat tactics as they walk down corridors in real-life. The list of fictional worlds is endless—from the mysterious building where *Donkey Kong* takes place (full of jumps and stairs and barrels and dangers for our little Mario) to the terrifying village of *Silent Hill*—and video games have relied upon these imagined spaces from their inception.

But what exactly is the relationship between fictional game worlds and the game experience? The work of Lisbeth Klastrup, presented in "Towards A Poetics of Virtual Worlds—Multiuser Textuality and The Emergence of Story," describes the differences between game worlds and social worlds, and argues that a game world's objects and space are all organized around the act of play.[7] Many of us have tried to open doors and windows that would not move in *Blade Runner*, or tried to climb the trees of *EverQuest*. The fictional world of games is like the stage of a play; it is meant for action, but many of the elements are there to be seen and not used. Only those objects directly related to gameplay will be "usable," although certain contemporary games with advanced physics offer the possibility of interacting with objects unrelated to the story (*Grand Theft Auto III* is a groundbreaking example). Games indicate which objects are relevant in different ways; in *Blade Runner*, for example, the cursor changes colour when the player moves it over a usable object. Others simply try to make as many objects "alive" as possible, in simulations that provide the illusion of a virtual reality. In *Grand Theft Auto III*, we move around in a city where all cars can be stolen, all people beaten up, and a lot of other things done that strictly have nothing to do with the missions we are given. The city, it seems, lives even without us. Designers have divided opinions as to what kind of world works best, but players' expectations are likely molded by a game's genre: we are more likely to try and explore every nook and cranny of an adventure game, and less likely to care about the surroundings in an action game.

The most important component of a game world is the game space,[8] understood as the setting for the gameplay. Game spaces are not realistic, but reductive; they reproduce some features of the real world, but create their own rules in order to facilitate gameplay (and to reduce the processing power required by a computer to run the game). For example, in *Myst* (see Chapter 4), the world around us seems open, but in actuality we are forced to follow a very specific route through the landscape, and can't stray off the path or explore.

Espen Aarseth looks at different kinds of spatial representation in video game history: from two dimensional to three dimensional, from open landscapes to landscapes where you can only move in a single direction, and from indoor corridors to space travel and everything in between. He argues that spatial representation is the most innovative aspect of video games. Following from his main point—that the spaces of video games are fundamentally different from real spaces—he makes an interesting distinction between space in single and multiplayer games. Single-player games often have landscapes that, as in the case of *Myst* above, seem to be open but are actually very restrictive. This is necessary because the game orchestrates the movement of the player in one direction, towards a final goal. Multiplayer landscapes, however, have to be open so that all players can move freely, and so that no player starts with an advantage. The challenge in these games is not the landscape (as it would be in a platform game), but the other players.

Figure 8.2 *Myth*

One of the most contested issues in relation to the fictional world of games has been cut-scenes, which are cinematic sequences used to relay information to the player. Many games with a sophisticated story use this technique to situate player actions in a fictional world that can thus be described with great authorial control. Play is interrupted and we watch a "film" where the game characters interact or something happens that is out of our control. Cut-scenes are used by designers to create narrative in a variety of ways.

First, they introduce a central narrative tension. Many arcade games used animated cut-scenes to introduce the central conflict of the game. These scenes were brief and served to give the player a chance to get ready for the actual game-play. As the need to get the player quickly through the game fell away, introductory cut-scenes grew longer and today's games often have extended movie sequences that introduce characters, and set the scene and the mood.

Second, cut-scenes shape the narrative in a certain direction. Often cut-scenes function to ensure that the game protagonist makes certain choices. The player is stripped of his or her influence and the narrative is moved along. In the game *Gabriel Knight 3*, for instance, Gabriel walks through a door, which triggers a cut-scene in which the player has no control over Gabriel's actions.

Third, they compensate for missing game narrative. Many games mark the passing of time within the game using cut-scenes. Sometimes these scenes illustrate a journey—where the protagonist is whisked to another location, for example—but often they merely convey new information. We may accept this convention because while jumping in time is not common in games, it is very familiar in movies. For instance, when the player of *Prince of Persia: Sands of Time* has performed a certain series of tasks the game jumps to a longish cut-scene showing the consequences of the prince having procured the dagger of time.

Fourth, they associate the game with cool modern cinema. A series of modern games apply brief cut-scenes that borrow from the modern cinema of Quentin Tarantino, Bryan Singer and others. In *Prince of Persia: Sands of Time*, for instance, certain actions trigger brief sequences characterized by dramatic sound and sophisticated "camera work." In *Max Payne 2*, new characters appearing trigger a brief cut-scene ending in a freeze frame with the name of the character superimposed (see Figure 8.4).

Figure 8.3 *New Zealand Story*

Fifth, they provide the player with information. Some modern games have integrated cut-scenes much more closely with the gameplay than was previously the norm. Here cinematics are used to convey useful information, often to serve as a kind of establishing shot describing the layout of a location. As the protagonist enters a new area, the "camera" may swoop through the scene showing the placement of enemies and objects.

Figure 8.4 *Max Payne II*

The rationale for using cut-scenes in games is disputed. Some hold it to be a case of cinema envy; others argue the technique compensates for game design incompetence, so that the fictional worlds are shown passively instead of letting the player discover them through gameplay.[9]

Others, however, see the attack on cut-scenes as a radical or purist attempt to (over)emphasize that which is special about games.[10] In his article "*In defense of cut-scenes*" Rune Klevjer argues that cut-scenes are a manifestation of the author's voice in the creation of the diegetic world, where he understands *diegesis* as "a fictional world, created by discourse."[11] The importance of cut-scenes is not only retrospective; as we have seen it also frames the world in which play takes place:

> The cut-scene may indeed be a narrative of re-telling . . . but more importantly: it is a narrative of pre-telling, paving the way for the mimetic event, making it a part of a narrative act, which does not take place after, but before the event. The cut-scene casts its meanings forward, strengthening the diegetic, rhetorical dimensions of the event to come.[12]

Apart from the settings presented in the game spaces and conveyed by cut-scenes, the other important ingredient when building fictional worlds is the characters that will populate them. We have talked about "actors" before, because many of these characters are capable of action, and indeed of interacting with the player. If we take a definition from a dictionary, characters are: "the people that the film, book, or play is *about*" (*Collins English Dictionary*, our italics). Let's see if we can we use this definition for video games.

It seems that games (when they have characters) would participate in both modes, the narrative and the dramatic: sometimes we read and imagine worlds (i.e. adventure games), sometimes we view worlds unfolding (i.e. cut-scenes in adventure games), but the revolution offered by video games is that we can play some characters ourselves, and that there are others that will react to us and do things to us that we can respond to. Characters in games are not just the people that the game is *about*, but also the people who are making action happen and thus producing different stories.

Mark J. P. Wolf considers characters as the driving force of narrative development in video games. He proposes that they be categorized by their function: playing characters, computer controlled characters and computer controlled characters with no action in the game (helpers, hinderers, beneficiaries, neutral characters or narrators[13]).

We propose our own typology of characters in video games which is related to the extent to which we can interact with these characters:

- *Stage characters*: they are just part of the scenario, moving around but with no personality or a function in the game. We cannot interact with them in any way.

- *Functional characters*: they are like stage characters but with a general function in the game, for example in *Grand Theft Auto III* it is the people walking around that we can attack and can attack us, and in *Vampire the Masquerade Redemption* the anonymous mortals that our vampire character needs to drink blood from once in a while.

- *Cast characters*: they are characters with a particular function in the game related to the story. They have personality in different degrees, for example, a minimal amount in the case of the *Blade Runner* bartender we have to interrogate for information in an isolated scene, and a great amount in the case of our first friend later enemy Sephiroth in *Final Fantasy VII*. These characters have their own agendas, and can be considered in Proppian[14] terms, as we will explain below.

- *Player characters*: the character controlled by the player (except in cut-scenes); we can usually control his actions but his motivations and missions are decided by the story.

Not many researchers have dealt with video game characters,[15] even though there is a rich tradition of character studies in literary criticism. If we think of how video game characters are created, we can see that the language of video games nearly allows for as much sophistication as that of literature and cinema. Characters can be constructed:

- Through description (what we can see on screen)

    ○ Symbolic (for example in the works of writer Thomas Mann, people with red hair are diabolic; this resource is not very much exploited in games).

    ○ Naturalistic (their appearance tells something about their inner self and personality; this is an oft-used resource, where villains are usually ugly, often monstrous; and heroes are good-looking).

    ○ A character has a model from real life. this is very much used in sports games, and even strategy games, where you can play Julius Caesar or other prominent historical figures. We can also include here licenses that make games featuring popular characters in other media, for example *Riddick* or *Garfield*.

- Through their actions: in certain games, actions define the character's position in the story, and may also define the outcome. In narrative they are static, meaning that the reader/viewer cannot alter their outcome. But a game allows us to take certain actions, and according to them we will sometimes be able to mold our character's personality, for example resorting to sneaking past the enemy instead of murdering him in *Metal Gear Solid*.

- Through their relationship to space: some characters are very linked to the fictional world, so that their life or death are attached to our actions in it. In *Donkey Kong*, Mario completes each level by breaking Donkey Kong's platform, which causes the gorilla to fall.

- Through other character's views: though common in literature, in video games non-playing characters are often desperately static and repetitive, and sometimes do not react to the player at all. Some games, however, use the eyes of others in an innovative manner. In *Titanic*, for example, non playing characters from your past (for example a girl called Georgia) react strongly to your presence, without you doing anything. The "cognition" of these non-playing characters gives a sensation of depth.

- *Through a meaningful name*: this is a very common technique, think of characters like Duke Nuke'm, Snake, Gabriel Knight or Max Payne.

These techniques are all used by designers to populate the fictional world with memorable characters of all kinds. But as to the player experience, the player-character is certainly the crucial one. Designer Toby Gard has proposed a typology of player characters, with three terms according to how easy it is for players to identify with them: from avatars to actors, with role-playing game characters in the middle:

> *Avatars* are a non-intrusive representation of ourselves, *actors* are always part of a story (or have a story, albeit minimal sometimes), and *roleplaying* characters have very different abilities that we can raise according to our performance.[16]

Typically, an avatar has no name and cannot be seen, as the game view is first person, so that the player merges with the character, such as in *Unreal*. Actors can usually be seen in third-person view and have their own biography that is integrated in the game story, such as Lara Croft of *Tomb Raider*. Roleplaying characters are "made" by players, who choose their name, appearance and abilities, and often can also choose between the first- and third-person views.

Recently, Tosca has added a fourth category: *iconic* characters. These are characters who are empty of personality but allow for the collective channeling of stereotyped expressions such as happiness in victory or dismay when losing, like the *Super Monkey Ball* monkeys.[17]

The importance of being able to identify with a game's characters is something of a recurrent theme in video game design manuals; there is a belief that the stronger the personality of the character, the easier it is for a player to feel alienated from it.[18] The implication—that designers should create characters with only vague attributes, is the opposite of a typical modern literary perspective, where characters are praised for their vivid uniqueness. The fear of alienation is also contradicted by some very popular video game characters, such as Lara Croft, who have very distinct personalities.

The last point we will consider in relation to characters is that of the creation of better (meaning more active) non-player characters, a problem directly related to the development of artificial intelligence[19] and one that has worried many developers for a long time. Brenda Laurel is in fact optimistic, and proposes simplification rather than more complexity:

> the fact is that, thanks to well-internalized dramatic convention, we can enjoy (and believe in) even one-dimensional dramatic characters. In fact, when a minor dramatic character possesses only one or two actionable traits, audience members will impute elaborate histories and motivations as needed to make it believable.[20]

She builds on the work of Meehan (1976), Lebowitz (1984) and others, who have established guidelines to create "functional and entertaining characters from a small cluster of well-conceived traits that are realized as goal-formulating and problem-solving styles."[21] Despite constant technological advancements and more and more complex games, good characters do not necessarily have to be life-like. The techniques mentioned above can allow for the creation of a very interesting array of characters of all categories (stage, functional, cast characters and player characters). It seems that the key to an enjoyable fictional world is not always the simulation of a real world, as successful "static" titles such as *Grim Fandango* demonstrate (a game that can be said to be more similar to a movie than a game, since the story is extremely linear, there is not much players can do, and the cut-scenes take up a lot of space). A combination of good cut-scenes that situate the game world effectively, simple but responsive non-playing characters and integrated story elements in the game spaces that the player can explore herself can do the trick. And of course there are the fascinating possibilities of interacting with the characters of fellow gamers in multiplayer titles, an interaction that has not been thoroughly explored in the research.

Mechanics: organizing narrative action

Now, let us examine what constitutes narrative action in video games, and ways of implementing it. A central preoccupation of game designers is the problem of linearity—literally, of how to get a player to move through a game in a way that is compelling. As the narrative possibilities of video games have become more complex, so too has the debate over the mechanics of the narrative. Designers now generally accept that forcing the player through the fictional world does not make a good video game, no matter how compelling the narrative. But if you don't force your player to do things, then how do you create a plot? This is the central question of narrative mechanics.

The basic concept designers use to organize narrative action is "branching." We can define branching as the existence of multiple paths in a narration. The question of branching leads to the problem of managing the exponential growth of nodes (or individual text spaces) in a narrative. This has been one of the most debated questions amongst hypertext theorists since the 1980s. Faced with the same problems, video game designers have generally allowed for moderate branching while implementing plot bottlenecks, through which all players have to go in order for the story to advance. For example in *Gabriel Knight: Sins of the Fathers*, the player has to visit a certain number of locations in order to finish each day; she can do it in a different order, but in the end, the day will finish in the same way. Jonas Heide Smith has illustrated the differences between the standard narrative progression of linear fiction (including novels and films) and the one for interactive fiction and narrative games.[22]

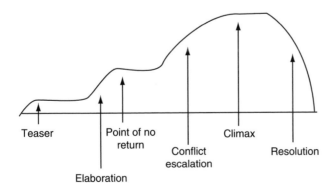

Figure 8.5 A model of classical linear fiction

As we can see, traditional fiction goes only one way—towards a resolution—and does not allow for interruptions or cuts. A traditional narration works is because it is a continuous line that plays with a reader's (or viewer's) expectations and orchestrates their emotional trip from beginning to end, controlling the important points such as the point of no return and the climax. If we applied the same model to a video game, we could not allow the player to do anything, as any deviation or delay would ruin our carefully planned emotional curve. Imagine the player dying in the middle of the narrative! But a game with such as narrative model would not be much of a game, which is why designers opt for another model:

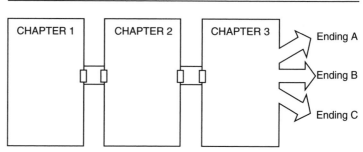

Figure 8.6 A model of interactive fiction

In this kind of fiction—typical of adventure and action-adventure games—there is no continuous curve. The player has to solve puzzles (or find objects, win battles, or talk to non-playing characters) within each chapter; usually there is some flexibility as to the order of the tasks, offering a small sense of freedom. With an emotional curve absent, designers rely on the emotional satisfaction—the "unambiguous sense of victory"—that solving the puzzles gives the player.[23] But ultimately, the player is *solving* a story instead of actively *creating* it. (This is true even if his actions can provoke a variety of endings, as is the case in *Myst*, for example.) The successive chapters work in a cumulative way so that at the end of each a climax or resolution is provided, usually preceded by a difficult "boss fight" to give a greater sense of achievement. As mentioned in Chapter 5, Jesper Juul calls these *progression* games, because the player has to complete a certain sequence of actions in order to get to the end, or endings, as sometimes these games allow for different resolutions according to the actions the player has taken before.

Not many progression games manage to give players a sense of freedom, but there are some notable attempts, such as the earlier mentioned *Blade Runner*. There are almost no puzzles, and instead the player just goes through different scenarios in search of clues. The player has a variety of options each time he confronts a replicant, the game's initial villains. Arresting, killing or letting them free each prompts complex responses through the game; ultimately, the player's actions decide if she turns out to be a replicant herself, which is one of the most interesting questions in the film that the game is based on. As Tosca writes,

> . . . With its game choices that don't matter and its emotional identity choices that are all important, *Blade Runner* creates a digital suspension of disbelief that players are willingly drawn into through the excitement of the different moral choices.[24]

Aside from progression games, the other dominant narrative structure—also defined by Juul—is *emergence* games. This type of game is nothing like the classical linear structure; instead of a prestructured sequence, there is a more active artificial intelligence (AI) where each object has behaviors. For example, in a progression game, the dragon will always attack the player when she steps into the cave, but in an emergence game, this might depend on how the player behaves towards the dragon, which is a more "active" object with a few possible different responses. Both for Juul and Smith, an emergent structure is preferable to give players a sense of freedom. Smith calls it "deistic narration," a kind of object-oriented narration where game designers become architects of space and situations:

> An example: A virtual living room is designed, the avatar is placed on a couch, and a dragon is placed under the couch. What we then *have* is not a story but a story is what we may *get*. What we have is a starting position with narrative potential but without direction[25]

The key to a successful mechanics is to make players feel that they are contributing to creating a plot; the most successful narrative experiences happen in games where our actions have noticeable plot consequences.

Beneath the narrative structure of an entire game, designers must also manage the smaller sequences of events that make up the arc of a game's plot. To explore these building blocks of narrative, game theorists have recently begun investigating quests.[26] Quests are small "missions" that players must perform; they structure a game's action and create opportunities for storytelling.

From the designer's point of view, a quest is a set of parameters in the game world (making use of the game's rules and gameplay) that creates a challenge for the player. From the player's point of view, a quest is a set of specific instructions for action; these can be a general goal (overthrow the evil king) or extremely precise (take this bucket to the well, fill it up and bring it back to me). After the quest has been completed it can be narrated as a story. Quests are a way of structuring the events that constitute a game, as they incarnate causality at two levels. On a semantic level, quests demonstrate how and why a player's actions are connected to each other and to the end of the game's story; and on a structural level, quests embody the cause and effect relationship between a plan of action and its results, or between the interaction of objects and events. These two levels can be perceived by both the player and the designer, and if the quests are well built, they enhance a player's emotional engagement. Ideally, quests are the *glue* where world, rules and themes come together in a meaningful way.

Most games with a narrative component employ quests, not only adventure games but even role-playing games or multiplayer role-playing games (where the massive presence of player characters does not leave a lot of possibilities for designer-controlled story production). In *World of Warcraft*, for example, at any given time of day or night, thousands of players around the globe are running around their fictional worlds, engrossed in their particular quests: find a book, kill a monster, take a letter to another city . . .

Game designers should ideally avoid quests that are boring or meaningless for the player. The two levels on which quests operate (the semantic and the structural, as discussed above), are also the two levels on which quests can fail. Quests generally do not work because they fail to integrate the storytelling elements in a particular game: if quests feel disconnected from the plot, the game-world or our characters, chances are that the bridging of the semantic and structural levels has not succeeded. There seems to be a fairly fixed and small number of typical quests that many games repeat (the exchange, the breach of contract, the discovery of the traitor, and saving the kingdom are among the most popular), and we might ask ourselves if it is desirable to explore new lands and devise new versions of these quests or search for entirely different ones. As Jill Walker suggests in her analysis of *World of Warcraft* quests,[27] some of the classic quests like taking a letter from a character to another can feel more significant if they reveal relationships between the non-playing characters that populate the world of the game. In other words, designers need not invest a lot of effort into making player characters a part of the quest-stories, a narrative can also be richer if the static world is better fleshed out than in most current games.

RECEPTION: THE PLAYER'S EXPERIENCE OF STORY

Reader response criticism or reception theory is a branch of literary theory that explores the experience of readers as they interact with texts, and tries to articulate the nature of the reading activity. It is a useful perspective as we study players' experiences when interacting with narrative video games. In what follows, we will argue that a reception-theory based analysis can explain the way that narrative and gameplay together determine the player experience in games that make use of stories. This approach can also answer the question: do we need to pay attention to the story in order to play this kind of game? A close analysis of the game *Resident Evil: Code Veronica X* will serve to introduce these ideas.

Released in 2001 for the PlayStation, *Resident Evil: Code Veronica X* is the fourth title in the very popular *Resident Evil* series. It is somewhere within the adventure genre and the subgenre of "survival horror." Along with other titles like *Silent Hill* and *Alone in the Dark* that fit this hybrid category, the player controls a character who has to get out of some enclosed place solving puzzles and destroying horrific monsters along the way. The overarching plot of *Veronica X* stretches across the whole *Resident Evil* series, and although they can be played independently, it is easier to understand what is going on if one knows the story. Most of the games contain complicated subplots that emerge from unsolved questions in previous games, all of which combine to create a vast fictional universe that partly explains the remarkable success of the series.

The story in *Resident Evil: Code Veronica X* is about a young woman, Claire Redfield, who travels to Europe to find her brother, Chris. Both siblings are survivors of previous games and enemies of the evil "Umbrella Corporation," which experiments with a biochemical virus that turn people into zombies and monsters. At the game's outset, Claire is captured by the company and sent to a prison in a monster-infected island, from which she will have to escape. Through the game, the player alternates between controlling three characters—Claire, her brother Chris and, for a short time, Steve Burnside (another prisoner in the island)—and uncovers yet more dark secrets of the evil corporation.

Let's begin our analysis with an initial concept, the "literary repertoire," because it will help us understand how readers (in this case, players) can start interpreting a story successfully—that is, how they get into it. The literary repertoire is described by Wolfgang Iser as "the familiar territory within the text,"[28] which can include anything that the reader might already know—references to earlier works, social norms, historical events. This repertoire brings context into the discussion without opening the door to excessively subjective interpretations or psychological particularities: the reader can only actualize[29] what is already in the text. Understanding the repertoire is a matter of competence, and it can affect both content (for example recognizing a quote) or form (being able to interpret the conventions of comic books). In the case of *Resident Evil: Code Veronica X*, the repertoire contains:

- knowledge of the survival horror genre of video games. This includes basic premises such as: kill all monsters; pick up all objects because they might help solve puzzles; there is a boss, or monster, that is especially difficult to kill at the end of each level or area.

- knowledge of the B-horror movies that inspired this kind of game. These movies place the game in the right cultural context, but also offer useful tips; horror devotees all know, for example, that zombies move really slowly, so you can probably dodge them instead of always fighting them (something that will prove particularly useful since it is easy to run out of ammunition).

- knowledge of how to cheat, since the player can become stuck, which stops the game. Savvy players will know to consult a "walkthrough," the detailed turn-by-turn summaries of games that we discussed in Chapter 7. They will also know where to find "cheats," such as pirate programs to optimize their performance in the game. (Note that just like in the case of the B-movies, here we are stretching the repertoire to include meta-elements—or elements beyond the game itself—but such "cheats" are now an established part of game communities.)

The repertoire is activated by "clues" in the game—everything from the creepy sounds when you go up the stairs to the dark rain on the fresh tombs—which indicate that we are immersed in a survival horror game. Even if we were to start the game knowing nothing about it, we would still be able to summon the right repertoire—the right mental category—soon enough, as we immediately have to face the creaking stairs, and a few minutes later we find ourselves in the first graveyard surrounded by zombies.

If our brains fail to recall the right repertoire—imagine, perhaps, that we had never played a similar game, or never seen a horror movie—the game cannot be appropriately enjoyed. In the first scene, for example, an injured soldier helps Claire out of her cell. If we wrongly summon the repertoire of "love story" to try to explain this, we will concentrate on the fact that he is wounded, and waste all our time either staying in the cell with him, or trying to find medicine to cure him (which will not happen until we have done many other things in the game). We will also be devastated when he dies later in the game, and perhaps lose sight of the more significant actions we need to accomplish.

This is not to say that players cannot summon the wrong repertoires on purpose; we could, for example, play the game as a friend to the zombies, and enact a "liberation of the oppressed" schema. This might be fun, but we would not get very far in the game, since it contradicts the game's mechanics; it is certainly a kind of play entirely unintended by the designers. Another important point is that summoning a repertoire need not be conscious. We can play a game using the conventions of the genre without being able to define the repertoire it fits into or isolate the individual clues.

In reader response criticism, the act of reading is vital as it transforms the literary text from artifact into aesthetic object. In other words, a text begins as a "dead" object with a lot of potential meanings that only become actualized through reading. Wolfgang Iser tries to explain how this happens through his theory of the "filling in the gaps." In a few words, it describes what happens when a reader starts from what the text says and figures out what it does not say. For example, if the text mentions that two new characters who meet in an elevator exchange hateful glances, the reader will wonder what the reason behind it is: maybe they know each other already and have had a fight, maybe they are ex-lovers, maybe they are fans of opposing football teams. As readers we tend to try and confirm these hypotheses as we read.[30]

We might assume that while playing a video game we would be tempted to "suspend" their interpretive, filling-in-the-gap abilities; it already is quite a lot of effort to concentrate on gameplay and try to solve the puzzles or get rid of your enemies. But this is not the case. Not only do we interpret plots in games in the same way as we do when they appear in other media, but we also have to deal with how to solve the game. Thus, our mind is busy with the story level and the action level at the same time. The first one, that we experience on the fly, can be narrated afterwards (it is tellable[31]) and makes sense as a story (complete with character motivation and feelings); the second is about solving action problems, and if it was to be narrated it would be a "walkthrough." To illustrate this, let us enter into *Veronica X*. The game opens with a cut-scene where our character, Claire, is captured by the Umbrella corporation men. The following description of this scene is written by Dan Birlew and Thomas Wilde, who have transposed the *Resident Evil* games into a series of stories.

STORY LEVEL

Slowly, someone clutching his stomach shambles into the room and stands outside Claire's cell door. Claire uses her lighter to see who it is, and is surprised to see the face of the man who took her prisoner in Paris.

The man unlocks her cell and opens the door. As Claire hesitantly steps outside her cell, he slumps into a nearby chair and pulls an empty bottle of medicine out of his pocket. He throws it against the floor in frustration. Not looking up, he tells Claire that the place is finished. They've been attacked by what he thinks is a "special forces team." Claire's free to leave the prison grounds, but he warns her that she has no chance of getting off the island.

Before leaving the cellblock, Claire picks up a knife, and notes that the man needs hemostatic medicine. A manifest on the desk tells her that the man's name is Rodrigo Juan Raval, and that he's a member of Umbrella's medical division. It's raining gently when Claire gets outside.[32]

The gaps here open and close as they do in any narrative: who is the guy? (open); Umbrella guard who captured me (close); why is he opening the door? maybe he will kill me, maybe he is a spy (open); he opens because the base is under attack and wants to give me a chance (close); do I believe him? (open) do I have a chance? (open) who is attacking us? (open). . . . We could continue. You get the idea: just like when reading a story, the gamer actively works to fill in the gaps.

But unlike in a novel (or a movie), as the story grows and readjusts in our minds, we also have to act. This walkthrough, written by CVXFREAK, demonstrates the choices a player must make as we decipher the game's clues:

ACTION LEVEL

CELLBLOCK ROOM—We are in a cellblock. Start off by going to your item screen. Go to the LIGHTER you see and use "Select" with the action button. This will prompt a cut-scene. After the cut-scene, go back into the cellblock and grab the ever important GREEN HERB. In the small corner of the room, grab the HANDGUN BULLETS. On the desk near the unconscious jailer is a COMBAT KNIFE. Once you have all the items, you may exit the room.

!!ALERT!!—Rodrigo is injured. You will need to find him HEMOSTATIC MEDI-CINE, which can be found in about an hour through the game. If you do not, you will miss out on some useful items.

CELLBLOCK HALLWAY—Run across the typewriter and grab the INK RIBBON from the desk. Do not save the game, though. Grab the box of HANDGUN BULLETS on the ground also. Run across the hallway, and un-equip the LIGHTER in your item screen, and equip the COMBAT KNIFE instead. Climb the stairs.[33]

This walkthrough gives a little too much away by foreshadowing Rodrigo's needs, rather than letting the player discover by herself that she can go back to him as the game unfolds. But walkthroughs are often full of spoilers, and to get a pure game experience, players. should only use them when totally stuck. As we can see, the walkthrough is full of things we *need to do* in order to get out of the cell and to the graveyard, but these things are not worth telling in the narration of the plot we had before (in the same way that what the guard says is not worth telling in the walk-through, that merely states "this will prompt a cut-scene").

When we say that both levels are "active" in our minds at the same time, we do not mean that they are as clearly separated as in our descriptions here. This is an abstraction necessary for analysis, but in fact, the act of playing is more than a sum of the two, since actual gameplay is full of doubts, ineffective movement, reloads, and at some point, likely death. This superfluous material is also an essential part of playing.

So the act of playing is informed by: our cognitive, and often-unconscious filling in-the-story-gaps, our sense of what we think that we have to do within the game, and the eye–hand coordination that gives us our playing ability. Below is my description, of the first time I played the opening scene of *Veronica X*, which demon-strates the messy reality of actual gameplay:

I walk around the cell in darkness, takes some time to find lighter and learn how to operate it. I watch the cut-scene, have no idea what the guy is talking about, they have been attacked shouldn't the attackers be on my side? Why does he say I have no chance? Maybe it is a trap, am not sure I should trust him but have no option. He doesn't talk anymore even though I try to click on him and approach him. (I don't see the herb they recommend to take in the walk-through). I get out, I explore the room outside and find the bullets, read the document about Rodrigo and find the knife. I also explore a lot of things with no result (try to open cupboard and get closer to the table for drawers, but it doesn't work). Since I know the game is about zombies and that the guy belongs to the evil corporation, I am not sure he won't turn into a zombie at any minute and kill me, so I stab him repeatedly to finish him off before leaving the cell. This has required equipping the knife instead of the lighter, something that needs several tries before I realize how you do it.

I am in the corridor, it is hard to control the character's movements and it takes forever to get out of the cell, move around, and go past corners. I find the ink ribbon and save the game (thus losing the first ink ribbon). I walk very slowly because I expect an attack any time, but nothing happens, I see the stairs but they are scary, so I go back to the cell. The guy is not moving, I am now think-ing that maybe I shouldn't have killed him, I want to shake him but the controls don't allow for that. Maybe I should put him in the cell to make sure he doesn't jump on me later, but I cannot move him. I want to search him to see if he has a gun but it can't be done. I walk out again and decide to go up the stairs, although it will probably be full of zombies and I still don't have a gun. When I start on the stairs there is a mini cut-scene with pounding heartbeat and creak-ing door. Spooky, I want to go back but can't control the character now. I am on the graveyard, the sound of the rain is soothing although I know something horrible will happen very soon.

Actual gameplay is full of trial and error—especially at the beginning of the game when we are not familiar with the interface or the story. My description of the endless things I attempted (moving the body, looking in the cupboards), and my rationale for killing Rodrigo (the implicit association with movies or other games in which the undead come back to haunt you), are all actions appropriate to the unfolding framework of the story. Though they differ from the sequence of actions recommended by the walkthrough above, they are not *wrong*; the player is simply using the information that she has at that moment, as she tries to fill in the gaps. The player will eventually fill the gaps in the right way and find the right sequence of actions to perform (alone or with help of a walkthrough); or, perhaps, she will quit the game in frustration. And here is a remarkable feature of narrative in video games: it is perpetually unfolding, constantly weaving back on itself, full of false starts and re-starts, as the player contributes to the story's creation with each action.

But let us come back to the question at the beginning of this section: can narra-tive games be played without paying attention to the story at all? As we have discussed, you can still play the game refusing to fill in the gaps of the story (for example by not watching the cut-scenes)—though you will not get very far in solving the puzzles. But more importantly, turning off our logical and deductive abilities prevents us from understanding the story, which is what the whole *Resident Evil* series is about.

When *Veronica X* starts, you do not know where you are, who has attacked the base, how to get off the island or whether your brother is alive or dead. While there is no doubt that the evil Umbrella Corporation must be behind everything and that a virus is responsible for the zombies and the rest of the monsters, the player does not know the story of the villain Ashfords, which is the central plot of this game. As she explores the island, she gradually finds information about the Ashford brother and sister, grandchildren of one of the founders of Umbrella. The player learns that the sister died some time before and the brother now has to control the military facility and laboratory in the island. Later the player gets hints that the sister is alive, but advancing in the game she discovers that it is actually Alfred, the brother, dressing up as her and playing both roles. Later still, the player finds out that the real sister is not dead but cryogenized incubating another terrible virus even worse than the one that makes people into zombies . . . It is a twisted plot embedded with subplots—what happened to the butler, whether Steve and Claire fall in love, whether Wesker can be alive? These try to keep the reader's expectations up so that when the killing of monsters becomes routine, there is the story to look forward to. At the end of the game, winning means escaping from the (second) Umbrella base, but also solving the mystery of the Ashfords and learning the truth about the rest of the questions in the subplots. Without attending to these intricacies, it is impossible to progress beyond the routinized killing of zombies that would surely get very boring after a while.

A concrete example of how the plot movements influence gameplay is the dragonfly sub-plot. At some point during your exploration of the island's mansion—home to the Ashfords—you will come across a video of your two enemies as children showing them pulling the wings off a dragonfly and putting it on top of an ant hill to be devoured. Later in the game, you will find a jewel dragonfly that you can turn into a key to open a secret door by pulling its wings off as you saw the Ashfords do in the video. Here is a puzzle that is actually based on the plot—you solve it because you've paid attention earlier on in the game—and therefore it feels meaningful. This is an improvement from other adventure games, where too many puzzles feel pointless and unrelated to the narrative. The famous rubber duck puzzle in *The Longest Journey* is a good example of a bad puzzle in an otherwise excellent adventure game.[34]

We hope to have demonstrated that a close reading of a video game is not only possible, but that it also yields interesting insights about how a game that makes use of stories is experienced by a player. Of course, one should keep in mind that the analysis presented here is very determined by the genre to which *Resident Evil-Code Veronica X* belongs just as any similar analysis will be tied to its subject. Different subgenres will require an adaptation of the concepts used here, but it is our belief that they are flexible enough to be extensively applicable. Using the notion of the "literary repertoire" demonstrates the vital importance of a game's cultural (literary, filmic) and gameplay context (knowledge from other games and genres). Similarly, exploring our innately human tendency to "fill in the gaps" of a story shows us that the interpretive process goes hand in hand with the skill-based operation of the game controls, which we also can call interactivity. Plumbing these and other insights of reader response criticism, we are given an intriguing perspective on narrative video games, one in which story and game are not opposed to each other but merge in a unique combination.

A BRIEF HISTORY OF LITERARY THEORY AND VIDEO GAMES

Just as we have examined above some of the practical applications of ideas about narrative to video games, here we will offer a historical look at the theoretical work that explicitly deals with questions of narrative, storytelling and fiction in relationship to video games. We will begin with a consideration of books, papers and articles published in the last two decades that deal with general questions about narrative. And then we follow with a brief examination of how video game designers have dealt with similar issues.

The choice of separating the historical overview of the field (this section) from the detailed discussion of the major theoretical issues (next section) is borne from a need for clarity, since many of these theories have been championed by individuals and are not part of a broader school of thought.

It is always arbitrary to isolate particular time periods, but there is a basic distinction between the works that appeared in the 1990s (or before) and those that appeared from 2000 on. The earlier ones tend to consider video games as part of more general theories about digital media, and the latter deal with video games as a unique object of study. We can even identify a third trend, as some game designers have touched upon theoretical questions related to narrative in their otherwise practical books. They have a different focus of interest that we could call normative or *poetic* in that they give guidelines to create better narratives in video games.

1990s digital theory

The 1990s was an exciting time in the nascent field of digital aesthetics: computers had become widespread, the Internet was beginning to be a major cultural focus and various forms of digital art, literature and games were emerging. A whole group of theorists was attracted to the new digital medium, determined to uncover how it was so special and different from previous media. Video games are not the main focus of these theorists—but only one more of the many new electronic texts (like the hypertext Afternoon or the interactive character Eliza). Games nevertheless play a significant part in their argumentation, be it as examples of qualities of the digital medium or as particular kinds of texts with their own properties. Their main interest areas in relationship to video games are:

- interactivity and the player's freedom;

- the opposition *video games vs. narratives*;

- the quality of video games (as works of art).

In what was to become a theoretical landmark in the study of new media and narrativity, Espen Aarseth's *Cybertext* (1997) performs a sharp analysis of the changes in textuality (the nature of the text) brought about by the digital era. Aarseth proposes a new model of textuality that can accommodate (among other things) print books, hypertexts and video games, which he classifies according to an innovative typology. According to Aarseth, video games are cybertexts, that is, "texts that involve calculation in their production of scriptons,"[35] which means that the participation of the reader/user is not trivial, and the degree of involvement goes beyond the activity of reading. Aarseth's foundation is theories of reader response and a solid understanding of narratological terms, which he translates into the digital medium. His main point is that reading a normal book requires an interpretive effort on the part of the reader, but engaging with a cybertext requires something more, as it is a configurative activity such as the one we described above for video games: with a print book, turning pages and understanding is enough, but with a game we need to interact for the story to advance. Cybertexts have existed for a long time (the

I-Ching, for example, a book that uses printed symbols to decode the tosses of a group of coins, has been around for nearly three millenia[36]), but only with the computer do their properties become widespread and easy to implement.

Cybertext examines the main genres of cybertextuality available at the time: hypertext, video games (in the form of adventure games), machine-generated literature, and MUDs. It was an important work in that it opened the textual paradigm to include the texts of the digital era, offering an attractive alternative to the dominant hypertext theory of the time (which emphasized the similarities of the new kinds of text with postmodern theories of dispersion).

The same year also saw the publication of the other landmark of the period, Janet Murray's *Hamlet on the Holodeck*.[37] This book takes its starting point in existing technologies (hypertext, virtual reality systems, artificial intelligence) and speculates about what the future of digital literature will be like. Janet Murray considers the computer as a new medium for storytelling because of its four properties: procedural, participatory, spatial and encyclopaedic, which we will go into later.

The last of the authors of this first wave of digital theory is the literary scholar Marie Laure Ryan, whose two main books open and close the period. Even though neither *Possible Worlds, Artificial Intelligence, and Narrative Theory* (1991) or *Narrative as Virtual Reality* (2001b),[38] are specifically about video games, Ryan touches on issues that are of interest to this field. *Possible Worlds, Artificial Intelligence, and Narrative Theory* is probably the best product of the "interactive fiction" tradition, as it connects literary theories of possible worlds to the realm of the digital, and remains a lasting inspiration for digital authors. In *Narrative as Virtual Reality*, she convincingly discusses some of the most contested terms of digital poetics, engaging with literary definitions of virtual reality, simulation and immersion in relationship to narrative. The book also includes a very useful typology of narrative structures,[39] and often uses video games as examples in argumentation, together with hypertext, interactive movies and other products of the digital age.

Video game theory since 2000

Our current decade is witness to the second wave of digital theory, and the first true wave of theory focused specifically on video games. This most recent scholarship is indebted to the pioneering work of the first generation, who have made it possible to publish books that exclusively examine video games.

The main interest of the second wave in relationship to video games are:

- to establish the independent status of video games as a medium;

- to describe video games as diegetic worlds;

- to argue for the legitimacy of literary approaches to video games.

The first attempt at describing video games as an independent medium comes from Mark J.P. Wolf, in his 2001 *The Medium of the Videogame*, which manages to situate video games within a framework of cultural and media history, and also considers the "formal aspects" of the video game (space, time and narrative). Wolf is very influenced by his own film studies background, which makes him disregard concepts such as gameplay, rules or interaction. This same background also means that narrative plays a prominent role in his analysis of the medium.

The status of video games as a fictional form is examined in a 2003 book by Barry Atkins, *More than a Game*. Atkin's method is the close reading of particular video games, a deep scrutiny of the works themselves. It is an interesting approach, but causes him to disregard previous theory, which damages his credibility when he tackles very contested issues in the field of digital culture—such as interactivity or immersion—as if for the first time.

Jesper Juul's "Half-Real—Video Games Between Real Rules and Fictional Worlds," published in 2005 has made a significant contribution. While earlier discussions were dominated by narrative defined as sequence of events, Juul's work establishes a concept of narrative akin to Henry Jenkins formulation of it as "any kind of general setting or fictional world."[40] Juul's argues that the essence of video games as a cultural product is the unique way in which they combine "the rules that the player interacts with in real time with a fictional, imagined world."[41]

Even though this second wave has centered around digital aesthetics and narrativity is shaped by **narratology** (a concept related to a structural understanding of stories, as we will see below) or the opposition between video games and stories,[42] there are other general literary perspectives related to the study of video games beyond narratology Though not a game scholar, Henry Jenkins, for example, has been quite influential with his concept of transmedial storytelling and his ideas of narrative architecture[43]

As introduced in the previous chapter on *Player Culture*, there has been a cultural turn in video games studies, which means that narrative questions have ceased to be the focus of scholars in the new field. The only recent publication with a story-centered agenda has been the 2007 *Second Person: Role-Playing and Story in Games and Playable Media*, which is an edited volume[44] that only tangentially deals with computer games. Other recent scholarship that touches upon the issue of narrative does so from a cultural perspective, such as Geoff King and Tanya Krzywinska do in their 2006 *Tomb Raiders and Space Invaders: Videogame Forms and Contexts*, where they explore the idea of cultural association, of how players actualize cultural knowledge when interacting with game narratives. They are more interested in how games reflect the values of the societies where they were created.

It is hard to predict what will happen in the field of gamestudies, which is already so diverse that a book like this is necessary to give an overview of the different currents, but it seems that narrative as an exclusive topic is a thing of the past. As examined above, researchers are now interested in the player's experience of narrative or in situating videogame narrative in the appropriate cultural contexts.

THE POETICS OF GAME DESIGN

Game designers have a long tradition of reflecting about their own practice, both in trade magazines (including *Game Developer*, *Gamasutra*) and conferences (including the annual meeting of the International Game Developers Association), and more recently in specialized books aimed at students of video games design.[45] Here we introduce a few of the ideas in the main books of the field to date; the term "poetics" is a useful description for these ideas because it is in origin a normative concept: how things should be in good literature, and game designers try to teach people how to make good games. Even though their reflection is mostly practice-oriented, they sometimes touch upon the more theoretical subjects that tend to interest scholars. The starting point of these published designers is that video games can tell stories, but they do so in their own unique way. As we explained in the introduction to this chapter, when video game designers refer to narrative or storytelling they are mostly alluding to the creation of what we have called fictional worlds, in contrast to how literary scholars use the term. Designers are primarily interested in: the ways in which video games tell stories; how to create better video games with better stories; and how to create practical design guidelines for this improved storytelling.

Andrew Rollings and Dave Morris stress the importance of settings and moods to immerse players into video games, and they devote an entire section of their *Game Architecture and Design* to "storytelling," to show how this can be done. They are against stories that "turn the player into a passive spectator,"[46] but in favor of others that let the player be a creator of the story, as it happens in *Half-Life*.[47] Though they do not explicitly define "active storytelling," their "toolbox of storytelling techniques"[48] offers a series of recommendations to make gameplay more engaging, by creating stories that offer different kinds of motivation for the player to attempt actions or solve quests.[49] As an example of their practical approach, here is a description of their *obstacles* "tool."

> A little old man runs into the inn where the hero is staying and says to him, "There is a vampire up at the castle. You have to kill it."

> Very poor. Try this instead. A fearful old man enters the inn and avoids the hero. When the hero asks what has frightened him, the old man gives no reply. Then he goes to a character sitting by the fire and begs him for something, but is refused. "You pawned it, you only get it back when you pay," he is told. If the hero pays on the man's behalf, he sees what the item is: a crucifix. "You should buy one yourself if you're going to stay in these parts," remarks the pawnbroker."[50]

In the first example, the player would just receive an order to accomplish a mission that had nothing to do with her. In the second, the fact that the player gets involved emotionally with the old man makes for a stronger motivation to try and find out what is happening in the village.

Game designers agree that one of the main reasons for playing video games is to fantasize; the concept of being someone else is a fundamental element of storytelling, as Richard Rouse explains in *Game Design: Theory and Practice*:

> Computer games, then, have the potential to be an even more immersive form of escapism. In games, players get the chance to actually be someone more exciting, to control a pulp-fiction adventurer, daring swordsman, or space-opera hero. [. . .] And, most importantly, the level of fantasy immersion is heightened from that of other art forms because of the interactive nature of gaming.[51]

Following this logic, games can also be "narrative play," as Katie Salen and Eric Zimmerman describe it in *Rules of Play—Game Design Fundamentals* (2004). Narrative as such is separated from the deep structure of games (such as rules), but creates an important connection to the "borders" of games, or how these games interact with the individual player and the society at large. Stories have a cultural dimension that places games in the general narrative repertoire of a society (where they exist alongside literature or film and relate to their established conventions and genres) and connects them to wider ideological issues like politics or gender representation. They also make the compelling argument that *everything* in a game can be "tools for crafting narrative experiences";[52] designers should not be limited, for example, to the use of cut-scenes, and the explanations provided by a game's opening screens, but should craft their game world in such a way that the player's action makes her discover a story: how the space is explored, what the non-playing characters reveal, even her actions can have a narrative meaning connected to the overarching story of the game.

Another way to integrate stories in video games is to apply Joseph Campbell's "hero's journey," describing the steps that mythical heroes tend to follow in their quests. These nine steps, which Campbell distilled from myths of cultures around the world, can be found in many Hollywood films, as Adams and Rollings summarize them:

1   existing in the ordinary world;

2   the call to adventure;

3   the refusal of the call;

4   the meeting with the mentor;

5   crossing the first threshold;

6   tests, allies, and enemies;

7   the approach of the innermost cave;

8   the ordeal;

9   the reward.[53]

Using the hero's journey is recommended by Andrew Rollings and Ernest Adams in *On Game Design* (2003). This structure is a good way (though not the only one) to organize narrative progress in a game as it links the advancement of the story with spatial advancement and a gradual overcoming of obstacles. These designers also document the various uses of stories in different genres, and how different kinds of games require different depth of story, from simple back-story to a full-fledged world. The authors rely on an Aristotelian plot development structure[54] and offer a useful section about how to organize the episodic delivery of a story.[55]

The most compelling quality of game design poetics is that designers have practical experience in trying to integrate stories with video games, and they have an intuitive understanding of what kinds of storytelling are acceptable and which are not. The key factor is whether the narrative is "flexible enough to allow it to become the player's story as well."[56] Their concerns thus mirror some of the most important theoretical discussions that we have examined: about how to make a story compatible with the interactive needs of a game, and the clear relationship between the quality of a video game's story and the player's experience.

MAJOR THEORETICAL ISSUES

Let us now look more closely at the issues introduced in the previous section. It would be difficult for any group of academics to find absolute consensus on what qualifies as the major issues of their field, but the issues discussed here have concerned a significant (if not all) number of the authors mentioned above. These major themes are very much framed by the typical theoretical problems of the digital era, that have kept hypertext theorists and digital aesthetic critics busy since the early 1990s:

- **ludology** versus narratology;

- interaction versus narrative;

- the interactive storytelling paradigm: in search of quality;

- the fictional status of video games.

The ludology versus narratology discussion

From our earlier discussion of literary theory, it seems like looking for stories in video games would be quite straightforward, utilizing the accumulated knowledge of literary theory in order to approach our new aesthetic object. But this approach has not been straightforward at all. Quite the opposite, the use of literary theory has caused the biggest clash of paradigms in our nascent field: the "war" between ludology and narratology.

Literature is one the oldest subjects of study in the humanities. Its study has been identified by different names in different times (from *poetics* to *literary criticism*) and contains a number of subfields (such as *metrics, narratology* and *semiotics*). Precisely because it is so well established, literary studies has been easily exported to the study of newer media, such as cinema, as the first steps in the creation of new disciplines usually are inspired by the old ones. We could say that the same has happened in the case of video games, as some early approaches to the study of games have centered on their representational quality, and thus authors have been able to apply literary and dramatic models to the description and cultural understanding of video games.[57]

However, some of these attempts have been rejected by a group of researchers, identified (alternately by themselves and by others) as "ludologists."[58] Their ambition is to consider video games *as games*, and not as narratives or anything else. The term *ludology* was introduced into video game studies by game theorist Gonzalo Frasca. He suggested that ludology be thought of as simply the "discipline that studies game and play activities."[59] In that broad sense there is no inherent opposition to literary approaches and indeed "ludology" is sometimes used to merely refer to "the study of games" (using any approach). Expanding on this stance, however, on his popular webpage Ludology.org, Frasca has since has specified that a ludological stance implies that "games cannot be understood through theories derived from narrative."[60]

Jesper Juul's article "Computer Games Telling Stories?" offers a balanced introduction to the debate. He argues that part of the problem arises from the indiscriminate use of the word narrative. If everything is a narrative, it is of course not very useful to say that video games also can be described as such. Juul also gives three reasons for why it is easy to confuse narratives with video games:

1   The player can tell stories of a game session.

2   Many video games contain narrative elements, and in many cases, the player may play to see a cut-scene or realise a narrative sequence.

3   Video games and narratives share some structural traits.[61]

But he argues that we should resist the temptation of confusing the two forms, because it is impossible to translate video games into stories and vice versa.[62] He also discusses how understanding narrative as simply a re-telling of events can be misleading, and that the experience of playing a game is very different from that of reading a story.

Ludologists have found a wide variety of reasons why subsuming video games under the headline of narrative is a bad idea; the most damning is that the approach can lead us to overlook the "intrinsic properties" of video games. The Finnish theorist Markku Eskelinen has taken over Frasca's less confrontational stance, and is at the vanguard of ludology's most radical anti-narrative stance. As he forcefully puts it:

> The old and new game components, their dynamic combination and distribution, the registers, the necessary manipulation of temporal, causal, spatial and functional relations and properties not to mention the rules and the goals and the lack of audience should suffice to set games and the gaming situation apart from narrative and drama, and to annihilate for good the discussion of computer games as stories, narratives or cinema.[63]

But the extremity of such a stance has further stoked the debate. The idea that games are first and foremost games—an argument bordering on the tautological— can be taken to mean that the formal properties of video games would thus be more important, more intrinsic, than the stories in the games (or the graphics, or the social activity that games promote). The debate has raged on for the last several years, where ludologists have attacked the supposed colonization of the new field of game studies from "alien" disciplines such as literature. Controversy is sometimes good, and from a pragmatic perspective we can say that this discussion has helped bring the study of video games into the spotlight.[64]

The debate continues amongst game scholars. Way back in 2003, the first DIGRA (Digital Games Research Association) conference included quite a handful of papers in topics related to video games and narrative; several presenters felt the need to position themselves in relation to ludology before starting their talks. It also included Gonzalo Frasca's paper, "Ludologists love stories too: notes from a debate that never took place," where he makes a defense of ludology and rejects the most extreme critiques by arguing that ludology's *raison d'être* is not at all to reject stories, but to focus on games. Two years later, at the next DIGRA conference, it was clear that Frasca's paper had not been the final word, as the discussion continued in a slightly altered form: the proponents or ludology were identified as "essentialists" while the importance of studying games as situated practices was now the preferred alternative.

Whereas ludologists have in the early days had difficulties pointing to the actual "enemy," many literary theorists have criticized the root of ludology, where stories are "just uninteresting ornaments or gift wrappings to games, and laying any emphasis on studying these kinds of marketing tools is just a waste of time and energy."[65] Scholars like Marie Laure Ryan, and later Julian Kücklich,[66] see ludology as a threat to the fruitful application of narrative concepts to the study of video games:

> Computer games functions as what Kendall Walton would call a "prop in a game of make-believe." It may not be the *raison d'être* of computer games, but it plays such an important role as a stimulant for the imagination that many recent computer games use lengthy film clips, which interrupt the game, to immerse the player in the game world.[67]

Paradoxically, certain ludologists have come to agree with the importance of stories. Juul, for example, has moved from his earlier radical position about the irrelevance of stories in relation to video games.

> On a formal level, games are *themable*, meaning that a set of rules can be assigned a new fictional world without modifying the rules. A game can always be changed from one setting to another; the gun can become a green rectangle, the players can control wooden figures rather than humanoid characters. But on an experiential level, fiction *matters* in games, and it is important to remember the duality of the formal and the experiential perspective on fiction in games.[68]

So even though fiction in video games is dependent on rules (and despite the fact that game rules can be discussed without referring to fiction), narrative remains an important part of the player's experience. Most ludologists have moved on but the debate is still heated; and it seems many concepts get mixed up in the heat of the theoretical battle, so that both sides talk about different things as if they were the same: a strict conception of narrative as fixed sequence of events (ludologists) and fiction in general (their "enemies"). It remains to be seen if ludology will continue to be defined negatively, that is, in opposition to narratology, instead of as a general term to apply to the study of video games in themselves as Frasca and other promoters originally intended. Beyond the squabbles, we should recognize that the ludology-narratology wars are a symptom of the struggle to define the new discipline of game studies, beyond the dominant paradigms—the hypertextual (Landow, 1992) and the cinematic (Manovich, 2001)—of the last two decades.

Interaction versus narrative

A game has to be interactive. This is the greatest innovation of video games, but also a great burden. So if the point of video games is that players do things (gameplay), the fact that in some video games they are forced to "sit and watch" (for example cut-scenes) is seen by some designers and others as an unwelcome invasion. And if designers are able to truly integrate stories into the game, how can narratives ever be fully engaging if they always have to offer the player the possibility of winning? And how can artificial intelligences ever become interesting fictional characters? All these questions are derived from the ongoing debate of interaction versus narrative.[69]

One solution to this problem is to conceive of video games as symbolic dramas, as Janet Murray does:

> In games, therefore, we have *a chance to* enact our most basic relationship to the world—our desire to prevail over adversity, to survive our inevitable defeats, to shape our environment, to master complexity, and to make our lives fit together like the pieces of a jigsaw puzzle. Each move in a game is *like* a plot event in one of these simple but compelling stories. *Like* the religious ceremonies of passage by which we mark birth, coming of age, marriage and death, games are ritual actions allowing us to *symbolically* enact the patterns that give meaning to our lives.[70] (italics are ours)

This comes after a discussion of the game *Myst*, where she wonders why the winning ending of the game (where you liberate the father) is less satisfying dramatically than the losing ending (where you liberate one of the evil brothers and are in turn imprisoned yourself). The question is if narrative satisfaction and game satisfaction are intrinsically opposed. This problem is thus translated to a different plane, as Murray does not answer the question, which would mean considering video games and stories at a same fundamental level. Instead she takes it to an abstract level, which might explain why we enjoy participating in the conflicts, posed by video games, but doesn't tell us much about how stories actually work *within* them. We could also say that it seems much easier to create symbolic dramas than real interactive stories (at plot level), since anything can be read as a symbolic drama. Even *Tetris*, *after all*, has "clear dramatic content."[71]

An alternative is Atkins's analysis of video games that effectively integrate narrative and gameplay. *More than a Game* is dedicated to four video games that he sees "as having a central narrative impetus, that develop story over time, rather than simply repeat with minimal difference in a move from level to level of increasing excess."[72] The chosen games are *Tomb Raider*, *Half-Life*, *Close Combat* and *SimCity*, which seem like strange choices as there are no adventure or role-playing video games among them, the two sub-genres with stronger narrative component.[73] Each of the four games is a good example of a different strategy to effectively integrate narrative and gameplay: *Tomb Raider* is a model of open-endedness and the use of quests. *Half-Life* employs innovative themes and perspective. *Close Combat* takes the concept of realism to new heights, and *SimCity*'s simulation rules can be read narratively, which means that game rules can have ideological implications. The book concludes with a discussion on the status of video games as a fictional form.

The narrative vs. interactivity debate also shows up in most video game design textbooks, although the authors might not identify it as such.[74] Richard Rouse, for example, in his textbook *Game Design: Theory and Practice* proposes to differentiate between the storytelling that occurs:

- out of game—through cut-scenes, mission briefings, documents "found" by the player, and the like;

- in-game: this is the most desirable kind, storytelling occurs through interaction with the game-world, through non playing characters' behavior, dialogue, etc.;

- external materials: such as a game manual or a website.[75]

Rouse argues that all out of game storytelling should be avoided, as it goes against the interactive experience of gaming. Rouse uses examples from bad cut-scenes (like in the game *Tekken*) to justify why they should always be avoided (or the player should be able to skip them), and to argue that they very often are not integrated into the game.[76] In-game storytelling is the preferable option, which Rouse describes as *showing*, compared to the *telling* that occurs with out-of-game narrative. In-game storytelling is achieved, for example, by creating a believable world that gives a context to the plot, and by non-player-characters who have personalities. *Deus-Ex* is a good example of how to achieve both narrative and interaction with its successful in-game storytelling, but the gameplay also offers the choice of acting in a violent or more pacifist way, so that players can create different stories as they go. "For in-game storytelling, players get to experience the story themselves instead of being told it second-hand." It also maintains the player's immersion in the game-world.[77]

Rouse, however, is not alone in proposing a way to use "storytelling" to thematize the rules in a game. All of the designers discussed offer their own techniques, which suggests that fiction might actually have a very important function in video games, as argued also by several theorists.[78] This connection is thoroughly explored by Jesper Juul, who is also interested in examples of "clashes" between rules and fiction, his term for the interesting combinations of these elements in video games where their differences are revealed. For example:

> In the Game of *Grand Theft Auto 3*, a blue arrow is placed over whatever object or target the player has to reach in a mission. Even though the game has been lauded for its elaborate world and detailed environments, the blue arrow clearly points to the *rules* of the game. This is at odds with a certain mode of thought that claims that a good game should never remind the player that he/she is playing a game. I claim that the player is always aware that the game is a game, and that this is part of the reason why we can accept incoherence in game worlds.[79]

Juul argues that the fictional world is also needed in video games in order for players to infer the rules (to let them know which repertoire applies)—which, in "good" games anyway, are hidden from immediate perception.[80] This compromise is a step forward from early ludological positions, and certainly shows a more effective way of reconciling literary theory and video games.

Perhaps further reconciliation is possible by re-examining our terminology. The idea that narrative and interactivity oppose each other springs from a definition of narrative as linear storytelling; while this is true in many instances, it is not very interesting, as Jonas Heide Smith remarks. There are other forms of narrative than the traditional sequence, and especially interesting possibilities have bloomed recently with the growth of multiplayer online games. We might even speculate that this argument will soon be a thing of the past, as we move past the dominant influence of single-player games. As we move forward, we might want to look at how narratives are produced in multiplayer environments, for example, where the parameters of the story are not all fixed by a designer and where new kinds of experiences arise due to the impredictability of the behaviour of the other players.[81]

In this same spirit, Henry Jenkins argues that games tell stories in their own unique way, and their narratives are not equivalent to a simplistic idea of linear story such as we find in films or novels.[82] Jenkins proposes, instead, that game stories are truly *spatial* and *environmental*. Spatial stories are related to those works of literature that tell a hero's odyssey, or travel narratives, in the case of computer games the travelling wouldn't only be done by the characters, but by the player. Environmental stories are related to the literature genres that focus on the depiction of worlds, such as fantasy or science fiction, in computer games, it is the player that does the exploring. In order to construct a world that tells a story, game designers are similar to creators of amusement park rides; they are not storytellers, but architects of narrative. Accordingly, Jenkins describes four ways in which narrative can appear in games:

- *Evoked narratives*: when video games reproduce a world that is known to players through other works of fiction, so that games are part of an encompassing system of meanings. For example, the game *Blade Runner* reproduces the world of the film and the novel, so that players will be able to "live out" the stories that existed in their imagination, just by visiting that world.

- *Enacted narratives*: where, as Jenkins puts it, "the story itself may be structured around the character's movement through space and the features of the environment may retard or accelerate that plot trajectory." This category encompasses the spatial and environmental stories mentioned above. These are typically not appreciated by literary scholars, as they privilege spatial exploration over plot development. This form is very well suited to video games, as a designer can create the world that the player will have to traverse and conquer.

- *Embedded narratives*: when "the game space becomes a memory palace whose contents must be deciphered as the player tries to reconstruct the plot." The classical embedded narrative would be a detective story, such as in adventure games, where players encounter a world of clues that have to be deciphered in order to find out about the story that has already happened. A good example of this is *Myst*.

- *Emergent narratives*: when "game spaces are designed to be rich with narrative potential, enabling the story-constructing activity of players." We have seen Juul's description of these narratives earlier, in the Mechanics section; both Juul and Heide Smith have called this object-oriented narration (see above), where the game space is filled with objects with their own behaviours, so that the player interaction creates unique combinations that feel significant. Henry Jenkins gives the example of *The Sims*, which allows the players to create their own stories.[83]

These four kinds of narratives don't address many of the elements discussed earlier, such as the sequential storytelling we find in quests, or other literary ingredients such as characterization. However, they might help move us beyond the frozen narrative versus interactivity discussion. Because these categories highlight other qualities of videogame stories, such as their spatial component and provide a way to introduce contextual elements such as in the evoked narratives category, they offer a different and fruitful use of literary theory in relation to video games.

The interactive storytelling paradigm: in search of quality

During the 1990s the theory of the "interactive narrative" had a certain prominence. It refers not to video games, nor hypertext (or other forms of digital literature), but rather to a sort of roleplaying where the computer can anticipate the player's reactions and give an illusion of total interactivity. It is considered an ideal form of digital storytelling, deeply engaging and immersive. Books have been written and conferences convened on the subject, usually dealing with the problems inherent to automatic generation of stories or how to improve artificial intelligence. Proponents of the "interactive narrative" frown upon the "game" label, as it for fear it would make their project less worthy of literary attention. This is represented for example by Janet Murray, who even though identifying video games as the greatest commercial success and creative effort in digital story-telling, has the following caveat: "The narrative content of these games is thin, and is often imported from other media or supplied by sketchy and stereotypical characters."[84]

Meanwhile, however, Murray's *Hamlet on the Holodeck* is an enthusiastic defense of the computer as the new storytelling medium, because of the way its four essential defining properties facilitate digital narration:

> . . . which separately and collectively make it a powerful vehicle for literary creation. Digital environments are *procedural, participatory, spatial and encyclopedic.* The first two properties make up most of what we mean by the vaguely used word interactive; the remaining two properties help to make digital creations seem as explorable and extensive as the actual world, making up much of what we mean when we say that cyberspace is *immersive.*[85] (our emphasis)

The *procedural* property refers to the computer's ability to execute rules in succession and thus generate behaviors; for Murray the computer character, Eliza, created by Joseph Weizenbaum in 1966 is a good example of how the procedural property can produce the illusion of a "living person." Eliza was able to converse with humans as if she was a psychologist that always turns your sentences against you For example, if you typed: "I am worried," the program would respond "what are you worried about?"

The second property, *participatory*, refers to the fact that we can influence the production of behavior when interacting with a computer; an example is the textual adventure game *Zork*, where the program would respond to the textual input of the player and produce lines of text that described her process in the game and thus created a story. Computers are also *spatial*, that is, able to represent naviga-ble space; this can be seen everywhere from graphic-based games such as *Pong* and *Pac-Man*, as well as well as the navigable "movie map" of Aspen, Colorado, made in 1978 by Nicholas Negroponte's group at MIT, plus the aforementioned textual spaces such as *Zork*. Finally, the *encyclopedic* property points to the storage capacity of computers, whose memories can keep enormous amounts of information and allow us to interact with information-rich environments from fan websites to MUDs to enormous games like *SimCity* and *Civilization*. Without going into a detailed discussion of the four properties, it is not hard to see that video games turn out to perfectly embody each of them, and thus, it could be argued, the perfect vehicle for digital storytelling.

Murray is inspired by the Holodeck, the entertainment system of the Star Trek universe. The Holodeck is a most immersive entertainment environment, a virtual reality machine that makes stories come to life and lets "readers"—this case the ship's crew—participate as actors in completely realistic virtual environments that make use of all five of the participant's senses. An example Murray gives is that of the female starship captain in the series *Star Trek: Voyager* who is entertained with a story inspired by *Jane Eyre*, in which she plays a nineteenth-century governess and nearly falls in love—in "real" life—with the virtual hero.[86]

Following the promise of the holodeck, Murray's dream is that of a *cyberbard*—a Homer or Shakespeare of the future, able to bend the computer to more artistic uses than those we know today. Murray's book is inspiring, filled with rich personal anecdotes about new media experiences, even though it also suffers from excessive utopianism; the book overstates the interest that interactive narrative might hold for average audiences, and projects the idea of the romantic author into the future. Janet Murray's inspiration was an earlier book by Brenda Laurel, *Computer as Theatre*, from 1991, which is about interface design and drama, although it also deals with video games and offers a dramatic model for computer-human interaction. She chooses *Spacewar*, to begin the book by explaining how our perception of the computer has shifted from considering it a powerful calculator to our current emphasis on its representational power. Her opinion of video games, however, regardless of their technological advancements, is not very positive: "I find most video games to be boring, frustrating and 'obstructionist' in the sense that they require players to solve puzzles primarily for the purpose of extending the duration of game play."[87]

Murray offers some guidelines for creating engaging interactive storytelling. To begin with, formulaic storytelling could make use of the same plots all stories are made of, combined in an interesting way that possibly involves powerful artificial intelligence.[88] Murray suggests that procedural storytelling could be similar to ancient oral storytelling (the bardic system), although how this inspiration can be used to combine the plots is not entirely clear. She also stresses the importance of using well-known genres (like mystery or science-fiction) in order to exploit knowledge that the user already has—similar to the "repertoire" concept of reader response theory.

Vladimir Propp's "morphology of the folktale" can be another tool to create digital stories. His system, created in 1928, describes how Russian folktales can be analyzed by isolating small narrative units that are combined in different ways but essentially repeat themselves in many tales (such as the hero leaves home or the hero gets a present). Murray argues that interactive narrative would benefit from reproducing his formulaic system of story elements, symbols and character functions. According to Murray, Propp's algorithm is much more complex than "most electronic computer games currently on the market," which are limited to two or three themes such as fight bad guy, solve puzzle, die. Without considering the economic reasons behind this simplicity, she thinks it is a problem that video games "do not allow substitution of thematic plot elements" that would require much more ambitious programming.[89]

The dubious opinions these scholars hold of video games are in part because they judge these games using the quality standards of other media, such as movies or print novels. They suggest that the simplicity of game narratives can be overcome in different ways, involving everything from complex artificial intelligence or more detailed fictional worlds. Mark J.P. Wolf, another author very worried about the quality of video games, seems to equate the emotional complexity of a player's experience with the level of detail in the games' visual imagery. He writes, for example, that *Myst* is a "turning point in the development of the video game's diegetic world," because of the light effects, that create a rich world, and which inspire "contemplative moods" in the player.[90]

But these criticisms might be more effective if video games were considered independently of other media, which appears easier now than it did in the 1990s when these works were written and the digital world was a myriad of different objects and theories. As the digital medium matures, computer games are now an established object of study and have been described extensively in their essential properties, so that maybe now the time is ripe for the kind of judgment of value that the proponents of interactive narrative attempted a bit too early.

The paradigm of the interactive narrative, however, does have a lot to offer our study of video games. In the relentless search for quality advocated by Murray and Laurel and others—in their insistence on the ways that narrative can be adapted to new technologies, we have to admire their enthusiasm for the possibilities of the new medium and their attempt at describing what is it with interactivity that people desire it so much.

The fictional status of video games

From the entire discussion above, it seems clear that fiction in video games does not work according to the same parameters as it does in representational media; it should also be clear that we cannot just apply literary theories wholesale to the study or design of video games without considering their specific properties. A variety of authors have begun to move beyond the quagmire of narrative, and instead have focused on what kinds of fictions video games are, and how we could delimit their fictional properties.

A foundational theoretical premise for these scholars is to decide what the gameworld is. Is the gameworld a prop for the player's imagination (in Walton's sense), or is the world as a virtual object or stage for the game to occur on? In Marie Laure Ryan's words:

> In an abstract sense, of course, most if not all games create a "game-world," or self-enclosed playing space, and the passion that the player brings to the game may be regarded as immersion in this game-world. But I would like to draw a distinction between "world" as a set of rules and tokens, and "world" as imaginary space, furnished with individuated objects. The pieces of a chess game may be labeled king, queen, bishop, or knight, but chess players do not relate to them as fictional persons, nor do they imagine a royal court, a castle, an army, and a war between rival kingdoms.[91]

One of the consequences of such a distinction is that the world as we imagine it in our head is not equivalent to the visual appearance of the virtual world of the game. Thus, we should consider the whole world experience and not just what has been called the "diegetic representation" of a world by authors like Wolf, which is just the "world on screen."[92] For Wolf, this is different from "extradiegetic narration," that is, how video games point to other diegetic worlds (television shows, movies, novels and the like). Wolf's examples of extradiegetic narration are of intro movies, cut-scenes, the intro screens and game manuals. However, the meta level of genre references not only points to stories in other media, they also call up the player's game *repertoire*[93]—as we saw using reader response theory—so that she can also infer how the world of that game will work. In other words, the world allows us to make inferences about the rules.

Salen and Zimmerman's concept of the "narrative descriptor" is a good example of these elements beyond the game. Narrative descriptors are "representations, which means that they are depictions of one or more aspects of the game world."[94] These can be graphics on the side of the arcade cabinet, manuals, soundtracks, cutscenes, etc. Let us for example look at their description of the action in *Asteroids*, by which players will be able to infer much about interaction and gameplay:

> Shoot the asteroids while avoiding collisions with them. Occasionally a flying saucer will appear and attempt to shoot you down with guided missiles. Destroy it or the missiles for more points.[95]

These few sentences remind us not only of a genre that is related to other media— "science fiction"—but also of typical video game conventions—in this case the reward system. Video game conventions, for example the fact of having several "lives," are very important for the gaming experience even if they wouldn't make sense in a traditional narration. Imagine an account of *Romeo and Juliet* where Romeo was allowed to start all over again after discovering his lover dead, as many times as it took for them to be together and live happy ever after. We would perceive this not only as incoherent, but also as a total destruction of the play's dramatic effect. Jesper Juul for one, argues that the incoherence and instability of video game fictions does not mean that these fictions are of lesser quality than those found in other media; rather, they just need to be considered from their own perspective:

> The worlds that video games project are often ontologically unstable, but the rules of video games are very ontologically stable. While we may not be able to explain *why* Mario reappears in *Donkey Kong*, we always know for certain how many lives we have left. That the majority of fictional game worlds are incoherent does not mean that video games are dysfunctional providers of fiction, but rather that they project fictional worlds in their own flickering, provisional, and optional way. Of all cultural forms that project fictional worlds, video games are probably unique in that it is meaningful to engage with a game while refusing to imagine the world that the game projects—the rules of a game are mostly sufficient to keep the player's interest.[96]

In a remarkable conjunction of ideas, authors from Henry Jenkins to Julian Kücklich have proposed literary approaches to the study of video games based on their fictionality, and not on their narrative qualities,[97] which takes us out of the cul de sac of the narratology-ludology debate. Perhaps this means the field is moving towards more stimulating discussions that also take into account more contemporary literary theory. However, postmodern literary theory has not been a part of the debate so far, and maybe it never will be.[98] Stories in computer games are still in their infancy, and the heavily loaded post-modernist theories about deconstruction or other dispersions of the text wouldn't be of much help at this stage.

Let us so return to the question we posed at the beginning of the chapter: are video games stories? Yes, we would answer. Many video games are stories, as well as games. Some games are more narrative than others, but even the most abstract usually include the sketched elements of a fictional world. And we need to take into account the narrative elements of a videogame if we are to fully understand the medium and how player interaction is shaped.

9 SERIOUS GAMES—WHEN ENTERTAINMENT IS NOT ENOUGH

ADVERTAINMENT/POLITICAL GAMES/TRADITIONAL GAMES FOR SERIOUS
PURPOSES/CATEGORIZING EDUCATIONAL COMPUTER GAMES/THE RATIONALE
BEHIND EDUTAINMENT/THE INSTRUCTIONAL APPROACH TO EDUTAINMENT/
THE MODERN APPROACH TO THE EDUCATIONAL USE OF COMPUTER GAMES/
THE EDUCATIONAL EFFECTIVENESS OF VIDEO GAMES/FINAL REMARKS

Can you name the seven wonders of the ancient world? If so, perhaps you are a trivia buff, or a world traveler. Or perhaps you are among the millions of people who have played *Civilization*, leading an entire people to glory and world domination. In this groundbreaking game, the player must develop a civilization of her choice, starting anywhere from a band of early American settlers to a modern nation spanning entire continents. Along the way, the player must absorb a wide range of historical knowledge while combining an understanding of geography, economics, and cultural history to adapt and prosper.

This chapter deals with one of the most nebulous and contested issues in the game world: the value of it all. We know that games serve, first and foremost, to entertain. As we contemplate the moneymaking juggernaut that is the gaming industry, it would be foolish to argue that anything is as important—read: profitable—as entertainment, although the other uses of games are growing these years. But beyond fun, what do players take away from video games? Not on a cultural level, but in terms of getting influenced on an individual level. Do players learn from video games, and if so, what do they learn? Is a video game capable of imprinting the Nike logo on a player's retina like in the ambitious Nike soccer game *Secret Tournament* developed for the World Cup in 2002? In the game you step into the shoes of world-class soccer players and have to survive a two a side soccer game staged in a cage. Could players be persuaded to join a political organization that advocated its message through video games like in the game *Ethnic Cleansing* where Jews, Mexicans and other ethnicities are offered as the only true enemies in an otherwise classical style first-person shooter game? However distasteful, the message is clear, and converting impressionable teenagers to a racist agenda is the clear goal. Can players learn about European history by playing *Europa Universalis* where through trade, diplomacy, colonization and war you have to carve out a place for your medieval nation?

Above are only a few of the titles and basic questions gathered under the umbrella term **serious games**. The term serious games was coined by the American academic Clark Abt in 1968, and was the title of his influential book.[1] Today, the label refers to a broad swathe of video games produced, marketed, or used for purposes other than pure entertainment; these include, but are not limited to, educational computer games, **edutainment** and advertainment (terms we'll define below), and also health games and political games. As we'll see, serious games span a wide area, and the games in question need not be originally conceived as "serious." In theory, any video game can be perceived as a serious game depending on its actual use and the player's perception of the game experience.

The breadth of what constitutes a serious game entails that very different research traditions and approaches converge on this topic. Early examples of research interest in serious video games are the work of psychologist Patricia Greenfield (1984) with her book *Mind and Media* that deal with the influence of among other things how computer games influence individuals' development; Thomas Malone (1980; 1987a; 1987b) with his work on motivation, education and video games; and psychologists Geoffrey and Elizabeth Loftus with *Mind at Play* (1983) on the cognitive learning gains from video games. In recent years interest has increased, with academic contributions from the fields of literacy with the work of James Paul Gee (2003) on basic learning principles of mainstream entertainment games, and socio-cultural theory by Kurt Squire (2004a) on the implications of actually using mainstream entertainment games in real classrooms. But in general it has been the discipline of education that has tried to understand educational use of games for example the work of Angela McFarlane *et al.* (2002), Marc Prensky (2001), John Kirriemuir (2002) and Simon Egenfeldt-Nielsen (2005).[2]

Before turning to educational games that dominate the field of serious games, it is worth examining other upcoming serious games areas like advertainment and political games. The research on these types of games is still very limited but this is changing.

ADVERTAINMENT

Advertainment is a fusion of advertising and entertainment, and refers to video games used for marketing purposes. Advertainment has grown considerably since its origins in the mid-1990s, led by an increasing interest from major companies around the world. Such growth has been facilitated by an abundance of new software, including Shockwave, Flash and Director, which require much less technical knowledge than earlier gaming tools that was mostly built in-house by game companies with limited documentation. The World Wide Web now means that anyone with a web page can "publish" a game, thus circumventing the traditional channels for reaching the game audience. Global brands in particular have been eager to produce advertainment titles, to attract traffic to their websites and increase brand awareness: a small sampling of recent games includes *The Beast*, developed for the Steven Spielberg movie *AI*, *Nokia Game* a returning game for Nokia, *Nike Goooal* for Nike, and *Stolichnaya* produced for the vodka company of the same name.

Companies like these especially appreciate the active participation required to play these games; while playing, we are relentlessly exposed to the companies' products—which are incorporated into the gameplay in more or less creative ways. While playing an advertainment title, in other words, we are literally helping to build the company's brand in our own and others' consciousness.[3] Gardner stresses the difference between integral games and giveaway games, which refers to a classic problem in using video games for serious purposes. Some serious games will not really integrate the message they want to get across with the gameplay. These are called the *giveaways* whereas the *integral games* integrate the message in the gameplay. Integral games are usually more difficult and expensive to develop, but also result in a stronger impression and user experience.

There is limited research into advertainment but it is considered one of the best means to draw visitors to web sites. And by making these interactive commercials fun for the consumer, these games facilitate exposure to the brand that can last a lot longer than a typical commercial. The global companies with leading online presence—like Lego, Nike, Disney, and Coca-Cola—continue to harness the potential of video games because they seem to work. Companies often keep the results to themselves but Toyota's *Adrenaline* racing game from 2000 was found to increase brand awareness considerably among consumers. According to company's own survey Toyota went from a number six ranking among major car brands to number two a mere three months after game launch.[4] Full-fledged video games are also increasingly considered a medium for mainstream advertising. And not just to reach reclusive adolescent boys but increasingly as a more mainstream advertising tool.

As video games reach a broader audience, product placement becomes a more appealing option for a wider variety of global brands. Product placement differs significantly from traditional advertainment games as product placements can in principle be implemented in any computer game, and not a specifically developed game as such. Though product placement began in racing and other sports games, as well as games that featured virtual worlds, today we encounter product placement in virtually any genre. We see product placement even in the abstract *Super Monkey Ball*, a game, which bears no resemblance to the world, we live in. The player picks up bananas labeled with the Dole brand name. The launch of *Super Monkey Ball* became part of a cross promotion with Dole to introduce a "luxury banana" in Japan.

Although a game may seem to feature product placement, that need not, of course, be the case. To increase realism, many video games try to model the game environment as closely as possible to the real world, leading to incidental product placement. Still, the last five years have seen an increased amount of actual product placement where companies are paying game publishers rather than the other way around. Product placement is also beginning to mature, as new companies now specialize in product placement and offer what they refer to as "dynamic implementation" of an ad product, which can be inserted and continuously updated across a number of titles that all have online access.[5]

Most advertainment is simply an extended version of product placement. However, sometimes advertainment *does* try to actually use video games to create a different advertising experience. One example is the home design game for high schools by the organization for interior architects. The intention behind this game was to bring new, talented people into the business by letting students experience what it is like to work as an interior architect. This provides a truly different user experience from other commercials by bringing users into the actual product, and letting them become part of it. The same is the case in the area of political games, where organizations attempt to bring users closer to their agenda, and participate in universes reflecting their world view.

POLITICAL GAMES

Political games are generally more ambitious in their game design than the advertainment titles we saw above, but also aim to affect the player through (more or less) hidden messages.[6] Some significant early attempts of constructing video games with a political agenda were *Nuclear War*, *Balance of Power*, *Hidden Agenda*, and the neo-Nazi game *Purging Germany*. All of these games tried to set a political agenda, and could in some sense be called educational; however their goals were quite special. Some served more as comic strips or propaganda leaflets than real games. They wanted to present a specific message, and this message had strong political undertones. In

Nuclear War, for example, the inevitable destructive consequences of nuclear war were caricatured in "Spitting Image" style, which is a cartoonist's caricature of world leaders. The subversive use of video games has always been present within game culture, but became less of a factor as the industry matured commercially during the 1990s.

However, political games have made a comeback in gaming subculture since the terrorist attacks on September 11, 2001. Many of these games have paralleled the fight on terrorism, and serve as part of an ideological crusade against Osama Bin Laden in particular. The subgenre is still emerging and research is quite limited, although news articles have hailed political games as "the next big thing," especially in connection with the 2004 U.S. presidential election.[7] Some recent well-known examples of using video games for political agitation are: *September 12th*, *Ethnic Cleansing*, *Michael Jackson Baby Game*, *Kaboom Kabul*, and *The Howard Dean Game for Iowa*.

September 12th, serves as a good example of this recent crop. In this simple, single-screen game, the player overlooks a village filled with both terrorists and civilians. The player's only option is to fire missiles to kill the terrorists or do nothing; the firing of the missile will inevitably result in civilian casualties. The deaths of innocent victims will draw mourners, who will also be drawn towards terrorism; the player watches as almost the entire village population become terrorists. The player cannot win the game, and does not get any points. All he can do is observe, and become more frustrated in his powerlessness. Circulated on the web in 2003 by Gonzalo Frasca, developer of the game and game researcher, *September 12th* is barely a game, but its criticism of the war on terror is clear.

One of the most discussed examples of political games is *Special Force*. Developed in 2003 by Hezbollah, the political party, social institution and/or terrorist group based in Lebanon depending on your source and outlook on the world, the player is set in the middle of the resistance against Israel in southern Lebanon. The goal—hinted at by the website's claim that the game includes "all that an anxious persons dreams of in order to participate in facing the Zionist enemy"—is to influence public opinion against the Israeli occupation.

These examples fit the informal definition of political games presented by Karlsson who writes that a political game

> . . . wants to communicate a specific message or perception of the world. Play becomes secondary. This does not mean that the gameplay necessarily lacks in any way. America's Army is hugely popular because of excellent gameplay, but play is still instrumental as regards to the U.S. Army's overriding goal.[8]

The game Karlsson refers to is one of the most successful efforts at political gaming, although some will deny its political connotations. Available free on its own homepage, it is explicitly offered as a promotional tool to "inspire" young men and women to join the U.S. army. However, its popularity has been a huge surprise for many, and some speculate partly in jest that without the game the United States would not have been able to continue the war in Iraq due to the lack of recruits.

Political games often overlap with the category usually referred to as news-gaming. At www.newsgaming.com, for instance, game designers try to illustrate conflicts in the current public debate—like airport security—through video games. Most controversial is Kuma Reality Games that develops episodic games allowing players to "Play accurate re-creations of real war events weeks after they occur." Here, players are able to play recent newsworthy event like the Iraq invasion or the Afghan fighting on their computers while receiving news analyses and video material. The games are built up as a classical first-person shooter. A more subtle and serious attempt of developing episodic games about current news is the collaboration between Persuasive Games and the *New York Times*. The popularity of this broad category of political games implies that at least some gamers do not mind a heavy-handed message as long as its delivered with something they can play.

Having covered the smaller areas of serious games we turn to educational computer games that are the main driver of games with an agenda beyond entertainment. This area has a long history, but before turning to the educational use of computer games it is important to consider the kinship with traditional, non-electronic games.

TRADITIONAL GAMES FOR SERIOUS PURPOSES

The serious games "movement" was born in the late 1950s with non-electronic, pen-and-paper and board games, although the term serious games was coined later. By the 1970s educational games had exploded in popularity, and were becoming an important pedagogical tool, especially for teaching in American businesses and the military. Then and now, the games used in such settings have primarily been simulations—which as we saw in Chapter 4, aim at precisely replicating a real-world event, from landing a plane to implementing city taxes—rather than the more broader category of fictional games including action, adventure and strategy where the replication of the real world can be less strict. One of the first educational non-electronic games, for example, was Inter-Nation Simulation from 1958, used in high school social studies classes to teach about international relations. Here, players control one of up to seven hypothetical nations, and need to negotiate with the other, nations in order to solve problems ranging from minor international crises to nuclear war. Another simulation, this one aimed at eleven-year-olds, was *The Sumerian Game* from 1961, where players learned about economic factors in Mesopotamia around 3500 B.C.

Since these initial efforts, the creation and use of these non-electronic—or "traditional"—games has been relatively stable. They were always quite popular with some teachers but never became a core feature of the educational system. Along with their popularity, research into the educational use of these traditional games is now well established in its own right, with peer-reviewed journals, well-known researchers, and substantial research topics. Over the last fifty years, researchers have addressed topics from the learning outcome of traditional games to the practical barriers of using such games. The majority of these findings have a bearing on the educational use of *video* games. Below we present the most important implications, with brief discussions of the key topics relevant to video games: effectiveness, motivation, debriefing, and the influence of teachers and setting.[9]

The number of studies on the effectiveness of traditional games in education is quite high, spanning more than thirty years of research, and offers good directions. The findings so far suggest that games are a viable alternative to traditional teaching, and provide approximately the same learning outcome—that is, a student has the same chance of learning a piece of material using a game than he does through another way of learning. Games cannot be said to be *more* effective than other teaching forms, although most studies have offered evidence of better retention over time. Students tend to subjectively rate their learning outcome higher when they use games, and to prefer gaming to other teaching methods. Thus, for good or bad, even though we cannot objectively measure an increased learning outcome, students often *feel* they have learned more. Indeed, the preference of students for games fits well with the increased motivation consistently found when examining the educational use of games.[10]

The effectiveness of traditional games relies heavily on how exactly they are used in a teaching environment. Debriefing—the process of reflection after the game has finished—is especially important. Researchers have found that students can make wrong assumptions based on their game experiences.[11] Therefore debriefing is of paramount importance, as the teacher needs to take time to correct any mistakes, clarify misconceptions and expand on the game experiences.[12]

The role of teachers and the setting for educational games have caused a number of problems in these studies. The school setting—with its physical limits in terms of classroom size and logistical limits in terms of available time for teaching—is not very appropriate for using games. In addition, most teachers have little experience using games, and this jeopardizes the learning experience. The teacher's theories of learning—not to mention their opinions about the value of alternative teaching strategies—may also hinder the effectiveness of games.[13] As we can see, the research into traditional games has addressed some of the tough questions of the proper role of games in education. Such research shows no sign of abating, as the use of games in education continues to grow these years. And now, more and more of these educational games are electronic. As we turn to video games, the thirty years of research into traditional games offers interesting insights in relation to games, and these are useful when we engage with video games. Especially, in more recent research on the educational use of computer games that challenge the dominance of edutainment, we see that a lot of the above ideas from traditional games make a comeback.

It is important to understand that there are different kinds of educational computer games, although the term edutainment is usually used as an all-encompassing term for educational computer games and the use of computer games for education.

CATEGORIZING EDUCATIONAL COMPUTER GAMES

An important distinction when determining the educational use of video games is the different game titles used. The first, most obvious category is commercial educational video games, often known as edutainment. Edutainment focuses on teaching the player certain specific skills: mostly algebra, spelling, problem solving, and other basic skills. Edutainment titles include *Pajama Sam*, *Castle of Dr. Brain* and *Mathblaster*. In *Mathblaster*, the player must shoot down the right answer to an arithmetical problem to progress in the game; with any luck, the player hopefully learns basic math along the way. Many of the edutainment games are consciously devised to mirror "normal" video games, in order to make them more appealing. However, usually it is a quite dated gameplay and graphics that are implemented. Edutainment titles have a strong educational component but often do not reflect the strong engagement present in commercial titles.[14]

The second category comprises commercial entertainment titles used fairly haphazardly for education. These rarely focus exclusively on one topic and on basic skills. Commercial entertainment video games in this category include *SimCity* and *Civilization*, titles used by several schools. In the game *SimCity* exemplary for commercial games with educational potential you have to plan and run a small city developing it from a hole in the ground to a busting metropolis. In order to build a metropolis you have to understand a lot of the basic principles of urban planning like zoning, sewage, land prices, pollution, crime and unemployment. The educational goals of commercial video games are mostly indirect rather than direct, goals that can lead to a skewed focus in the learning process. However, their strength is that the motivational part is well documented through success on the commercial entertainment market. When commercial games like SimCity get it right they are an unbeatable educational experience.

The third category is research-based educational video games; these often challenge the existing formula of edutainment (e.g. Hancock and Osterweil, 1996; Malone and Lepper, 1987a). Edutainment originating from research often presents new approaches and has strong documentation for learning outcomes. However, these titles often lack the budgets and technical quality to compete with the more commercial titles. They make a greater impact only if published on the commercial market with some modifications. Exemplary titles are *Oregon Trail, Logical Journey of the Zoombinis, Phoenix Quest* and *Global Conflicts: Palestine*. In *Global Conflicts: Palestine* you play a journalist arriving in Jerusalem. You have to write stories and in the process find sources, information and recognize different perspectives and agendas to get the right story. The research-based educational computer games are still far between but show that there is a way to combine to strength of commercial entertainment games with education without necessarily limiting oneself to edutainment. Even though we find different expressions of educational computer games, edutainment has come to dominate the area with a very particular approach, which we shall describe below as problematic and limiting.

THE RATIONALE BEHIND EDUTAINMENT

According to legend, founder of Electronic Arts Trip Hawkins in 1984, coined the term "edutainment," to refer to any electronic games that use entertainment in the service of education. The label was used with great success for the top-seller *Seven Cities of Gold* about the Spanish colonization of Latin America in the sixteenth century.

While edutainment in the public refers broadly to any electronic use of entertainment for educational purposes, it is manifested in a variety of ways depending on your learning approach. Historically, edutainment started out in the United States in the 1970s as a very fragmented field with different developers picking their own favorite theory from the major learning approaches (behaviorism, cognitivism and constructivism). Early on edutainment drew strongly on existing traditions within educational media, but it became even more marked in the early 1980s. By the 1980s, edutainment basically relied on the learning principles of behaviorism, articulated first by John Watson in 1919. Today, we still have edutainment titles that are similar to the ones in the 1970s and 1980s. The behaviorist approach cares less about the actual connection between the game and the learning experience; the game often simply serves as a reward for learning. This baggage strongly shapes the way video games are developed and used for education even today. So although edutainment does not have to be behaviorist it is often so today, which has increasingly led researchers of educational use of games to look at using commercial computer games. Here they rely on the lessons learned from non-electronic games and simulations, where for example debriefing is critical. Indeed the limited research on commercial computer games finds very similar results to the extensive research on traditional, non-electronic games discussed previously in this chapter.[15]

So while edutainment started as a serious attempt to create video games that could teach children various subjects it was quickly marred. The reliance on behaviorism resulted in games that relied heavily on simple game mechanics, quite traditional learning principles to the detriment of researchers and many parents.[16] Today edutainment tend to focus on simple game structures, which provide a limited learning experience for younger children because edutainment feed the player information, rather than encouraging curiosity and exploration.

We must also acknowledge that edutainment has, from the very start, primarily been driven by business interests. This pedagogically mostly unambitious perspective has arguably undermined the market by producing a long string of low-quality games that simply aren't very engaging to play.[17] The edutainment category also includes a number of titles with questionable educational content, developed by opportunists seeing a chance to capitalize on parents' hopes for such games. These are often found attached to a license like Disney of Garfield that have fielded some of the more spurious of many examples, as the games focus on the same basic games that offer little that is new in the way of teaching math and spelling that remain among the most popular topics.[18]

The formula settled on by must edutainment titles in the 1980s that are still with us today can be defined by the following characteristics:

- *Little intrinsic motivation*: edutainment relies on extrinsic motivation—the promise of rewards—rather than intrinsic motivation arising from the game activity per se. Extrinsic motivation is not related to the game but consists of arbitrary rewards, like getting points for completing a level; intrinsic motivation, on the other hand, might be a feeling of mastery from completing a level. It is considered more pedagogically valuable because research shows that this leads to stronger learning experiences (especially in Malone's research that we will discuss a bit later). Where intrinsic motivation is in short supply for edutainment, it is evident when we look at the educational use of commercial video games. Intrinsic motivation is also quite strong in the research-based educational computer games, although with large variations.

- *No integrated learning experience*: usually edutainment is unable to integrate the experience of playing with the experience of learning, so the latter is subordinated beneath the more palpable experience of play. The player will often concentrate on playing the game rather than learning from the game. This problem is most evident in entertainment computer games used for educational use, where the entertainment experiences are not necessarily closely related to any accidental learning contents, skills or competences. The research-based titles often excel in this area, as they are capable of finding unique game mechanics that work as significant learning activities.

- *Drill-and-practice learning*: the learning principles in edutainment are inspired by drill-and-practice thinking rather than understanding. Games encourage the player to memorize the answers—for example, that two plus two equals four—but don't necessary teach the underlying rules that make this true. Again, we will see that research-based games and entertainment computer games used in education rely on quite different learning principles. Here we find that discovery, exploration, problem solving and experience-based learning are much more appropriate for describing the game and learning experience.

- *Simple gameplay*: most edutainment titles contain simple gameplay, often from classic arcade titles or a simple adventure game with a world you can move around in. The simple gameplay can be effective, especially for younger and less avid game players. However, increasingly, we need to deliver more advanced and innovative game experiences to be able to keep educational games engaging and motivating compared to the rapid developing entertainment titles. Especially, entertainment computer games are of course quite strong when it comes to developing new formats.

- *No teacher presence*: edutainment hardly demands anything of teachers or parents; it assume that students can simply be put in front of a given game title, and through gameplay alone will learn the given content or skills. This is a very problematic assertion given recent research for example by Egenfeldt-Nielsen (2005) and Squire (2004a). In the research on educational use of *Civilization III* and *Europa Universalis II* in high schools the teacher is crucial to facilitating students' appreciation of key experiences in the game and expand these experiences beyond the game world.

It is a common problem in edutainment that the video games and the educational material used is completely separated. In the commercially successful edutainment title *Chefren's Pyramid* the player might read something about the pyramids, and then play a bit of *backgammon*. This hardly facilitates a meaningful learning experience. A way to overcome this would be for games to implicitly use educational material as part of the basic conflict (or goal) of the game, as suggested by Malone (1980). Or in technical terms, the game's victory conditions would require the desired learning outcome, so the player would have to utilize the desired knowledge in order to win. For instance, gaining geographical knowledge in *Civilization* is crucial to take full advantage of the map and the historical development of a certain region is beneficial in *Europa Univeralis II*. Whether you get this information before, during or after playing the game is not important. However, it is important that you will actually need educationally relevant contents, skills or attitudes to succeed in the game, because you will then find it relevant and meaningful while playing the game, and worth "holding" onto. However, often a fruitful connection between educational content and the basic game structure remains difficult to construct. The simple structure of video games limits the amount of material one can include and this material must be integrated with the core game activities. Otherwise the player risks only learning one thing, namely to play the game.

Consequently, the attitude among educators, researchers, and game developers towards edutainment titles is often one of deep skepticism. The game design, the learning principles, and the graphics are all criticized heavily by both children and parents.[19] Practically none of the current edutainment titles are built on research that verifies their educational benefits.

However, the ghettoized position of edutainment games may be changing. An understanding is emerging among developers, educators and researchers that to make successful edutainment games one may have to turn to be inspired more closely by the commercial games industry. The minimal success of edutainment titles over the last ten years implies that children are unlikely to be attracted to discount games. The game titles which dominate the entertainment games sales charts are not discount products, but rather state-of-the-art in all areas, from programming to visualizing to animating (not to mention marketing!).[20]

THE INSTRUCTIONAL APPROACH TO EDUTAINMENT

The principles of behaviorism continue to influence edutainment, but other theories are influential concerning educational computer games. The growing importance of cognitivism during the late 1980s supplemented with behaviorism leads to what we can refer to as the "instructional approach." This approach attempts to describe how video games can best affect the player and how to deal with various obstacles to learning. The main learning principles within the instructional approach come from the laws of exercise and effect developed within a behaviorist framework. The law of exercise says that repetition is crucial to learning something which is surely true for learning a number of basic skills like reading, writing and spelling. The law of effect states that we can strengthen a response by providing a reward.[21] These basic principles have been expanded within the field of cognitive theory, which has articulated a number of potential obstacles to learning—limits like *attention, processing speed, interfaces,* and *motivation.*

During the 1980s, the cognitive theorist Thomas Malone elaborates on the instructional approach, and stresses that to be effective the gameplay and educational content must be integrated. Malone identifies a number of factors relevant to designing educational video games, and especially stresses the need for intrinsic motivation in a game. In 1987, Malone and Mark Lepper (1987a, 1987b) write arguably the most influential papers in the research on educational video games. However, much of Malone's work does not have a lasting effect on the development of edutainment. They list the elements needed to achieve intrinsic motivation in a game, which is one of the shortcomings of edutainment, but crucial to achieve strong educational computer games that are comparable to entertainment computer games:

- *Fantasy*: the game activity can increase intrinsic motivation by using fantasies as a part of the game universe. All entertainment games rely heavily on building fantasies for players to explore and educational games should be similar rather than be abstract and distant games like finding the missing letters in a word and getting points for that. A fantasy can be internal or external to the game. In a missing letters game you can easily provide an external fantasy that you need to find the letter to free the princess. However, an internal fantasy is more motivating but it also requires that the fantasy is tied more closely to the actual gameplay and not merely an *ad hoc* story. This is almost impossible to accomplish in an abstract game.

- *Control*: the player gains the overall feeling of being the controlling party while playing. The sense of feeling in control is present in most entertainment games, and many fans of the bestseller *Grand Theft Auto* series describe the control and freedom as the defining element of the series. All games have a sense of control given their interactive nature, but the degree of control can vary widely. Basically, as Raph Koster (2004) would say, games are about verbs not nouns, things you can do, and many educational computer games are just way more limiting than their entertainment counterparts.[22]

- *Challenge*: the activity should be of the appropriate level of difficulty for the player to be pushed to the limit of his or her capacity. Here again we see that most entertainment games do this extraordinarily well, whereas many educational computer games have to rely on the lowest common denominator among players. They make it too easy (or sometimes too hard). Indeed, balancing a game is always a very hard assignment.

- *Curiosity*: the information in the game should be complex and unknown to encourage exploration and re-organization of the information. So games must always have more to show whether literally in the exploration of a visual universe, conversations or events in role-playing games or in strategy games' relationships between variables and the dynamics of the underlying system. Here entertainment games are also ahead of educational computer games as they provide more areas to explore and reconcile, whereas many educational computer games (especially edutainment) make the mistake of serving information well chewed and ordered to the player.

Over the years, the above principles served as guidelines to many researchers and some game designers. It seems, however, that although the contribution is important their focus is too narrow on the game structure itself. The principles leave little room for the social dynamics around the game and learning experience, which we will explore further a bit later in this chapter. Although later revisions of Malone and Lepper's work tried to integrate the collaboration around video games, the context around the game is arguably downplayed in this framework. The instructional approach still influences the majority of edutainment titles out there, although the principles are not applied to their fullest extent.

THE MODERN APPROACH TO THE EDUCATIONAL USE OF COMPUTER GAMES

The last decade's criticism of edutainment has largely emerged from constructionist circles. Constructivism is particularly critical of the industry's reliance on behaviorism and cognitive learning theory. Constructivist theorists stress different elements such as the player's freedom to explore the game universe and the process of constructing knowledge in a meaningful and personal way. For some constructionist thinkers, video games hold fantastic promise; they make it possible for the learners to approach a subject in an active way and construct their own representations. In an ideal game, constructivists argue, the learning experience of the students draws on different perspectives, gives rise to a variety of actions, and offers a fuller understanding of the given topic.

For these thinkers, the main focus is the actual construction process of knowledge facilitated by interaction with the game; as a consequence, constructivist-based research has focused on open-ended games, on students making their own simple games and on so-called microworlds. A microworld is a simulation of a system—anything from small universe with laws of physics to a city with basic urban planning actions -, which is simplified and constructed so that a player can work with the system's concrete objects. When players interact with objects in a video game, they are learning about the properties of these objects, their connections and applications. In a constructionist perspective, this is an optimal way to learn.[23]

From the behaviorist perspective, the challenge of educational video games is transmitting information from the video game to the player. The context of this information is irrelevant, and the transmission of content relies on conditioning and reinforcement (much like "drill-and-practice"). From a constructivist position, the transmission of information is not sufficient for a successful educational experience. Players must actively engage in a video game and construct their own knowledge using the artifacts of the game world.

Among the most noticeable early constructivist contributions within this field, the work by Yasmin Kafai remains central. In the mid-1990s, Kafai researched how to use the actual game design process as a new way for students to engage with a subject. Seymour Papert, often seen as the father of constructivism, inspired Kafai's work. Kafai envisioned children not just as players of games, but as the actual designers of these games hereby turning children into producers of knowledge and in a very concrete way let them play with knowledge.[24]

Today the socio-cultural approach is becoming a stronger alternative within the educational use of computer games, and is championed by James Paul Gee, David Williamson Schaffer and Kurt Squire in particular. In a socio-cultural perspective, video games are tools for constructing viable learning experiences. Games mediate discussion, reflection, and analysis. The video game experience is facilitated by the surrounding classroom culture and the student's identity. This approach is argued to be very useful for understanding video games that are surrounded by strong social networks, which facilitate the learning experience.[25] Here, the content of a video game is less significant than its way of initiating new explorations and journeys into knowledge.

Gee (2003) has given the strongest account of the area and presents five main areas of interest concerning video games for educational purposes. He does not see these as limited to school settings but as intrinsic qualities found in video games:

- *Semiotic domains*: like other activities in life, video games are a semiotic domain— a realm of signs and symbols—that one slowly learns to interpret. The player learns to make sense of and navigate through a video game, and in doing so is pointed to other interesting domains, like science and history.

- *Learning and identity*: when the student is involved with the material, video games give new opportunities for learning experiences. Namely, video games are quite good at creating agency and identification: they develop the player's sense of control and encourage the player to identify with other people. Both of these spark critical thinking and deepen the learning experience.

- *Situated meaning and learning*: video games are well suited for new forms of learning where the player is situated in the domain and understands it from the inside. Players can interact with the game world through probing, can choose different ways to learn, and can see a topic in its larger context.

- *Telling and doing*: games can amplify the important elements in an area to facilitate easier understanding, and represent subsets of domains enabling the player to practice in a safe environment with constant feedback. Games also lend themselves well to transferring between domains, so that you can apply facts you learned about astronomy in a video game to real-life stargazing. This is due to the fact that games are virtual worlds with meaningful, concrete and rich audiovisual learning experiences rather than abstract bits of concepts put together in a textbook.

- *Cultural models*: the content in games represents ways of perceiving the world, and uses a lot of information implicit in the game universes. This content also has bearing on other domains of life, and can be both good and bad depending on your values and norms.

Gee's contribution is currently one of the strongest, but also symptomatic of the area's broader problems: he does not engage with earlier research on traditional games, or with other findings within educational computer games research. This weakens his claims, and increases the fragmentation of the field.

Though each theory offers its own problems, the field of educational use of computer games has made great strides in the last two decades, and offers a host of engaging research. Let us now turn our attention to four of the foundational issues facing the field today.

Learning vs. playing

The recent research on the educational use of video games is concerned with a series of basic problems. Some researchers question the viability of packaging education as fun. They fear that using video games for learning sends the implicit message that learning is not necessarily hard work, but must always be fun.[26] However, this problem seems to spring more from these researchers' beliefs on education, as they are not supported by any direct studies.

But a related, and more crucial, issue is the potentially inherent contradiction between learning and playing. Researchers increasingly suggest that a student should clearly see that a particular game is about learning a specific topic and appreciate the expected result. Without explicitly framing the experience as educational, the goals and rules in play take over. The play and learning clash is evident when the game goals work against the learning goals. This is all too often the case as much educational use of video games relies on commercial titles, and many edutainment titles split the game and learning parts.[27]

Another problem between playing and learning relates to students' interest and engagement, which will vary considerably between lessons. Students see the experiences with games as a playful, voluntary activity, an activity that they control. Within a game the player remains in control, very different from the more explicit demands that traditional classroom learning makes on a student. The player feels that the control should not be tainted by outside interference, but may also criticize the lack of direct educational interventions. On one hand, player control is a critical characteristic in video games stressed by all researchers, but it is also a fact that many studies show the benefit of carefully guiding, supporting, scaffolding, introducing and debriefing the player after the video game experience. This guiding is actually part of most game cultures but becomes problematic in school settings. The lack of a firm setting confuses students that are uncertain of the expectations when playing and learning. Ultimately, students are unsure whether to approach the video game as play or learning.[28]

Indeed, sometimes the playful approach may ruin the educational experience. On a very basic level, relying on games means that some students will not trust the experience, while others may trust it too much. Research indicates that when students experience a contrast between their own knowledge and information presented in the game, they stick with their own knowledge.[29] Other studies indicate that students sometimes have a blind belief in the game.[30] Neither approach is very beneficial. Blind belief is a poor starting point for critical reflection and complete denial is similarly problematic.

Drill-and-practice vs. microworlds

Today, most researchers seem to shy away from a narrow focus on drill-and-practice games found in behaviorist edutainment; but many designers still indirectly assume that parts of the game have drill-and-practice elements that can transfer facts and support development of different skills. In fact, research indicates that drill-and-practice can be useful, but works best in combination with other teaching forms.[31] Maria Klawe (1998) stresses that video games should be used for math activities that are otherwise hard to introduce in a classroom while specifically pointing to the limitations of drill-and-practice.

> Most of the early mathematical video games focused on drill and practice of simple number operations and concepts. Such games are easy to develop. Moreover, playing such games are an effective and motivating method of increasing fluency for many students. However, drill and practice is only one of many components of mathematics learning and can be achieved via a variety of non computer-based methods.[32]

The preference for drill-and-practice is understandable: it replicates the rote repetition that is the basic part of many traditional classrooms, and thus must feel familiar to many designers; and furthermore, drill-and-practice games are easy to develop compared to the design challenges facing other types of titles. Microworlds, for example, have proven significantly harder to design than classic drill-and-practice games.[33]

In Microworlds the player is confronted with a virtual world that contain a condensed version of the most important variables and characteristics of a given domain. This could be a physics environment where you explore the different mechanics and interrelationships between atoms by constructing strings of molecules. It could also be a simulation of Williamsburg in colonial times where you get a look into the important elements of everyday life, interactions and routines.

Immersion vs. transfer

In discussing the challenges of the game design process, Klawe (1998) raises some of the central problems with educational video games. Most of her conclusions are backed up by an earlier study by Kamran Sedighian and Andishe Sedighian (1996), the researchers responsible for the *Super Tangram* component of *E-Gems* series of educational titles. Klawe points out that the immersive effect of video games lead to a lack of awareness of the mathematical structures and concepts integrated in the video game. This results in a weak transfer of game experience to other contexts. Students may learn some content or skills in the game universe and apply them in the game context, but most games are not constructed in a way to make the knowledge accessible in other contexts. In an earlier study, Klawe and Eileen Phillips (1995) found that when students wrote down math problems on paper simultaneous with playing a math video game, they were more successful in transferring the video game skills to other classroom practice. The engagement with paper and pencil, these researchers found, forces the students to construct the knowledge actively.

The transfer of knowledge seems to represent a double bind. On one hand, many researchers assume that the learning experience must be undetectable by children—that an educational video game should resemble a traditional video game. It should not give itself away as children will then shy away from the educational title.[34] On the other hand, it seems that if the players are not aware that the learning elements, the learning experience—and especially the student's ability to transfer the information elsewhere—will be undermined. The transfer of game skills to other contexts has to be made explicit (and here, as we'll see below, the teacher can play a crucial role).

Teacher intervention

Contemporary research consistently shows that teachers play an important role in facilitating learning with video games: teachers steer the use of a game in the right direction, and provide an effective debriefing that can catch misperceptions and important differences in students' experiences while playing. Many edutainment titles adhering to behaviorism neglect the teacher's role, and assume that no outside intervention is necessary for learning. In more recent titles that are designed with a constructivist approach (although far between), the teacher is made essential.

Many researchers argue that video games should not be thought of as explicitly educational, but as tools, which provide opportunities for interested teachers. Thus, the teacher's role is imperative to create the learning experience. This is especially true regarding commercial entertainment titles which find their way into educational settings—like *The Sims* and *Civilization*—which have not been developed with curriculum explicitly in mind.[35]

THE EDUCATIONAL EFFECTIVENESS OF VIDEO GAMES

The question that continues to haunt the educational use of games is whether it is really worth the trouble. The research findings regarding the effectiveness of video games for educational use are still sparse but at least thirty studies address the issue directly.[36] So far, one thing seems relatively clear: just as we saw earlier with the use of traditional games, players seem to learn the same things when using video games as when taught by other methods, although a student's retention may be better with the former. Also, motivation, relevance and engagement are stronger when using computer games in education compared to traditional teaching. An example is a 2005 quasi-experimental study of *Europa Universalis II* in a high school history class. On a multiple-choice exam of European history from 1500 to 1700 given immediately after the course ended, the students who used the video game had lower scores than the group who had learned via a traditional classes and case studies. However, when the students took a similar test five months later, the scores of the two groups were equal.[37] This study also revealed that students found the computer game to be more engaging and motivating, although not all found it to contain relevant historical information. However, the question of relevance seemed tied to specific issues in this empirical study.

One problem with the research is that most studies are content with proving that it is possible to learn from video games. Few have the opportunity and persistence to actually compare video games with traditional teaching methods. From several decades of theoretical speculation and practical research it seems obvious that we can learn *something* from video games, but the questions are *what* and *how*, and *whether it is different from what we learn with traditional teaching methods*. These questions still remain largely unanswered, although there is support for better retention and higher motivation when using games compared to more traditional teaching forms.

Some small-scale qualitative studies have failed to find educational effects of video games, and question the general merits of the educational use of video games. These researchers point out that the content in video games is understood and mediated in the game context in ways that are not appropriate for education. The risk is for example present in *Civilization*, where a player may understand the building of the the Hanging Gardens of Babylon, one of the seven wonders of the ancient world as nothing more than providing a reward of one extra happy face. This is hardly an adequate description of their historical and cultural significance. Others have also found mixed evidence for the effectiveness of video games.[38]

A fundamental difficulty of our assessment of games is that defining "educational effectiveness" is incredibly difficult. Measuring the *learning outcome* of a given activity is never easy, but video games make such quantification even harder. We also need to acknowledge that different kinds of computer games aspire to different forms of knowledge that is not easy to measure. Some of these knowledge forms will largely go unnoticed if we rely on, for example, simple multiple choice tests. Computer games are dynamic systems and each player will have a different experience.

In the ambitious educational strategy game *Making History: The Calm and The Storm* by Muzzy Lane, one student may not acquire the information about the Japanese occupation of Manchuria in 1931, whereas another player will get this information. This makes it very hard to compare learning outcomes between students and classes, and also causes concern for teachers. What is one to measure, and will students learn the right things? To some degree, this problem stems from a narrow focus on education as knowledge acquisition. Let's see what happens when we expand our search to include the "softer"—but no less valuable—cognitive skills.

Cognitive learning outcomes

Some researchers have argued that we should not look for a direct relationship between game playing and the assimilation of specific knowledge; instead, they have suggested that video games could improve general cognitive skills. Over the last twenty years, eye–hand coordination, spatial ability, and problem-solving have received a lot of attention.

Starting in early 1980s researchers attempted to connect eye–hand coordination and game play,[39] but with disappointing results. This limited number of studies all found that there do not seem to be any differences between non-players and players in respect to eye–hand coordination, although anecdotal evidence remained popular in and outside research circles.[40]

The area of spatial ability is more thoroughly researched than the question of eye–hand coordination, and positive effects of game play have been found both on a long-term basis[41] and in terms of short-term improvement.[42] After playing video games, subjects were able to perceive more quickly the construction of objects in 2D/3D space. A major controversy in research on educational video games revolved around the question of whether one can transfer skills learned in video games to other areas. Although the area of spatial skills gives some indications of transfer there are severe methodological problems. A frequent source of error in the studies on spatial ability is the measurement methods. The test of spatial skills is conducted on a computer screen, the native platform for video games. Hence, the test is administered in an environment favoring the video game players. The favorable results for the video games group may therefore be a consequence of familiarity with the test platform rather than improved spatial ability.

The third and final cognitive area—problem-solving in relation to computer games—has received the most research over the past thirty years. Problem-solving is often linked to adventure games, a game genre popular among teachers, journalist, parents, players, and researchers alike.[43]

Most of these studies have methodological problems of their own—particularly in the testing methods used to measure problem-solving—but the conclusions of the most ambitious studies are consistent: problem-solving skills can be improved by playing one game and then transferred to another video game. They also found that general problem-solving skills are a predictor of performance in video games, which implies that video games may potentially be used to test a subject's existing problem-solving skills.[44] However, the studies did not find that real problem-solving will be improved by playing computer games.

The results of this research to date are mixed, but lend some support to the belief that video games influence cognitive skills (although, we should note, often not significantly more than other activities like making a small puzzle). However, all of these studies are hindered by the difficulty of documenting the transfer of skills obtained in a video game to other areas of life. Still, we believe that edutainment would benefit from broadening its definition of effectiveness in education. If we focus not just on the acquisition of specific facts, but consider the many skills required to play games, then perhaps we can more adequately understand the variety of benefits that might come from play.

FINAL REMARKS

There are positive research results on the benefits of educational use of computer games, but it still seems that the real breakthrough is some years away, when it is known that the majority of teachers use computer games in an educational setting.

Unfortunately many publishers and developers within the area are stuck with the edutainment formula that provides much low hanging fruit, but also has a lot of limitations as described above. This far from implies that these games do not work, but rather that there is much room for further improvement.

The barriers blocking the educational use of video games seem to be numerous. Research on edutainment has provided little clear direction where the field should head. Taken as a whole, the results of these studies suggest that students can acquire knowledge from a video game, but that this acquisition may not be any more effective than a teacher's presentation, or reading a textbook. Furthermore, it is evident that edutainment is at a dead end where the formula remains unchanged. We, therefore have to look to the use of commercial computer games and research-based educational computer games to find new ways for the area.

We must also acknowledge that contemporary education may simply be a poor fit for video games. The foundations of primary and secondary education today— lesson plans and strictly divided subjects—hardly facilitate the use of video games. To this we can add the clash between game expectations and school expectations on the part of both students and teachers. Many teachers are curious about games, but with their strong pop culture connotations it is also easy distrust their educational benefits—few teachers will accept that killing monsters can be educational, and in the eyes of many non-gamers, killing monsters is what most games are all about.

Some researchers have argued that we should be careful about investing large sums of money into expensive educational video games before we have evidence that they are worth the investment.[45] On the other hand, it is very hard to actually gain the necessary experience to develop effective titles without experimental use and research. Though to date it is still difficult to prove conclusively that serious games are worth the investment, it would be premature to dismiss the potential of educational video games.

The market is seeing more ambitious attempts like *Making History: The Calm and The Storm* and *Global Conflicts: Palestine*, where video games are integrated more deeply into current educational praxis. The new momentum in research circles towards what video games entail educationally is beginning to give way to a better appreciation of their real potential.

10 VIDEO GAMES AND RISKS

TWO RESEARCH PERSPECTIVES/THE ACTIVE MEDIA PERSPECTIVE/THE ACTIVE
USER PERSPECTIVE/OTHER QUESTIONS/FINAL REMARKS

This chapter explores the risks involved with playing video games—or, in popular parlance, the (alleged) harmful effects of video game play. This is an issue that everyone in the industry—and just as many people who have nothing to do with video games—seems to have an opinion about. For angry parents and determined teenagers, for dismissive developers to anxious educators, and for seemingly everyone in between, the video games seem to contain an element of danger. Over the years, the question of harm has received massive attention in both public debate and in research circles.

Was the Columbine High School shooting of 1999 aided by the killers' fondness for violent video games? Can violent video games make you more aggressive? Questions like these never seem far from the public agenda, and researchers of various stripes have for the last decades tried to answer questions like these.

We discuss this Pandora's box by contrasting two competing research perspectives: the *Active User* perspective and the *Active Media* perspective. The discussion will make clear that the link between violent games and player aggression has received the most attention but that underneath this issue lie even more basic disagreements about how we experience and perceive video games.

As we have seen throughout this book, academic research has been conducted on many elements of video games; however, the study of dangers in connection with games remains a key research avenue, as it continuously receives massive media attention, and is still an arena of heavy controversy. As mentioned, research within this area has primarily been centered on the question of whether video games lead to increased aggression in players. This concern has been inspired by regular bursts of public concern in relation to violent video games, most noticeable upon the release of *Death Race* in 1976, *Mortal Kombat* in 1994, and *Grand Theft Auto III* in 2001.

Until the late 1990s, the majority of funded game research contained a risk perspective. In this century it has become somewhat of an orphan in games research, as more than a few researchers have flatly refused to participate in studying risk. These researchers, as we'll discuss further below, typically feel that video games as a medium are treated unfairly—that the discussion of games and aggression is essentially an attempt to turn games into a scapegoat for more complex societal problems; they also fear that the link to aggression is a precursor to censorship not leveled at other media. Scholars who refuse to engage in this debate may well be interested in aggression question in *itself*, but just resent what they see as an unfair criticism of video games, and suspect that these opponents of games may have ulterior motives.

TWO RESEARCH PERSPECTIVES

The Active Media perspective refers to a school of thought that believes that the media actively influence a mostly passive recipient, the player. Its proponents typically use "classical" methods of research, often based in a laboratory, and are influenced mainly by social psychology and behaviorism. This perspective mostly exists outside mainstream games research; "risk" researchers do not consider themselves games researchers, do not attend games conferences, and do often not play games etc.). This split has at times led to problematic research, lacking a basic knowledge of (or interest in) video games.

In contrast, the Active User perspective refers to a school of thought that stresses the active interpretation and filtering players exhibit when playing video games. The Active User perspective will get their empirical data from natural settings and tend to look to anthropology, cultural studies and media theory for theoretical ammunition.

We should note that the distinction between Active Media perspective and active user perspective is an artificial one set up by us to recognize some basic differences between researchers examining the risks of computers games. In the following pages, the Active Media perspective and the Active User perspective are both discussed in a way, which provides the necessary knowledge for understanding the debate on risks both in research circles and in the general press. The chapter should also give the reader a starting point for conducting studies in both areas with an eye for potential problems and limitations.

Over the last thirty years, more than fifty studies have been conducted to try and understand the relationship between video games and risk. Taken as a whole, this body of knowledge has been influenced more by the Active Media perspective than the Active User perspective. The former has imbued this research with a social psychological perspective, and a reliance on what Active Media researchers refer to as "the effect tradition," that is, an almost automatic relationship between playing violent video games and becoming more violent. In the Active Media perspective, video games are conceived as having a direct, objective, and measurable effect on players.

An Active User perspective, which takes the opposite starting point, has over the last ten years increasingly challenged this tradition. According to researchers from this latter perspective, video games do not have the same effect on everybody but are mediated by a variety of factors like playing context, genre expectations, and the individual player's interpretation. The player is not seen as a passive recipient of the content in video games but rather as an active, selective, and critical user.

Below we present a typical research design for each perspective. It should be stressed that in principle the two perspectives (or "theories") are not directly linked to specific academic fields, although researchers within each are typically allied with certain methodologies, as we'll see below. These research designs summarize the specific ways that each group prefers to conduct a scientific study. By examining a standard example of these two research perspectives, we hope to show that the way you formulate and examine the question of harmful video games will to a large extent decide what answers you get.

A typical research design in the Active Media perspective

A typical study in this tradition will start out with two groups of subjects; they can number anywhere from eight to 100. One group plays a violent video game (for instance, the action game *Quake*) while the other group plays a non-violent video game (for instance, the racing game *Need for Speed*). Before each group of subjects starts playing, their level of aggression is measured by different methods from a standard multiple-choice psychological questionnaire to physiological test taking swabs of saliva and testing for the amount of cortisol in the player's body. This measurement is then repeated for both groups after the groups have played their game. The assumption is that any difference in the change in aggression levels between the two groups can be attributed to the difference between the two games. The effect of one violent game can then be generalized to other violent video games that these groups might play.

Typical research design in the Active User perspective

In a classic study following an Active User perspective, the researchers observe and interview a group of children playing different video games in a natural setting (such as an after school club) over a longer period (say, three months). Through their observations the researchers note behavioral characteristics such as verbal and physical violence. The questions could range from the children's perception of dying in a game to whether they have bad dreams. The researchers aim to describe the full experience of gameplay and the context in which these children play games; the ultimate goal is to understand how the players integrate video games into their daily life (how the player *uses* the games).

The effect of playing certain games (or types of games) is just one potential focus of an Active User study, and is rarely looked for specifically. When incidences of aggression are found, for example, they are analyzed in the specific context in which they arose; researchers hesitate to generalize actions or behaviors to other situations because they believe that each player perceives each game differently and the context of play is important for the player's perception. Furthermore, because everything that the children do is seen as dependent on the context (in this case, the after school program, and the particular group of subjects, and the specific games they play), the researchers are not able to isolate "violence" as a variable.

The focus of these two research designs makes all the difference. The Active Media perspective looks at what a video game does to a player whereas the Active User perspective is interested in what the players do with the video game. This crucial difference stems from a very basic theoretical disagreement on how we should understand people's psychological functioning. This split also runs through a number of other disciplines and may be exemplified by the disagreement evident in the following statements:

An Active Media proponent concludes, based on laboratory studies:

> . . . exposure to violent video games is significantly linked to increases in aggressive behaviour, aggressive cognition, aggressive affect, and cardiovascular arousal, and to decreases in helping behaviour.[1]

Compare that to the following statement from a group of Active User proponents:

> Many scholars believe that trying to understand the media's impact on human development through laboratory measurements and other numerical methods is inherently flawed.[2]

	Active Media Perspective	Active User Perspective
Scientific and theoratical starting point	Behaviorism, social psychology, experimental psychology	Anthropology, ethnography, literary studies/semiotics, cultural studies, media theory
Research methods	Predominantly, quantitative (controlled studies)	Predominantly qualitative (interview and observation)
Main interest	The effects of media on attitude and behavior	Meaning, role and function of media
Research object	The video game (what effect the game has on the player)	The player (what the player does with the game)

Table 10.1 Differences between the Active Media perspective and the Active User perspective

Though the following graph simplifies each perspective slightly, laying out their basic characteristics side by side gives us a graphic appreciation of their differences.

Whereas the Active Media perspective wants to generalize, researchers within the Active User perspective usually abstain from making general claims. The Active Media perspective wants to examine the specific influence of violent video games but the Active User perspective wants to examine video games in a broader way.

Researchers within the two perspectives do share some notions of what qualifies as science—they both agree, for example, that logic, arguments and reasoning are pillars of science. However, it is quite unlikely that studies with an Active Media perspective will ever fully convince Active User researchers, and vice versa. As we look at the basic assumptions of the two groups, it is less likely they are directly disagreeing with another, and more likely they are having different conversations. Their theoretical assumptions are just dramatically different from each other. Attempts have recently been made to combine the approaches for a stronger research design and to facilitate a better dialogue between the two perspectives.[3]

Traditionally, the two research positions have seldom engaged in direct discussions of each other's research; the occasional public debates are centered on the Active User perspective's skepticism towards the basic premises of the Active Media perspective. Within the last five years, however, the Active Media perspective has begun to engage with the criticism from the Active User perspective, trying to refute some of the critique.[4] Media researcher David Buckingham criticizes both positions for building barriers but also states that:

> Despite the more complex views of meaning which have been developed . . . much of the work on violence has remained stubbornly tied to behaviourist assumptions.[5]

Let us deepen our understanding of risk by exploring the thinking behind each of these perspectives, as well as the relevant criticisms of each. We will begin with the Active Media perspective, since it remains the most dominant perspective.

THE ACTIVE MEDIA PERSPECTIVE

The Active Media perspective has set the agenda for research into the risks of video games since the early 1980s; though it is less dominant today, its influence continues to be felt, with more than fifty published studies in the last two decades. The Active Media perspective has its theoretical roots in North American psychology, and the "behaviorist tradition" constitutes an important part of its foundation. Another basic building block is communication theory (often defined as who says what to whom in what channel with what effect,) particularly the branches more inspired by classical social sciences than by hermeneutic approaches to media use.

With its 1910s origins, behaviorism conceptualized human beings as fairly simple systems that responded to the stimuli around them; classical behaviorists avoided discussing inner mental processes. Active Media perspective relies on behaviorism, especially in its use of theory for understanding empirical results, but is offering still more sophisticated theoretical frameworks to guide predictions and interpretations.

Active Media research can technically employ most types of methodologies like experimental studies to cross section-correlation. Nevertheless, these studies share a basic assumption that a particular medium (like video games/violent video games) has one particular effect on people (who are basically similar); this assumption often leads to experiments with a fairly standard research design, similar to the example presented earlier.

The most used research design is usually referred to as an *experimental study*. Ideally these take place in a laboratory setting, and by filtering out confounding variables the researcher aims to measure the exact effect of a given variable. The two other typical research designs are cross-section correlations studies and longitudinal correlation studies.

Cross section-correlation studies look at a group's use of video games and level of aggression at a given point in time. A correlation is said to exist if the players of violent video games are more aggressive than the non-players. So, if a group of gamers plays more violent video games and is more aggressive than others while playing or immediately after, this denotes a correlation.

Longitudinal-correlation studies typically follow a given group of people over a number of years. If, over time, a correlation is ascertained between the fact that those who played violent video games also exhibit more aggressive behavior (and that behavior was not present at the start) then there is a *causal* correlation: violent video games in those cases lead to aggressive behavior. No studies of this type have been undertaken, even though they would offer the strongest evidence for establishing a clear cause and effect correlation between violent video games and aggressive behavior.

After a lot of criticism, research designs have been improved and attempts have been made to review earlier research in the related field of meta-studies (which we'll discuss below). There seems to be common agreement among researchers within the field that the results from these three typical effect studies are not strong enough by themselves to give a final verdict on whether video games promote aggression. We will return to some concrete research results after we have looked at common theories in the Active Media perspective.

Theories and methods

Researchers within the Active Media perspective have a variety of theoretical starting points. Albert Bandura's social learning theory from the 1970s has often been preferred, but over the years other approaches have been applied. Below, we will introduce the most important ones: catharsis theory, cultivation theory, social learning theory, general arousal theory, the cognitive neo-association model of aggression and the general aggression model. See Dill and Dill (1998) or Calvert (1999) for other introductions.

Catharsis theory:[6] the idea of catharsis has a long history in psychology, dating back to Sigmund Freud in the late 1890s, but in video games research a newer version of the theory is often used. Seymour Feshbach and Robert Singer proposed this theory in the early 1970s pointing out that experiencing depictions of violence in media (whether video games, movies or television) can actually reduce aggressive feelings. The idea is that one's own aggressive feelings will be mirrored in the media, and experiencing them will reduce internal tension. In video games, the active role of the player further enhances this effect as the aggressive feelings are not only seen on the screen but also actively performed by moving the avatar on the screen.

The application of the catharsis theory within the Active Media tradition is limited to a few studies, but the theory is often used in less scientific discussions. The limited interest in catharsis as an explanatory theory could also be attributed to the inclination among effect researchers to focus on the dangers of video games; thus they are less likely to seek out arguments that games *reduce* aggression. In the last decade, the catharsis theory has also become less acceptable in psychology in general.[7]

Cultivation theory:[8] this theory is built on television research, and attempts to explain to what degree media lead to a distorted perception of social reality, for example through stereotyped perceptions. The theory has been less used in relation to video games; and though there are certainly characters in video games that are based on ethnic or gender stereotypes, it is still uncertain what stereotypes, if any, video games can produce in the player.

Social learning theory:[9] behavior is learned through imitation of attractive models with attached rewards. Supporters of social learning theory stress that video games exemplify this model of learning: they demand the player's full attention and entail active identification with characters on the computer screen. Furthermore, rewards are attached directly to the performance of symbolic violence (getting points, for example, by killing opponents). Therefore, it is more likely that these aggressive actions are transferred to the outside world.

The general arousal theory:[10] this theory claims that video games will increase the player's arousal level and thus increase his energy and the intensity of his actions. The increased arousal will not necessarily lead to different player actions but more likely a heightened intensity in these actions. Supporters of this theory point out that especially violent video games give the necessary arousal to facilitate more aggressive behavior. Getting into an argument with a friend while playing a violent video game may accelerate into a fierce discussion, or you may be more likely to get irritated when someone pokes you after playing a game than after talking on the phone or washing dishes.

Cognitive neo-association model of aggression:[11] the theory points out that violent media lead to hostility and aggression due to reinforcement of association nodes in the brain that are related to hostility and aggression. These nodes can be created and strengthened by video games; through these nodes aggressive thoughts will be transformed into physical action.

General aggression model:[12] the general aggression model (GAM) is one of the newest theories in the field and combines earlier theories on aggression with cognitive schemata theory. The cognitive schemata theory suggests that we order our experiences in different schemata that we use when we perceive new experiences. According to the model, violent media content causes aggressive behavior by influencing the person's internal state which researchers measure by looking at a variety of cognitive, affective, and arousal variables. Violent media content increases aggressive behavior in several concrete ways: by teaching the player how to perform aggressive actions, by influencing underlying aggressive and cognitive schematas, by increasing arousal and by creating an emotional and aggressive mental state.

From the descriptions above it should be clear that most theories refer to media in general; the one exception is the general aggression model, which was developed with video games in mind. The theories, mostly developed in the 1970s and 1980s, reflect the strong influence of behaviorism and cognitivism at that time. This is also true of most of the research questions posed, research designs constructed, and methods used. They are also heavily inspired by research on television and violence.

Important studies

In the last ten years, Active Media research has to a large extent consisted of meta-analyses of earlier studies; in other words, looking at previous studies and combining their results to make a stronger case for the risks associated with video games. There have, however, been some notable exceptions.[13] As we noted earlier, the total number of studies is at least fifty, but it is hard to estimate, and depends on what one chooses to include as a research study. In his meta-analysis, Anderson (2004) includes about forty-four studies on aggressive behavior covering most studies within the Active Media Perspective.

In their 2000 study Anderson and Dill (2000) examine video games in relation to aggressive thoughts, feelings, and behavior both in the artificial setting of a laboratory and by data on real life behavior. This study consists of two parts; the first part is the most interesting, as it represents a classic research design and typical findings from the effect perspective.

More than 220 psychology students participated in the first part of the study; a majority were women, the average age was nineteen, and the students were awarded course points for participating.

The subjects filled out a questionnaire describing their five favorite games, and their experience with the content, violence, and playing style of the game. The students were also asked about the amount of time they spent playing. From these questionnaires the researchers extrapolated information about the subjects' aggressive behavior, criminal record, game habits, and general worldview.

The results showed that male players felt more secure, played more violent video games, and spent more time playing than women. The more a participant played violent games, the more likely it was that he or she had engaged in criminal activities. Academic achievements were also hampered by a high playing time. Those who played *violent* video games did even worse academically, and were more involved in aggressive crimes like theft. The second part of the study consisted of an experimental study. It confirmed that violent video games reinforce aggressive thoughts, with men being the more aggressive than women. The overall conclusion was that there is a causal relationship between realistic violent video games, aggressive behavior, and crime.

In their 2002 study, Active Media researchers Steve Durkin and Bonnie Barber (2002) examined a number of links between video games and adolescents. One thousand three hundred and four adolescents participated, covering a broad socio-demographic profile; their average age was sixteen. The study captured both positive and negative effects of video games. The researchers divided the adolescents into three groups based on their video game usage, and rated them according to the following variables: family closeness, activity involvement, positive school engagement, positive mental health, substance use, self-concept, friendship network, and disobedience. The overall conclusion is that "computer games can be a positive feature of a healthy adolescence."[14] Though noting the potential negative impact of video games, Durkin and Barber also found that games can offer a variety of positive effects in the lives of adolescents; the optimism of their work gives surprisingly different results than traditional studies within the Active Media perspective.

The study measured the game use of youngsters on a scale from 1 to 7 (1= never; 7= daily). Looking closer at the results, it is clear that the group which has low usage of video games (defined as answering 2, 3 or 4), rates better than both the group that does not play video games and the group which plays video games regularly (defined as answering 5, 6 or 7). The results indicate that the group with low usage of video games has less depressed moods, better self-esteem, and better academic achievement. The group that does not play video games at all is more deviant and is more prone to criminal behavior. The study did not find differences between the groups in relation to self-reported aggression.

Quite often, research from the Active Media perspective is criticized heavily for only looking at the short-term effect. However, one 2005 study has examined the effect of violent games one month after play. The study was conducted with 213 participants aged 14 to 68 (the average age was 28) playing *Asheron's Call* 2 for one month. The study found no increased aggression on any measure after the trial period.[15]

A 2001 study by Thomas N. Robinson, Marta L. Wilde, Lisa C. Navracruz, Farish Haydel and Ann Varady stands out for its untraditional research design: it looks at what happens when we change children's media habits. The study involves children from two different schools, with an average age of nine years. The goal was to reduce media consumption (television, video, and video games) and examine the consequences. The participants were split into two groups: the first group maintained its normal level of media usage, without outside interference. The second group was allowed to maintain its normal media habits, but was educated about media use during a six-month-long course. The course used social learning theory to help the children explain what happened to their behavior and emotions when they used media. It also introduced *turn-off television* days, parents' information campaign, and discussions in general. After the course, the children were encouraged to reduce their media consumption to around seven hours a week.

The results showed that the trained group was perceived as less aggressive by their friends and showed less verbal aggression. Researchers also witnessed a tendency towards less physical aggression, but the decrease was not statistically significant. The study is particularly interesting because it points to realistic ways to limit the influence of aggression by educating players of video games to become critical and self-aware. This is quite different from the traditional Active Media perspective, where players are seen as helpless victims in the hands of video games It also turns the research design upside-down in comparison with traditional Active Media research designs. Instead of measuring what happens when one plays video games, it measures what happens when one does not. Of course the problem with the above study is that it doesn't focus exclusively on video games, but media use in general.

Another recent trend in examining the effect of violent video games is to apply more advanced statistical analysis than previous studies. These new studies reveal interesting problems with earlier research. Earlier research has primarily looked at whether there was any relation between playing violent video games and measures of aggression—not how big the effect of playing violent video games was. So, basically early studies said that yes you become more violent when playing video games. However, they did not say anything about the strength of the video games compared to other factors like parents' involvement. Attempts to remedy this problem are seen in recent studies, for example Gentile *et al.* (2004) and Funk *et al.* (2004).

Studies in the last five years have attempted to introduce more subtlety to their analyses. Douglas Gentile and his colleagues in 2004 found that adolescents who played more video games with more violence were more hostile, got into more arguments with teachers, and were more involved in physical fights compared to their contemporaries who didn't play violent video games to the same extent. These adolescents also seemed to perform worse in school. The superficial evidence pointed to a damning correlation between video game violence and a broad spectrum of problematic behavior.

However, when the researchers complicated their study with additional variables—especially the gender of the subjects and involvement of their parents—the results were radically different. When these factors are considered the effect of violent video game exposures on physical fights practically disappears. The way it works is that when you simply look at the relationship between violent video games and violence there may actually be underlying variables that are so to speak hidden. For example let's say that less parental involvement leads to more playing of violent video games. Let's also say that less parental involvement leads to more violence. Then you would in simple statistical analysis find that violent video leads to more violence. However, as the example shows this is not really a valid relationship as it is really the parental involvement that is the explanatory factor.

These findings stress the importance of looking for additional variables, rather than limiting studies to focus exclusively on the relation between playing violent video games and aggression. Ultimately, the study indicated that parental involvement and gender differences were a more powerful underlying explanation for aggression than video games. In some way this lends some support to the Active User perspective that criticizes the Active Media perspective for having too simple models for humans and their behaviors.

Meta studies

As mentioned earlier, a large number of meta-studies (studies combining the results of previous Active Media studies) have been conducted in the past ten years. Though they all seek a larger sample, and thereby a stronger dataset for making statistical analysis, these meta-studies vary in their intentions. Some simply review different earlier studies and look for overall tendencies. The more ambitious ones collect all the original data in earlier studies and make new statistical analyses. Below we present examples of both types as they have different strengths. The conclusions from the newest ones, conducted within the last ten years, are not clear-cut. The main difference between the meta studies is how seriously one should take the method problems documented and criticized over the years.[16]

From their 2001 meta-study, the two psychology professors Craig Anderson and Brad Bushman offer a straightforward and potent conclusion: "Violent video games increase aggressive behavior in children and young adults."[17] This conclusion is supported focusing on the difference between flawed experiments and stronger experiments. Anderson finds that the effect size (the actual harmful impact of video games not just the strength of the relationship) increases as the strength of a study's methodology increases: that the current combination of correlation studies and experimental studies provide strong evidence that violent video games lead to aggressive behavior in real-life. Communication researcher John Sherry does not disagree although he is less convinced. He stresses that the effect of video games is smaller than that of violent television.[18] British psychology professor Mark Griffiths (1999) is even less convinced, stating that the only consistent finding from the many studies he has analyzed is that young children are affected by violence more than teenagers and older youngsters.

Psychologist Jonathan Freedman stresses that the research is limited and finds it very problematic that strong claims are made. He states, "I cannot think of another important issue for which scientists have been willing to reach conclusions on such a small body of research. Even if the research had been designed and conducted perfectly, there is far too little evidence to reach any firm conclusions."[19]

Despite the strong stand by Anderson and Bushman, the majority of active media researchers favor Freedman's cautious approach.[20] The exceptions are usually in research studies either co-authored by Craig Anderson, or by his colleagues.[21] Furthermore, it is noteworthy that a large number of associations within health care have made strong claims on the risk involved with video games for example the American Psychology Association has spoken out against video games, although here there is also disagreement.[22] As late as 2007 the American Psychiatrist Association has refused to include video games in the diagnostics system DSM due to limited and inconclusive research: ". . . the APA does not consider 'video game addiction' to be a mental disorder at this time."[23]

Overall, the meta studies do not provide a clear picture; ultimately, the results are too mixed to warrant any strong conclusions. In line with common research practice, it would be premature to conclude that there is a link between violent video games and aggression. However, there are enough indications to warrant further studies. And those who prefer can conclude from these studies that a cautious stand is the safest: they will avoid violent video games, because we know that no harm will come to a player from not playing these games, and by avoiding them the player avoids any potential (though not yet proven) aggressive side effects.

Criticism

Criticism of the effect perspective has grown with surprising intensity over the last ten years. These critiques been more explicit than those leveled against the Active User perspective. The criticism has been aimed at different levels of studies, spanning basic differences in ontological approach to humans, disagreement on what constitutes scientific evidence, and specific faults with methodology. The critique directed at the competing Active User perspective has, however, grown stronger over the last five years. Psychology in general has broadened its approaches and challenged basic assumptions about how to do research and what methods to use. Some are inclined to disqualify all published Active Media studies due to severe method problems. The influential comparative media scholar, Henry Jenkins, is very skeptical of the simplistic conclusions often put forward. He cautions us against looking for links in studies that do not reflect real life media use. Below are the primary faults that have been leveled against the Active Media perspective.

Laboratory versus everyday situations

The Active Media perspective relies heavily on laboratory studies to establish a relationship between video games and aggression. However, the laboratory is not similar to everyday situations, and although the differences may seem obvious, Active Media researchers continue to apply results in an experimental setting to real life behavior. The majority of laboratory studies do a very bad job at replicating the phenomena they want to study. Important variables—like the social experience around the video game, the player's control of the situation and the desire to play video games—are absent in the experimental setting. Usually, the players are not in charge of how long they play, what they play or how they play. This is hardly representative of an activity that is mostly driven by pleasure.

Another distortion created by the laboratory is that the length of the play session in these studies can vary from 4 to 75 minutes. This range could very well have an important bearing on how the video game is experienced. The players with brief play periods are abruptly interrupted, and although this may also happen when you play normally, the short time span is not representative of most play. In any case, the interruption is arbitrary, and not linked to the actual experience of playing violent games. Participants given a long play time may also experience something different from real-life, where they may be used to taking turns or playing for shorter periods. The longer playtime may, especially for inexperienced players, lead to tiredness. This tiredness then becomes a confounding variable, which can distort the results. Sherry's meta analysis (2001) finds that less aggressive behavior is exhibited the longer one plays. This seems counter-intuitive, and could unintentionally demonstrate how the artificial setting of the laboratory might lead to an increase in aggressive behavior. In long play sessions, on the other hand, the players might be less aggressive because they get used to the artificial situation and hence do not feel uncomfortable.

Within the structures of the laboratory, participants are inevitably led in specific directions by a study; there is always the danger that they might anticipate what the researchers are looking for and distort their answers accordingly. Though we can't prove a connection, look at the different results from the studies we examined earlier by Durkin and Barber (2002) and Anderson and Dill (2000). Each research team began with different expectations; how can we be sure that these expectations didn't influence the different results they obtained? Due to their starting point the majority of Active Media researchers expect to find a negative effect; not surprisingly, the majority of them do.

Problems of causality

The validity of the laboratory setting is further compounded by problems of causality. Even within the carefully controlled laboratory environment, we cannot be certain how to explain a given effect. If players of violent games exhibit aggressive behavior, how do we know this isn't because they weren't able to choose the game themselves, and were "forced" to play a title they didn't like? Such problems are even more pronounced in cross section-correlation studies. Here, a study may find that people who show a preference for violent games exhibit more aggressive behavior than those who play more peaceful games, or who do not play at all. But from this result alone causality cannot be established: aggression could be caused by the violent games *or* the preference for violent games could be caused by the person's aggressive tendencies. In the case of longitudinal correlation, this problem is less acute. However, such studies cannot completely assure validity. The gaming variable may theoretically be tied to other variables—anything from parental involvement to gender as we saw earlier-which may in fact be the actual cause of the increased aggression. Theoretically, we can even go so far as to say that the aggression could be caused by the social stigma assigned to players of violent games, rather than by the games themselves.

Defining aggression

Another basic problem in studies within the Active Media perspective is the inconsistent use of the term aggression: both what constitutes aggression and how it is measured. This problem is not limited to media studies, but applies to studies of aggression in general.[24] Researchers have used all of the following as measure of aggression: aggressive thoughts, hitting a doll, playing patterns, verbal aggression, aggressive behavior, physical fights or the more obscure willingness to donate money for charity. These different variables in turn draw on different theoretical traditions that can be contradictory in their theoretical assumptions and unclear in their measurement criteria.

It is interesting to note that Geen (2001, p. 3) offers a very simple working definition of aggression: actions that *do harm or intend to do harm*. This very proposition disqualifies a number of studies performed on the effect on video games, which instead look for violent thoughts or preferences for certain aggressive words. However, he acknowledges that underlying variables can mediate aggression, like those presented by Anderson and Bushman in their General Aggression model. Aggression continues to be an ambiguous concept, and the exact relation between aggressive schemata, aggressive play, verbal aggression, and physical aggression is unresolved.

Video games are a rich and varied phenomenon

The Active Media perspective does not approach video games as a varied phenomenon, but implies that video games are homogenous, with only slight differences in their content. For most researchers within the Active Media perspective, the only relevant difference seems to be whether this content is violent or non-violent. This approach would be problematic even with other media. To compare the effect of a non-violent soap opera with a violent action movie, for example, would hardly make sense. They use very different artistic effects, and aspire to different goals, and one runs the risk of not measuring violent content but simply the general impact of different formats.

The enormous differences between video games are obvious to video game researchers, but seem less clear to psychologists and other Active Media participants from other traditions. Despite the evolution of game research over the last twenty years, a certain degree of ignorance remains about even the most basic differences between video games. A somewhat dated study by Anderson and Dill (2000) loses its persuasiveness when the researchers choose to compare *Wolfenstein* 3D (a violent action game) with *Myst* (a peaceful adventure game). When we recall the large differences between the adventure genre and the action genre, we cannot help but doubt the study's implication that the only important difference between the games is the level of violence.

Criticism of basic assumptions

Throughout this chapter, we have argued that the Active Media perspective starting point for examining the effect of video games is problematic. When a researcher wants to look for a relation between video games and aggression, opponents of active media have argued that the researcher ought to look at the places where aggression is actually found. The researcher may, as a starting point, interview hard-ened youth criminals, look at whether video games trigger fights in clubs or bars, or visit the local arcade. Beginning with actual events (rather than in a laboratory) results in a hypothesis informed by empirical data. The researcher can then analyze this data and devise further tests to see if the results can be generalized to other real-life situations.

Strangely, Active Media researchers do not examine the actual places where a direct link between video games and violent behavior might be found. It is interesting, as Jenkins (2000) points out, that in the few studies of arcade, we find very little violence in the actual places where games are played. We still need to establish an real world link between playing video games and real life violence, beyond the often over-hyped media descriptions of single, tragic events like the Columbine shootings, where on closer examination the link to video games is at best sketchy.

Professor David Gauntlett (2001) has also suggested that the Active Media Perspective offers a conservative perception of children and young people, one that runs contrary to modern developmental psychology. In modern psychology, as has been mentioned earlier, the context is essential for framing an experience; individuals, far from passive, construct their understanding of a situation. The basic ability of humans to interpret experiences is lacking in Active Media research. For Active Media researchers it seems irrelevant whether a player is killing someone to save the world or killing someone for the fun of it.[25]

Ultimately, one may have to accept the fundamental assumptions of positivism and behaviorism if the Active Media perspective is to be meaningful. But in the United States and much of Europe, as well as many other places around the world, these theoretical assumptions are no longer the dominant psychological approach. The Active Media perspective remains haunted by its internal method problems mentioned above, and by a sustained and withering critique of its basic theoretical assumptions. Though its legacy remains strong, these problems have limited the impact that Active media research has had on the video game research community.

THE ACTIVE USER PERSPECTIVE

If we can generalize, the video game research community typically approaches their work from an angle closer to this perspective. The Active User community consists mostly of researchers from the humanities, particularly from the fields of cultural studies, anthropology and pedagogy; though the academy contains endless variations, these researchers share many of the same theoretical assumptions about people, methods and what research entails. The Active User perspective has, when dealing with video games and risks, drawn on methods from the humanities and certain parts of the social sciences, with a preference for qualitative methods like interviews and field observations. This approach highlights the attitude that players are competent and selective, not just passive recipients of information. In other words, agency belongs to the player: the player, and not the media, is in charge.

No two people experience a book, a film, a game or any other media in exactly the same way. The experience largely depends on their personal background and the context in which they "absorb" the media. An individual's experience with media can be completely unpredictable for researchers, no matter how thoroughly the media product itself has been analyzed and dissected. Thus, Active User researchers hesitate to draw a direct line between a media product's content and a change in the behavior or attitude of the user.

Specifically, when someone plays a video game, the activity cannot be understood without considering the context he is playing in. The player may have friends hanging around, be alone in a big house or just passing by the local game café. It seems problematic, these researchers argue, to insist that certain games are dangerous, as the meaning of playing a game is not a static entity to be discovered by looking at the game. As Carsten Jessen states:

> Computer games primarily acquire their meaning and content through their concrete use in concrete situations. In this sense they are more a kind of tool for social relations than a means for communication of the message one normally look for in the media. . . . we cannot interpret content outside the concrete practice which also provides the framework of understanding.[26]

When an outsider views a video game, assumptions are the easiest thing to make. A well-meaning researcher—not to mention an anxious parent—sees a child playing a video game, gleefully shooting other children, and eventually being shot himself. The adults may be horrified. For the child, this is play. The player is not really killing other children but competing against the like-minded, exploring worlds of intrigue and adventure, and socializing with others through a fascinating medium. If this defense of video games seems hard to stomach, remember that violent, unspeakable acts are abundant in fairy tales, which hardly raise an eyebrow.

Theories and methods

The Active User perspective cannot be understood as a close-knit research community, but rather as a wide group of different researchers with a shared mindset. The perspective has been strongest in the Nordic countries and the U.K. Researchers tend to draw on a variety of theories and methods, and do not see them as mutually exclusive.

Literary Theories of reader response and reception

"Reader response" theories originate in literary studies, and assign more interpretive agency to the reader (or user) than to the text itself. This approach began with the early work on theories of aesthetic response by Hans Robert Jauss and Wolfgang Iser in the 1970s. These authors proposed that readers create meaning by engaging with texts in a variety of ways. As we have seen, for example, readers unconsciously "fill in the gaps" while reading; they are able to follow the plot even though usually some information is missing. Readers do a lot of mental work when reading, using their encyclopedic knowledge of the world and their ability to relate cause and effect to interpret texts.

Another interesting branch of reader response theory is represented by Stanley Fish, who makes the radical proposal that texts have no meaning other than what they are assigned by interpretive communities. For example, if a reader believes that Shakespeare is the peak of all literature, his ardor will unavoidably affect his reading.

All these perspectives insist, although in different ways, in the active participation of readers. Reader response theories have been exported to other media, like television, partly to contest the common view of audiences as passive consumers. It is also easy to export this point of view to video games. Theories of the Active User perspective all take for granted that engaging with video games is a worthwhile activity, and that a game's meaning is built only with a player's active participation.

Play as meta-communication[27]

Gregory Bateson points out humans are capable of communicating that actions should be interpreted based on the context and that play is crucial for developing this ability. The concept of frame refers to the context we use for interpreting a given activity; as a result, the meaning of a given activity depends on the persons involved. When a group of children is play fighting in the backyard, a bystander may see it as aggressive and dangerous behavior. But for the children it can just as well be play; should someone be hurt by accident, it would not be interpreted as aggression but as an unfortunate side effect of playing. It is not possible to interpret another person's behavior without taking into account his own interpretation and perspective.

The Children's Perspective[28]

Flemming Mouritsen (2003) and Carsten Jessen (2001) attempt to get closer to children's use of video games. They see children as capable of constructing a frame around their play and culture that is almost impenetrable by adults. According to some researchers of children's culture, it is almost impossible for adults to see beyond their own frame of reference and approach video games with an open mind. Still, many studies from the Active User perspective attempt to understand the meaning of video games by seeing these games through children's eyes. The difficulty of this approach is obvious, but Active User researchers believe that the only way to really understand children's use of video games is to be a part of children's game culture—by observing, participating, and thus opening themselves as researchers up to other interpretations.

Though the above theories vary widely in their origins and uses, all prioritize the individual, internal perspective of each human being, and stress that the creation of meaning as central for any media experience, including video games. As opposed to the Active Media perspective's positivist approach, the scientific standpoint of Active User researchers is hermeneutic: the aim of research is to constantly revisit a problem and construct an increasingly valid interpretation. The goal is not so much to generalize the results to all people, but rather to offer reflections, insights, and understanding of a specific phenomenon that will be increasingly convincing although never conclusive.

Most researchers in the wide Active User group will draw on some of these theoretical perspectives, although their influence may be implicit. Fish's theory, for example, is often seen as too extreme, but Iser's foundational reader response work still has an impact although researchers may not explicitly mention him.

Important studies

It should be noted that the number of Active User studies that directly examine video games and risks are quite limited. Compared to the fifty studies coming from the Active Media camp over the last generation, Active User researchers have only made limited forays into the topic. As mentioned at the chapter's opening, many game researchers shy away from this subject as they find it hard to generalize from a single media object. Video games are so diverse, and mean so many different things to different people, that from an Active User perspective it hardly makes sense to ask the broad question: "Are video games dangerous?" or even a more humble question like: "Do violent video games lead to aggression?" For one five-year-old, a video game may be conceived as dangerous, violent, and scary, but another child can perceive the same game completely differently at the same age. Instead, the goal is to create a multi-faceted picture of video games, rather than limiting the research by replicating existing stereotypes and assumptions. We can see the Active User perspective at work through a few key examples.

In 2001, Birgitte Holm Sørensen and Carsten Jessen[29] studied thirty-one children in Denmark, aged from five to seventeen years. The children were interviewed in small groups, and then the researchers observed about twenty of them playing video games. The goal was simple: to arrive at a picture of children's perception of playing video games, their ability to distinguish between fiction and reality, and their appreciation of interactivity. The study found that the potential negative-influence from violent content in video games is smaller than that of violence in other media. The researchers also see video games as close to ordinary play activities, and concluded that the children used video games as yet another toy.

Several other studies have turned their focus on adults, and found that adults often have a stereotyped and limited knowledge of video games. They can therefore not predict how a person will understand a specific media product. They have little experience with video games and often approach the medium with a wish to censor, regulate, and alter the experience into something they know and understand. From this perspective, computer games will seldom fulfill an adult's conception of acceptable activities for children. As we saw in Chapter 3, adults have a knack of idealizing children's play, which means that adults understand video games in relation to how they think children should play and behave.

An adult's interpretation may thus be very far away from how children themselves understand the activity of playing video games.[30] Active user researchers insist that violent video game content cannot be taken at face value. Video games may on the surface look like simple, bloody fighting games, while in fact they utilize basic story lines that help us handle the difficult realities of life. In a hostile and scary world, video games may be just what a lot of children need to address their fears and insecurity (Jones, 2002).

In the large European research project "Children, Young People and the Changing Media Environment," organized by Sonia Livingstone (2002), video games play a central part. The study looks at twelve European countries, and combines qualitative and quantitative methods. In total, close to 15,000 children aged between six and sixteen participated. The researchers find that media increasingly plays a central role in private homes, and video games are prominent.

Another important contribution to the field is the American psychologist Sherry Turkle's work, which is presented in the books *The Second Self* (1984) and *Life on the Screen*.[31] Turkle examined different perceptions of technology and tried to assess what computers and virtual worlds mean for us as human beings. She performed a range of studies inspired by ethnography, and although the results are perhaps stretched too far, they are interesting. Turkle points out how computers inspire the user to think non-linearly, and how the computer's interactive capacity forces the user to reconsider the relation between nothing less than man and machine, and life and death. According to Turkle (1995), people think that technology is merely a useful tool, and certainly technology is often useful. However, we fail to appreciate the more subtle ways it influences our lives every single day. Technology, including games, offers new ways for children of thinking and relating to each other. Turkle finds that technology can have an effect, but that this is probably neither predominantly positive nor negative. This effect does not exist in a vacuum but is a part of everyday interactions and formed by each child and its surroundings.

In a more recent study, the ambiguity of media is also attested to by Laura Ermi and Frans Mäyrä (2003). They maintain that video games can captivate children through strong features like challenges, vast virtual worlds, and freedom. It may be the very freedom and chance to get away from the restrictions of the real world that lead children to prefer video games to other play activities. This preference is a conscious one, as the researchers found even their ten- to twelve-year-old-subjects could engage in a debate concerning the adverse effects of video games:

> In conclusion, the image of a child in contemporary game culture that emerges from our research is not one of helpless victim. On the contrary, many children seem to be very articulate about their preferences and capable of sharply criticizing games . . . .[32]

The above sampling makes clear that risk is far from central to the Active User perspective. However, the field's research does have some bearing on the relationship between video games and risk. Video games are used very differently and it is too simple to talk of general media effects.

Criticism

It seems that there is a double standard at work. When Active User researchers criticize the effect perspective, they challenge the reliability and validity of the research results. This is leveled at all areas of Active Media research, right from the basic theoretical assumptions about how humans work to the concrete ways of measuring effect. These rigorous demands are, however, rarely applied in Active User researchers' own studies. This leads the Active Media perspective to adopt a dismissive attitude towards Active User studies. The former considers the experimental designs of the latter as fuzzy and lacking in scientific rigor; some Active media proponents consider Active User work a lesser form of research (or worse yet, not research at all).

More concretely, the criticism of the Active User perspective is aimed at the limited scope of results and a typical weakness in documentation. This criticism, however, is usually not explicitly brought forward by the competing perspective. The Active Media perspective seems to have a limited interest in Active User studies, and finds that attacking the findings is really not worth much time and effort. As described earlier, Active User researchers, on the other hand, are quite ready to deliver criticism in the other direction.

It is clear that the theoretical framework outlined above makes it very hard (or even desirable) for Active User researchers to generalize from their results. These researchers believe that observations of a group of children's reactions towards violence do not necessarily apply to other children. Still, data is sometimes stretched to make general conclusions. This is problematic when you use qualitative research methods that are not capable of being—nor intended to be—stretched into broader conclusions. A researcher may have performed observations in an after school program over a couple of weeks, and formed an opinion on the children's interactions. These results cannot, however, be easily generalized as we have no way of knowing if these students are representative. The sample of Active User studies is not random, and it is almost always too small a sample given the full population it generalizes to. Furthermore, it is seldom possible for others to gain access to the exact data that forms the researcher's opinions, and this makes it hard to test the conclusions of a given study.

OTHER QUESTIONS

The Active Media perspective has primarily examined the effect of violent video games on aggression in children and adolescences. However, other topics have been examined in relation to risks associated with video games and these are presented below.

The content of video games

More and more people—academics and pundits alike—have questioned the unbalanced content of video games as evident from the studies below. The most pressing question is whether games present a stereotyped, perhaps even discriminative, picture of the world.

The models for solving problems, stereotyped game universes, and frequent depictions of violence are just a few examples of problematic content. The Active Media studies examining this question offer various conclusions: they find that aggression is often a part of games, although the degree of violence depicted varies significantly both between video games and between the researchers analyzing content. Karen Dill *et al.* (2005) find that 79–85 percent of all video games contain violence, but Schierbeck and Carstens (1999) stress that only 5 percent contain extreme violence. It makes a difference whether we are talking about the "war game", chess or the almost vicious beat'em up *Mortal Kombat*. On the other hand, the labeling of released titles still more often end up with an M for mature on the U.S. market.[33]

Social relations, gender and exposed groups

Another question currently popular is whether some groups are more exposed to the effects of video game than others. From the start, video games have appealed more to males than females, and there are clear gender differences in video game preferences. As we saw in Chapter 4, the lack of strong female game characters has been lamented until (and also since) Lara Croft entered the scene. The difference gender makes has been closely investigated, especially in Justine Cassell's and Henry Jenkins *From Barbie to Mortal Kombat* published in 1998. In the last five years, these questions have not remained as high on the research agenda, as video games usage has become increasingly gender balanced.

The studies on gender differences from the Active Media Perspective have conflicting results. Some studies[34] find that females become more aggressive playing violent video games than males, while others do not find this effect (i.e. Durkin and Barber, 2002). The stronger response of some women might be a result of female test subjects being less used to video games in general. They may therefore find it more intense, alien, and overwhelming to play a violent video game, which could trigger a more aggressive reaction.

Researchers from both the Active Media and Active User perspectives have stressed that age may play an important role in how someone is influenced by video games. Developmental psychology argues that young children (below eight years) can have trouble distinguishing between reality and fiction. The lack of this ability is especially problematic if we look at children from the social learning theoretical perspective. From a social learning perspective, the inability to discriminate is especially problematic, as children may imitate in real life what they see in video games. At least one Active User study, however, stresses that children may be capable early on of telling fiction from reality.[35] Dill and Dill (1998) challenge this claim stating that the case for media-competent children may be exaggerated.

Extending this argument, Active Media researchers have claimed that video games affect our perception of the surrounding world. The results are remarkably in agreement, and show that violent video games result in a more negative perception of the real world.[36] A consequence of this finding is that players may perceive the world as a more hostile and dangerous place. They may also transfer behaviors from the game to the real world leading to what can be labeled as crime.

The increases in crime have been speculated to be a consequence of video games, although most studies supporting a link between crimes and video games are based on arcade games (and violent crime in the U.S. has been decreasing for some time). Arcade games cost money to play, and therefore could give an incentive to find what we might call alternative funding sources. This is however entirely different with most current video game playing, where one can play without great cost. Some studies have also found that academic achievement can be affected by video games but others failed to find a relation.[37]

On the positive side, some have pointed out that players with low self-esteem may improve their sense of self by mastering video games. The relevant studies are now relatively old and have contradictory results. The conclusion—not surprisingly—is often that the relationship between self-esteem and video games varies depending on the player.[38] These correlations, however, have only been explored to a limited extent to date.

Addiction

Addiction to video games is a research topic on the rise, but the number of completed studies remains limited, and is primarily performed by the British psychologist Mark Griffiths and his co-researchers. The definition of addiction causes a number of problems for these Active Media studies, and a satisfactory definition has yet to be found. The most serious attempt is based on DSM-IIIR, a scale used for psychiatric diagnosis of gambling disorder.

Addiction to video games does not have the same repercussions as other addiction forms. The secondary consequences that are normally associated with addiction, such as crime and debt, are not part of the pathology of video game addiction. Thus, labeling a person, as a video game addict often seems to be based more on subjective values than scientific rationale. A reasonable conclusion on addiction is presented by Mark Griffiths:

> . . . it is this author's belief that videogame addiction does indeed exist but that it affects only a very small minority of players. There appears to be many people

who use video games excessively, but are not addicted as measured by these (or any other) criteria.[39]

Different definitions of addiction result in quite different estimates of addicted players. In one study, 19.9 percent of players are found to display addictive behavior in relation to video games[40] while another study—by the same researcher, no less—arrives at the significantly higher figure of 37.5 percent.[41] However, both of these numbers are adjusted downwards by the researchers, as most addicted players do not seem troubled by their playing pattern—nor does gameplay seem to harm their lives or their relationships. In a recent article, Griffiths and Davies settle on the assertion that 7 percent of the total number of video game players are addicted, which follows the symptoms from the revised DSM-IIIR protocol, and play more than thirty hours a week.

FINAL REMARKS

The potential adverse effect of video games has long been the subject of debate. This debate intensified in the 1990s as certain games became still more realistic and detailed in their depictions of violence. In recent years, a number of violent incidents have been linked—especially in public debate—to the perpetrators' fascination with violent games. At the same time, more realistic audio and graphics, as well as more complex games, have reactivated worries about whether video games could damage those who play them.

We have summarized the volumes of research into the risks associated with video games, focusing specifically on the keystone of this research over the past two decades: the relationship between *violent video games* and *increased aggression in gamers*. The results have, however, often pointed in different directions. Whereas some researchers feel that they have found clear signs of aggressive behavior caused by video games, others have not been able to replicate their results, and still others have been strongly critical of the methods and underlying theories used in these studies.

This tangle of conflicting conclusions can be maddening, especially for parents desperate to protect their children, and governments eager to defend against any threats to a country's youth. But as we have seen, by dividing the research into two ideological camps, we gain a much better understanding of the nuts and bolts of this disagreement.

The *Active Media perspective* is based on medical and psychological traditions. The researchers usually try to study the question with the help of specially staged experiments, in which people are exposed to different types of games under controlled (but not very realistic) conditions. The perspective has the strong support of certain academic groups in the U.S.

The *Active User perspective* derives inspiration from ethnography and culturally oriented media studies. Researchers in this paradigm stress the fact that the user constructs meaning from each piece of media, and the process is always dependent on the *context*. According to this perspective, it is not possible to study the potentially adverse effect of violent video games in artificial settings, or without attempting to understand the player's own perspective. The Active User perspective has a strong position in Scandinavia and Great Britain.

These two academic traditions are in strong disagreement about how (and even whether) to answer the question: "Do video games cause players any harm?" The majority of Active User researchers either answer that video games do not seem to cause harm in any direct sense, or, more likely, that the question is quite simply too general to answer. Some Active Media researchers, by contrast, answer in the affirmative, while others say that there might be is a connection between video games and harm, but we are uncertain to what extent.

We may never be able to provide a definitive answer, to this and to many other knotty problems. But after more than four decades of video games, decades of academic research, and untold hours of gameplay, we do know a few things. Video games are here to stay. From the first, almost embarrassingly abstract pixels, they have sunk deep into our imaginations, forced us to reach deep into our wallets, and carved a place in cultures around the world.

Video games have been successful because they are beguiling. They inspire the full gamut of emotional reactions, from fear and hatred to utter devotion. As they become more and more a part of our lives, and as they grow in directions we can today only barely imagine, the field of video game studies will need new talent, both to develop these creations and to seek to understand them. We hope that this book has given you a feel for the key avenues to understanding video games. And if you are intrigued, we invite you to explore further this astounding medium.

DISCUSSION QUESTIONS

CHAPTER 1 STUDYING VIDEO GAMES

1) There is a move away from linear media (such as television) and towards interactive media (such as video games and the internet). What causes this trend? Is it simply that technology offers new forms of interaction with media or is this move tied to larger changes in society?

2) What are the challenges and pitfalls of opening up a whole new field of academic study like Video Game Studies? What considerations should one be aware of when entering territory where very little previous research exists?

3) How should a student of games whose research focuses on one type of analysis deal with the existence of other types of analysis? Is it necessary, in every case, to address all of the major perspectives on a video game phenomenon?

CHAPTER 2 THE GAME INDUSTRY

1) Marketing material for games and consoles has changed considerably over the years. Find video game ads from the past and present—in print or online via the related websites—and discuss the development of advertising themes and messages in your examples.

2) What does the astonishing success of the Nintendo Wii console tell us about player preferences and likely future developments in the game industry?

3) What are the risks and benefits of inviting large numbers of beta testers to test a not-yet-completed game?

CHAPTER 3 WHAT IS A GAME?

1) Consider Marshall McLuhan's idea of games as cultural reflections, and discuss how your own experience matches with the idea that games somehow reflect larger cultural (or personal) phenomena.

2) Game and media critic Henry Jenkins has argued that game designers should "concentrate on exploring the aesthetics of action instead of trying to imitate other media." Do you agree with this statement? Why or why not? Consider several recent video games and discuss how the design of current games reflects this issue.

3) Using data available online, find out what are the current best-selling games. Discuss to what extent these titles borrow from movies, whether in terms of form or content. Could any of these titles function as movies or could they only really function as games?

CHAPTER 4   HISTORY

1) Many game types have analog predecessors, but massively multiplayer games arguably bear only little resemblance to previous media forms. From what other areas or fields may one borrow inspiration for the design of MMORPGs? Discuss examples of MMORPGs that seem to draw inspiration from other media.

2) From a publisher's perspective, what are the pros and cons of having one's game labeled "controversial," "violent," or even "morally depraved"?

3) In the future, which games will be the most popular—games incorporating more sophisticated or less sophisticated storytelling than is the norm today? Why?

CHAPTER 5   VIDEO GAME AESTHETICS

1) In what sense are game rules like real-life laws of nature?

2) What are the dangers of discussing a game only in terms of its rules?

3) It seems that most games are very concretely tied to the physical world (few games are entirely abstract). Although game developers can control the game world physics entirely, they often use real-world, Earth-like principles of gravity, avatar forms, etc. Why do you think that is?

4) What game genres, in your opinion, benefit from using 3D graphics instead of 2D graphics? Discuss using examples of past and present games.

CHAPTER 6   VIDEO GAME CULTURE

1) Think about your media consumption. What do you expect of the different media, such as newspapers, books, music, television, and film? Compare them to video games: what can other media forms do that video games can't, and what can video games do that other media can't?

2) Why do you think parts of the public are so worried about the violent content in video games? What is your perception of video game violence?

3) Why do you play? Make a list of the different motivations mentioned by students in your class and see which are the most common.

4) Find examples of the influence of video games on other cultural forms like cinema or painting (other than the ones introduced in the chapter), and discuss them.

CHAPTER 7   PLAYER CULTURE

1) Think about your identity as a player. Do the people close to you know you play video games? Why or why not? Is it something you talk about with new people you meet?

2) What kind of feelings do you experience when playing games? How do they relate to other players? How is playing games different from other kinds of socializing in this respect?

3) Discuss the differences between games that require heavy participation in a community and those that can be played casually. Hard-core gamers versus casual gamers: what defines a player?

4) Select a few recent games you all know and discuss: a) the way they represent women and the actions the female characters can perform in the game; b) do women like to play them and why?

5) Does your online (video game) life affect your offline life? If yes, how? If not, why not?

CHAPTER 8   NARRATIVE

1) Think about a game you have played where you liked the story. How is it different from other kinds of stories like those in books or movies? What do you like and dislike in video game stories?

2) Think about a remarkable video game character (including player characters) and tell each other why you remember him/her. How are characters in games different from characters in other media?

3) What makes a good quest in a game? Why? Use examples.

4) Give each other a summary of a good story-based game you have played. What do you leave out when you tell it? Why?

5) Are interactivity and narrative totally opposed? In other words, can a game designer give options to her players while at the same time making sure they experience a good story? Discuss using theory from the chapter but also examples from your player experience.

CHAPTER 9 SERIOUS GAMES

1) How do "serious games" such as edutainment titles compare to "regular" video games?

2) What challenges do you see in using games for other purposes than entertainment?

3) What is the potential for using games for other purposes than entertainment?

4) Do advertising and political games presents game developers with ethical and moral dilemmas?

CHAPTER 10 VIDEO GAMES AND RISKS

1) What research perspective is best supported?

2) How would you criticize the Active User perspective?

3) How would you criticize the Active Media perspective?

4) What, if anything, makes video games more complex to study than other media?

VIDEO GAME TIMELINE

3500 B.C.   Egyptians are playing the board game Senet
1952   PhD student A.S. Douglas develops a version of *Noughts and Crosses* for the EDSAC
             computer at the University of Cambridge.
1954   Physicist William Higinbotham runs the electronic (but non-
             computerized) game *Tennis For Two* as a demonstration tool at Brookhaven National
             Laboratory in Upton, New York.
1961   Steven Russell and friends develop the two-player space shooter *Spacewar* at MIT.
1971   The first arcade game, *Computer Space*, is released. The game, inspired by *Spacewar*, is
             not a great success, most likely because it is too difficult to play.
1972   Influential early game developer Atari is founded in California.
             Atari releases the *Pong* arcade game which is hugely successful.
             Magnavox launches the Odyssey console.
             Hunt the Wumps
1974   The *Dungeons & Dragons* table-top role-playing game is commercially
             launched.
1976   *Night Driver*
             Death Race
             Adventure
1977   Atari launches the Video Computer System, one of the first game consoles to use
             cartridges (and is thus able to play games not built into the system). The machine
             later becomes known as the Atari 2600.
1978   *Space Invaders*
             Empire
1979   *Asteroids*
             Galaxian
             Mystery House
1980   *Battlezone*
             Pac-Man
             Defender
             Zork
             Space Panic
             Ultima
             MUD (first persistent online multiplayer game)
1982   *Microsoft Flight Simulator*
1983   *Dragon's Lair*
             Mario Bros.
             Elite
             Nintendo's Famicom console (to be known in the West as the Nintendo
             Entertainment System) is launched in Japan.
1984   A severe crash in sales, beginning the previous year, leads many to doubt the
             future of the game industry.
             King's Quest
1985   Mary Ann Buckles writes PhD dissertation entitled *Interactive Fiction: The Computer
             Storygame 'Adventure'*.
             Tetris

1985	*Gauntlet*
	Balance of Power
	Habitat
1986	The Nintendo Entertainment System is launched in the U.S.
	The Sega Master System console is launched.
	Meridian 59
1987	*Leisure Suit Larry in the Land of the Lounge Lizards*
	Maniac Mansion
	Ultima Online
1989	Nintendo launches the Game Boy handheld console.
	The Sega Genesis console is launched.
	Herzog Zwei
	SimCity
1990	*The Secret of Monkey Island*
1991	The Super Nintendo Entertainment System console is launched.
	Sid Meier's Civilization
1992	*Wolfenstein 3D*
	Mortal Kombat
	Dune II
1993	*Doom*
	The 7th Guest
1994	*Myst*
	The Entertainment Software Rating Board is created.
	Sony's PlayStation console is launched in Japan (to be launched in the U.S. the following year).
1995	The Nintendo 64 console is launched in Japan (to be launched in the U.S. the following year).
1996	*Tomb Raider*
1998	Sega's Dreamcast console is launched in Japan.
	Dance Dance Revolution
1999	The Columbine High School shootings lead to increased worry over violent video games.
	EverQuest
2000	Sony's PlayStation 2 console is launched in the U.S.
	The Sims
2001	*Grand Theft Auto III*
	Microsoft launches the Xbox console.
	The peer-reviewed *Game Studies: The International Journal of Game Studies* is launched.
2003	First large-scale international conference of DiGRA, the Digital Games Research Association is held.
2004	Nintendo launches the Nintendo DS handheld console.
	World of Warcraft
2005	Sony launches the PlayStation Portable handheld console.
	Microsoft launches the Xbox 360 console.
2006	Sony launches the PlayStation 3 console.
	Nintendo launches the Wii console.
	The peer-reviewed *Games and Culture* journal is launched.
2007	*Halo 3* is launched and becomes the fastest selling game in history.

GLOSSARY

1337 sp3@k Pronounced *leet speak*. A dialect of online communication (typically between gamers) which is written using certain rules of substitution (e.g. "3" for "E") and can be very difficult to understand for anyone who is not active in online communities.

3D-shooter Action games in which the action is seen through the eyes of the protagonist and where the graphics are three dimensional (and often constructed of polygons). [*Synonym:* First-Person Shooter]

Action games Games focusing on speed and physical drama which make high demands on the player's reflexes and coordination skills.

Adventure games Games focusing on puzzle solving within a narrative framework. These games typically demand strict, logical thought.

Aesthetics (of a video game) All aspects of a video game which are experienced by the player, whether directly – such as audio and graphics - or indirectly – such as rules (note that aesthetics is an ambiguous term used in many ways across disciplines).

AI (artificial intelligence) Often used to describe the behavior patterns of computer opponents.

Arcade Public gaming facility offering computer games (arcade games). Arcades were highly popular in the early eighties where a game would typically begin when the player inserted the equivalent of a U.S. quarter. Action games were especially well suited for arcades.

Arcade game Game played on dedicated "arcade" machines. The player inserts coins to play and a game is typically quite brief.

Autofire Feature of certain joysticks sending "fire" impulses to the game with short intervals.

Avatar Graphical representation of the user in an online forum, especially role-playing games.

Boot (verb) To *boot* or to *kick* a player is to exclude him or her from an online game.

Bot Computer controlled ally or opponent (typically in action and strategy games).

Camper 1 In multi-player team games: a player who only values his or her own survival without caring for the condition of other team members.
2 player who hides in a safe place taking down the enemy as he approaches without placing himself in any real danger.

CGI (computer-generated imagery) Special effects (in movies, for instance) created by computer graphics.

Clipping The act of removing graphics that move outside the player's logical line of vision.

Console A computer designed with the sole purpose of playing games, often sold without a keyboard.

Controller The hardware through which the player sends his or her input to the game, typically a "pad" with a number of buttons which can be mapped to perform various functions depending on the game.

Cut-scene Dramatically important sequence, often displayed without the interaction of the player. The scene is typically shown to motivate a shift in the "plot" of the game and displayed outside of the game engine.

DOT (damage over time) Refers to damage dealt to players or computer controlled characters in combat games. Damage over time is a type of damage that occurs at set intervals over a limited period of time such as poisonous effects

Dynamics The processes and events of a game which are generated by the relationships between rules, game world physics, player input, etc.

Edutainment Combination of the terms "education" and "entertainment." Label for games with a pronounced educational ambition.

Emergence 1 the phenomenon wherein a complex, interesting high-level function is produced as a result of combining simple low-level mechanisms in simple ways.

	2 the phenomenon wherein a system is designed according to certain principles, but interesting properties arise that are not included in the goals of the designer.
Engine	The basic code that defines the relation between game objects and determine the limits of graphics and sound.
Flow	The flow state is described as the feeling of optimal experience. It is felt when we feel in control of our own fate and have sense of exhilaration and enjoyment.
FPS	1 frames per second or the number of images displayed on a screen every second to display the illusion of motion (frames per second is often referred to as framerate).
	2 first-person shooter, a shoot-'em-up game which plays from a first-person perspective (or from the view of the character).
Frag	A kill in an action game, typically a 3D-shooter.
Game community	Players who interact with a high frequency around a game and may develop a particular set of norms and forms of interaction.
Game object	A separate entity in a game world, such as a character, a sword, or a car. Does not refer to things like background graphics, sounds, interface details, etc.
Gameplay	Ambiguous term for the total effect of all active game elements. Refers to the holistic game experience and the ability of the game to command the attention of the player.
Gamespace	The entire space (or world, or universe) which is presented by a game.
Genre	A category (of video games) based on certain shared characteristics.
Hardware	Tangible elements of a computer/console such as processor, graphics card, hard drive (as opposed to *software*).
HUD	Heads-Up Display. Usually shows the player's remaining health, ammo count, and armor level.
Interactive fiction	Contested label for types of fiction based on high user participation. Normally the term refers to computer-based types of fiction but role-playing games such as *Dungeons & Dragons* and special forms of paper-based literature may also deserve the label "interactive." (Sometimes used to refer solely to textual adventure games.)
Interactivity	The term is used in many fields but typically as a measure of user influence. The higher the degree of interactivity the more influence the user has on the form and course of a media product.
Interface	The graphical or textual form of interaction between user and software. Through the interface the user may give commands to the software which are then translated into instructions that the computer can interpret.
Joystick	A type of *controller* in which the player chooses "direction" by manipulating a stick (as in a fighter airplane).
KS (kill steal)	The act of killing an enemy who was already the target of another human player thereby gaining the credit for the kill. This is considered rude.
Lag	Decreased game speed, typically due to low bandwidth.
Latency	In online multi-player games: the time it takes to transmit data from the player's machine to the server and back.
Ludology	The study of games, particularly computer games. Ludology is often defined as the study of game structure (or gameplay) as opposed to the study of games as narratives or games as a visual medium.
Mechanics	Ambiguous term often referring to events or actions which the game design allows for; for instance: driving, regaining health or shooting. May be thought of as the "verbs" of a game, i.e. that which the player can do.
MMORPG (massively multiplayer on-line role-playing game)	*see Online role-playing game.*

Mod (modification)	A piece of software which modifies the appearance and/or rules of an existing game. Mods are often made and published by enthusiastic players.
MUD (multi-user dungeon)	A system for virtual role-playing. Can be conceived of as a thematically charged chat-room with a focus on role-playing. Certain types—so-called MOOs—operate with objects that the players/users can interact with (and sometimes alter/create). Many online role-playing games are direct descendents of MUDs.
Narratology	The study of narratives. Within computer game research narratology is often seen as opposed to ludology. Non-player characters (NPCs), or characters in games (mostly RPGs) that are controlled by the computer that are either not controlled by human players or are controlled through a very limited range.
Online role-playing games	Game type where several (typically several thousand) players act simultaneously in the same server based world. Users normally pay a monthly fee and connect by their Internet account. An online role-playing game is a graphically illustrated MUD. This type of game is often termed an MMORPG (Massively multiplayer on-line role-playing game).
Parser	The function that interprets the (adventure game) player's textual input.
Play	Ambiguous term often (when contrasted to "games") referring to the relatively unstructured, relatively goal-less activity of children's (or adults') playful behavior.
Player character (PC)	In-game characters controlled by human players (usually in RPGs), as opposed to non-player characters (NPCs).
Player-killing	One player killing another (typically in MMORPGs). Sometimes considered a serious problem.
Player versus environment (PVE)	Usually refers to a type of online role-playing game, where human players only fight computer controlled opponents.
Player versus player (PVP)	Usually refers to a type of online role-playing game, where human players can fight each other.
Polygon	Geometric figure; a closed plane figure bounded by straight lines. 3D graphics usually consist of polygons and are therefore not dependent upon a fixed perspective.
Real-time strategy game	Strategy game in which the action is played out continuously without breaks (as opposed to turn-based strategy games).
Serious games	Games intentionally created with a primary agenda other than entertainment.
Shoot-'em-up	Action game with extreme focus on shooting down enemies. Seldom used to describe 3D-shooters and often refers to more abstract games using third-person perspective.
Simulation games	Games focusing on realism. Typically they set heavy demands on the player's ability to understand and remember complex principles and relations.
Source code	Basis instructions describing how a game works. The source code reveals the secrets of a piece of software and is therefore often guarded zealously.
Spawning	The event of someone or something appearing in a game.
Strategy games	Games focusing on the ability to deal with dynamic priorities, typically in a context of resource shortage. Strategy games may be divided into: *real-time strategy games and turn-based strategy games*.
Text game	Game which only uses textual input and output. These are often adventure games (where the textual form was popular in the 1980s).
Turn-based strategy games	Strategy games divided into "turns" similar to those in board games (and as opposed to rea time strategy games). Typically, one player makes a move, and then the next player makes a move, and so on.
Vector graphics	Graphics defined and generated on the basis of mathematical statements, whereby the perspective becomes flexible.
Virtual world	Multi-player (or multi-user) system which is presented as having a large-scale geography. May be divided into game worlds and social worlds, the latter having no objective goals.

GAMES CITED

Format: Developer, *Title*, Year. Publisher

2015, *Medal of Honour: Allied Assault*, 2002. Electronic Arts Games

Access Software, *Under a Killing Moon*, 1994. Access Software

Action Graphics, *Winter Games*, 1986. Epyx

Activision, *Aliens*, 1986. Activision

Activision, *Decathlon*, 1983. Activision

Activision, *Ghostbusters*, 1984. Activision

Activision, *Little Computer People*, 1985. Activision

Alexey Pajitnov, *Tetris*, 1987. Tetris

Amusement Vision, *Super Monkey Ball*, 2001. Sega

Atari, *Pong*, 1972. Atari

Anim-X, *Majestic*, 2001. Electronic Arts, Inc.

Archetype Interactive, *Meridian 59*, 1986. The 3DO Company

Ashby Computers and Graphics, *Knight Lore*, 1984. Ashby Computers and Graphics

Atari Games, *Indiana Jones and the Temple of Doom*, 1985. U.S. Gold

Atari, *Asteroids*, 1979, Atari

Atari, *Gauntlet*, 1985. Mindscape

Atari, *Lunar Lander*, 1979. Atari

Atari, *Marble Madness*, 1984. Atari

Atari, *Night Driver*, 1976. Atari

Atari, *North and South*, 1989. Atari

Atari, *Paperboy*, 1984. Atari

Atari, *Pole Position*, 1982. Atari

Atari, *Pong*, 1972. Atari

Atari, *Shark Jaws*, 1975. Atari

Atari, *Space Race*, 1973. Atari

Atari, *Tempest*, 1980. Atari

Atari, *Xevious*, 1982. Atari

Atari. *Battlezone*, 1983. Atari

Atomic Games, *Close Combat*, 1996. Microsoft Game Studios

Baer, Ralph, *Fox and Hounds* 1966.

Bally Midway, *Space Invaders*, 1978. Bally Midway

Bally Midway, *Spy Hunter*, 1983. Bally Midway

Bally/Midway, *Ms. Pac-Man*, 1983. Atarisoft

Bartle, Richard and Roy Trubshaw, *MUD*, 1978.

Bethesda Softworks, *The Elder Scrolls III: Morrowind*, 2002. Bethesda Softwork

Big Huge Games, *Rise of Nations*, 2003. Microsoft Game Studios

BioWare Corporation, *Neverwinter Nights*, 2002. Infogrames

BioWare Corporation, *Star Wars: Knights of the Old Republic*, 2003. LucasArts

BioWare, *Baldur's Gate II: Shadows of Amn*, 2000). Interplay

BioWare, *Baldur's Gate*, 1998. Interplay

Bizarre Creations, *Project Gotham Racing*, 2002. Microsoft Game Studios

Black Isle Studios, *Planescape: Torment*,1999. Interplay

Blizzard Entertainment, *Diablo*, 1996. Blizzard Entertainment

Blizzard Entertainment, *StarCraft*, 1998. Blizzard Entertainment

Blizzard Entertainment, *Warcraft II: Tides of Darkness*, 1995. Blizzard Entertainment

Blizzard Entertainment, *WarCraft III: Reign of Chaos*, 2002. Blizzard Entertainment

Blizzard Entertainment, *Warcraft: Orcs and Humans*, 1994. Blizzard Entertainment

Blizzard Entertainment, *World of Warcraft*, 2004. Blizzard Entertainment

Blue Sky Productions, *Ultima Underworld: The Stygian Abyss*, 1992. Origin Systems

Blue Fang Games, *Zoo Tycoon*, 2001. Microsoft Game Studios

BlueSky Software, *SoftPorn*, 1981. On-Line Systems

Bright, Walter, *Empire*, 1978.

Broderbund Software, *Where in the World is Carmen Sandiego?* 1985. Broderbund Software

Broderbund, *Prince of Persia*, 1989. Broderbund

Bullfrog Productions, *Populous*, 1989. Electronic Arts

Bungie Software, *Halo 2*, 2004. Microsoft Game Studios

Bungie Software, *Halo: Combat Evolved*, 2001. Microsoft Game Studios

Capcom Entertainment, *Ghost'n'Goblins*, 1985. Elite Systems

Capcom Entertainment, *Resident Evil 2*, 1998. Capcom Entertainment

Capcom Entertainment, *Resident Evil X: Code Veronica X*, 2001. Capcom Entertainment

Capcom Entertainment, *Resident Evil*, 1996. Capcom Entertaiment

Capcom Production Studio 4, *Resident evil 4*, 2007. Capcom

Capcom, *1942*, 1984. Capcom

Capcom, *Street Fighter*, 1998. Capcom

Centuri, *Time Pilot*, 1982. Centuri

Cherry, Wes, *Microsoft Solitaire*, 1981. Microsoft

Chris Crawford, *Balance of Power*, 1985. Mindscape

Cinematronics, *Space Wars*, 1977. Cinematronics

Cinemaware, *Defender of the Crown*, 1986. Cinemaware

Cinemaware, *King of Chicago*, 1987. Cinemaware

Cinemaware, *Lords of the Rising Sun*, 1988. Cinemaware

Core Design, *Tomb Raider II: The Dagger of Xian*, 1997. Eidos

Core Design, *Tomb Raider*, 1996. Eidos

Volition Incorporated, *Freespace II*, 1999. Interplay Productions

Criterion Games, *Burnout 3*, 2004. Electronic Arts

Crowther, Will and Woods, Don, *Adventure*, 1976.

Crytek, *Far Cry*, 2004. Ubisoft Entertainment

Cyan Worlds, *Myst*, 1994. Broderbund Software

Cyan Worlds, *Riven*, 1997, Broderbund

Cyberflix, *Titanic: Adventure Out of Time*, 1996. GTE Entertainment

Data East Corporation, *Commando*, 1985. Capcom,

Data East Corporation, *Karate Champ*, 1986. Data East Corporation

Data East, *Bump'n'Jump*, 1983. Bally/Midway

Datasoft, *Bruce Lee*, 1984. Datasoft

Davidson and Associates, *Math Blaster*, 1986.

Davidson and Associates
Digital Domain, *Barbie Fashion Designer*, 1996.
Mattel
Digital Extrems, *Unreal*, 1998. GT Interactive
Software Corporation
Digital Illusions, *Battlefield 1942*, 2002. Electronic
Arts
Digital Illusions, *Sub Battle Simulator*, 1987.
Epyx
Digital Pictures, *Night Trap*, 1992. Sega
Distinctive Software, Inc. *Test Drive*, 1987.
Accolade.
DMA Design, *Grand Theft Auto III*, 2001. Rockstar
Games
DMA Design, *Grand Theft Auto*, 1997. BMG
Interactive
DMA Design, *Lemmings*, 1990. Psygnosis
EA Tiburon, *Madden NFL 2007*, 2006. Electronic
Arts
E-Gems, *Phoenix Quest*, 1994. E-Gems
E-Gems, *Super Tangrams*, 1994. E-Gems
Electronic Arts Canada *FIFA 2005*, 2004. Electronic
Arts
Electronic Arts Canada, *FIFA 2004*, 2003. Electronic
Arts
Electronic Arts Canada, *Need for Speed*, 1994.
Electronic Arts
Electronic Arts, Canada, *SSX 3*, 2003. Electronic
Arts
Electronic Arts Pacific, *Command and Conquer:
Generals*, 2003. Electronic Arts
Electronic Arts, *007: Everything or Nothing*, 2004.
Electronic Arts
Electronic Arts, *688 Attack Sub*, 1989. Electronic
Arts
Ensemble Studios, *Age of Empires II: Age of Kings*,
1999. Microsoft Game Studios
Ensemble Studios, *Age of Empires II: The
Conquerors' Expansion* 2000, Microsoft Game
Studios
Ensemble Studios, *Age of Empires*, 1997.
Microsoft Game Studios
Ensemble Studios, *Age of Mythology*, 2002.
Microsoft Game Studios
Ensemble Studios. *Age of Empires III*, 2005.
Microsoft Game Studios
Epic Games, *Unreal Tournament*, 1999. GT
Interactive Software Corporation
Epyx *Summer Games*, 1984. Epyx
Epyx, *Impossible Mission*, 1985. Epyx
Epyx, *Summer Games II*, 1985. Epyx
Epyx, *Pitstop 2*, 1984, U.S. Gold
Epyx, *Pitstop*, 1983. Epyx
Evolution Studios. *MotorStorm*, 2006. Sony
Computer Entertainment
Exidy, *Death Race*, 1976. Exidy
Firaxis Games, *Civilization III*, 2001. Infogrames
Firaxis Games, *Civilization IV*, 2005. 2K Games
Firaxis Games, *Pirates*, 2004. Atari
Firaxis Games, *Sid Meier's Civilization III: Play the
World*, 2002. Infogrames
Firebird Software, *Elite*, 1985. Firebird Software
Framfab Denmark, *Nike Goooal*, 2004. Nike
Funcom Oslo, *Dreamfall: The Longest Journey*,
2006. K.E. Media
Funcom, *Anarchy Online*, 2001. Funcom
Funcom, *The Longest Journey*, 1999. IQ Media
Nordic
Gary Gygax, *Advanced Dungeons and Dragons*,
1977. TSR

Gonzalo Frasca, *Kaboom Kabul*, 2002.
Newsgaming
Gonzalo Frasca, *September 12th*, 2003.
Newsgaming
Gravity Corporation, *Ragnarok Online*, 2002.
Gravity Corporation
Gray Matter Interactive Studios, *Return to Castle
Wolfenstein*, 2001. Activision Publishing
Harrison, Bill Baer, Ralph and Bill Rusch,
Firefighter, 1967.
Hezbollah, *Special Force*, 2003. Hezbollah
Humongous Entertainment, *Pajama Sam*, 1996.
Humongous Ent. (PC)
Id Software, Doom II: *Hell on Earth*, 1994. Atari
Id Software, *Doom*, 1993. Id Software
Id Software, *Doom III*, 2004. Activision
Id software, *Quake*, 1996. Id Software
Id Software, *Wolfenstein 3D*, 1992. Apogee
Software
Ignited Minds, *America's Army*, 2002. U.S. Army
Imotions, *Alone in the Dark*, 1993). Infogrames
Infocom, *Deadline*, 1982. Infocom
Infocom, *Planetfall*, 1983. Infocom
Infocom, *Stationfall*, 1987. Infocom
Infocom, *Suspect*, 1984. Infocom
Infocom, *The Witness*, 1983. Infocom
Infocom, *Zork: The Great Underground Empire*,
1980. Infocom
Infogrames, *North and South*, 1989. Infogrames
Interplay, *Fallout*, 1997. Interplay
Interplay, *Tales of the Unknown, Volume I: The
Bard's Tale*, 1985, Electronic Arts
Introversion Software, *Darwinia*, 2005.
Introversion Software
IO Interactive, *Hitman: Codename 47*, 2000. Eidos
Interactive
Ion Storm, *Deus Ex*, 2000. Eidos Interactive
ION Storm, *Thief: Deadly Shadows*, 2004. Eidos
Irem, *Moon Patrol*, 1982. Irem
Jagex, *Runescape*, 2001. Jagex Ltd.
JC Entertainment, *Hongyue*, World Games, 2001
K-byte, *World Games*, 1986. Epyx
Kee Games, *Sprint 2*, 1978
Kee Games, *Tank*, 1974. Kee Games
Konami Corporation, *Silent Hill*, 1999. Konami
Corporation
Konami, *Adventures of Bayou Billy*, 1988.
Konami
Konami, *Beatmania*, 1988. Konami
Konami, *Dance Dance Revolution*, 2001. Konami
Konami, *Metal Gear Solid*, 1998. Konami
Konami, *Metal Gear Solid: Twin Snakes*, 2004.
Konami
Konami, *Scramble*, 1981. Konami
Konami, *Track and Field*, 1983. Konami
Konami, *Yie Ar Kung-Fu*, 1984. Imagine Software
Kuju Entertainment, *Microsoft Train Simulator*,
2001. Microsoft
Kuma Reality Games, *Kuma War*, 2004. Kuma
Reality Games
Legend Entertainment Company, *Unreal II: The
Awakening, 2003*. Infogrames
Linden Lab, *Second life*, 2003. Linden Lab
Lionhead Studios, *Black and White*, 2001.
Electronic Arts
LucasArts Entertainment Company, *Star Wars:
Episode I—Racer*, 1999. LucasArts Entertainment
Company
LucasArts, *Day of the Tentacle*, 1993. LucasArts
LucasArts, *Grim Fandango*, 1998. LucasArts

LucasArts, *Indiana Jones and The Last Crusade*, 1989. LucasArts

LucasArts, *Star Wars Episode I: Racer*, 1999. LucasArts

LucasFilm Games, *Maniac Mansion*, 1987. LucasFilm Games

LucasFilm Games, *Zak McKracken and the Alien Mindbenders*, 1988. LucasFilm Games

LucasFilms Games, *Loom*, 1990. LucasFilms Games

LucasFilms Games, *The Secret of Monkey Island*, 1990. LucasFilms Games

LucasFilms. *Habitat*, 1985. LucasFilms

Madblast, *Michael Jackson Baby game*, 2002. Madblast

Magnetic Fields, *Lotus Esprit Turbo Challenge*, 1990. Gremlins Graphics Software

Magnetic Fields, *Super Cars II*, 1991. Gremlins Graphics

Magnetic Scrolls, *Myth*, 1989. Rainbird Software

Maxis Software, *The Sims Online*, 2002. Electronic Arts

Maxis Software, *SimCity*, 1989. Broderbund Software

Maxis Software, *The Sims*, 2000. Electronic Arts

Maxis Software, *SimCity 2000*, 1993. Maxis Software

Maxis Software, *SimEarth*, 1990. SimEarth

MC2-Mycroïds, *Syberia*, 2002. MC2-Mycroïds

MECC, *Oregon Trail*, 1985. MECC

Merril, Rick, *Hamurabi*, 1978

MicroProse Software, *Pirates*, 1987. MicroProse Software

MicroProse Software, *Railroad Tycoon*, 1990. MicroProse Software

MicroProse Software, *Sid Meier's Civilization*, 1991. MicroProse Software

MicroProse Software, *Sid Meier's Pirates!* 1987. MicroProse Software

MicroProse, *Civilization*, 1988. Activision

MicroProse, *Darklands*, 1992. MicroProse

Microprose, *X-COM: UFO Defense*, 1994. Microprose

Microsoft Game Studios, *AI*, 2001. Warner Bros

Microsoft, *Microsoft Solitaire*, 1995 (1988). Microsoft

Microsoft, *The Beast*, 2001. Microsoft

Midway Games, *E.T.: The Extra-Terrestrial*, 1982. Midway Games

Midway Games, *Gremlins*, 1984. Atari

Midway Games, *Mortal Kombat*, 1993. Acclaim Entertainment

Midway Games, *West Battle Zone*, 1983. Atarisoft

Midway, *Gorf*, 1981. Midway

Midway, *Gun Fight*, 1975. Midway

Midway, *Pac-Man*, 1980. Midway

Milton Brailey *Frogger*, 1981. Sega

Muse Software, *Castle Wolfenstein*, 1983. Muse Software

Muzzy Lane, *Making History: The Calm and The Storm*, 2007. Strategy First

Mythic Entertainment, *Dark Age of Camelot*, 2001. Vivendi/Abandon Entertainment

n/a. *Stunt Car Racer*, 1988, Microstyle

Namco, *Galaxian*, 1979. Namco

Namco, *Pac-Land*, 1985. Namco

Namco, *Soul Calibur* 1999. Namco

Namco, *Tekken*, 1995. Namco

NanaOn-Sha, *Parappa the Rapper*, 1996. SCEI

Nana-On-Sha, *Vib Ribbon*, 1999. SCEI

Naughty Dog, *Crash Bandicoot 2: Cortex Strikes Back*, 1997. SCEA

Ncsoft, *Lineage II: The Chaotic Cronicle*, 2004. Ncsoft

Ncsoft, *Lineage the Bloodpledge*, 2001. Ncsoft

New World Computer, *Nuclear War*, 1989. New World Computer

Nihilistic Software, *Vampire The Masquerade: Redemption*, 2000. Activision Publishing

Nihon Bussan/AV Japan, *Kung-Fu Master*, 1984. Nihon Bussan/AV Japan

Nintendo Corporation, *Mario Bros.*, 1983. Nintendo Corporation

Nintendo EAD, *Mario Kart*, 1992. Nintendo Corporation

Nintendo EAD, *The Legend of Zelda: The Wind Waker*, 2002. Nintendo Co., Ltd.

Nintendo, *Donkey Kong*, 1981. Nintendo

Nintendo, *Mario Bros.*, 1983. Nintendo

Nintendo, *Pikmin*, 2001. Nintendo

Nintendo, *Super Mario Bros.*, 1985. Nintendo

Nintendo, *Super Mario Kart*, 1992. Nintendo

Nokia, *Nokia Game*, 1999–2003. Nokia,

Nova Logic, *Delta Force*, 1998. Nova Logic

Nutting Associates, *Computer Space*, 1971. Nutting Associates

Online Systems, *Mystery House*, 1990. Online Systems

Origin Systems, *Ultima Online*, 1997. Electronic Arts

Ozark Softscape, Seven Cities of Gold, 1984. Electronic Arts

Panlogic, *Lap of Honour*, 2004. The Daily Telegraph

Paradox Entertainment, *Europa Universalis II*, 2001. Strategy First

Paradox Entertainment, *Europa Universalis*, 2000. Strategy First

Paradox Entertainment, *Hearts of Iron*, 2002. Strategy First

Persuasive Games, *Airport Security*, 2006. Shockwave.com

Persuasive Games, *The Howard Dean game for Iowa*, 2003

Persuasive Games, *The Howard Dean game for Iowa*, 2004. Dean For America Campaign Site

Polyphony Digital, *Gran Turismo*, 1997. SCEI

Psygnosis, *Blood Money*, 1990. Psygnosis

Ralph Baer, *Firefighter*, unknown year.

Rare, *California Games*, 1998. Epyx

Raven Software, *Hexen*, 1996. Atari

Reflections Interactive, *Shadow of the Beast*, 1990. Psygnosis

Relic Entertainment, *Warhammer 40,000: Dawn of War*, 2004. THQ

Remedy Entertainment, *Max Payne II: The Fall of Max Payne*, 2003. Rockstar Games

Resistance Records, *Ethnic Cleansing*, 2002. Resistance Records

Retro Studios, *Metroid Prime*, 2002. Nintendo of America

Revolution Software, *Broken Sword: The Sleeping Dragon, 2003*. THQ

Richard Garriot, *Akalabeth*, 1980. California Pacific Computer

Richard Garriott, *Ultima*, 1980. California Pacific Computer

Rockstar North, *Grand Theft Auto III: Vice City*, 2002. Rockstar Games

Rockstar North, *Grand Theft Auto: San* Andreas, 2004. Rockstar Games

Rockstar North, *Manhunt*, 2003. Rockstar Games

Rockstart North, *Grand Theft Auto: Vice City*, 2002. Rockstar Games,

Russell, Steward, Graetz, Martin, Russell, Stephen and Wiitanen, Wayne, *Spacewar*, 1962.

SCEE, *Spice World*, 1998. SCEE

SCEI, *Fluid*, 1996. SCEI

Sega Entertainment, *Golden Axe*, 1989. Virgin Games

Sega Entertainment, *Hang-On*, 1985. Sega Entertainment

Sega, *Out Run*, 1986. Sega

Sega, *Wonder Boy*, 1986. Sega

Sega/Gremlin, *Zaxxon*, 1982. Gremlin

Serious Games Interactive, *Global Conflicts: Palestine*, 2007. Serious Games Interactive

Shiny, *Enter the Matrix*, 2003. Atari.

Sierra On-line, *Phantasmagoria*, 1995. Sierra On-line, Inc

Sierra Online, *3-D Helicopter Simulator*, 1987. Sierra Online.

Sierra Online, *Gabriel Knight 3: Blood of the Sacred, Blood of the Damned*, 1999. Sierra Online

Sierra Online, *Gabriel Knight: Sins of the Fathers*, 1993. Sierra Online

Sierra On-Line, Inc. *Phantasmagoria*, Sierra On-Line,

Sierra Online, *King's Quest*, 1984. Sierra Online

Sierra Online, *Leisure Suit Larry 3: Passionate Patti in Pursuit of the Pulsating Pectorals*, 1989. Sierra Online

Sierra Online, *Leisure Suit Larry in the Land of the Lounge Lizards*, 1987. Sierra Online

Sierra Online, *Space Quest: Roger Wilco in the Sarien Encounter*, 1991. Sierra Online

Sierra On-Line, *The Beast Within: A Gabriel Knight Mystery*, 1995. Sierra On-Line

Sierra Online, *Ulysses and the Golden Fleece*, 1981. Sierra Online

Sierra, *Castle of Dr. Brain*, 1991. Sierra (PC)

Simtex, *Master of Orion*, 1994. Microprose

Sir-tech Software, *Wizardry: Proving Grounds of the Mad Overlord*, 1981. Sir-tech Software

Skive Creative and Revolver Communication, *Stoli Brides*, 2004, Stolichnaya

Smilebit, *Jet Set Radio*, 2000. Sega

Smoking Car Productions, *The Last Express*, 1997. Broderbund Software

Sonic Team, *Sonic the Hedgehog*, 1991. Sega

Sony Online Entertainment, *Star Wars Galaxies: An Empire Divided*, 2003. LucasArts

Sports Interactive, *Championship Manager 4*, 2003. Eidos Interactive

Square Co., *Final Fantasy VII*, 1997. Square Co

Square Co., *Final Fantasy*, 1987. Square Co

Square Enix, *Final Fantasy XI*, 2003. Sony Online

SSG Strategic Studies Group, *Warlords*, 1990. SSG Strategic Studies Group

SSI, *Champions of Krynn*, 1990. SSI

SSI, *Kampfgruppe*, 1985. SSI

SSI, *Storm Across Europe*, 1989. SSI

SSI, *Sword of Aragon*, 1989. SSI

SSI. *Gettysburg: The Turning Point*, 1986. SSI

Stainless Steel Studios, *Empires: Dawn of the Modern World*, 2003. Activision

Starbreeze studios, *The Chronicles of Riddick*, 2004. Vivendi

SubLOGIC, *Microsoft Flight Simulator*, 1982. Microsoft Game Studios

Synapse Software, *Blue Max*, 1983. Synapse Software

System 3 Software, *International Karate+*, 1985. System 3 Software

Taito Corporation, *New Zealand Story*, 1989. Imagine Corporation

Taito, *Elevator Action*, 1985. Nintendo

Taito, *Operation Wolf*, 1988. Ocean Corporation

Taito, *Qix*, 1981. Taito

Taito, *Rainbow Islands*, 1988. Taito

Taito, *The New Zealand Story*, 1989, Ocean

Take-Two Interactive Software, *Ripper*, 1996. Take-Two Interactive Software

TATI Mixedia, *Backpacker*, 1995. BMG Interactive

Techno Soft, *Herzog Zwei*, 1989. Techno Soft

Technos Japan Corp, *Double Dragon*, 1987. Technos Japan Corp.

Technos, *Double Dragon*. 1987. Taito

Tehkan, *Bomb Jack*, 1984. Tehkan

The Learning Company, *Logical Journey of the Zoombinis*, 1996. Brøderbund (PC)

There Inc. *There.com*, 2003. There Inc

Toaplan Arcade Games, *Zero Wing*, 1991. Toaplan Arcade Games

Tool Factory, *Chefren's Pyramid*, 2001. Alega Skolmateriel

Torus Games, *Carmageddon*, 1997. SCI

Trans Fiction System, *Hidden Agenda*, 1988. Springboard

Trilobyte, *The 7th Guest*, 1997. Virgin

Turbine Entertainment Software, *Asheron's Call*, 2001. Microsoft Studios Games

Turbine Entertainment Software, *Asheron's Call 2: Fallen Kings*, 2002. Microsoft

Ubisoft Montpellier Studios, *Beyond Good and Evil*, 2002. UbiSoft

Ubisoft Montreal, *Prince of Persia: Sands of Time*, 2003. Ubisoft Entertainment

United Game Artists, *Rez*, 2001. SCI

Universal, *Space Panic*, 1980. Universal

Unknown developer, *Purging Germany*, unknown year

Valve Corporation, *Half-Life II*, 2004. Vivendi Universal Games

Valve Corporation, *Half-Life*, 1998. Sierra Online

Valve, *Counter-Strike*, 2000. Sierra Online

Verant Interactive, *EverQuest*, 1999. 989 Studios

Volker Morawe and Tilman Reiff, *Pain Game*, 2001. Volker Morawe and Tilman Reiff

Westwood Studios, *Blade Runner*, 1997. Virgin Interactive Entertainment

Westwood Studios, *Command and Conquer*, 1995. Virgin Interactive

Westwood Studios, *Dune II: The Building of a Dynasty*, 1992. Virgin Games

Westwood Studios, *Eye of the Beholder*, 1990. Strategic Simulations

Wild Tanget, *Secret Tournament*, 2002. Nike

Wildtangent, *Adrenaline*, 2000. Toyota

Williams Entertainment *Joust*, 1982. Atarisoft

Williams, *Defender*, 1980. Williams

NOTES

INTRODUCTION

[1] Film scholar Joseph Anderson in *The Reality of Illusion*, 1996 has argued interestingly that play-behavior is a biological adaptation. This also explains why we like movies.

[2] One source is Kafai, 1998.

CHAPTER 1

[1] Aarseth, 2001.

[2] Williams, 2003a; Williams, 2003b.

[3] Williams, 2003b, p. 521.

[4] Ducheneaut and Moore, 2004; Ducheneaut *et al.*, 2004.

[5] Tosca, 2003.

[6] Juul, 2003b.

[7] Salen and Zimmerman, 2004.

[8] Atkins, 2003; Tosca, 2003c.

[9] Kerr, 2003; Taylor, 2003; Wright *et al.*, 2002.

[10] For example, Consalvo, 2003.

[11] Juul, 2003a; Salen and Zimmerman, 2004; Aarseth, 1997.

CHAPTER 2

[1] The ESA, 2006.

[2] OECD's Directorate for Science, Technology and Industry, 2005.

[3] The reader is referred to trade organizations such as the Entertainment Software Association (US) and ELSPA (Europe) for updated numbers.

[4] "Wireless games" refers primarily to games for mobile phones, see OECD's Directorate for Science, Technology and Industry, 2005.

[5] OECD's Directorate for Science, Technology and Industry, 2005.

[6] See for example Williams, 2002.

[7] Snow, 2007.

[8] Nexgen Wars, 2007.

[9] Gamezone.com, 2006.

[10] ign.com, 2005.

[11] MobyGames, 2007b.

[12] MobyGames, 2007a.

[13] Increasingly, PC games can also be purchased for download which can change the role of the distributor and entirely cut off the retail link.

[14] Kahn, 2004.

[15] Based on Tim Ryan's article *The Anatomy of a Design Document*, see Ryan, 1999a; Ryan, 1999b.

[16] Mencher, 2003.

[17] A game must be as easy as possible to *use* (i.e. have high usability) but must of course be fun and appropriately challenging rather than easy to *play* (i.e. it must have high playability, be attractive to play).

[18] For further details on roles in the industry see Kelley, 2002; Mencher, 2003.

CHAPTER 3

[1] Wittgenstein, 1953/1967: §67.

[2] Huizinga, 1938/2000.

[3] Huizinga in fact merely uses the concept as an *example* of how a game can be delimitated from the outside world. Within game studies, however, the term has come to refer to the more general idea that games take place within special spaces set aside from the outside world.

[4] Castronova, 2004, p. 7.

[5] Crawford, 1982.

[6] Salen and Zimmerman, 2004.

[7] See also Caillois, 1958/2001, Juul, 2003a, p. 11.

[8] Juul, 2003a, p. 11.

[9] See also Juul, 2003a.

[10] Juul, 2003a.

[11] Newman, 2004.

[12] McLuhan, 1964, pp. 208–209.

[13] McLuhan, 1964, p. 212.

[14] Avedon and Sutton-Smith, 1971, p. 7.

[15] Avedon and Sutton-Smith, 1971, p. 7.

[16] Nietzsche, 2005, p. 80.

[17] Jung, 1928, p. 107.

[18] Mead, 1967, p. 152.

[19] Mead, 1967, p. 152.

[20] Jenkins, 2005.

[21] Seldes, 1957.

[22] Jenkins, 2005.

[23] Jenkins, 2005.

[24] Parlett, 1999.

[25] Suits, 1978, p. 34.

[26] Available at http://www.mindsim.com/MindSim/Corporate/artCGD.pdf

[27] Crawford, 1982, p. 1.

[28] Crawford, 1982, p. 7.

[29] Crawford, 1982, p. 14.

[30] Crawford, 1982, p. 8.

[31] Salen and Zimmerman, 2004, p. 80.

[32] Juul, 2003b, p. 35.

[33] Juul, 2005.

[34] See also Rollings and Morris, 2000, p. 61.

[35] Smith, 2006b, pp. 65–66.

[36] Modding is slang for "modifying" a game. Common ways of modding games include inserting new graphics or creating alternate levels. Some game developers encourage players to mod, by providing their game engines as open source software while other modifications are done without the developer's consent.

[37] Hunicke *et al.*, 2004.

[38] Wolf, 2001.

[39] Aarseth, 1997; Aarseth *et al.*, 2003.

[40] Wolf, 2001, p. 114.

[41] Wolf, 2001, p. 115.

CHAPTER 4

[1] See Leeson, 2005.

[2] Hasbro, 2006.

[3] An EDSAC emulator for various operating systems is available at http://www.dcs.warwick.ac.uk/ledsac/

[4] Graetz, 1981.

[5] Java emulation available at http://lcs.www.media.mit.edu/groups/el/projects/spacewar/

[6] Burnham, 2003.

[7] Fine, 2002.

[8] Sometimes referred to as *Advent* or *Colossal Cave*.

[9] DeMaria and Wilson, 2002.

[10] Hunter, 2000.

[11] Novak, 2007.

[12] Morrison, 2005.

[13] DeMaria and Wilson, 2002.

[14] Lebling, 1980.

[15] Rothstein, 1983.

[16] LucasFilm Games, 1990.

[17] The one notable exception is Sierra's 1982 publication of the RPG *Ultima II: Revenge of the Enchantress*.

[18] Microsoft Game Studios, 1982.

[19] Morningstar and Farmer, 2003.

[20] King and Borland, 2003.

[21] A version of *Dungeons and Dragons* published in parallel and featuring more player options and more sophisticated rules.

[22] A "persistent" game world is one which lives on when any individual player logs off. Such a world may be either fully persistent (i.e. keep evolving as long as the game exists) or reset with intervals, the latter being a rarity for modern virtual worlds.

[23] Stevenson and Berkowitz, 2004.

[24] The ESA, 2006.

[25] The ESA, 2006.

[26] Often "exclusive" titles do appear on other consoles after a few years and are often released in PC versions as well closely following their console debut.

[27] Expansion packs are quite widespread in the game industry, and are usually a small sequel to a popular game that sells at less than the original game. Often expansion packs require the original game but provides more characters, levels or scenarios, which extends the lifespan of the original game.

[28] IDSA, 2003.

[29] Schiesel, 2007a.

[30] gamespy.com, 2003.

[31] Bartle, 2003.

[32] Woodcock, 2006.

[33] MMORPGs (massively multi-player online role-playing games) are a subset of MMOGs (massively online games) which include other genres.

[34] White, 2007.

CHAPTER 5

[1] Badham, 1983.

[2] Salen and Zimmerman, 2004, p. 128.

[3] Sniderman, 1999, p. 2.

[4] Sniderman, 1999, p. 2.

[5] The reader is encouraged to consult Jesper Juul's "Half-Real—Video Games between Real Rules and Fictional Worlds" (Juul, 2003a) and Katie Salen and Eric Zimmerman's *Rules of Play—Game Design Fundamentals* (Salen and Zimmerman, 2004) for details and more elaborate arguments.

[6] Juul, 2003a.

[7] Salen and Zimmerman, 2004, p. 120.

[8] Friedman, 1995.

[9] Sniderman, 1999, p. 2.

[10] Salen and Zimmerman, 2004.

[11] Frasca, 2001a, p. 9.

[12] Juul, 2003a, pp. 66–67.

[13] The concepts of *perfect* and *complete* information derive from the field of mathematical game theory in which they refer to slightly different things. Technically, perfect information means that all events having passed prior to one's next move are known while complete information means that players know the entire gamespace and the goals of all other players. See Smith, 2006b.

[14] This comes very close to the meaning of "dynamics" in the MDA model.

[15] The reader interested in game balance is advised to also consult Rollings and Morris's *Game Architecture and Design* Rollings and Morris, 2004 and Rollings and Adams' *Andrew Rolling and Ernest Adams on Game Design* Rollings and Adams, 2003.

[16] Rollings and Adams, 2003, p. 247.

[17] Smith, 2006a.

[18] See http://www.stud.ntnu.no/~havarmor/progr/pacman3d/index.php

[19] Though hardly impossible. The point here is mainly that such a design choice would be unlikely.

[20] Obviously, not all games let themselves be so strictly defined. In Bullfrog's *Dungeon Keeper*, for instance, the strategic third-person view was substituted during battle scenes for a first-person sequence, as the player (taking on the role of evil dungeon keeper) assumed control of an individual minion.

[21] Järvinen, 2002.

[22] Note that isometric perspective can also be used alongside 3D graphics—as demonstrated, for instance, in *Age of Mythology*.

[23] But see Juul, 2004; Rau, 2001.

[24] Juul, 2004.

[25] While the graphical style may lean towards realism, the gameplay itself does not. For instance, armies and cities are somewhat arbitrarily symbolized by quite few buildings or units.

[26] Järvinen, 2002.

[27] Järvinen, 2002, p. 123.

[28] A design copied by cell phone manufacturers under names such as *Erix*.

[29] Hawkins, 2005.

[30] Järvinen, 2002, p. 124.

[31] It is telling that Richard Rouse's otherwise recommendable book *Game Design—Theory and Practice* (2001) does not dedicate one single subsection to audio.

[32] In movies, sound originating from the fictive world is usually labelled "diegetic" while sound effects or music which do not have an in-movie source are labelled "non-diegetic."

[33] Weir, 2000.

[34] As it is put in the movie *Demolition Man*: "This isn't the wild west. The wild west wasn't even the wild west." If we saw real footage from the old west we might not find it realistic, since our concept of the time is mostly constructed by Hollywood. For a list of semi-realistic movie sound clichés, many of which are accepted as realistic see http://www.filmsound.org/cliche/. In a video game context, see Hämäläinen, 2002.

[35] O'Donnell, 2002.

[36] Holland, 1998; Johnson, 2001.

[37] See for instance http://www.bitstorm.org/gameoflife/

[38] Smith, 2001.

[39] Herz, 1997, p. 154.

[40] Juul, 2002.

[41] Juul, 2002, p. 324.

[42] Juul, 2002, p. 324.

[43] But since arcade games are/were never process-oriented, we see cooperative multi-player games of the progression type in this format (e.g. Golden Axe and Double Dragon).

CHAPTER 6

[1] McLuhan, 1964, p. 199.

[2] Bourdieu, 1987.

[3] Jenkins, 2005.

[4] See for example Schiesel, 2007b.

[5] Langway, 1981.

[6] About this controversy see for example Kent in his "The Ultimate History of Video games," pp. 90–92.

[7] Anderson and Dill, 2000.

[8] Griffiths, 2005.

[9] The arcade version was from 1992.

[10] From Gagne, 2001.

[11] http://www.esrb.org/

[12] Each ESRB rating is based on the consensus of at least three specially trained raters who view content independently of one another.

ESRB raters work on a part-time basis and are recruited from one of the most culturally diverse populations—the New York metropolitan area. They must be adults, and typically have experience with children through their profession, education or by being parents or caregivers themselves. They are not required to have advanced skills as computer and video game players since their job is to review content and determine its age-appropriateness, not to assess how challenging or entertaining a particular game is to play. To ensure their objectivity ESRB raters are kept anonymous, and they are not permitted to have any ties to or connections with any individuals or entities in the computer/video game industry

(from the ESRB website, accessed June, 3 2007. http://www.esrb.org/ratings/faq.jsp#14).

[13] PEGI stands for (Pan European Game Information), and it was established in 2003 by the ISFE, Interactive Software Federation of Europe, the trade group for European game publishers. They rate games according to an age rating system and content labels, much as the ESRB. The difference between the two organizations (apart from diverging individual rating of games) is that the ESRB has agreements with some companies, who pledge themselves not to sell adult rated games to children. PEGI ratings are totally voluntary and not enforced by European law, so that children will be able to buy adult rated game without problems. Twenty-nine countries are members. Germany isn't because they have their own, much more strict, rules for video game content.

[14] About this and other controversies see for example GAMEINFORMER, 2006.

[15] Developed by Dutch modder Patrick Wildenborg.

[16] Around $24.5 million according to own estimate. http://www.gamespot.com/news/6152490.html

[17] See for example BBC News, 2004.

[18] Jenkins, 2000.

[19] Williams, 2003a, Williams, 2003b.

[20] Ibid., p. 241.

[21] Ibid., p. 242.

[22] For reference see the commercials at: http://www.theoldcomputer.com/Libarary's/tv_adverts_summary.htm

[23] Commercials for the different Sega Genesis/Megadrive games would include a sound clip of a masculine voice screaming: "Sega!" very loudly, usually at the end of the commercial. This was a very effective branding manoeuvre.

[24] The launch of a new console is often framed in warlike terms by manufacturers, as the newcomer boasts of better technology than its predecessor: Mattel's Intellivision vs. Atari, Sega vs. Nintendo, etc.

[25] For reference see the commercials at: http://www.goodcowfilms.com/farm/games/commercials/

[26] See for example BBC News, 2002.

[27] The "Jump Rope" advert won a Silver Lion at the 2006 Cannes advertising festival.

[28] Chee and Smith, 2003.

[29] CBS, 2002.

[30] Gluck, 2002.

[31] BBC News, 2003.

[32] BBC News, 2003.

[33] Wang, 2005.

[34] Goodwins and Loney, 2002.

[35] Games Press, 2005.

[36] See Sutton-Smith and Kelly-Byrne, 1984.

[37] Sutton-Smith and Kelly-Byrne, 1984.

[38] Pellegrini, 1995.

[39] Ackerman, 1998.

[40] Schousboe, 1993.

[41] Jones, 2002.

[42] From ELSPA's white paper "The cultural life of computer and video games: a cross-industry study." All of ELSPAs white papers are available at: http://www.elspa.com/?c=/menu/&m=press&l=whitepapers

[43] King, 2002.

[44] Hunt, 2002, p. 203.

[45] Hunt, 2002, p. 195.

[46] Grieb, 2002, p. 161.

[47] ELSPA, 2003.

[48] ELSPA, 2003.

[49] http://www.c-level.cc/tekken/

[50] http://www.pacmanhattan.com/

[51] http://www.opensorcery.net/velvet-strike/

[52] From the *Velvet Strike* website: http://www.opensorcery.net/velvet-strike/about.html

[53] http://www.metacortechs.com/

[54] McGonigal, 2003.

[55] Before them, there had been a number of specific accounts about games from an ethnographic point of view, where descriptions of individual games and the practices around them helped understand a particular culture, many of which are described in the Avedon and Sutton-Smith's co-edited volume *The Study of Games* Avedon and Sutton-Smith, 1971.

[56] By cultural object here we understand an object that not only has a practical use, but also a symbolic significance, that is, we can talk about its meaning.

[57] Huizinga, 1938/2000, p. 73.

[58] Huizinga, 1938/2000.

[59] Squire, 2004b.

[60] Caillois, 2001, p. 4.

[61] Sutton-Smith, 1997, p. 11.

[62] There is no real agreement between cultural theorists about the precise definition of "popular culture." As John Storey has remarked, the term is always defined in contrast to other concepts (Storey, 2001, pp. 1–16).

[63] Evans, 2001.

[64] Evans, 2001, p. 60.

[65] Evans, 2001, pp. 164–180.

CHAPTER 7

[1] Estallo, 1995.

[2] Morris, 1999.

[3] Wright et al., 2002.

[4] Csikszentmihalyi, 1990, p. 67.

[5] Csikszentmihalyi, 1990, pp. 48–67.

[6] By this we mean that the game's challenges usually start being small, giving the player a chance to get used to the interface and the rules, and gradually get more and more difficult as the player masters the game. For example you can start a warrior character at *World of Warcraft* and begin by killing boars with your sword while you learn how the combat system works; as you go up in levels the enemies become more powerful and you need to use more weapons in more complex ways.

[7] To this, we could add the fact that video games are different, so that the pleasures of playing *Donkey Kong* are very different from those afforded by a game like *Anarchy Online*. The joy of successful hand-eye coordination in a platform game has nothing (or very little) to do with that of performance in a role-playing game, even though both activities could prompt players into a state of flow.

[8] Turkle, 1995.

[9] Baron, 2004.

[10] Talin, 2002.

[11] Smith, 2003.

[12] http://www.worldcybergames.com/6th/history/Halloffame/Hall_main.asp.

[13] e.g. Hughes, 1999; Jessen, 1995.

[14] Bell, 2001, pp. 92–110.

[15] Erickson, 1997.

[16] Even though there is some real life interaction when people meet physically to play for example in championships or conventions.

[17] As Richard Bartle describes of the different styles people adapt while playing, Bartle, 1996.

[18] Even though trading was later allowed for *EverQuest II* (2005).

[19] Taylor, 2002.

[20] These words are usually synonyms, referring to an organized group of players that takes action together in the game. Some games call them guilds and others, clans.

[21] For an explanation of *camping* and examples see the next section.

[22] Chee and Smith, 2003.

[23] Some definitions do leave out conflict, e.g. Juul, 2003b.

[24] Salen and Zimmerman, 2004, p. 80.

[25] Avedon and Sutton-Smith, 1971.

[26] Battle.net, 2003.

[27] Smith, 2003.

[28] Kim, 1998; King and Borland, 2003.

[29] Rollings and Adams, 2003, p. 527.

[30] Andy Kuo's student paper "A (very) brief history of cheating" is often referred to; see also Kücklich, 2004.

[31] Foo and Koivisto, 2004.

[32] Foo and Koivisto, 2004, p. 2.

[33] King and Borland, 2003, pp. 161–162.

[34] http://aok.heavengames.com.

[35] Sherblom-Woodward, 2002.

[36] Leetspeak, originating tellingly from a version of the word "elite," mainly works by a series of specific alternative spellings (like using *z* instead of certain *s*es) and the liberal use of non-alphabetic characters to stand for (more or less similarly shaped) letters. Thus leet itself is often written l33t, *ub3r* means über and newbie is often written *n00b*.

[37] Buckingham *et al.*, 2005.

[38] For an example of a walkthrough, see Chapter 8.

[39] By UNSC Trooper, posted on July 2007 to: http://halosn.bungie.org/fanfic/?story=UNSC_Trooper0704071531331.html

[40] http://www.planettribes.com/allyourbase/AYB2.swf

[41] Available at his website at: http://www.alxlen.com

[42] Sotamaa, 2003, pp. 4–6 His works present a thorough examination of modding varieties and the academic interest for modding.

[43] Postigo, 2003.

[44] Morris, 1999.

[45] http://www.worldcybergames.com/6th/inside/WCGC/WCGC_structure.asp, accessed June 3, 2007.

[46] http://news.teamxbox.com/xbox/11963/Team-USA-to-Defend-World-Cyber-Games-Crown/

[47] http://www.esportsea.com/

[48] http://www.esportsea.com/

[49] Ibid.

[50] Krotoski, 2004.

[51] Schott and Horrell, 2000.

[52] Yee, Nicholas, 2001.

[53] Kafai, 1998.

[54] Schott and Horrell, 2000, p. 50, this is consistent with the ELSPA report findings, also based on in-depth interviews with women players. Reasons for women's satisfaction with games were "The presence of a good plot, rich characterisations, choice in how they pursue goals, freedom of self-expression, novelty in challenges, immersion in atmospheric virtual environments, pick-up-and-play capabilities and flexibility," Krotoski, 2004.

[55] Dietz, 1998; Ramirez *et al.*, 2002.

[56] Carr, 2002; Flanagan, 1999.

[57] Dietz, 1998.

[58] Replicating a study by Provenzo, see Provenzo, 1991.

[59] Ramírez *et al.*, 2002.

[60] Cassel and Jenkins, 1998; O'Riordan, 2001.

[61] Kennedy, 2002.

[62] Flanagan, 1999, p. 78.

[63] Jansz and Martins, 2003.

[64] While studying topics of gender, researchers such as Dietz, 1998; Jansz and Martins, 2003; Trunnel, 2002 have stressed the overrepresentation of Caucasian characters, even in games produced by Asians. As Trunnel herself puts it: "Research has not been conducted on representations of race in video games. However, while more research needs to be conducted in order to fully assess how race is being represented in video games, it seems that most games rarely address racial issues. Some games attempt to depict diversity in racial and cultural backgrounds by placing a 'token' African American, Hispanic or Asian individual as a character in the game," meaning a secondary positive character that doesn't really have any gameplay transcendence (see Trunnel, 2002).

[65] Jenkins, 2000.

[66] Jenkins, 2001.

[67] Schott and Horrell, 2000.

[68] Krotoski, 2004.

[69] Public gaming spaces such as gaming competitions or LAN parties follow similar patterns and can therefore easily be considered to be masculine—i.e. male dominated—spaces. This perception contributes to a constraint on female access and participation in public gaming activities. Such exclusion may be reinforced by the stereotypical and offensive behavior of males toward females in public game spaces ranging from belittlement as "only girls," to patronizing female competitors through the well meaning provision of prize giving, or objectification via the display of pornography at the event. (p. 249)

[70] Rutter and Bryce, 2006.

[71] Kerr, 2003, p. 270.

[72] Research indicates that women between 35 and 49 "spend more time on online games than any other demographic," referring to the very lucrative online games market of puzzle, card and trivia-based portals, see Krotoski, 2004, p. 12.

[73] Taylor, 2003, p. 40.

[74] Rutter and Bryce, 2006, pp. 149–150,162.

[75] King and Krzywinska, 2006, p. 38.

[76] Castronova, 2001.

[77] Castronova, 2004.

[78] Ward, 2003.

[79] Lyman, 2003.

[80] Harmon, 2004.

[81] Lastowka and Hunter, 2004.

[82] Taylor, 2006, p. 153.

[83] "Consider the range of material productions players are engaged in: the creation of game guides, walk-throughs, answers to frequently asked questions (FAQs), maps, object and monster databases, third-party message boards and mailing lists, play norms, server guidelines, modifications, plug-ins, strategies and strategy guides, auctions/trading, tweaks to user interfaces (UI), macro sharing, fanfic, game movies, counter-narratives, comics, and fan gatherings" (Taylor, 2006, p. 155).

CHAPTER 8

[1] From the game package of Westwood's *Blade Runner*. Just like the film, the game is set in Los Angeles in 2019, and the player has the role of a rookie blade runner named Ray McCoy, who has to deal with several dangerous replicants.

[2] http://www.lucasarts.com/products/starwarsracer/default.htm

[3] About the similarity of *The Sims*, and doll house play, see Flanagan, 2003; Krotoski, 2004, p. 12.

[4] The following distinction builds on Rimmon-Kenan, 2002.

[5] As Rimmon-Kenan herself notes, these distinctions have been given different names by different literary theorists, for example Genette's *histoire*, *récit* and *narration*. This is not the place to discuss them and compare them, as we are only interested in that which will help us understand computer games.

[6] Tosca, 2003b.

[7] Klastrup, 2003, p. 19.

[8] Aarseth, 2000.

[9] Rouse, 2001, p. 223.

[10] Klevjer, 2002; Wolf, 2001.

[11] Klevjer, 2002, p. 198. This definition follows Gérard Genette, for whom *diegesis* would be the narrative of a work of fiction, that is, the story, so that everything that didn't belong to the main story would be "extradiegetic." Later, in film theory, *diegesis* has been understood in the same way as the elements that belong to the main story (so that they for example would include the background of the characters that has led to the present situation).

12 Klevjer, 2002, p. 200.

13 Wolf, 2001, p. 98. Unlike characters in other media, who are deeper and capable of development, characters in video games follow a goal, that can be "score oriented, conflict oriented, task oriented or some combination of these." However, his argument suffers from a confusion between the personality of the fictitious characters (in many cases absent) and the actions that players have to take when controlling them. There is no reason why a playing character cannot be a narrator, for example.

14 Vladimir Propp published his *Morphology of the Folk Tale* in 1928, where among other things he offered a typology of characters according to their function in these narratives: the hero, the villain, the donor, the dispacher, the false hero, the helper, the princess and the father (of the princess). Propp, 1969.

15 It is mostly designers, see for instance Saltzman, 2000 and Meretzky, 2001.

16 Gard, 2000.

17 Tosca, 2003b.

18 Rouse, 2001, p. 235.

19 Bringsjord, 2001.

20 Laurel, 1993, p. 145.

21 Laurel, 1993, p. 146.

22 Smith, 2000a.

23 Smith, 2000a.

24 Tosca, 2005.

25 Smith, 2000b.

26 Tosca, 2003c; Tronstad, 2001; Aarseth, 2003. The following is based on Tosca, 2003c.

27 Walker, 2007.

28 Iser, 1979, p. 69.

29 Actualize here means to understand the cues provided by the text and call for the relevant repertoire, in other words, make the appropriate projections. This is because as we explain in the chapter, the text doesn't say it all.

30 Iser, 1979, p. 169.

31 In Marie Laure Ryan's sense (1991).

32 This text has been written by Dan Birlew and Thomas Wilde, it is a 135-page document entitled "A detailed plot analysis of the Resident Evil Videogame Series," where the authors turn the games into stories. It is available at http://db.gamefaqs.com/console/psx/file/resident_evil_plot.txt

33 This walkthrough by CVXFREAK can be found at http://db.gamefaqs.com/console/dreamcast/file/resident_evil_code_veronica_complete.txt

34 The puzzle is as follows: in order to pick up a key from the subway track, you need to have picked up a rubber duck and a clamp in an earlier screen. The duck has a band aid that needs to be removed. The band-aid covers a hole in the duck, so when you remove it, it will deinflate quickly. Before it loses all air, you need to combine it with the clamp and a clothesline to form a tool that will allow you to pick up the key.

35 Aarseth, 1997, p. 75. *Scriptons* are the text units than the reader sees on-screen after having manipulated the text. They are different from *textons*, which are all the units that make up the text, but are not necessarily visible to the reader, for example the programming language.

36 The I-*Ching* is a multiple-authored text whose current written version was probably written around 800 years before Christ. It consists of sixty-four symbols, each of which contains a main text and six small ones. Readers have to toss three coins in order to combine these fragments, so that the random result (1 out of 4,096 possible) is used in predictions and future-telling. Aarseth, 1997, p. 75.

37 Murray, 1997.

38 We include a 2001 book in this period because it is not about computer games, but deals with the problems that are typical of the 1990s' digital research.

39 Ryan, 2001b, pp. 246–258.

[40] Jenkins, 2003a, Jenkins, 2003b.

[41] Juul, 2005, p. 145.

[42] This trend still continues, particularly for those worried about improving the narrative quality of computer games, or "interactive stories." For example, see Lindley, 2002.

[43] Jenkins, 2003a, Jenkins, 2003b.

[44] Wardrip-Fruin and Harrigan, 2007. They are interested in how different "playable media" tell stories in different ways.

[45] Rollings and Adams, 2003; Rollings and Morris, 2000; Rouse, 2001; Salen and Zimmerman, 2004.

[46] Rollings and Morris, 2000, p. 109.

[47] Rollings and Morris, 2000, p. 110.

[48] Rollings and Morris, 2000, pp. 110–120.

[49] This toolbox includes the following items: obstacles, foreshadowing, personalization, resonance, resistance, plot points, suspense, theme, resolution and change.

[50] Rollings and Morris, 2000, pp. 110–111.

[51] Rouse, 2001, p. 7.

[52] Salen and Zimmerman, 2004, p. 381.

[53] Rollings and Adams, 2003, pp. 115–119.

[54] Meaning a classic story with beginning, middle and end, and only one narrative linear progression; and not a modernist or postmodern story that can begin anywhere and doesn't necessary end, or that has many story lines open at the same time.

[55] Rollings and Adams, 2003, pp. 115–119.

[56] Rouse, 2001, p. 218.

[57] Laurel, 1993; Murray, 1997; Ryan, 1991; Ryan, 2001b; Aarseth, 1997.

[58] See Frasca, 2003b, for a history of the use of the concept. *Ludus* means "game" in Latin, therefore *ludology* would be the study of games. The (mostly Scandinavian) researchers associated with this term are Markku Eskelinen, Gonzalo Frasca, Aki Jaarvinen, Jesper Juul and Espen Aarseth.

[59] Frasca, 1999.

[60] Frasca, 2001b.

[61] Juul, 2001.

[62] Although he doesn't mention adaptation of fictional universes, which is certainly possible as in the case of the *Blade Runner* game, even though the same sequence of events is not maintained.

[63] Eskelinen, 2001.

[64] A good summary of the history of the controversy can be found in Frasca, 2003b.

[65] Eskelinen, 2001.

[66] Kücklich, 2002; Kücklich, 2003a.

[67] Ryan, 2001a.

[68] Juul, 2003a, p. 168.

[69] This problem is inherited from earlier discussions about the status of digital literature, mostly from the field of hypertext theory, in which authors like Landow, 1992 or Douglas, 1992 wonder about the break with traditional narrative brought about by hyper-text narrative.

[70] Murray, 1997, p. 143.

[71] Murray, 1997, p. 144.

[72] Atkins, 2003, p. 20.

[73] There might be a historical explanation though, as the classic genre of adventure computer games is not so popular any more but its characteristics have been incorporated into others such as the sub-genres of action-adventure or survival horror.

[74] Salen and Zimmerman call this opposition: *crafted story* versus *emergent experience*, see Salen and Zimmerman, 2004, pp. 383–384.

[75] Rouse, 2001, pp. 219–228.

[76] Rouse, 2001, p. 223.

[77] Rouse, 2001, p. 227.

[78] Such as Ryan (2001a); Wolf (2001, pp. 109–110) or Laurel, who talks about goals as framework for action, Laurel, 1993, p. 106.

[79] Juul, 2003a, p. 146.

[80] Juul, 2003a, p. 163.

[81] Smith, 2000b.

[82] Jenkins, 2003a.

[83] Jenkins, 2003a.

[84] Murray, 1997, p. 51.

[85] Murray, 1997, p. 71.

[86] In the episode "Persistence of Vision" of the said series, see Murray, 1997: Chapter 1.

[87] Laurel, 1993, p. 167.

[88] Murray, 1997, p. 186.

[89] Murray, 1997, p. 197.

[90] Wolf, 2001.

[91] Ryan, 2001b, p. 307. Jesper Juul also makes this distinction between "the worlds we find in computer games and how computer games cue the players into imagining worlds" Juul, 2003a, p. 109.

[92] Wolf, 2001, p. 94.

[93] Tosca, 2003c.

[94] Salen and Zimmerman, 2004, p. 399.

[95] Salen and Zimmerman, 2004, p. 400.

[96] Juul, 2003a, p. 169.

[97] Jenkins, 2003a; Kücklich, 2003b.

[98] Ludologists, narratologists and everybody in between would seem to agree with Atkins's caveat: "it is not always necessary, or even advisable, to turn immediately to the work of critics such as Baudrillard, Jameson, Hassan or Umberto Eco (. . .) when confronted with the formal novelty of the computer game" (Atkins, 2003, p. 19).

CHAPTER 9

[1] Abt, 1968.

[2] The diverse backgrounds of these researchers may have had the unfortunate result that earlier research on the topic, published in a variety of journals, has not always been acknowledged. The most noticeable omission is the research on non-electronic educational games.

[3] Gardner, 2001; Lindstrøm, 2003; Rodgers, 2004; Tønner, 2000.

[4] Youn et al., 2003.

[5] Book, 2003; Emery, 2002; Lienert, 2004; Wong, 2004.

[6] Delwiche, 2007; Frasca, 2009.

[7] Erard, 2004.

[8] Karlsson, 2004, p. 4.

[9] Greenblat and Duke, 1981.

[10] Clegg, 1991; Randel et al., 1992; Van Sickle, 1986; Wentworth and Lewis, 1973.

[11] Egenfeldt-Nielsen, 2006.

[12] Lederman and Fumitoshi, 1995.

[13] Saegesser, 1981.

[14] Facer et al., 2003; Leyland, 1996.

[15] The most significant research on commercial computer games used in education is by Squire (2004a) and Egenfeldt-Nielsen (2005).

[16] Buckingham and Scanlon, 2002; Leyland, 1996.

[17] Buckingham and Scanlon, 2002; Egenfeldt-Nielsen, 2005.

[18] Buckingham and Scanlon, 2002; Egenfeldt-Nielsen, 2005.

[19] Buckingham and Scanlon, 2002.

[20] Buckingham and Scanlon, 2002.

[21] Good and Brophy, 1990.

[22] To a large extent this is a consequence of the fact that the feeling of control and freedom are by far the most expensive parts of game development.

[23] Rieber, 1996.

[24] Kafai, 1996.

[25] Gee, 2003; Jessen, 2001; Linderoth, 2002; Shaffer, 2006; Squire, 2004b.

[26] Healy, 1999; Kafai, 2001; Okan, 2003.

[27] Egenfeldt-Nielsen, 2005; Grundy, 1991; Healy, 1999; Magnussen and Misfeldt, 2004.

[28] Egenfeldt-Nielsen, 2005; Jillian et al., 1999; Leutner, 1993; Squire, 2004a.

[29] Egenfeldt-Nielsen, 2005.

[30] Grundy, 1991.

[31] Cotton, 1991; Loftus and Loftus, 1983.

[32] Maria M. Klawe, 1998, p. 9.

[33] Kafai, 1995; Kafai, 2001; Papert, 1998.

[34] Brody, 1993.

[35] Cavallari et al., 1992; Egenfeldt-Nielsen, 2005; Grundy, 1991; Klawe, 1998; Squire, 2004a.

[36] See Egenfeldt-Nielsen, 2007 for an overview.

[37] Egenfeldt-Nielsen, 2005.

[38] McFarlane et al., 2002; Squire, 2004a.

[39] Egenfeldt-Nielsen, 2003.

[40] Funk and Buchman, 1995; Gagnon, 1985; Gibb et al., 1983; Griffith et al., 1983.

[41] Gagnon, 1985; Green and Bavelier, 2003; Greenfield et al., 1996; Lowery and Knirk, 1983.

[42] Dorval and Pepin, 1986; Gagnon, 1985; Green and Bavelier, 2003; Lowery and Knirk, 1983; Okagaki and French, 1996; Subrahmanyam and Greenfield, 1996.

[43] J. Gee, 2003; Greenfield, 1984; Herring, 1984; Whitebread, 1997; Grundy, 1991; Jillian et al., 1999; Ko, 2002.

[44] Ko, 2002.

[45] Grundy, 1991; Jillian et al., 1999.

CHAPTER 10

[1] C. Anderson, 2004, p. 1.

[2] Heins, 2001, unpaginated.

[3] Williams, 2003b.

[4] Anderson, 2003.

[5] Buckingham, 2001, p. 67.

[6] Feshbach and Singer, 1971.

[7] Bushman et al., 1999.

[8] Chandler, 1995; Gerbner, 1973.

[9] Bandura, 1977.

[10] Zillmann, 1979.

[11] Berkowitz, 1984.

[12] Anderson and Bushman, 2001.

[13] Anderson and Dill, 2000; Durkin and Barber, 2002; Lynch et al., 2001; Robinson et al., 2001.

[14] Durkin and Barber, 2002, p. 373.

[15] Williams and Skoric, 2005.

[16] Bensley and Van Eenwyk, 2001; Emes, 1997; Freedman, 2001; Robinson et al., 2001.

[17] C.A. Anderson and Bushman, 2001, p. 353.

[18] Sherry, 2001.

[19] Freedman, 2001, p. 2.

[20] Bensley and Van Eenwyk, 2001; Dill and Dill, 1998; Freedman, 2001; Goldstein, 2001; Ivory, 2001; Sherry, 2001.

[21] Anderson *et al.*, 2004; Anderson and Bushman, 2001.

[22] Grossman and DeGaetano, 1999, for a summary.

[23] American Psychological Association, 2007.

[24] Geen, 2001.

[25] Gauntlett, 2001.

[26] Jessen, 1998, unpaginated.

[27] Bateson, 1972.

[28] Jessen, 1998.

[29] Jessen, 2001; Sørensen and Jessen, 2000.

[30] Jessen, 1998.

[31] Turkle, 1995.

[32] Ermi and Mäyrä, 2003, p. 244.

[33] Taylor, 2003.

[34] For example Cooper and Mackie, 1986.

[35] Buckingham, 2000.

[36] Anderson and Dill, 2000; Kirsh, 2003; Lynch *et al.*, 2001.

[37] Durkin and Barber, 2002; Harris, 2001.

[38] Harris, 2001.

[39] Griffiths and Davies, 2005.

[40] Griffiths and Hunt, 1998.

[41] Griffiths, 1997.

BIBLIOGRAPHY

Aarseth, E. (1997). *Cybertext: Perspectives on Ergodic Literature*. London: Johns Hopkins University Press.

Aarseth, E. (2000). Allegories of Space: The Question of Spatiality in Computer Games. In M. Eskelinen and R. Koskimaa (eds.), *Cybertext Yearbook 2000*. Jyväskylä: University of Jyväskylä.

Aarseth, E. (2001). Computer Game Studies, Year One. *Game Studies*, 1(1).

Aarseth, E. (2003). Beyond the Frontier: Quest Computer Games as Post-Narrative Discourse. In M. L. Ryan (Ed.), *Narrative Across Media*. Lincoln: University of Nebraska Press.

Aarseth, E., Sunnanå, L., and Smedstad, S. M. (2003, November 4–6). A Multi-Dimensional Typology of Games. Paper presented at the Level Up—Digital Games Research Conference, Utrecht.

Abt, C. (1968). Games for Learning. In E. O. Schild (Ed.), *Simulation Games in Learning*. London: Sage Publications.

Ackerman, D. (1998). *Deep Play*. New York: Vintage Press.

Adams, E. (2004, July 9). Postmodernism and the Three Types of Immersion. *Gamasutra.com*, Available online: http://www.gamasutra.com/features/20040709/adams_01.shtml#.

Almanac, C. I. (2003). *Worldwide Cumulative PC Sales Exceed 1 billion.PCs-In-Use tops 200M in USA. Cumulative PC Sales Surpass 400M*, from http://www.c-i-a.com/pr0203.htm

American Psychological Association, (2007). *Statement of the American Psychiatric Association on "Video Game Addiction"*. Retrieved 3 August, 2007, from http://www.psych.org/news_room/press_releases/07–47videogameaddiction_2_.pdf

Anderson, C. (2003). *Violent Video Games: Myths, Facts, and Unanswered Questions*. Retrieved 9 August, 2004, from http://www.apa.org/science/sb-anderson.pdf

Anderson, C. (2004). An Update on the Effects of Playing Violent Video Games. *Journal of Adolescence*, 27, 113–122.

Anderson, C.A. and Dill, K.E. (2000). Video Games and Aggressive Thoughts, Feelings, and Behavior in the Laboratory and in Life. *Journal of Personality and Social Psychology*, 78(4), 772–791.

Anderson, C.A. and Bushman, B.J. (2001). Effects of Violent Video Games on Aggressive Behavior, Aggressive Cognition, Aggressive Affect, Physiological Arousal, and Prosocial Behavior: A Meta-Analytic Review of the Scientific Literature. *Psychological Science*, 12(5), 353–359.

Anderson, C., Funk, J., and Griffith, M. (2004). Contemporary Issues in Adolescent Video Game Playing: Brief Overview and Introduction to the Special Issue. *Journal of Adolescence*, 27, 1–3.

Anderson, J. (1996). *The Reality of Illusion: An Ecological Approach to Cognitive Film Theory*. Carbondale: Southern Illinois University Press.

Atkins, B. (2003). *More Than a Game: The Computer Game as a Fictional Form*. Manchester: Manchester University Press.

Avedon, E.M., and Sutton-Smith, B. (1971). *The Study of Games*. New York: John Wiley and Sons Inc.

Aycock, Alan (1988) "Gens Una Sumus": Play as Metaculture. *Play & Culture*, 1(2), 124–137.

Badham, J. (Director) (1983). *WarGames* (movie). USA.

Bandura, A. (1977). *Social Learning Theory*. Englewood Cliffs: Prentice-Hall.

Baron, J. (2004). Glory and Shame: Powerful Psychology in Multiplayer Online Games. In J. Mulligan and B. Patrovsky (eds.), *Developing Online Games: An Insider's Guide*. Boston: New Riders Media.

Bartle, R. (1990). *Interactive Multi-User Computer Games*. London: British Telecom.

Bartle, R. (1996). *Hearts, Clubs, Diamonds, Spades: Players who Suit MUDs*. Retrieved November 27, 2003, 2003, from http://www.mud.co.uk/richard/hcds.htm

Bartle, R. (2003). *Designing Virtual Worlds*. Indianapolis: New Riders.

Bateson, G. (1972). *Steps to an Ecology of Mind*. Chicago: University of Chicago Press.

Battle.net (2003, September 30). *StarCraft, Diablo II, and Warcraft III Accounts Closed*. Retrieved November 14, 2003, from http://www.battle.net/news/0309.shtml

BBC News (2002). "Shocking" Xbox advert banned [Electronic Version]. Retrieved August 3, 2007 from http://news.bbc.co.uk/2/hi/entertainment/2028725.stm.

BBC News (2003, July 8). Thailand restricts Online Gamers. *BBC News*.

BBC News. (2004). Police reject game link to murder [Electronic Version]. *bbc.co.uk*. Retrieved August 3, 2007 from http://news.bbc.co.uk/1/hi/england/leicestershire/3538066.stm.

BBC News (2005, July 26). Uproar grows over GTA Sex Scenes. *BBC News*.

Bell, D. (2001). *An Introduction to Cybercultures*. London: Routledge.

Bensley, L. and Van Eenwyk, J. (2001). Video Games and Real-Life Aggression: Review of the Literature. *Journal of Adolescent Health*, 29(4).

Berkowitz, L. (1984). Some Effects of Thoughts on the Anti- and Prosocial Influences of Media Events: A cognitive neoassociationistic analysis. *Psychological Bulletin* (95), 410–427.

Book, B. (2003). "These bodies are FREE, so get one NOW!": Advertising and Branding in Social Virtual Worlds, *Interactive Media Forum: Identity and Cultures in Cyberspace*. Miami University in Oxford, Ohio: SSRN.

Bourdieu, P. (1987). *Distinction: A Social Critique of the Judgement of Taste*. Boston: Harvard University Press.

Bransford, W. (1998). The Past Was No Illusion. In C. Dodsworth (ed.), *Digital Illusion. Entertaining the Future with High Technology*. Boston: ACM Press/Addison Wesley.

Briceno, H., Chao, W., Glenn, A., Hu, S., Krishnamurthy, A., and Tsuchida, B. (2000). *Down From the Top of Its Game—The Story of Infocom, Inc*. Cambridge, MA: The MIT Press.

Bringsjord, S. (2001). Is it Possible to Build Dramatically Compelling Interactive Digital Entertainment (in the Form, e.g. of Computer Games)? *Game Studies*, 1(1).

Brody, H. (1993). Video Games that Teach? *Technology Review*, 96(8), 51–57.

Bryce, J. and Rutter, J. (2002). Killing Like a Girl: Gendered Gaming and Girl Gamers' Visibility. In F. Mayrä (ed.), *CGDC Conference Proceedings*. Tampere: Tampere University Press.

Buckingham, D. (2000). *After the Death of Childhood: Growing Up in the Age of Electronic Media*. London: Polity Press.

Buckingham, D. (2001). Electronic Child Abuse? Rethinking the Media's Effects on Children. In M. Barker and J. Petley (Eds.), *Ill Effects—the Media/Violence Debate*. London: Routledge.

Buckingham, D. and Scanlon, M. (2002). *Education, Edutainment, And Learning in the Home*. Buckingham: Open University Press.

Buckingham, D., Carr, D., Burn, A., and Schott, G. (2005). *Video Games: Text, Narrative, Play*. Cambridge: Polity Press.

Burnham, V. (2001). *Supercade: A Visual History of the Videogame Age 1971–1984*. Cambridge, MA: The MIT Press.

Burnham, V. (2003). Television Gaming Apparatus. In *Supercade—A Visual History of the Videogame Age 1971–1984* (pp. 52–55). Cambridge, MA: The MIT Press.

Bushman, B.J. (2002). Does Venting Anger Feed or Extinguish the Flame? Catharsis, Rumination, Distraction, Anger, and Aggressive Responding. *Personality and Social Psychology Bulletin* (28).

Bushman, B.J., Baumeister, R.F., and Stack, A.D. (1999). Catharsis, Aggression, and Persuasive Influence: Self-Fulfilling or Self-Defeating Prophecies? *Journal of Personality and Social Psychology*, 76(3), 367–376.

Caillois, R. (1958/2001). *Man, Play and Games*. Urbana: University of Illinois Press.

Calvert, S.L. (1999). *Children's Journeys through the Information Age*. Boston: McGraw-Hill.

Carr, D. (2002). Playing with Lara. In T. Krzywinska (ed.), *ScreenPlay. Cinema/Video Games/Interfaces*. London: Wallflower Press.

Cassell, J. and Jenkins, H. (1998). *From Barbie to Mortal Kombat: Gender and Computer Games*. Cambridge, MA: The MIT Press.

Castronova, E. (2001). Virtual Worlds: A First-Hand Account of Market and Society on the Cyberian Frontier. *The Gruter Institute Working Papers on Law, Economics, and Evolutionary Biology*, 2(1), 1–68.

Castronova, E. (2004, August 3). *Virtual World Economy: It's Namibia, Basically*, from http://terranova.blogs.com/terra_nova/2004/08/virtual_world_e.html

Cavallari, J., Hedberg, J., and Harper, B. (1992). Adventure Games in Education: A Review. *Australian Journal of Educational Technology*, 8(2), 172–184.

CBS (2002, 18 October). Addicted: Suicide Over Everquest? *CBS News*.

Chandler, D. (1995). *Cultivation Theory*. Retrieved 20th of January, 2004, from http://www.aber.ac.uk/media/Documents/short/cultiv.html

Chee, F. and Smith, R. (2003). Is Electronic Community an Addictive Substance? Paper presented at the Level Up—Digital Games Research Conference, Utrecht.

Clegg, A.A. (1991). Games and Simulations in Social Studies Education. In J.P. Shaver (ed.), *Handbook of Research on Social Studies Teaching and Learning*. New York: Macmillan.

Consalvo, M. (2003). It's No Videogame: News Commentary and the Second Gulf War. In M. Copier (ed.), *Proceedings of Level-Up Conference*. Utrecht: University of Utrecht Press.

Cooper, J. and Mackie, D. (1986). Video Games and Aggression in Children. *Journal of Applied Social Psychology*, 16(8), 726–744.

Cotton, K. (1991). *Computer-Assisted Instruction*: Northwest Regional Educational Laboratory.

Crawford, C. (1982). *The Art of Computer Game Design*. Berkeley: McGraw-Hill.

Crawford, C. (2003). *Chris Crawford on Game Design*. Boston: New Riders.

Csikszentmihalyi, M. (1990). *Flow: The Psychology of Optimal Experience*. New York: Harper Perennial.

Delwiche, A. (2007). From The Green Berets to America's Army: Video-games as a Vehicle for Political Propaganda. In P. Williams and J.H. Smith (eds.), *The Players' Realm: Studies on the Culture of Video Games and Gaming*. Jefferson, NC: McFarland Press.

DeMaria, R. and Wilson, J.L. (2002). *High Score!: The Illustrated History of Electronic Games*. New York: McGraw-Hill/Osborne.

Dibbell, J. (2003, December 2003). The Unreal Estate Boom. *Wired* 11.01, Available online: http://www.wired.com/wired/archive/11.01/gaming.html.

Dietz, T. (1998). An Examination of Violence and Gender Role Portrayals in Video Games: Implications for Gender Socialization and Aggresive Behavior. *Sex Roles: A Journal of Research*, 38, 425–442.

Dill, K.E. and Dill, J.C. (1998). Video Games Violence: A Review of the Empirical Literature. *Aggression and Violent Behavior: A Review Journal*, 3(4), 407–428.

Dill, K.E., Gentile, D.A., Richter, W.A., and Dill, J.C. (2005). Violence, Sex, Race and Age in Popular Video Games: A Content Analysis. In D.J. Henderson (ed.), *Featuring Females: Feminist Analyses of the Media*. Washington, DC: American Psychological Association.

Dorval, M. and Pepin, M. (1986). Effect of Playing a Video Game on a Measure of Spatial Visualization. *Perceptual Motor Skills*, 62(1), 159–162.

Douglas, J.Y. (1992). Print Pathways and Interactive Labyrinths: How Hypertext Narratives Affect the Act of Reading, Doctoral Thesis. New York: New York University.

Ducheneaut, N. and Moore, R.J. (2004, November 6–10). The Social Side of Gaming: A Study of Interaction Patterns in a Massively Multiplayer Online Game. Paper presented at the CSCW2004, Chicago.

Ducheneaut, N., Moore, R.J., and Nickell, E. (2004). *Designing for Sociability in Massively Multiplayer Games: An Examination of the "Third Places" of SWG*. Paper presented at the Other Players conference, IT University of Copenhagen.

Durkin, K. and Barber, B. (2002). Not so Doomed: Computer Game Play and Positive Adolescent Development. *Applied Development Psychology*, 23(4), 373–392.

Dyer, R. (2002). *Only Entertainment* (2nd edn). New York: Routledge.

Egenfeldt-Nielsen, S. (2003). *Keep the Monkey Rolling: Eye-Hand Coordination in Super Monkey Ball*. Paper presented at the Digra—Level up, Utrecht University.

Egenfeldt-Nielsen, S. (2005). Beyond Edutainment: Exploring the Educational Potential of Computer Games. Unpublished PhD thesis, IT University of Copenhagen, Copenhagen.

Egenfeldt-Nielsen, S. (2006, May 3). Case Study of Global Conflicts. Paper presented at the Games@IULM, Milan, Italy.

Egenfeldt-Nielsen, S. (2007). *Educational Potential of Computer Games*. New York: Continuum International Publishing Group.

Eladhari, M. (2003, May 2). *Trends in MMOG development*. Retrieved January 14, 2004, from http://www.game-research.com/art_trends_in_mmog.asp

ELSPA (2002). *Screen Digest: Interactive Leisure Software Report 4th Edition*. Retrieved March 21, 2004, from http://www.elspa.com/serv/screendigestintro.asp

ELSPA (2003). *The Cultural Life of Computer and Video Games: A Cross Industry Study*. Retrieved 2004, May, 2004, from http://www.elspa.com

Emery, G. (2002). What's in a Name: Product Placement in Games, *USA Today*.

Emes, C. (1997). Is Mr Pac Man Eating Our Children? A Review of the Effect of Video Games on Children. *The Canadian Journal of Psychiatry*, 42(4), 409–414.

Erard, M. (2004). In These Games, the Points Are All Political, *The New York Times*.

Erickson, T. (1997). Social Interaction on the Net: Virtual Community as Participatory Genre. In J.F.J. Nunamaker and R.H.J. Sprague (eds), *IEEE 13th Proceedings* (Vol. 6). Los Alamitos, CA: IEEE Computer Society Press.

Ermi, L. and Mäyrä, F. (2003). Power and Control of Games: Children as the Actors of Game Cultures. In J. Raessens (ed.), *Digital Games Research Conference*. Utrecht University: Utrecht University.

Eskelinen, M. (2001). The Gaming Situation. *Game Studies*, 1(1).

Estallo, J.A. (1995). *Los videojuegos. Juicios y prejuicios*. Barcelona: Planeta.

Evans, A. (2001). *This Virtual Life: Escapism and Simulation in our Media World*. London: Vision.

Faber, L. (1998). *Re:play*. London: Lawrence King Publishing.

Facer, K., Furlong, J., Furlong, R., and Sutherland, R. (2003). "Edutainment" Software: A Site for Cultures in Conflict. In R. Sutherland, G. Claxton and A. Pollard (eds.), *Learning and Teaching Where Worldviews Meet*. London: Trentham Books.

Fagen, R. (1995). Animal Play, Games of Angels, Biology, and Brian. In A.D. Pellegrini (ed.), *The Future of Play Theory: A Multidisciplinary Inquiry into the Contributions of Brian Sutton-Smith*. Albany: State University of New York Press.

Feshbach, S. and Singer, R. (1971). *Television and Aggression*. San Francisco: Jossey-Bass.

Fine, G.A. (1982/2002). *Shared Fantasy: Role-Playing Games as Social Worlds*. Chicago: University of Chicago Press.

Flanagan, M. (1999). Mobile Identities, Digital Stars and Post-Cinematic Selves. *Wide Angle: Issue on Digitality and the Memory of Cinema*, 21(1), 77–93.

Flanagan, M. (2003). Une maison de poupée virtuelle capitaliste? The Sims: domesticité, consommation, et feminité. In D. Desjeux (ed.), *Consommations sociétés: Cahiers pluridisciplinaire sur la consommation et l'interculturel*. Paris: L'Harmattan

Foo, C.Y. and Koivisto, E.M.I. (2004). Defining Grief Play in MMORPGs: Player and Developer Perceptions. Paper presented at the International Conference on Advances in Computer Entertainment Technology (ACE 2004), Singapore.

Frasca, G. (1999). *Ludology meets Narratology: Similitude and Differences between (Video) Games and Narrative*. Retrieved 29th of March, 2004, from http://www.jacaranda.org/frasca/ludology.htm

Frasca, G. (2001a). Video games of the Oppressed: Video games as a Means for Critical Thinking and Debate. Unpublished Masters thesis, Georgia Institute of Technology.

Frasca, G. (2001b). *What is Ludology? A Provisory Definition*. Retrieved 29th of March, 2003, from http://rludology.org/article.php?story=20010708201200000

Frasca, G. (2003a). *Ideological Video Games: Press Left Button to Dissent*. Retrieved 9. august, 2004, from http://www.igda.org/columns/ivorytower/ivory_Nov03.php

Frasca, G. (2003b, November 4–6). Ludologists Love Stories, Too: Notes from a Debate that Never Took Place. Paper presented at the Level Up—Digital Games Research Conference, Utrecht.

Freedman, J.L. (2001, October 26–27). Evaluating the Research on Violent Video Games. Paper presented at Playing by the Rules—The Cultural Policy Challenges of Video Games, Chicago.

Friedman, T. (1995). *Making Sense of Software: Computer Games and Interactive Textuality*. Retrieved 8th of Februrary, 2004, from http://www.duke.edu/~tlove/simcity.htm.

Funk, J. and Buchman, D. (1995). Video Game Controversies. *Paediatric Annals*, 24(2), 91–94.

Funk, J.B., Baldacci, H.B., Pasold, T., and Baumgardner, J. (2004). Violence Exposure in Real-life, Video Games, Television, Movies, and the Internet: Is There Desensitization? *Journal of Adolescence*, 27(1), 23–39.

Gagne, K.A. (2001). Moral Panics Over Youth Culture and Video Games. Unpublished Major Qualifying Project Report, Worcester Polytechnic Institute.

Gagnon, D. (1985). Video Games and Spatial Skills: An Exploratory Study. *Educational Communications and Technology Journal*, 33(4), 263–275.

Game Concept and Proposal. *Gamasutra*, Available online: http://www.gamasutra.com/features/19991019/ryan_01.htm.

Gameinformer (2006). *The Ratings Game: The Controversy Over the ESRB* [*Electronic Version*]. Gameinformer. Retrieved August 3, 2007 from http://www.gameinformer.com/News/Story/200610/N06.1004.1635.57594.htm?Page=1.

Games Press. (2005). *Hearts of Iron II* [*Electronic Version*]. *GamesIndustry.biz*. Retrieved August 3 2007 from http://www.gamesindustry.biz/content_page.php?aid=6159.

gamespy.com. (2003). Twenty-five Most Overrated Games of All Time. Retrieved July 17, 2007, from http://archive.gamespy.com/articles/september03/25overrated/index.shtml

Gamezone.com. (2006). *EA's Madden NFL 07 Returns Opening Week Kick-Off with Biggest Retail Performance Ever*. Retrieved 8 July, 2006, from http://pc.gamezone.com/news/09_01_06_12_52PM.htm

Gard, T. (2000). *Building Character*. *Gamasutra*, Available online: http://www.gamasutra.com/features/20000720/gard_pvf.htm.

Gardner, P. (2001). *Games with a Day Job: Putting the Power of Games to Work*. *Gamasutra*, Available online: http://www.gamasutra.com/features/20010601/gardner_02.htm.

Gauntlett, D. (2001). The Worrying Influence of "Media Effects" Studies. In J. Petley (ed.), *Ill Effects—The Media/Violence Debate*. London: Routledge.

Gee, J.P. (2003). *What Video Games Have to Teach Us about Learning and Literacy*. New York: Palgrave Macmillan.

Geen, R.G. (2001). *Human Aggression*. (2n edn). Buckingham: Open University Press.

Gentile, D.A., Lynch, Paul J., Linder, J.R., and Walsh, D.A. (2004). The Effects of Violent Video Game Habits on Adolescent Hostility, Aggressive Behaviors, and School Performance. *Journal of Adolescence*, 27(1), 5–22.

Gerbner, G. (1973). Cultural Indicators—The Third Voice. In G. Gerbner, L.P. Gross and W.H. Melody (eds.), *Communications Technology and Social Policy*. New York: Wiley.

Gibb, G., Bailey, J., Lambirth, T., and Wilson, W. (1983). Personality Differences Between High and Low Electronic Video Game Users. *The Journal of Psychology*, 114, 159–165.

Gluck, C. (2002, November 22). South Korea's Gaming Addicts. *BBC News*.

Goldstein, J. (2001, October 27). Does Playing Violent Video Games Cause Aggressive Behavior? Paper presented at the Playing by the Rules Conference, Chicago, Illinois.

Good, T.L. and Brophy, J.E. (1990). *Educational Psychology: A Realistic Approach*. Fourth Edition. New York: Longman.

Goodwins, R. and Loney, M. (2002, 3 September). In Greece, Use a GameBoy, Go to Jail. *CNET News.com*.

Graetz, J.M. (1981). *The Origin of Spacewar*. *Creative Computing* 8, Available online: http://www.wheels.org/spacewar/creative/SpacewarOrigin.html.

Green, C.S. and Bavelier, D. (2003). Action Video Game Modifies Visual Selective Attention. *Nature* (423), 534–537.

Greenblat, C. and Duke, R.E. (1981). *Gaming-Simulation: Rationale Applications*. London: Sage Publications.

Greenfield, P. (1984). *Mind and Media: The Effects of Television, Video Games, and Computers*. Cambridge, MA: Harvard University Press.

Greenfield, P.M., Brannon, C., and Lohr, D. (1996). Two-Dimensional Representations of Movement Through Three-Dimensional Space: The Role of Video Game Experience. In P.M. Greenfield and R.R. Cocking (eds.), *Interacting With Video* (pp. 169–185). New Jersey: Ablex Publishing.

Grieb, M. (2002). Run Lara Run. In G. King and T. Krzywinska (eds.), *ScreenPlay. Cinema/Video games/Interfaces*. London: Wallflower Press.

Griffith, J.L., Voloschin, P., Gibb, G.D., and Bailey, J.R. (1983). Differences in Eye-Hand Motor Coordination of Video-Game Users and Non-users. *Perceptual Motor Skills*, 57, 155–158.

Griffiths, M. (2005). Video Games and Health. *British Medical Journal* (331), 122–123.

Griffiths, M.D. (1997). Computer Game Playing in Early Adolescence. *Youth and Society*, 29(2), 223–237.

Griffiths, M.D. (1999). Violent Video Games and Aggression: A Review of the Literature. *Aggression and Violent Behavior*, 4(2), 283–290.

Griffiths, M.D. and Hunt, N. (1998). Dependence on Computer Games by Adolescents. *Psychological Reports*, 82(2), 475–480.

Griffiths, M.D. and Davies, M. N. O. (2005). Videogame Addiction: Does It Exist? In J. Raessens (ed.), *Handbook of Computer Game Studies*. Boston: The MIT Press, 359–373.

Grossman, D. and DeGaetano, G. (1999). *Stop Teaching Our Kids to Kill: A Call to Action Against TV, Movie and Video Game Violence*. New York: Crown Books.

Grundy, S. (1991). A Computer Adventure as a Worthwhile Educational Experience. *Interchange*, 22(4), 41–55.

Hämäläinen, P. (2002). *3D Sound Rendering and Cinematic Sound in Computer Games*, Helsinki: HUT, Telecommunications Software and Multimedia Laboratory.

Hancock, C. and Osterweil, S. (1996). Zoombinis and the Art of Mathematical Play. *Hands On!*, 19(1).

Harmon, A. (2004, January 15). A Real-Life Debate on Free Expression in a Cyberspace City. *The New York Times*.

Harris, J. (2001). *The Effects of Computer Games on Young Children—A Review of the Research*. London: Home Office.

Hasbro, (2006). History of the Monopoly Game. Retrieved July 9, 2007, from http://www.hasbro.com/monopoly/default.cfm?page=history.

Hawkins, M. (2005). *Go To Synesthesia . . . Jake Kazdal's Journey Through The Heart of Rez*. Retrieved June 19, 2007, from http://www.gamasutra.com/features/20050506/hawkins_01.shtml.

Healy, J.M. (1999). *Failure to Connect: How Computers Affect Our Children's Minds*. New York: Touchstone.

Heins, M. (2001). *Re: AAP's New Policy on Media Violence*. Retrieved 20 January, 2004, from http://www.fepproject.org/news/aapviolenceltr.html.

Herring, R. (1984). *Educational Computer Games*. Retrieved 3 August, 2007, from http://www.cyberroach.com/analog/an19/edu_games.htm.

Herz, J.C. (1997). *Joystick Nation: How Video Games Gobbled our Money, Won our Hearts, and Rewired Our Minds*. London: Abacus.

Holden, S. (2002, March 15). They May Be High-Tech, But They're Still the Undead. *The New York Times*.

Holland, J.H. (1998). *Emergence: From Chaos to Order*. Reading, MA: Addison-Wesley.

Hughes, L.A. (1999). Children's Games and Gaming. In B. Sutton-Smith, J. Mechling, T.W. Johnson and F.R. McMahon (eds.), *Children's Folklore*. Logan: Utah State University Press.

Huizinga, J. (1938/2000). *Homo Ludens: A Study of the Play-Element in Culture*. London: Routledge.

Hunicke, R., LeBlanc, M., and Zubek, R. (2004). *MDA: A Formal Approach to Game Design and Game Research*. Retrieved August 9, 2004, from http://www.cs.northwestern.edu/~hunicke/pubs/MDA.pdf.

Hunt, L. (2002). "I Know Kung Fu!" The Martial Arts in the Age of Digital Reproduction. In T. Krzywinska (ed.), *ScreenPlay. Cinema/Video Games/Interfaces*. London: Wallflower Press.

Hunter, W. (2000). The Dot Eaters—Video Game History 101. Retrieved November 23, 2003, from http://www.emuunlim.com/doteaters/

IDATE (2004). *Video Games—NextGen Gaming: On its Way and Here to Stay* (Market Research). Paris: IDATE.

IDSA (2003). *Essential Facts About the Computer and Video Game Industry*. Washington, DC: The Interactive Digital Software Association.

ign.com. (2005). *The Sims Franchise Celebrates its Fifth Anniversary*. Retrieved July 8, 2007, from http://games.ign.com/articles/585/585856p1.html.

Iser, W. (1979). *The Act of Reading—A Theory of Aesthetic Response*. London: Johns Hopkins University Press.

Ivory, J.D. (2001, August). Video Games and the Elusive Search for their Effects on Children: An Assessment of Twenty Years of Research. Paper presented at the Association for Education in Journalism and Mass Communication's Annual Convention, Washington, DC.

Jakobsson, M. and Taylor, T.L. (2003). The Sopranos Meets EverQuest: Social Networking in Massively Multiplayer Online Games. *FineArt Forum*, 17(8).

Jansz, J. and Martins, R. (2003). The Representation of Gender and Ethnicity in Digital Interactive Games. In J. Raessens (ed.), *Level Up. Digital Games Research Conference Proceedings*. Utrecht: Utrecht University Press.

Järvinen, A. (2002). Gran Stylissimo: The Audiovisual Elements and Styles in Computer and Video Games. Paper presented at the Computer Games and Digital Cultures, Tampere.

Jenkins, H. (1992). *Textual Poachers. Television Fans and Participatory Culture*. New York: Routledge.

Jenkins, H. (2000). *Lessons from Littleton—What Congress Doesn't Want to Hear About Youth and Media*. Retrieved January 13, 2004, from http://www.nais.org/pubs/ismag.cfm?file_id= 1267&ismag_id=14.

Jenkins, H. (2001). *From Barbie to Mortal Kombat: Further Reflections*. Retrieved May, 2004, from http://culturalpolicy.uchicago.edu/conf2001/papers/jenkins.html.

Jenkins, H. (2003a). Game Design as Narrative Architecture. In N. Wardrip-Fruin and P. Harrigan (eds.), *First Person*. Cambridge, MA: The MIT Press.

Jenkins, H. (2003b, January 15, 2003). Transmedia Storytelling. *Technology Review*.

Jenkins, H. (2005). Games, the New Lively Art. In J. Raessens and J. Goldstein (eds.), *Handbook of Computer Game Studies*. Cambridge: The MIT Press.

Jessen, C. (1995). Children's Computer Culture. *Dansk Paedagogisk Tidsskrift* (5).

Jensen, J.F. (1997). "Interactivity" Tracking a New Concept in Media and Communication Studies. Paper presented at the The XIII Nordic Conference on Mass Communication Research, Jyväskla.

Jessen, C. (1998). *Interpretive Communities: The Reception of Computer Games by Children and the Young*. Retrieved August 9, 2004, from http://www.carsten-jessen.dk/intercom.html.

Jessen, C. (2001). *Børn, leg og computerspil*. Odense: Odense Universitetsforlag.

Jillian, J.D., Upitis, R., Koch, C., and Young, J. (1999). The Story of Phoenix Quest: How Girls Respond to a Prototype Language and Mathematics Computer Game. *Gender and Education*, 11(2), 207–223.

Johnson, S. (2001). *Emergence: The Connected Lives of Ants, Brains, Cities, and Software*. London: Penguin Books.

Jones, G. (2002). *Killing Monsters—Why Children Need Fantasy Super Heroes, and Make-Believe Violence*. New York: Basic Books.

Jung, C.G. (1928). On Psychic Energy. In C.G. Jung (ed.), *Collected Works 8: The Structure and Dynamics of Psyche*. New Jersey: Princeton University Press.

Juul, J. (2001). Computer Games Telling Stories? A Brief Note on Computer Games and Narratives. *Gamestudies*, 1(1).

Juul, J. (2002). The Open and the Closed: Games of Emergence and Games of Progression. Paper presented at the Computer Games and Digital Cultures Conference, Tampere, Finland.

Juul, J. (2003a). *Half-Real—Video Games Between Real Rules and Fictional Worlds*. Unpublished PhD dissertation, IT University of Copenhagen, Copenhagen.

Juul, J. (2003b). The Game, The Player, The World—Looking for a Heart of Gameness. Paper presented at the Level Up—Digital Games Research Conference, Utrecht.

Juul, J. (2004). Introduction to Game Time. In N. Wardrip-Fruin and P. Harrigan (eds.), *First Person: New Media as Story, Performance, and Game*. Cambridge, MA: The MIT Press.

Juul, J. (2005). *Half-Real: Video Games Between Real Rules and Fictional Worlds*. Cambridge, MA: The MIT Press.

Kafai, Y. (1995). *Minds in Play: Computer Game Design as a Context for Children's Learning*. Hillsdale, NJ: Lawrence Erlbaum Associates.

Kafai, Y. (1996). Software by Kids for Kids. *Communications of The ACM*, 39(4), 38–40.

Kafai, J.B. (1998). Video Game Design by Girls and Boys: Variability and Consistency of Gender Differences. In J. Cassell and H. Jenkins (eds.), *From Barbie to Mortal Kombat. Gender and Computer Games*. Cambridge, MA: The MIT Press.

Kafai, Y.B. (2001). The Educational Potential of Electronic Games: From Games-To-Teach to Games-To-Learn. Paper presented at the Playing by the Rules, Cultural Policy Center, University of Chicago.

Kahn, C. (2004). *Worldwide Boxoffice*. Retrieved December 1, 2004, from http://www.worldwideboxoffice.com.

Karlsson, Ø.N. (2004). First Person Politics—Computer Games as Political Communication. Unpublished manuscript, Copenhagen.

Kelley, H. (2002). *Breaking In*. Retrieved August 16, 2004, from http://www.igda.org/breakingin/career_paths.htm.

Kennedy, H.W. (2002). Lara Croft: Feminist Icon or Cyberbimbo? On the Limits of Textual Analysis. *Gamestudies*, 2(2).

Kent, Steven L. (2001). *The Ultimate History of Video Games. From Pong to Pokemon, the Story Behind the Craze that Touched our Lives and Changed the World*. New York: Random House.

Kerr, A. (2003). Women Just Want to Have Fun—A Study of Adult Female Players of Digital Games. Paper presented at the Level Up, Utrecht.

Kim, A.J. (1998). Killers Have More Fun. *Wired*, 6.05, 6.05, Available online: http://www.wired.com/wired/archive/6.05/ultima.html?topic=gaming&topic_set=newmedia.

King, B. and Borland, J. (2003). *Dungeons and Dreamers: The Rise of Computer Game Culture from Geek to Chic*. New York: McGraw-Hill.

King, G. (2002). Die Hard/Try Harder: Narrative, Spectacle and Beyond from Hollywood to Videogame. In T. Krzywinska (ed.), *ScreenPlay. Cinema/Video games/interfaces*. London: Wallflower Press.

King, G. and Krzywinska, T. (2006). *Tomb Raiders and Space Invaders: Videogame Forms and Contexts*. London: I.B. Tauris.

Kirriemuir, J. (2002). Video Gaming, Education and Digital Learning Technologies. Relevance and Opportunities. *D-Lib Magazine*, 8(2).

Kirsh, S.J. (2003). The Effects of Violent Video Games on Adolescents: The Overlooked Influence of Development. *Aggression and Violent Behavior*, 8(4), 377–389.

Klastrup, L. (2003). Towards a Poetics of Virtual Worlds—Multiuser Textuality and the Emergence of Story, Ph.D. thesis, IT University of Copenhagen.

Klawe, M.M. (1998). When Does the Use Of Computer Games and Other Interactive Multimedia Software Help Students Learn Mathematics? Unpublished manuscript.

Klawe, M.M. and Phillips, E. (1995). A Classroom Study: Electronic Games Engage Children as Researchers. Paper presented at the CSCL 1995, Bloomington, Indiana.

Klevjer, R. (2002, June 6–8). In Defense of Cutscenes. Paper presented at the Computer Games and Digital Cultures Conference, Tampere.

Ko, S. (2002). An Empirical Analysis of Children's Thinking and Learning in a Computer Game Context. *Educational-Psychology*: 22(2), 219–233.

Koster, Raph (2004). *Theory of Fun for Game Design*. Scottsdale: Paraglyph Press.

Krotoski, A. (2004). *Chicks and Joysticks. An Exploration of Women and Gaming*. London: ELSPA.

Krzywinska, T. (2002). Hands-On-Horror. In T. Krzywinska (ed.), *ScreenPlay. Cinema/Video Games/Interfaces*. London: Wallflower Press.

Kücklich, J. (2002). The Study of Computer Games as a Second-Order Cybernetic System. In F. Mayrä (Ed.), *CGDC02 Conference Proceedings*. Tampere: Tampere University Press.

Kücklich, J. (2003a). Perspectives on Computer Game Philology. *Gamestudies*, 3(1).

Kücklich, J. (2003b). The Playability of Computer Games versus the Readability of Computer Games: Towards a Holistic Theory of Fictionality. In J. Raessens (ed.), *Level-Up Conference Proceedings*. Utrecht: Utrecht University Press.

Kücklich, J. (2004). Other Playings—Cheating in Computer Games. Paper presented at the Other Players—a conference on multiplayer phenomena, Copenhagen.

Kuo, A. (2001). *A (Very) Brief History of Cheating*. Retrieved august 23, 2005, from http://shl.stanford.edu/Game_archive/StudentPapers/BySubject/A-I/C/Cheating/Kuo_Andy.pdf.

Kushner, D. (2003). *Masters of Doom: How Two Guys Created an Empire and Transformed Pop*. London: Piatkus.

Landow, G. (1992). *Hypertext. The Convergence of Contemporary Critical Theory and Technology*. Baltimore: Johns Hopkins University Press.

Langway, L. (1981, November 16). *Invasion of the Video Creatures. Newsweek*, 90−94, Available online: http://www.gamearchive.com/General/Articles/ClassicNews/1981/Newsweek11−16−81.htm.

Lastowka, G. and Hunter, D. (2004). The Laws of the Virtual Worlds. *California Law Review*, 92(1), 1−73.

Laurel, B. (1993). *Computers as Theatre*. Reading, MA: Addison-Wesley.

Lebling, P.D. (1980, December). *Zork and the Future of Computerized Fantasy Simulations. Byte*, Available online: http://www.csd.uwo.ca/Infocom/Articles/byte.html.

Lebowitz, M. (1984). Creating Characters in a Storytelling Universe. *Poetics*, 13, 171−194.

Lederman, L.C. and Fumitoshi, K. (1995). Debriefing the Debriefing Process: A New Look. In K. Arai (ed.), *Simulation and Gaming Across Disciplines and Cultures*. London: Sage Publications.

Leeson, B. (2005). *Origins of the Kriegsspiel*. Retrieved August 25, 2005, from http://myweb.tiscali.co.uk/kriegsspiel/kriegsspiel/origins.htm.

Leutner, D. (1993). Guided Discovery Learning with Computer-Based Simulation Games: Effects of Adaptive and Non-Adaptive Instructional Support. *Learning and Instruction*, 3(2), 113−132.

Leyland, B. (1996). How Can Computer Games Offer Deep Learning and Still be Fun? Paper presented at Ascilite, Adelaide, Australia.

Lienert, A. (2004, February 15 2004). Video Games Open New Path to Market Cars: Gamers are Influencing New Vehicle Designs, Advertisements. *Detroit News*.

Linderoth, J. (2002, August 19−22). Making Sense of Computer Games: Learning with New Artefacts. Paper presented at the Toys, Games and Media, London.

Lindley, C.A. (2002). The Gameplay Gestalt, Narrative and Interactive Storytelling. In F. Mayrä (ed.), *CGDC02 Conference Proceedings*. Tampere: Tampere University Press.

Lindstrøm, M. (2003). *Brand Games: Your Move*. Retrieved august 9, 2004, from http://www.martinlindstrom.com/index.php?id=writing&archive_id=77.

Livingstone, Sonia (2002). *Young People and New Media: Childhood and the Changing Media Environment*. London: Sage.

Loftus, G. and Loftus, E. (1983). *Mind at Play: The Psychology of Video Games*. New York: Basic Books.

Lowery, B. and Knirk, F. (1983). Micro-Computer Video Games and Spatial Visual Acquisition. *Journal of Educational Technology Systems*, 11(2), 155−166.

LucasFilm Games. (1990). Loom manual. Washington.

Lyman, J. (2003, December 19). Gamer Wins Lawsuit in Chinese Court Over Stolen Virtual Winnings. *TechNewsWorld*.

Lynch, P.J., Gentile, D.A., Olson, A.A., and Brederode, T.M. von (2001, April). The Effects of Violent Video Game Habits on Adolescent Aggressive Attitudes and Behaviors. Paper presented at the Biennial Conference of the Society for Research in Child Development, Minneapolis, Minnesota.

McFarlane, A., Sparrowhawk, A., and Heald, Y. (2002). *Report on the Educational Use of Games. Teachers Evaluating Educational Multimedia*. Cambridge, MA: TEEM.

McGonigal, J. (2003). A Real Little Game: The Performance of Belief in Pervasive Play. Paper presented at the Level Up—Digital Games Research Conference, Utrecht.

McLuhan, M. (1964). *Understanding Media: The Extensions of Man*. New York: The New American Library, Inc.

Magnussen, R. and Misfeldt, M. (2004, 6–8. December). Player Transformation of Educational Multiplayer Games. Paper presented at the Other Players, Copenhagen.

Malone, T.W. (1980). What Makes things Fun to Learn? Heuristics for Designing Instructional Computer Games. Paper presented at the Symposium on Small Systems archive., Palo Alto, California, United States.

Malone, T. W. and Lepper, M. (1987a). Intrinsic Motivation and Instructional Effectiveness in Computer-based Education. In R.E. Snow and M.F. Farr (Eds.), *Aptitude Learning, and Instruction*. London: Lawrence Erlbaum Associates Publishers.

Malone, T.W., and Lepper, M. (1987b). Making Learning Fun: A Taxonomy of Intrinsic Motivation for Learning. In Snow and Farr (eds.), *Aptitude Learning, and Instruction*. London: Lawrence Erlbaum Associates Publishers.

Manovich, L. (2001). *The Language of New Media*. Cambridge, MA: The MIT Press.

Mead, G.H. (1934/1967). *Mind, Self and Society—From the Standpoint of a Social Behaviorist*. Chicago: The University of Chicago Press.

Meehan, J.R. (1976). *The Metanovel: Writing Stories by Computer*. New Haven: Yale University Press.

Mencher, M. (2003). *Get in the Game! Careers in the Game Industry*. Boston: New Riders Publishing.

Meretzky, S. (2001, November 20, 2001). Building Character: An Analysis of Character Creation. *Gamasutra*.

Microsoft Game Studios (1982). Microsoft Flight Simulator manual.

Mmogchart.com (2005). *An Analysis of MMOG Subscription Growth*. Retrieved August 26, 2005, from http://www.mmogchart.com/.

MobyGames (2007a). Halo 2. Retrieved June 4, 2007, from http://www.mobygames.com/game/xbox/halo-2/credits

MobyGames. (2007b, June 4 2007). SimCity. Retrieved June 4, 2007, from http://www.mobygames.com/game/dos/simcity/credits.

Morningstar, C. and Farmer, F.R. (2003). The Lessons of Lucasfilm's Habitat. In N. Wardrip-Fruin and N. Montfort (eds.), *The New Media Reader*. Cambridge, MA: The MIT Press.

Morris, S. (1999). *Online Gaming Culture. An Examination of Emerging Forms of Production and Participation in Multiplayer First-Person-Shooter Gaming*. Retrieved 2003, December, 2003, from http://www.game-culture.com/articles/onlinegaming.html.

Morrison, M. (2005). *Beginning Game Programming*. Indianapolis, IN: SAMS.

Mouritsen, F. (2003). *Childhood and Children's Culture*. Portland: International Specialized Book Service Inc.

Mulligan, J. and Patrovsky, B. (2003). *Developing Online Games: An Insider's Guide*. Indianapolis: New Riders.

Murray, J. (1997). *Hamlet on the Holodeck—The Future of Narrative on Cyberspace*. Cambridge, MA: The MIT Press.

Newman, J. (2004). *Video games. Routledge Introductions to Media and Communications*. London: Routledge.

Nexgen Wars. (2007). Console sales. Retrieved July 8, 2007, from http://nexgenwars.com/.

Nietzsche, F. (1891/2005). *Thus Spake Zarathustra*: Abbaci Books.

Novak, J. (2007). *Game Development Essentials: An Introduction* (2nd edn.). Clifton Park: Thomson/Delmar Learning.

O'Donnell, M. (2002). Producing Audio for Halo. Retrieved January 23, 2004, from http://www.gamasutra.com/resource_guide/20020520/odonnell_01.htm.

OECD's Directorate for Science, Technology and Industry (2005). *Digital Broadband Content: The Online Computer and Video Game Industry*: Organisation for Economic Co-operation and Development.

Okagaki, L. and French, P. (1996). Effects of Video Game Playing on Measures of Spatial Performance: Gender Effects in Late Adolescence. In P. Greenfield and R. Cocking (eds.), *Interacting With Video*. New Jersey: Ablex Publishing.

Okan, Z. (2003). Edutainment: Is Learning at Risk? *British Journal of Educational Technology*, 34(3), 255–264.

O'Riordan, K. (2001). Playing with Lara in Virtual Space. In S.R. Munt (ed.), *Technospaces. Inside the New Media*. London: Continuum.

Papert, S. (1998, June). Does Easy Do It? Children, Games and Learning. *Game Developer*, 87–88, Available online: http://papert.org/articles/Doeseasydoit.html.

Parlett, D.S. (1999). *The Oxford History of Board Games*. Oxford: Oxford University Press.

Pearce, C. (2005). Theory Wars: An Argument Against Arguments in the So-called Ludology/Narratology Debate. Paper presented at the DIGRA 2005—Changing Views: Worlds in Play, Vancouver.

Pellegrini, A.D. (1995). *The Future of Play Theory: A Multidisciplinary Inquiry into the Contributions of Brian Sutton-Smith*. Albany: State University of New York Press.

Postigo, H. (2003). From Pong to Planet-Quake: Post-Industrial Transitions from Leisure to Work. *Information, Communication and Society*, 6(4), 593–607.

Postman, N. (1986). *Amusing Ourselves to Death: Public Discourse in the Age of Show Business*. New York: Penguin Books.

Prensky, M. (2001). *Digital Game-Based Learning*. New York: McGraw-Hill.

Propp, V. (1969). *Morphology of the Folktale*. Austin: University of Texas.

Provenzo Eugene, F. (1991). *Video Kids: Making sense of Nintendo*. Cambridge, MA: Harvard University Press.

Ramrez, S.U., Forteza, B.R., Hernando, J.L.O., and Martorell, S.G. (2002). El rol de la figura femenina en los videojuegos. Edutec. *Revista Electrónica de Tecnología Educativa*, 15.

Randel, J.M., Morris, B.A., Wetzel, C.D., and Whitehill, B.V. (1992). The Effectiveness of Games for Educational Purposes: A Review of Recent Research. *Simulation and Gaming*, 23(3), 261–276.

Rau, A. (2001, March 1–2). Reload—Yes/No. Clashing Times in Graphic Adventure Games. Paper presented at Computer Games and Digital Textualities, IT University of Copenhagen.

Rieber, L.P. (1996). Seriously Considering Play: Designing Interactive Learning Environments Based on the Blending of Microworlds, Simulations, and Games. *Educational Technology Research and Development*, 44(2), 43–58.

Rimmon Kenan, S. (1983/2002). *Narrative Fiction*. London: Routledge.

Robinson, T.N., Wilde, M.L., Navracruz, L.C., Farish, H.K., and Varady, A. (2001). Effects of Reducing Children's Television and Video Game Use on Aggressive Behavior: A Randomized Controlled Trial. *Archives of Pediatrics and Adolescent Medicine*, 155(7), 17–23.

Rodgers, Z. (2004, July 28). Chrysler Reports Big Brand Lift on Advergames. *ClickZ News*, Available.

Rollings, A. and Adams, E. (2003). *Andrew Rollings and Ernest Adams on Game Design*. Boston: New Riders Publishing.

Rollings, A. and Morris, D. (2000). *Game Architecture and Design*. Scottsdale: Coriolis.

Rollings, A. and Morris, D. (2004). *Game Architecture and Design—A New Edition*. Boston: New Riders.

Rothstein, E. (1983, May 8). Reading and Writing: Participatory Novels. *The New York Times Book Review*.

Rouse, R. (2001). *Game Design: Theory and Practice*. Plano, TX: Wordware.

Rutter, J. and Bryce, J. (2006). *Understanding Digital Games*. London: Sage Publications.

Ryan, M.L. (1991). *Possible Worlds, Artificial Intelligence, and Narrative Theory*. Bloomington: Indiana University Press.

Ryan, M.L. (2001a). Beyond Myth and Metaphor. The Case of Narrative in Digital Media. *Gamestudies*, 1(1).

Ryan, M.L. (2001b). *Narrative as Virtual Reality. Immersion and Interactivity in Literature and Electronic Media*. Baltimore: Johns Hopkins University Press.

Ryan, T. (1999a). The Anatomy of a Design Document, Part 1: Documentation Guidelines for the Game Concept and Proposal [Electronic Version]. *Gamasutra*. Retrieved October 19 from http://www.gamasutra.com/features/19991019/ryan_01.htm.

Ryan, T. (1999b). The Anatomy of a Design Document, Part 2: Documentation Guidelines for the Functional and Technical Specifications [Electronic Version]. *Gamasutra*. Retrieved December 17 from http://www.gamasutra.com/features/19991217/ryan_01.htm.

Saegesser, F. (1981). Simulation-Gaming in the Classroom. Some Obstacles and Advantages. *Simulation and Games*, 12(3), 281–294.

Salen, K. and Zimmerman, E. (2004). *Rules of Play—Game Design Fundamentals*. London: The MIT Press.

Saltzman, M. (2000). *Game Design: Secrets of the Sages*. Indianapolis, IN: Brady Games.

Schierbeck, L. and Carstens, B. (1999). *Gennemgang af computerspil udgivet i Danmark i 1998*. Copenhagen: The Media Council for Children and Young People.

Schiesel, S. (2007a). P.E. Classes Turn to Video Game That Works Legs [Electronic Version]. *New York Times*. Retrieved July 17 2007 from http://www.nytimes.com/2007/04/30/health/30exer.html?ex=1184817600&en=0d289da4bf2732e9&ei=5070.

Schiesel, S. (2007b). Video Games Conquer Retirees [Electronic Version]. *The New York Times*. Retrieved August 3 2007 from http://www.nytimes.com/2007/03/30/arts/30seni.html?ex=1332907200&en=071aee3567f7bb9b&ei=5088&partner=rssnyt&emc=rss.

Schott, G. and Horrell, K. (2000). Girl Gamers and their Relationship with the Gaming Culture. *Convergence*, 6(4), 36–54.

Schousboe, I. (1993). Den onde leg—en udvidet synsvinkel på legen og dens funktioner. *Nordisk Psykologi*, 45(2), 97–119.

Sedighian, K. and Sedighian, A.S. (1996). Can Educational Computer Games Help Educators Learn About the Psychology of Learning Mathematics in Children? Paper presented at the 18th Annual Meeting of the International Group for the Psychology of Mathematics Education, Florida.

Seldes, G. (1957). *The Seven Lively Arts*. New York: Sagmore Press.

Sherblom-Woodward, B. (2002). Hackers, Gamers and Lamers—The Use of l33t in the Computer Sub-Culture. Unpublished Masters thesis, University of Swarthmore, Swarthmore.

Shafter, David W. (2006). *How Computer Games Help Children Learn*. New York: Palgrave Macmillan.

Sherry, J.L. (2001). The Effects of Violent Video Games on Aggression: A Meta-Analysis. *Human Communication Research*, 27(3), 409–431.

Smith, H. (2001). *The Future of Game Design: Moving Beyond Deus Ex and Other Dated Paradigms*. Retrieved December 16, 2004, from http://www.igda.org/articles/hsmith_future.php.

Smith, J.H. (2000a). The Dragon in the Attic [Electronic Version]. *Game Research*. Retrieved 3 August 2007 from http://game-research.com/index.php/articles/the-dragon-in-the-attic-on-the-limits-of-interactive-fiction/.

Smith, J.H. (2000b). The Road not Taken—The Hows and Whys of Interactive Fiction [Electronic Version]. *Game Research*. Retrieved August 3, 2007 from http://game-research.com/index.php/articles/the-road-not-taken-the-hows-and-whys-of-interactive-fiction/.

Smith, J.H. (2003). Avatars You Can Trust—A Survey on the Issue of Trust and Communication in MMORPGs [Electronic Version]. *Game Research*. Retrieved August 3, 2007 from http://game-research.com/index.php/articles/avatars-you-can-trust-a-survey-on-the-issue-of-trust-and-communication-in-mmorpgs/.

Smith, J.H. (2004). Playing Dirty—Understanding Conflicts in Multiplayer Games. Paper presented at the 5th annual conference of The Association of Internet Researchers, The University of Sussex.

Smith, J.H. (2006a). The Games Economists Play: Implications of Economic Game Theory for the Study of Computer Games. *Game Studies: The International Journal of Computer Game Research*, 6(1).

Smith, J.H. (2006b). Plans and Purposes: How Videogame Goals Shape Player Behaviour. Unpublished PhD dissertation, IT University of Copenhagen, Copenhagen.

Sniderman, S. (1999). Unwritten Rules. *The Life of Games*, 1(1), 2–7.

Snow, B. (2007). Wii Outsells the Mighty PS2 for the Same Period. Retrieved July 8, 2007, from http://www.infendo.com/gamecube/wii-outsells-the-mighty-ps2-for-the-same-period/.

Sørensen, B.H., and Jessen, C. (2000). It Isn't Real—Children, Computer Games, Violence and Reality. In C. von Feilitzen and U. Carlsson (eds.), *Children in the New Media Landscape—Games Pornography Perceptions*. Göteborg: The UNESCO International Clearinghouse on Children and Violence on the Screen at Nordicom.

Sotamaa, O. (2003). Computer Game Modding, Intermediality and Participatory Culture. Unpublished manuscript.

Squire, K. (2004a). Replaying History. Unpublished Ph.D. dissertation. Indiana University.

Squire, K.D. (2004b). Civilization III as a World History Sandbox. In M. Bittanti (ed.), *Civilization and its Discontents. Virtual History. Real Fantasies*. Milan, Italy: Ludilogica Press.

Stevenson, R. and Berkowitz, B. (2004). Video Game Industry Faces "Crisis of Creativity" [Electronic Version]. *Forbes.com*. Retrieved 17 July 2007 from http://www.forbes.com/business/newswire/2004/03/26/rtr1313656.html.

Storey, John (2001). *An Introduction to Cultural Theory and Popular Culture*. Athens, GA: University of Georgia Press.

Subrahmanyam, K. and Greenfield, P. (1996). Effect of Video Game Practice. In P. Greenfield and R. Cocking (eds.), *Interacting With Video*. New Jersey: Ablex Publishing.

Suits, B. (1978). *Grasshopper: Games, Life, and Utopia*. Toronto: University of Toronto Press.

Sutton-Smith, B. (1997). *The Ambiguity of Play*. Cambridge, MA: Harvard University Press.

Sutton-Smith, B., and Kelly-Byrne, D. (1984). The Idealization of Play. In P.K. Smith (ed.), *Play in Animals and Humans*. Oxford: Basil Blackwell Inc.

Talin (2002). Managing Deviant Behavior in Online Worlds. In J. Mulligan and B. Patrovsky (eds.), *Developing Online Games. An Insider's Guide*. Boston: New Riders.

Taylor, J. (2003). *Home Interactive Entertainment Market Update 2002–2003*. Portland: Arcadia Investment Corp.

Taylor, T. (2003, 4–6 November). Power Gamers Just Want To Have Fun? Instrumental Play in a MMOG. Paper presented at the Level Up: Digital Games Research Conference 2003, Utrecht, Holland.

Taylor, T.L. (2002). Whose Avatar is This Anyway? Negotiating Corporate Ownership in a Virtual World. In F. Mayrä (ed.), *CGDC 02 Conference Proceedings*. Tampere: Tampere University Press.

Taylor, T.L. (2003). Multiple Pleasures. Women and Online Gaming. *Convergence*, 9(1), 8–18.

Taylor, T.L. (2006). *Play Between Worlds: Exploring Online Game Culture*. Cambridge, MA: The MIT Press.

The ESA (2004). *Essential Facts about the Computer and Video Game Industry 2004*. Washington: The Interactive Digital Software Association.

The ESA (2006). *Essential Facts About the Computer and Video Game Industry 2006*. Washington: The Interactive Digital Software Association.

Tønner, U. (2000). *Reklamespil på nettet er effektiv branding*. Retrieved August 9, 2004, from http://design.emu.dk/artik/00/36-branding.html.

Tosca, S.P. (2003a). Reading Resident Evil: Code Veronica X. *Proceedings of DAC03*. Melbourne: RMIT Press.

Tosca, S.P. (2003b). The Appeal of Cute Monkeys. In J. Raessens (ed.), *Level-Up Conference Proceedings*. Utrecht: Utrecht University Press.

Tosca, S.P. (2003c). The Quest Problem in Computer Games. *TIDSE 03 Proceedings*. Darmstadt: Fraunhofer IRB Verlag.

Tosca, S. (2005). Implanted Memories or the Illusion of Free Action. In W. Brooker (ed.), *The Blade Runner Experience*. London: Wallflower Press.

Tronstad, R. (2001). Semiotic and Non-Semiotic MUD Performance. *Proceedings of COSIGN 01*. Amsterdam.

Trunnel, D. (2002). Reality in Fantasy: Violence, Gender and Race in Final Fantasy IX. from http://www.communication.ilstu.edu/activities/CSCA2002/Reality_in_Fantasy.pdf.

Turkle, S. (1984). *The Second Self: Computers and the Human Spirit*. London: Granada.

Turkle, S. (1995). *Life on the Screen—Identity in the Age of the Internet*. London: Phoenix.

Van Sickle, R. (1986). A Quantitative Review of Research on Instructional Simulation Gaming: A Twenty-Year Perspective. *Theory Research in Social Education*, 14(3), 245–264.

Verant, I. (1999). *EverQuest: 989 Studios*.

Walker, J. (2007). A Network of Quests in World of Warcraft. In P. Harrigan and Noah-Wardrup-Fruin (eds.), *Second Person: Role-Playing and Story in Games and Playable Media*. Cambridge, MA: The MIT Press.

Wang, F. (2005, August 3). China Bans Minors under 18 from Playing Online Games that Allow Players to Kill Other Players. *Interfax China*.

Ward, M. (2003, September 29, 2003). Does Virtual Crime Need Real Justice? Retrieved November 11, 2003, from http://news.bbc.co.uk/1/hi/technology/3138456.stm.

Wardrip-Fruin, N. and Harrigan, P. (2007). *Second Person: Role-Playing and Story in Games and Playable Media*. Cambridge, MA: The MIT Press.

Weir, P. (2000). *Satisfaction with Interaction: Future Prospects for Interactive Audio*. Retrieved January 21, 2004, from http://www.earcom.net/article_BAFTA.htm.

Wentworth, D.R. and Lewis, D.R. (1973). A Review of Research on Instructional Games and Simulations in Social Studies Education. *Social Education*, 37, 432–440.

White, P.V. (2007). MMOGData. Retrieved July 17, 2007, from http://mmogdata .voig.com/Home.html.

Whitebread, D. (1997). Developing Children's Problem-Solving: The Educational Uses of Adventure Games. In A. McFarlane (Ed.), *Information Technology and Authentic Learning*. London: Routledge.

Williams, D. (2002). Structure and Competition in the U.S. Home Video Game Industry. *The International Journal on Media Management*, 4(1), 41–54.

Williams, D. (2003a). Trouble in River City: The Social Life of Video Games. Unpublished PhD dissertation, University of Michigan, Michigan.

Williams, D. (2003b). The Videogame Lightning Rod. Constructions of a New Media Technology, 1970–2000. *Information, Communication and Society*, 6(4), 524–549.

Williams, D. and Skoric, M. (2005). Internet Fantasy Violence: A Test of Aggression in an Online Game. *Communication Monographs*, 22(2), 217–233.

Wittgenstein, L. (1953/1967). *Philosophical Investigations*. Oxford: Blackwell.

Wolf, M.J.P. (2001). *The Medium of the Video Game*. Austin: University of Texas Press.

Wong, M. (2004, October 18, 2004). *Advertisements Insinuated Into Video Games*. Retrieved January 27, 2005, from http://www.bizreport.com/news/8204.

Woodcock, B.S. (2006, September 2004). An Analysis of MMOG Subscription Growth—Version 21.0. Retrieved July 17, 2007, from http://www.mmogchart.com/.

WorldwideBoxOffice (2004) from http://www.worldwideboxoffice.com.

Wright, T., Boria, E., and Breidenbach, P. (2002). Creative Player Actions in FPS Online Video Games. *Game Studies*, 2(2).

Youn, S., Lee, M., and Doyle, K.O. (2003). Lifestyles of Online Gamers: A Psychographic Approach. *Journal of Interactive Advertising*, 3(2).

Zillmann, D. (1979). *Hostility and Aggression*. Hillsdale, NJ: Erlbaum.

INDEX